THE
SERVICE REVOLUTION
IN SOUTH ASIA

THE
SERVICE REVOLUTION
IN SOUTH ASIA

EDITED BY
EJAZ GHANI

OXFORD
UNIVERSITY PRESS

OXFORD

UNIVERSITY PRESS

YMCA Library Building, Jai Singh Road, New Delhi 110 001

Oxford University Press is a department of the University of Oxford.
It furthers the University's objective of excellence in research, scholarship,
and education by publishing worldwide in

Oxford   New York

Auckland   Cape Town   Dar es Salaam   Hong Kong   Karachi
Kuala Lumpur   Madrid   Melbourne   Mexico City   Nairobi
New Delhi   Shanghai   Taipei   Toronto

With offices in
Argentina   Austria   Brazil   Chile   Czech Republic   France   Greece
Guatemala   Hungary   Italy   Japan   Poland   Portugal   Singapore
South Korea   Switzerland   Thailand   Turkey   Ukraine   Vietnam

Oxford is a registered trademark of Oxford University Press
in the UK and in certain other countries

Published in India
by Oxford University Press, New Delhi

© World Bank 2010

The moral rights of the author have been asserted
Database right Oxford University Press (maker)

First published 2010

The findings, interpretations, and conclusions expressed herein are those of the
author(s) and do not necessarily reflect the views of the Executive Director of
the International Bank for Reconstruction and Development/The World Bank or
the governments they represent. The World Bank does not guarantee the accuracy
of the data included in this work. The boundaries, colours, denominations,
and other information shown on any map in this work do not imply any
judgment on the part of The World Bank concerning the legal status of
any territory or the endorsement of acceptance of such boundaries.

ISBN-13: 978-0-19-806511-1
ISBN-10: 0-19-806511-6

Typeset in Adobe Garamond Pro 10.5/12.7
by Eleven Arts, Keshav Puram, Delhi 110 035
Printed in India by Artxel, New Delhi 110 020
Published by Oxford University Press
YMCA Library Building, Jai Singh Road, New Delhi 110 001

Contents

III   INFRASTRUCTURE

Tables and Figures

FIGURES

Preface

The growth experience of India and other South Asian countries suggests that a Service Revolution—rapid income growth, job creation, gender equality, and poverty reduction led by services—is now possible. What is Service Revolution? Can service be as dynamic as manufacturing? Can latecomers to development take advantage of the globalization of service? Can service be a driver of sustained growth, job creation, and poverty reduction? What kind of policies and institutions do developing countries need to benefit from a service-led growth? This book answers these questions from three different spatial perspectives—within country, regionally, and globally. It compares and contrasts the roles of different sectors in growth and poverty reduction.

South Asia's growth pattern of jumping straight from agriculture to service, sidestepping manufacturing, and sustaining rapid growth over the last two decades, is remarkable. It contradicts a seemingly iron law of development that has held true for almost two hundred years since the start of the Industrial Revolution. This law—which is now conventional wisdom—says that industrialization is the only route to rapid economic development. This is no longer the case. In this book, we show that growth in South Asia has in fact been led by service, that labour productivity levels in service are above those in industry, and that productivity growth in service sectors in India match labour productivity growth in manufacturing sectors in China. Furthermore, services-led growth has been effective in reducing poverty.

So can a service-led growth be sustained? A service-led growth is sustainable because the globalization of service is just the tip of the iceberg. Service is the largest sector in the world, as it accounts for more than 70 per cent of global output. The Service Revolution has altered the characteristics of services. Services can now be produced and exported at low cost. The old idea of services being non-transportable, non-tradable, and non-scalable no longer holds for a host of modern impersonal services. Developing countries can sustain a service-led growth as there is a huge room for catch-up and convergence.

Education, telecommunication, and connectivity are the keys to ignite and sustain a service-led growth. The infrastructure needs of services differ from manufacturing. Services rely less on ports and roads and more on telecommunication and electricity. Maintaining and upgrading both the quantity and quality of its telecommunication infrastructure is crucial for ensuring the possibility of engaging in trade in services in the first place. Given that the skill requirements in services are higher than in manufacturing, investing in education is of paramount importance. Globalization of services has increased the demand for skilled workers and return to education, which in turn, has increased the demand for education. This can become a virtuous circle.

Is service-led growth a panacea for South Asia? Services cannot substitute for industrial job creation. South Asia has a young population. More than 150 million new workers will join the labour force in the next decade. Many of them will indeed find jobs in services. But South Asia cannot afford to ignore the manufacturing sector. Neither should it blindly follow the East Asian model of manufacturing-led growth.

South Asia's development experience offers hope to latecomers to development. The marginalization of Africa during a period when China and other East Asian countries grew rapidly led some to wonder if latecomers to development like Africa and South Asia were doomed to failure. The process of globalization in the late twentieth century led to a strong divergence of incomes between those who industrialized and broke into global markets and a 'bottom billion' of people in some 60 countries where incomes stagnated for twenty years. It seemed as if the 'bottom billion' would have to wait their turn for development, until the giant industrializers like China became rich and uncompetitive in labour-intensive manufacturing.

The promise of the Service Revolution is that countries do not need to wait to get started with rapid development. There is a new boat that development latecomers can take. The globalization of service provides alternative opportunities for developing countries to find niches, beyond manufacturing, where they can specialize, scale up, and achieve explosive growth, just like the industrializers. The core of the argument in this volume is that as the number of goods and services produced and traded across the world expand with globalization, the possibilities for all countries to develop based on their comparative advantage expand. That comparative advantage can just as easily be in services as in manufacturing or indeed agriculture. We do not argue for services against manufacturing or agriculture, but do argue against the long-held proposition that industrialization is the *only* route to economic development.

EJAZ GHANI

The Service Revolution in South Asia

An Overview

Ejaz Ghani and Homi Kharas[#]

The story of Hyderabad—the capital of the Indian state of Andhra Pradesh—is truly inspiring for latecomers to development. Within two decades, Andhra Pradesh has been catapulted straight from a poor and largely agricultural economy into a major service centre. It has transformed itself from a lagging into a leading region. Fuelled by an increase in service exports of forty-five times between 1998 and 2008, the number of information technology (IT) companies in Hyderabad increased eight times, and employment increased twenty times.

Service-led growth has mushroomed in other parts of India and South Asia as well. Indeed, growth in the service sector has enabled South Asia to grow almost as fast as East Asia in this century, with growth of just under 7 per cent annually between 2000–7. Growth rates in South Asia and East Asia have converged (Ghani and Ahmed 2009). The two fastest growing regions in the world, however, have very different growth patterns. While East Asia is a story of growth led by manufacturing, South Asia has thrived on service-led growth.

[#]We are grateful to Lakshmi Iyer for her contribution to the overview, and to Saurabh Mishra for research support. We would also like to thank a number of colleagues for useful comments at the review meeting including S. Ahmed, R. Anand, P. Banerjee, D. Biller, C. Dahlman, S. Devarajan, P. Dongier, M. Engman, M. Haddad, M. Kawai, Justin Yifu Lin, E. May, A. Mattoo, I. Nabi, M. Pigato, J. Sebastian Saez, S. Yusuf, E. Lim, and G. Zannini. The views expressed here are not necessarily those of the World Bank. Any remaining errors are our responsibility.

The South Asian experience of growth in the twenty-first century is remarkable because it contradicts a seemingly iron law of development that has held true for almost 200 years since the start of the Industrial Revolution. This law—which is now conventional wisdom—says that industrialization is the only route to rapid economic development. It goes further to say that as a result of globalization the pace of development can be explosive. But the potential for explosive growth has until now been distinctive to manufacturing (UNIDO 2009). This is no longer the case. The South Asian experience suggests that a services revolution—rapid growth and poverty reduction led by services—is now possible. This can fundamentally change the pattern of development for many developing countries.

What is this services revolution and what has led to it? Can services be a driver of growth, job creation, and poverty reduction? What are the location and spatial characteristics of services? Is there a role for exports in sustaining service-led growth over the long run? What kind of infrastructure, including education, do developing countries need to sustain service-led growth? This volume is all about answering these questions based on a fresh look at what has happened in South Asia over the last two decades.

The services revolution could upset three long-held tenets of economic development. First, services have long been thought to be driven by domestic demand. They could not by themselves drive growth, but instead followed growth. In the classical treatment of services, any attempt to expand the volume of services production beyond the limits of domestic demand would quickly lead to deterioration in the price of services, hence a reduction in profitability, and hence the impulse towards expanded production would be choked off.

Second, services in developing countries were considered to have lower productivity and lower productivity growth than industry. It is hard to improve the labour productivity of a symphony (or, as it turns out, of a government which increasingly dominates the service sector). As economies became more service oriented, their growth would slow. For rich countries, with high demand for various services, the slowdown in growth was an acceptable consequence of the higher welfare that could be achieved by a switch towards services. But for developing countries, such a trade-off was thought to be inappropriate.

Third, services jobs in developing countries were thought of as menial, and for the most part poorly paid, especially for low skilled workers. As such, service jobs could not be an effective pathway out of poverty.

It is these three beliefs that the services revolution that has started across South Asia challenges. In this volume we show that growth has in fact been led by services, that labour productivity levels in services in South Asia are above those in industry, and that productivity growth in South Asia's service sector matches labour productivity growth in manufacturing in successful East Asian countries. Further, we suggest that services-led growth in South Asia has been effective in reducing poverty.

South Asia's experience offers hope that globalization can indeed be a force for development in many more countries. The marginalization of Africa during a period when China and other East Asian countries grew rapidly led some to wonder if latecomers to development were not doomed to failure. The process of globalization in the late twentieth century led to a divergence of incomes between those who industrialized and broke into global markets and a 'bottom billion' of people in some sixty countries where incomes stagnated for twenty years (Collier 2007). It seemed as if the 'bottom billion' would have to wait their turn for development, until the giant industrializers like China became rich and uncompetitive in labour-intensive manufacturing.

The promise of the services revolution is that countries do not need to wait to get started with rapid development. There is a new boat that development latecomers can take. The globalization of service exports provides alternative opportunities for developing countries to find niches, beyond manufacturing, where they can specialize, scale up, and achieve explosive growth, just like the industrializers. The core of our argument is that as the number of goods and services produced and traded across the world expands with globalization, the possibilities for all countries to develop based on their comparative advantage expand. That comparative advantage can just as easily be in services as in manufacturing or indeed agriculture. We do not argue for services and against manufacturing or agriculture, but do argue against the long-held proposition that industrialization is the *only* route to economic development.

THE SERVICES REVOLUTION

Services have characteristics that differ significantly from goods. Goods are physical things that can be put in a box and traded. They can be made anywhere, at any time, and at any scale. More and more goods are produced each year as firms develop new products and as production processes are broken down into individual parts and components. With a growing number of goods, productivity can rise because of specialization (a finer division of labour) and scale (falling unit costs of production). Trade in goods allows even small countries to find a niche in global markets where they can be competitive. The East Asian countries are exemplars of countries which have developed rapidly on the basis of this simple proposition.

Services are difficult to place in a box because they are bound by time and proximity. For example, eating in a restaurant, getting a haircut, having a medical check-up, or seeking a loan from a bank, all require face-to-face transactions (Baumol 1967). This makes it difficult to trade services. They are produced where and when demand is present.

However, technological changes (telephone and internet) and what Bhagwati (1984) has called splintering and disembodiment of services have made many services tradable, just like manufactured goods. These services, called modern impersonal progressive services (Baumol 1985), include communication, banking, insurance, and business-related services. They are being created by three global forces—technology, transportability, and tradability—the 3Ts that are driving the services revolution.

Technology, especially information and communication technology (ICT), has given services a physical presence. They can be produced and stored as a series of ones and zeros in digital format. Banking and loan transactions can now be conducted online. A medical check-up may still require a meeting with a doctor, but the results of an X-ray may be reviewed by a radiologist in a different country, the details of the examination may be transcribed by a person working in a different time zone, and medical records may be stored and updated on a remote server.

Thanks to telephone lines and the internet, these modern services can also be easily transported today over long distances with little or no degradation in quality (Baumol 1986). This is the second T, transportability, which has meant that services are no longer restricted by time and space. One indicator of the cost of transporting services is the average cost of an international telephone call to the United States (Figure 1). For most developing countries, this has fallen by 80 per cent or more over the last decade, a decline in cost which is much more rapid than the fall in transport costs for goods. Even more significant is the decline in cost and increased access of broadband internet. Perhaps as important as cost is the speed, clarity, and reliability with which information can now be transported.

The third T, tradability, refers to the fact that many modern services, which are transported digitally, face few government barriers when they are moved from one country to another. There are no borders, customs, or tariffs on the international exchange of most modern impersonal services.[1]

[1]United States Schedule of Specific Commitments under the General Agreement on Trade in Services (GATS) shows that there are no 'tariff' barriers per se on trade in modern impersonal services. Pricing and tax related measures may apply, but there are

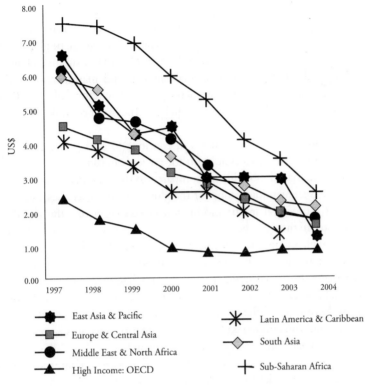

US$

8.00
7.00
6.00
5.00
4.00
3.00
2.00
1.00
0.00

1997   1998   1999   2000   2001   2002   2003   2004

East Asia & Pacific
Europe & Central Asia
Middle East & North Africa
High Income: OECD

Latin America & Caribbean
South Asia
Sub-Saharan Africa

FIGURE 1   **Average Cost of Telephone Call to the US**
(US$ per 3 minutes)

Source: Chapter 3, this volume.

The 3Ts have unleashed a services revolution riding on the wave of the internet age. Service exports from developing countries almost tripled in the last ten years, growing by 11 per cent annually from about US$ 240 billion in 1997 to US$ 692 billion in 2007. Service exports now account for 5 per cent of developing countries' gross domestic product (GDP) (total GDP of developing countries was US$ 14.3 trillion in 2007).

---

no 'at the border' tariffs, because modern impersonal services delivered electronically are difficult to monitor, especially mode 1 (cross-border) flow of services. Traditional services (modes 2, 3, 4—see Chapter 1 for details) might have a tariff component, or a regulatory related payment that can be considered to be equivalent to a tariff. For example, in air transport services, foreign-owned freight aircraft might have to pay a higher airport fee, and the difference between airport fees for foreign and domestic providers can be said to be a tariff equivalent.

We have only witnessed the tip of the iceberg (Blinder 2006). The internet age will continue to transform more services into modern impersonal services. The range of business processes that can be globalized and digitized is constantly expanding: processing insurance claims; desktop publishing; the remote management and maintenance of IT networks; compiling audits; completing tax returns; transcribing medical records; and financial research and analysis. The list of possible activities is almost endless.

The globalization of services will continue to be a strong force for two reasons. First, services account for more than 70 per cent of global GDP, more than double in size compared to the manufacturing sector. So, there is tremendous scope for the globalization of services. Second, the cost differential in the production of services across the world is enormous. In the past, the only option to narrowing such cost differentials was through migration, but migration has been heavily regulated and global international migration has remained steady at about 3 per cent for decades. Now that service providers can sell services without crossing national borders by making use of the internet (outsourcing), the scope for exploiting cost differentials is much higher. What is more, it is very hard for governments to regulate modern impersonal services, so prospects for rapid expansion in service exports are good.

Modern impersonal services have many features in common with manufacturing. Like manufacturing, they benefit from technological advances that generate productivity growth year after year. They exhibit similar tendencies for scale and agglomeration economies. Service producers can bring down unit costs by expanding operations. They benefit from being in close proximity to one another as that creates a pool of well-trained workers. They are labour intensive.

But there are also differences. Modern services are more skill intensive than other types of economic activity. They require excellence in telecommunications. While traded goods move by ship, air, and road, globally traded modern impersonal services are delivered using telephone lines or the internet.

What the services revolution has done is to open up many more niches for countries through which they can leverage the global economy. Each country should try its best to take advantage of these opportunities, whether in manufacturing or services, exploiting comparative advantages. What the South Asian experience shows is that the opportunities in modern services are sufficiently large to drive development of the whole economy.

As yet, modern impersonal services are only a small part of the total services. The sector is still dominated by traditional personal services which include trade, hotels, restaurants, beauty shops, barbers, transport, and public administration. The only way for these services to be traded is for the service providers themselves to move to where the demand is located. But migration faces many barriers. It is costly and subject to major government regulation. Yet South Asia benefits handsomely from its ability to send migrants abroad and receive remittances from them.

SERVICES-LED GROWTH

The modern service sector has become an important driver of growth in both developed and developing countries. Figure 2 compares what has happened in 134 countries between 2000 and 2005 in terms of real GDP growth, shown on the vertical axis, and service value-added growth, shown on the horizontal axis. Each point represents one country. The positive relationship between the two variables implies that countries with high growth in services also tend to have high overall

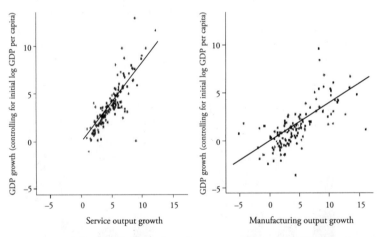

FIGURE 2   GDP Growth and Service Value-added Growth (2000–5)

FIGURE 3   GDP Growth and Manufacturing Value-added Growth (2000–5)

Source: Chapter 1, this volume (author's calculation using data from the World Bank 2008).

Note: Each point in the chart corresponds to a five-year growth during 2000–5 for a specific country. GDP growth rates control for level of initial income per capita. All values are in constant US$ 2000. Growth rates are compounded annual averages. The sample consists of 134 countries.

economic growth or conversely that countries with high overall economic growth have high services growth. One cannot identify causality from a regression like this. If services have a high income elasticity of domestic demand, then we would expect higher overall growth to be associated with higher service sector growth. But we will also show later that high service growth is also associated with high service export growth. This suggests that it is services that have been driving overall economic growth rather than vice versa.

Exactly the same exercise is shown in Figure 3 for the relationship between manufacturing growth and overall economic growth. Again, there is a positive relationship which probably runs from manufacturing growth to overall growth. This is the relationship which has been reported to emphasize the importance of manufacturing for growth (UNIDO 2009). Comparing the two graphs, it is clear that the slope is steeper in Figure 2. This suggests that the effect of services growth seems to be stronger than the effect of manufacturing growth on aggregate economic growth.

The service sector has become particularly important in South Asia, growing from less than 40 per cent of GDP in 1980 to more than 50 per cent of GDP in the region in 2005 (Figure 4). This is not limited to a specific country: the share of services in GDP was more than 50 per cent in India, Pakistan, Bangladesh, and Sri Lanka and 49 per cent in Nepal. The trend over time to a higher service sector share shows that

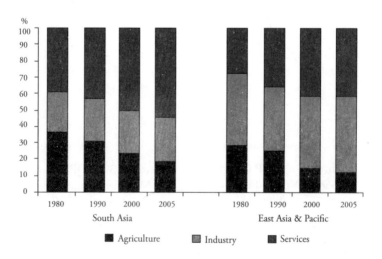

FIGURE 4   Share of Sectors in GDP in Asia

Source: Chapter 2, this volume.

higher real growth in services has not been offset by price declines. Figure 4 also shows that South Asia has a higher share of services and a more rapid service sector growth than East Asia, although the latter is richer and has grown faster over time. This suggests that services are not simply responding to domestic demand (which would be higher in East Asia), but also to export opportunities.

Not only does the service sector form the bulk of the economy, but services are the largest contributor to GDP growth as well. The service sector accounted for more than 50 per cent of GDP growth in all South Asian countries (Figure 5). Its contribution to GDP growth is nearly twice that of industry. Further, the contribution of services to overall GDP growth has increased over time in India, Pakistan, and Sri Lanka. This is in sharp contrast to the East Asian countries shown in Figure 5 (China and Korea) where industry contributes between 40–50 per cent to GDP growth.

The differences and similarities in service-led growth in South Asia and manufacturing-led growth in East Asia are explored in Chapter 1 by Ejaz Ghani. He shows that while there is some evidence of convergence in growth patterns, there are also significant differences between the regions. In East Asia, services are also growing rapidly as a natural progression to improve the efficiency of inputs needed to sustain a dynamic manufacturing base. Finance, logistics, and trade services

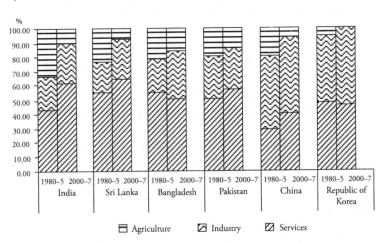

FIGURE 5   Contribution of Services to GDP Growth in South Asia
(1980–5, 2000–7)

Source: Chapter 2, this volume.

linked to manufacturing exports have grown rapidly. But manufacturing demand has not been the driver of growth in services in South Asia. India has a small manufacturing base and an even smaller manufacturing export platform. Yet, its services have exploded. In fact, India's services growth has fuelled an expansion of manufacturing to satisfy the growing domestic demand for goods as incomes rise. Thus the difference between manufacturing growth and services growth in both East and South Asia has narrowed, but the drivers of growth remain distinct.

But how dynamic is the service sector in South Asia? Can services productivity be as high as manufacturing productivity? Chapter 2 by Barry Bosworth and Annemie Maertens documents in detail the contribution of the service sector to economic growth and employment generation in South Asia. Services were once thought of as stagnant and low productivity growth areas, without the dynamic externalities attributed to manufacturing. That was one reason why services were not thought of as a potential leading sector for development. In fact, the finding is that absolute levels of labour productivity are the highest in the service sector for South Asian countries (Figure 6). Labour productivity is higher in the service sector than in the manufacturing sector for India, Nepal, Pakistan, and Sri Lanka, in stark contrast to East Asian countries where the industrial sector has substantially higher productivity levels. Only Bangladesh and Bhutan in South Asia have higher labour productivity in industry than in services. Given that the process of development is one of transferring resources (largely labour) from low productivity areas to high productivity areas, it makes sense to interpret rapid South Asian growth as one of moving labour from low-productivity agriculture to high-productivity services.

Along with high levels of labour productivity in services, South Asia's growth experience shows that the service sector displays significant productivity growth. In the post-2000 period, labour productivity growth has been higher in the service sector than in the manufacturing sector for India, Pakistan, and Sri Lanka (Figure 7). This is an important finding, since there needs to be high and sustained productivity growth in order for services to be a transformational growth engine for the whole economy.

We should note that the relatively recent development of the 3Ts—technology, transportability, and tradability—of services means that the ability of services growth to drive overall economic growth is also a relatively new phenomenon. Tradability in particular means that there is a large global market available for services, and that prices will not

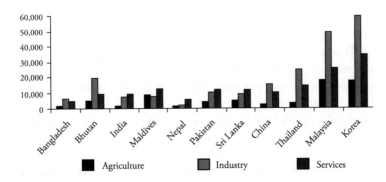

FIGURE 6   **Labour Productivity Levels by Sector (2005)**
(*PPP international dollars per worker*)

Source: World Bank (2008a).
Notes: Data for China is from 2004. The utilities industry in Malaysia is included in services rather than industry. Labour productivity = value added by sector/ employment in that sector.

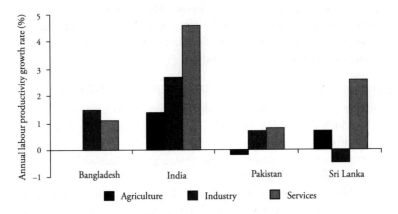

FIGURE 7   **Labour Productivity Growth in the Service Sector (2000–6)**

Source: Chapter 2, this volume.

decline even if volumes rise rapidly. In one of the most careful studies of total factor productivity (TFP) growth in China and India, Bosworth and Collins (2008) find that India managed to record a TFP growth of 2.4 per cent in services between 1980 and 2006—a level that could sustain rapid aggregate growth and twice the level of TFP growth in either agriculture or industry. By contrast, China, despite more rapid aggregate growth over this period, managed a service sector TFP growth of only 2 per cent per year, slower than that in either agriculture or industry.

One reason for rapid productivity growth in services in South Asia is that these economies are starting from a low technological base compared to international best practices. There can thus be rapid catch-up just like in manufacturing. Beyond this, services also display potential for productivity gains from learning, networking, and knowledge spillovers. Modern impersonal services tend to cluster together to take advantage of scale economies and externalities.

It is easier for service firms to cluster than for manufacturing firms. Service firms take up less space, do not cause traffic jams when shipping their goods, and pollute less. This is not only true for developed countries, with notable tradable services hubs in New York, London, Silicon Valley, but also in developing countries, like in Hyderabad.

These issues are explored in Chapter 3 by Bosker and Garretsen. They show that thick markets for services attract more service firms and workers. Service corridors arise, just like manufacturing clusters. These benefit from externalities such as knowledge spillovers between firms, workers, and universities. Productivity enhancing externalities are far more prominent in service corridors compared to goods clusters, as services tend to be 'non-rival' goods.

SERVICE-LED GROWTH AND POVERTY REDUCTION

Despite concentrated locations, the benefits of service growth appear to be widely distributed. Globally, there is cross-country evidence from some fifty developing countries that poverty reduction is associated more strongly with growth in the service sector than with growth in manufacturing or agriculture.

Table 1 reports the cross-country regression results of change in poverty headcount regressed on growth in agriculture, manufacturing, and services output. Growth in services output is significantly associated with poverty reduction in developing countries, whereas growth in agriculture and growth in manufacturing is not significant. The regression controls for initial conditions. When countries are richer initially, the speed of poverty reduction is lower (row 1); when they have higher initial poverty, they make faster progress in poverty reduction (row 2). Controlling for all variables, South Asian countries like India and Sri Lanka have, however, had lower rates of poverty reduction than expected, based on other countries' experiences.

TABLE 1   Cross-country Results on Change in Poverty Headcount (1990–2005) (Regressed on Agriculture, Manufacturing, and Services Output Growth, for Fifty Developing Countries)

	(1)	(2)	(3)	(4)	Sectoral Output Growth Weighted by Initial Share of Sector in GDP	
					(5)	(6)
Log GDP per capita initial			9.99***	9.82***	14.59***	13.87***
			(3.07)	(3.36)	(3.84)	(4.26)
Initial level of poverty	–0.17*	–0.17*				
	(0.08)	(0.09)				
Growth in agriculture output	0.55	0.58	0.51	0.55	0.02	0.02
	(0.97)	(1.04)	(0.91)	(0.97)	(0.02)	(0.02)
Growth in manufacturing output	–0.06	0.08	–0.01	0.11	–0.03	0.001
	(0.46)	(0.44)	(0.54)	(0.53)	(0.02)	(0.02)
Growth in services output	–2.30***	–2.11**	–1.92**	–1.74*	–0.02**	–0.04***
	(0.86)	(0.89)	(0.88)	(0.91)	(0.01)	(0.01)
India indicator		9.44**		8.83**		10.63***
		(4.22)		(3.71)		(3.64)
China indicator		–24.48***		–23.01***		—27.51***
		(5.48)		(5.35)		(8.84)
Bangladesh indicator		–3.99		–4.24		–2.06
		(4.19)		(3.24)		(3.72)
Sri Lanka indicator		4.51**		7.76***		9.25****
		(1.98)		(2.35)		(2.58)
Control for time period	Yes	Yes	Yes	Yes	Yes	Yes
Observations	50	50	50	50	50	50

Source: Chapter 1, this volume.
Notes: Robust standard errors are reported in parenthesis. *** represents significance at 1 per cent, ** at 5 per cent, and * at 10 per cent. Country size is measured by area in square kilometres. The dependent variable is percentage of population below US$ 1 (PPP) per day.

Visually, we can plot the change in poverty between 1990 and 2005 against the growth of services (Figure 8).

These results are further confirmed when we examine the impact of sectoral growth patterns on poverty reduction within India, using a panel of Indian state data from 1994 to 2005. Our results show that the trend growth in the service sector among Indian states is associated with a decrease in the trend of the headcount poverty rate of almost 1.5 points

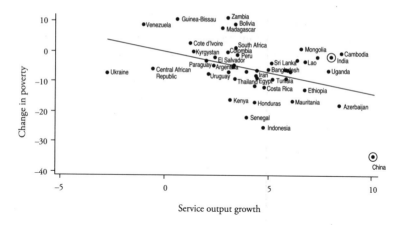

FIGURE 8   Change in Poverty and Growth in Service Outputs
(1990–2005)

Source: Chapter 1, this volume.
Notes: Change in poverty (1991–2005) after controlling for initial level of poverty, and growth in agricultural output, manufacturing output, and service output. Poverty is defined as percentage of population below US$ 1 (PPP) per day.

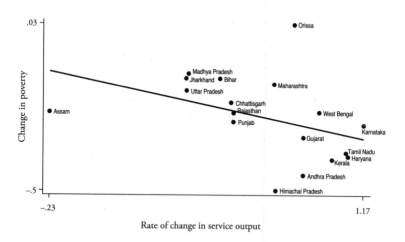

FIGURE 9   Change in Poverty and Service Outputs at the State Level
in India (1994–2005)

Source: Chapter 1, this volume.

during the sample period. In fact, the service sector is the only sector showing a statistically significant association with poverty reduction. Similar results are found when differentiating into rural and urban poverty. Service sector growth is strongly associated with a reduction in both urban and rural poverty rates. Some states like Andhra Pradesh, Karnataka, and Tamil Nadu have experienced a significant decrease in urban poverty that is associated with an increase in their service sector share. In contrast, other states like Orissa that have experienced a weaker services growth have experienced a more disappointing record of poverty alleviation (Figure 9).

Services have emerged as a key driver of poverty reduction in South Asia. Historical evidence in India from the 1970s to the early 1990s shows agricultural growth to be a major factor in reducing poverty. Indeed for decades, poverty reduction in India was synonymous with rural and, in particular, agricultural growth. But since the 1990s agriculture has lagged other sectors, shrinking in its contribution to GDP, while the contribution of services to overall GDP growth has exploded. That poverty reduction has continued despite a slowdown in agriculture points to the emergence of new drivers of poverty reduction.

Services are contributing to poverty reduction via two channels. Directly, they provide the largest source of new job growth. Indirectly, they provide the income that, when spent, drives further demand for goods and services and jobs to produce these. Figure 10 shows that the service sector in India and Pakistan has had the fastest growth in the number of jobs created in recent years, while for Bangladesh and Sri Lanka job creation in services is somewhat slower than in manufacturing. A recent World Bank study on India also reported faster changes in employment away from agriculture and into construction and trade, hotels and restaurants, and transport and communications (World Bank 2008b): by 2006, 26 per cent of all jobs in India were in the service sector. Chapter 2 provides further details on the job creation trends in all South Asian countries.

In addition to direct job creation, some estimates suggest that the indirect effect of a growing service sector can be larger than the direct effect. For instance, India's IT industry association NASSCOM estimates that for every job created in the IT sector, four additional jobs are created in the rest of the economy due to high levels of consumption spending by professionals employed in this sector (NASSCOM and CRISIL 2007).

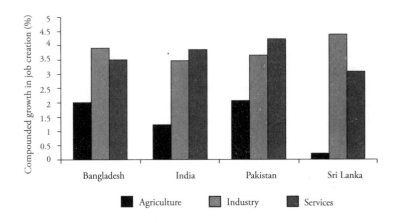

FIGURE 10   Job Creation Rates in Agriculture, Industry,
and Service Sectors (1990–2006)

Sources: Bangladesh—Labour Force Surveys, in *Key Findings of Labour Force Survey and Statistical Yearbook,* various editions. India—Sivasubramanian, *The Sources of Economic Growth in India: 1950–1 to 1999–2000,* for earlier years, and Bosworth et al. (2007) for the more recent period. Pakistan—LABORSTAT, ILO (2008) and *Handbook of Statistics on Pakistan Economy.* Sri Lanka—KILM, ILO (2008) for data up to 1989; from 1990 onwards *Labour Survey Reports,* various editions.

Service jobs are good jobs. Wage growth has been higher in the service sector than in manufacturing and agriculture in recent years in India (Figure 11). While manufacturing wages fell in the early 2000s in both rural and urban areas despite rapid economic growth, service sector wages in utilities, trade, transport, and even rural finance improved. In fact, in many sectors rural wages may have increased faster than in urban areas, possibly reflecting the rising rural–urban migration over time that is taking place in India.

It is this internal rural–urban migration and links between rural and urban labour markets that allow the modern impersonal service sector in India to contribute to overall poverty reduction, even though modern services are concentrated in urban areas.

Currently South Asia suffers from one of the lowest female labour force participation rates in the world. Only around one-third of all women of working age in India, Pakistan, and Sri Lanka are actually working or looking for work. Internationally, countries with high employment in services tend to have the highest participation of women in the labour market (Figure 12). The development of service industries, therefore,

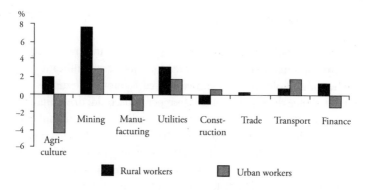

FIGURE 11   Growth in Average Daily Earnings,
India (1999–2000/2004–5)

Source: Kundu and Mohanan (2009).
Note: Agriculture includes agriculture, forestry and fishing; mining includes mining and quarrying; utilities include electricity, gas, and water supply; trade includes trade, hotels, and restaurants; transport includes transport, storage, and communications; finance includes financial intermediation, real estate, and business.

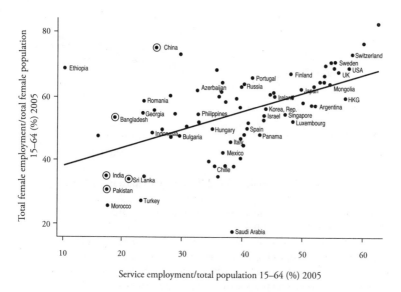

FIGURE 12   Increased Service Employment and
Female Labour Force Participation

Source: Chapter 1, this volume.

brings new workers into the labour force, making the contribution to aggregate growth even larger.[2]

The employment of women has a special role in poverty reduction. Incomes of households where women have jobs are significantly higher. Higher household incomes and enhanced economic status for women in turn reduce the number of children per household, drive higher levels of education and healthcare for children, and increase household savings and the ability to accumulate assets that generate additional income.

In both India and Pakistan, women are going into service sector jobs at a much faster rate than into manufacturing or agriculture (Figure 13). Between 1985 and 2002, female employment in services in Pakistan grew by 7 per cent per year, compared to 6 per cent female employment growth in industry.

Domestic jobs do not capture the full extent of the contribution of services to poverty reduction. Many localities also benefit from remittances received from international migrants (so-called mode 4 service exports).

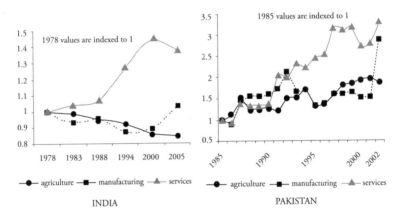

INDIA

PAKISTAN

FIGURE 13   Female Labour Force Participation by Sector

Sources: India—National Sample Survey, respective years. Pakistan—Labour Force Survey and KILM, ILO (2007).

Note: For India, the service sector employment includes trade, restaurant, transport and communications, and other services category. The figure represents the sum of employment figures for rural and urban areas. Female employment is reported as number of females employed per 1000 employed persons.

[2]In this, services play a similar role to labour-intensive manufacturing exports in East Asia. There, assembly jobs in garments and electronics have been largely filled by women moving out of low-productivity self-employment on family farms.

These remittances are often channelled directly to poor households and have become a major source of income and asset accumulation for poor households across South Asia. In Nepal, between a fifth and half of the decline in poverty between 1995 and 2004 has been attributed to increased internal and international migration. In rural Pakistan, school enrollment rates increased by 54 per cent for girls in migrant households as opposed to only 7 per cent for boys in migrant households. Children of Sri Lankan migrant-sending households had higher birth weight and spent more on private tuition, a possible contributor to better education outcomes.

SERVICE EXPORTS—MODERN AND TRADITIONAL

South Asia is not well integrated with the global economy but it has adopted more liberal policies towards the service sector. All South Asian countries are more open to trade in services than they were two decades ago. Liberalized services like business and telecommunication services have attracted significant domestic and foreign investment. In India, a majority of the foreign direct investment (FDI) inflows are concentrated in the service sector, and in particular modern impersonal services (Gordon and Gupta 2004).

Service exports can be delivered in four different ways:

1. Services being provided remotely across borders, such as IT and IT-enabled service (ITES) exports (mode 1), which account for some 28 per cent of global trade in services
2. Consumption abroad such as tourism and travel (mode 2) which account for some 14 per cent of global trade in services
3. Commercial presence through FDI (mode 3) which account for some 57 per cent of global trade in services
4. Movement of natural persons which brings in remittances (mode 4) which account for some 1 per cent of global trade in services

For South Asia, however, not all four modes of service export delivery are important. There are two important types of service exports. First is IT and ITES exports (mode 1), or modern impersonal service exports, where services are exported electronically over long distances, without the provider of the service crossing national borders. These are skill intensive sectors, and are mostly exported from India, although they are also picking up from other South Asian countries. The growth of the modern service export or IT industry in South Asia is explored in detail in Chapter 4 by Rafiq Dossani.

Service exports seem to be closely related to service sector growth. The relationship in the recent past (2000–5) is charted in Figure 14.

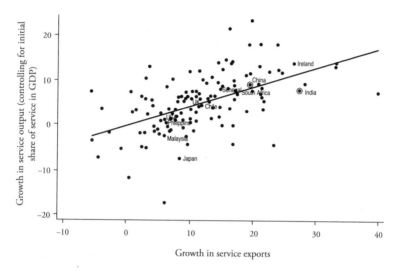

FIGURE 14   Service Value Added and Service Exports Growth (2000–5)

Source: World Bank (2008a).
Notes: Each point represents a country. Reported figure for 130 countries. Y-axis is growth in service output controlling for initial share of service in GDP. All values are in current US$ terms.

The strong positive correlation shows that countries which have had faster service sector value-added growth have also had faster service sector exports over this period. This association suggests that services cannot be viewed as responding principally to domestic demand. If that were the case, and if services were really non-tradable as conventional wisdom suggests, then there would be no relationship between services value added and services export growth. Of course, just like is the case for manufacturing, the positive relationship does not imply causality. It may be the case that countries with more successful, rapidly growing, service firms end up exporting more, or it could be the case that because of specialized service exports, the aggregate growth of service value added is raised. More microeconometric evidence would be needed to identify this causality. But in both cases, the fundamental point remains that the service sector should not be treated any longer as a domestic demand-driven, non-tradable sector.

The second important type of service exports from South Asia involves movement of natural persons across borders to provide services to a consumer (mode 4). This has typically involved less skill intensive activities and is a key contributor to the traditional service export from South Asia. Migration, and the resulting inflow of remittances, is explored in Chapter 5 by Sanket Mohapatra and Çağlar Özden.

Recently, both types of service exports have been growing rapidly. Since the 1980s, the global trade in services has grown faster than the global trade in merchandise goods. Figure 15 compares the trend in share of service trade in service value added for developing and developed countries for the period 1985–2005. What stands out is that the ratio of service trade in service output for developing countries has increased much faster than it has for developed countries. This suggests that developing countries are more focused on production of services which can be traded, rather than for domestic consumption. Modern impersonal service exports (computer and information services, financial services, business services, communication, or mode 1) are growing much faster than traditional personal service exports (migration, travel, and transport). However, within developing countries, some regions have benefitted more than the others in modern service trade.

South Asia has experienced an exponential increase in service exports at a rate which exceeds even the rapid growth of East Asian manufactured exports (Figure 16). This suggests that service exports are

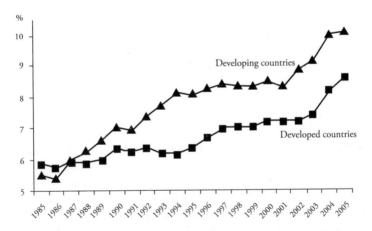

FIGURE 15   Exports of Services as a Share of Service Value Added
(*per cent*)

Source: World Bank (2008a).
Note: Developing countries are defined as middle and low income countries. Developed countries are high income Organisation for Economic Co-operation and Development (OECD) countries.

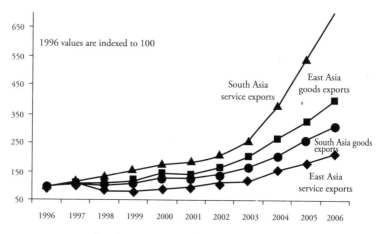

FIGURE 16   Comparing South Asia's Service Exports with
East Asia's Goods Exports

Source: IMF (2008).

Notes: Exports are in current US$ terms. East Asia includes developing countries such as Cambodia, China, Indonesia, Malaysia, the Philippines, Thailand, and Vietnam. South Asia includes Bangladesh, India, Maldives, Nepal, Pakistan, and Sri Lanka.

a key component of service-led growth. Within South Asia, the fastest growing segment of exports has been in the IT and ITES sectors.

South Asia has exhibited a clear comparative advantage in services while East Asia has shown a comparative advantage in goods. A comparison of revealed comparative advantage (RCA) in service and goods exports for South Asia and East Asia is shown in Figure 17. It shows that South Asia's comparative advantage in service exports has exploded while its comparative advantage in goods exports has declined slightly.

In the last few years, South Asia (predominantly India) has increased its comparative advantage in modern impersonal service exports, while losing comparative advantage in traditional service exports like tourism (Figure 18). This is perhaps not surprising. The infrastructure requirements for traditional services—moving people around the country—are similar to those required for moving goods, something which South Asia, and India in particular, is notoriously poor at doing. But India has an excellent telecommunication network, and so its modern impersonal service export sector has boomed. The exact reverse is seen in East Asia. There, the region had a slight comparative advantage in modern services exports in 1997,

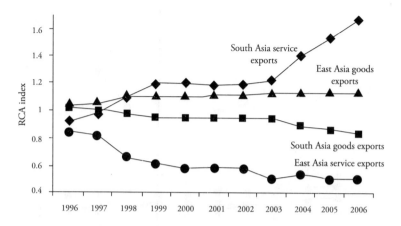

FIGURE 17   Revealed Comparative Advantage—A Comparison of
East Asia and South Asia in Service and Goods Exports

Sources: IMF (2008) and the World Bank (2008a).
Notes: The RCA index is calculated using the following concept: $RCA=(E_{CJ}/E_{CT})/(E_{WJ}/W_{WT})$ where E=exports, C=country index, J=specific sector index, W=world, T=total exports of goods and services. Data is in current US$ terms.

but this quickly eroded after the crisis, perhaps because much of the East Asian service sector exports like finance, transport, and logistics were linked to trade in goods. Traditional service exports like tourism have shown a gradual decline in East Asia's RCA. Many East Asian countries still lack the educational and language skills, broadband connectivity, and clustering of firms that has helped Indian firms exploit the new global niches in modern IT-enabled impersonal service exports

Chapter 4 by Rafiq Dossani examines the growth of the software industry in detail. It presents an overview of the region's growth in IT and ITES. The chapter includes an analysis of Pakistan, Bangladesh, Sri Lanka, and Nepal which is of interest since typically the focus has been on India because of its large absolute size. This allows a regional comparison of why some countries succeeded in modern service exports, while others floundered.

Chapter 4 reports that the modern service industry took root in South Asia due to a combination of idiosyncratic factors: the presence of qualified engineers and returning engineers from abroad. However, the subsequent growth of software exports depended crucially on the supply of qualified workers, and the lowering of communication costs,

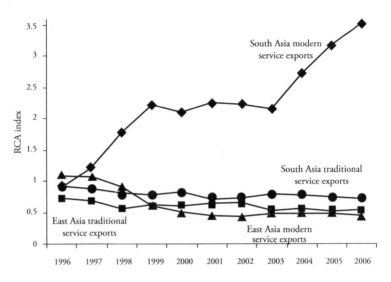

FIGURE 18   Comparative Advantage of South Asia in
Modern and Traditional Service Exports

Sources: IMF (2008) and the World Bank (2008a).

Note: The RCA index is calculated using the following concept: $RCA = (M_{CJ} / E_{CT})/(M_{WJ}/W_{WT})$ where M=modern or traditional service exports, C=country index, J=specific sector index, W=world, T=total services exports. Modern services are communication, insurance, financial, computer, information, and other business services. The remaining services such as travel, transport, royalties, license fees, construction, and personal, cultural, recreational, and government services are traditional services.

and an improved business environment. In this respect, policies such an encouraging private participation in the education sector, and telecom deregulation were helpful to the growth of the IT industry, while other targeted initiatives such as tax breaks were not particularly helpful.

While India has shown an explosive growth in IT and ITES, other South Asian countries have lagged behind. Sri Lanka was held back by its education policy which disallowed private provision. Bangladesh was held back by its restrictive bandwidth policy. Pakistan and India followed similar policies but had different political/business environments leading to lower trust levels for work done in Pakistan. South Asian countries would benefit if they were to change their higher education and bandwidth policies, and business environment in a way that encourages multinational entry, protects intellectual property rights, and lowers initial establishment costs. India's currently restrictive labour laws have not adversely affected the high-end service industry because employees mostly belong to the managerial class owing to their relatively high wage rates, and IT industries have been exempted from restrictive labour laws.

While modern impersonal service exports are important to India, traditional personal service exports are even more important to other South Asian countries. Many countries in South Asia notably Bangladesh, Sri Lanka, Nepal and, to a lesser extent, India and Pakistan are increasingly relying on manpower exports as a strategy for addressing the unemployment problem at home, and at the same time generating large foreign-currency flows of remittances. Decreasing dependency ratios in several countries are expanding the size of domestic labour markets. Lower transactions, transportation, and communication costs are facilitating the formation of migrant networks and channels for labour mobility across borders.

Chapter 5 by Mohapatra and Özden examines migration and remittances in detail. Traditional service exports have increased rapidly, as measured by remittance inflows (Figure 19). It is estimated that over 22 million people, or 1.5 per cent of the South Asian population, lived outside their country of birth in 2005. Intra-regional migration (34.5 per cent) covers the largest share of international migration movement in South Asia, while high-income non-OECD countries (25.3 per cent) and

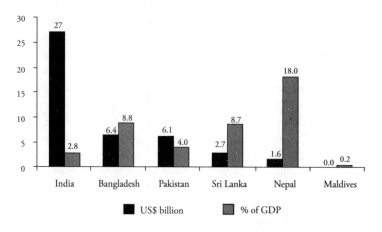

FIGURE 19   Remittances in South Asia (2007)

Source: Chapter 5, this volume (data taken from worldbank.org/prospects/ migrationandremittances).

high-income OECD countries (20.3 per cent) are the second and third largest destinations. Bangladesh–India and India–United Arab Emirates are the top two migration corridors in the region. South Asia also has a large immigrant population (about 11.2 million).

Remittances are the largest source of external fund flows in South Asia. In 2006, remittances in South Asia were almost twice as large as private debt and portfolio equity, three times as large as FDI, and seven times as large as official development assistance. Compared to other regions, remittances in South Asia are a far more important form of external fund flows than FDI. The official remittance inflows to South Asia have been increasing continuously over the past decade from US$ 5.6 billion (1.4 per cent of GDP) in 1990 to US$ 43.8 billion (3.2 per cent of GDP) in 2007. In 2007, the top recipient countries of recorded remittances in South Asia were India (US$ 27.0 billion), Bangladesh (US$ 6.4 billion), and Pakistan (US$ 6.1 billion), collectively making the South Asian region the third largest regional recipient of remittances in the world after Latin America and the Caribbean and East Asia and the Pacific. As a share of GDP, however, Nepal receives the largest formal remittance inflows (16 per cent), followed by Bangladesh (9.0 per cent), and Sri Lanka (8.7 per cent). The true size, including unrecorded flows through informal channels, is believed to be significantly larger.

Remittances improve a country's access to capital. By generating a steady stream of foreign exchange earnings, remittances can improve a country's credit worthiness and enhance its access to international capital markets. The ratio of debt to exports, a key indebtedness indicator, increases significantly when remittances are excluded. While capital flows tend to rise during favourable economic cycles and decline in bad times, remittances tend to be counter-cyclical relative to recipient countries' economic cycles. They are likely to rise when the recipient country suffers an economic downturn following a financial crisis, natural disaster, or political conflict as migrants transfer more funds during hard times (and when home currencies depreciate) to help their families and friends. In addition to bringing the direct benefit of higher wages earned abroad, migration helps households diversify their sources of income and thus reduces their vulnerability to risks.

There are also downsides to remittances. At a macroeconomic level, large and sustained remittance flows may lead to currency appreciation with adverse consequences for exports. Households receiving large amounts of remittances may become dependent on this source of income, and may prefer to reduce work efforts. Remittance channels, particularly the so-called hawala and other informal channels, may be misused for money laundering and the financing of terrorism.

In terms of policy, Mohapatra and Özden find that lowering the cost of sending remittances can have several beneficial effects (cost of sending remittances to South Asia remains high compared to the cost of sending remittances to the Philippines and Mexico), and that South Asian countries are also developing innovative ways to leverage the presence of the large diaspora abroad, such as the issuance of diaspora bonds. Similarly, more can be done to improve the earning potential of migrant workers such as setting up migrant welfare funds (as several South Asian countries have already done) to negotiating labour standards and transparent employment contracts for migrant workers. The leading country in improving migration conditions has been the Philippines, which also provides pre-departure training and facilities for re-integration of returning migrants.

SERVICE INFRASTRUCTURE

In order for service-led growth to work, countries need an appropriate infrastructure. As identified by various chapters, the key inputs for service-led growth are education, telecommunication, aviation, and connectivity. A series of chapters evaluate the status of these key factors across South Asian countries, examine their evolution over time, and provide policy recommendations.

Education

The service sector is more skill intensive than industry or agriculture in all South Asian countries. This makes higher education a critical input into the growth of the modern service sector. Chapter 6 by Carl J. Dahlman provides an in-depth look at the education sector in South Asia.

The dramatic success of modern service exports from India illustrates the importance of education with depth and talent, and this can be easily scaled up. India has benefitted from globalization of services because it has a large number of highly skilled graduates. India is known for its Indian Institutes of Technology (IITs) and for the English language ability of its service workers.

The demand for skilled engineers and other higher education graduates is immense in India. Since the formal education sector is not able to provide the number of quality graduates needed, the private IT sector in India took its own initiative. The IT industry has been working with the government to establish twenty new IITs based on a public-private partnership model. The government is also expanding the number of IITs and Indian Institutes of Management (IIMs) and other high quality higher education institutions.

The dramatic success of service exports from India illustrates the potential for creating a dynamic virtuous circle of higher education leading to the growth of service exports, leading back to faster growth and more investments in higher education. Nevertheless, the example of the Indian modern service industry also illustrates the need to reform and update antiquated and dysfunctional educational systems.

There are many problems in the higher education sector in South Asian countries. These include access, quality, relevance, financing, and governance. Policymakers should note that higher education has a long gestation period. Countries need to invest both in expanding higher education as well as in expanding access to and quality of basic education. South Asian governments should consider charging higher tuitions for elite public higher education such as at the IITs and IIMs. The government also has to develop alternative funding mechanisms, including developing a more effective student loan system.

Telecommunication

South Asia is well known for its poor infrastructure. But the infrastructure that matters to service trade is in better shape. For South Asia in the 1990s, there was faster growth in service-relevant infrastructure such as personal computers and telecommunication, compared to manufacturing-relevant

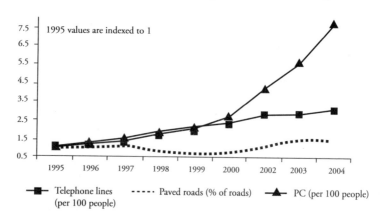

FIGURE 20   Growth of Service-relevant Infrastructure in South Asia

Source: World Bank (2008a).

infrastructure such as roads (Figure 20). The telecommunication sector has experienced major investment and competition and this has improved the electronic delivery of services tremendously. The telecommunication sector is explored in Chapter 7 by Caroline Cecot and Scott Wallsten.

Telecommunication growth is the most powerful symbol of the vitality of the service sector and, at the same time, is critical for further development of the other parts of the economy. While there has been a dramatic transformation of this sector, some policy issues remain. A key issue in the region is the design of universal access regimes to provide better connectivity and greater competition at a regional level. The policy priorities at the national level, with varying emphasis in each country, should be to reform the incumbent operator; strengthen the regulator and enhance its independence from both the incumbent and the government; eliminate barriers to entry other than those dictated by scarcity of spectrum; and establish an effective universal access scheme that widens access to services in poor and remote areas.

Civil Aviation

A few years ago, a passenger who wanted to travel from Colombo to Karachi had to go via Dubai, and a passenger who wanted to travel from Colombo to Dhaka had to go via Bangkok. In recent years, deregulation and the resulting competition in the airlines market has spawned the emergence of low cost carriers, making air travel more direct and less expensive. Chapter 8 by Yahua Zhang and Christopher Findlay documents that many barriers still remain in the civil aviation sector and the extent of liberalization varies from country to country.

India is leading the aviation reforms in South Asia, initiating deregulation as early as the 1980s, especially on international routes. Landlocked countries may be victims of geography but their isolation is sometimes deepened by their own policies, as well as those of their neighbours. Nepal's unquestioned comparative advantage in tourism is being eroded by the poor state of international and domestic aviation. Sri Lankan Airlines has benefited since it was privatized.

There are three obvious priorities for policy. The first political challenge is to prepare national airlines for a more competitive environment. Drawing upon the transforming experiences of Sri Lankan Airlines (a joint venture with Emirates), serious consideration should be given to possible joint ventures with foreign airlines, which could inject the necessary capital as well as technological and managerial improvements. At the same time, countries should push for more liberal

Bilateral Air Service Agreements which do not restrict capacity or flight frequency and grant fifth freedom rights, or even opt for more open sky agreements. Finally, there is a need for regulatory reform, in particular to enhance both the independence and capacity of the departments of civil aviation.

ORGANIZING FOR SERVICES

South Asia presents an unusual growth pattern, with a large share of the economy devoted to the service sector, and the service sector providing much of the economic growth in the last decade. The result has been rapid economic growth accompanied by significant reduction in poverty. This pattern stands in sharp contrast to conventional wisdom in development thinking. That conventional wisdom holds that labour-intensive manufacturing is the only sustainable way to promote rapid, sustained growth.

So is South Asia's growth pattern sustainable? We argue that it is because of a global services revolution that has altered the characteristics of services. Thanks to the ICT revolution, there is now a much wider array of new products that can be produced and exported at low costs. This array of products increasingly includes modern, impersonal services, and South Asia has taken advantage of these possibilities, with India establishing a clear comparative advantage in service exports. India's experience may be particular, but it points to a rapid change in the world that has important implications for all developing countries—namely the globalization of services. Other countries may or may not also have a comparative advantage in some service sectors. What is certain is that the old idea of services being non-tradable and non-scalable because of inelastic demand no longer holds for a host of modern impersonal services. Instead, it seems that under the right circumstances the service sector can demonstrate significant labour and TFP growth.

It is perhaps surprising that modern, high-skilled service exports could be beneficial for poverty reduction. Indeed, there seems to be suggestive evidence across countries and across states within India that services growth is even better for poverty than manufacturing growth. This is a topic on which more work is required, but the evidence explored in this volume suggests where further research might focus. Service sector wages appear to have risen faster than wages in the other sectors. Also, services disproportionately provide job opportunities for women, encouraging greater labour force participation among this group. Rapid services growth might also tighten labour markets within a state, leading to more rapid urbanization of people in search of jobs. The precise channel is as yet unclear, but each of the preceding effects seems to be present in India.

The link between service output growth and service export growth also appears robust, at least in the twenty-first century. This suggests that services are now also part of the broad trend towards globalization. It also suggests that service sector development typically goes hand in hand with service export development. In this, there is no difference in pattern between services and manufacturing.

This pattern of growth and poverty reduction has important implications for policy. In the case of South Asia, luck and history may have played a part in the development of services. South Asia's English language heritage, its strong traditions of higher education, its computer savvy diaspora, and its embrace of modern telecommunication infrastructure provided a basis for service exports. Perhaps as important, its notorious problems with infrastructure like power and transport, its complex logistics, and heavy licensing regimes militated against development of industry. It was natural for comparative advantage to shift towards services.

That said, the policy discussion in the region can now usefully be expanded to ask how to build on this comparative advantage. Until now, it was assumed that the critical task was how to organize for industrial growth. Growth diagnostics, business environment assessments, competitiveness studies, innovation audits, and product space analyses have become standard tools for policymakers, but all these focus exclusively on how to improve conditions for manufacturing firms. The experience of South Asia suggests that there may be other issues that need attention to support the service sector, and these issues should not be neglected. Education, telecommunication, and connectivity are the keys to ignite a service-led growth revolution.

REFERENCES

Baumol, William J. 1967. 'Macroeconomics of Unbalanced Growth: The Anatomy of Urban Crisis', *American Economic Review*, 57(3): 415–26.

————. 1985. 'Productivity Policy and the Service Sector', in R.P. Inman (ed.), *Managing the Service Economy: Prospects and Problems*. Cambridge: Cambridge University Press.

————. 1986. 'Productivity Growth, Convergence and Welfare: What the Long-run Data Show', *American Economic Review*, 76(5): 1072–85.

Bhagwati, Jagdish N. 1984. 'Splintering and Disembodiment of Services and Developing Nations', *The World Economy*, 7: 133–44.

Blinder, Alan S. 2006. 'Offshoring: The Next Industrial Revolution?', *Foreign Affairs*, 85(2): 113–28.

Bosworth, Barry and Susan M. Collins. 2008. 'Accounting for Growth—Comparing China and India', *Journal of Economic Perspectives*, 22(1): 45–66.

Bosworth, Barry, Susan Collins, and Arvind Virmani. 2007. 'Sources of Growth in the Indian Economy', in *India Policy Forum*. Washington, D.C.: Brookings. Available at http://www.brookings.edu/papers/2006/0715globaleconomics_bosworth.aspx.

Collier, Paul. 2007. *The Bottom Billion: Why the Poorest Countries are Failing and What Can Be Done About It?* New York and Oxford: Oxford University Press.

Ghani, Ejaz and Sadiq Ahmed. 2009. *Accelerating Growth and Job Creation in South Asia*. New Delhi: Oxford University Press.

Gordon, James and Poonam Gupta. 2004. 'Understanding India's Services Revolution', International Monetary Fund Working Paper WP/04/171, IMF, Washington, D.C., September.

International Monetary Fund. 2008. *Balance of Payments Yearbook*. Washington, D.C.: IMF.

Kundu, Amitabh and P.C. Mohanan. 2009. 'Poverty and Inequality Outcomes of Economic Growth in India: Focus on Employment Pattern during the Period of Structural Adjustment', presentation at OECD Seminar on 'Employment Outcomes and Inequality: New Evidence, Links and Policy Responses in Brazil, China and India'. Available at http://www.oecd.org/dataoecd/60/42/42560797.pdf, accessed in May 2009.

NASSCOM and CRISIL. 2007. 'The Rising Tide: Output and Employment Linkages of IT-ITES'. Available at http://www.nasscom.in/upload/51269/NASSCOM_CRISIL.pdf.

United Nations Industrial Development Organization (UNIDO). 2009. *Breaking In and Moving Up: New Industrial Challenges for the Bottom Billion and the Middle Income Countries*, Industrial Development Report. Vienna: UNIDO.

World Bank. 2008a. *World Development Indicators 2008*. Washington, D.C.: World Bank.

———. 2008b. 'India's Employment Challenges—Creating Jobs, Helping Workers', Report Number 35772-IN.

———. 2009. 'Reshaping Economic Geography', *World Development Report 2009*. Washington, D.C.: World Bank.

I
Role of Service in Development

I

Role of Service in Development

1

Is Service-led Growth a Miracle for South Asia?

Ejaz Ghani[#]

Services represent the fastest growing sector of the global economy and account for two-thirds of global output. World Trade Organization (2009)

South Asia, land of curry, cricket, and the Taj Mahal, has come of age. It is the new kid on the block in the area of development. Over the last twenty-five years, South Asia has grown twice as fast as the world economy. It is the second fastest growing region in the world after East Asia.[1] India has consistently ranked in the top 10 per cent of all countries in growth performance since the 1980s. While India has attracted global attention, the other South Asian countries, including Bangladesh, Pakistan, and Sri Lanka, have also done well. South Asian countries have maintained high growth rates, despite episodes of natural disasters, crises, and conflicts in the region.

Although both South Asia and East Asia are rapidly growing economies, their growth patterns are dramatically different. South Asia is a service-led growth story. East Asia is a manufacturing-led growth miracle.

[#] I am grateful to Lakshmi Iyer for her contribution to this chapter, and to Saurabh Mishra for valuable research support. I would also like to thank R. Ananad, A.Flaaen, N. Yoshida, C. Dahlman, C. Raddatz, P. Goopta, P. Banerjee, and A. Panagaria for suggestions. Any errors are my responsibility.
[1] See Ghani and Ahmed (2009).

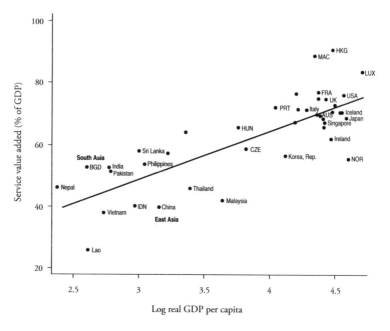

FIGURE 1.1   The Service Sector in South Asia (2005)

Source: World Bank (2008a).

Figure 1.1 shows the size of service value added in Gross Domestic Product (GDP) in South Asia, East Asia, and the Organisation for Economic Co-operation and Development (OECD) countries, as a function of the level of GDP per capita (see Annexure 1A for defintion and sources of data). We should note that in all South Asian countries—India, Pakistan, Bangladesh, Sri Lanka, and Nepal—the service sector accounts for more than 50 per cent of GDP. All these countries are above the regression line in Figure 1.1, which means that they have a much bigger share of service in GDP relative to their level of real GDP per capita. All East Asian countries are below the line, that is, they have a smaller service sector in GDP, despite higher real GDP per capita. South Asia resembles the growth patterns of Ireland and Norway, rather than that of China and Malaysia. Despite being a low-income region, South Asian countries have adopted the growth patterns of middle/high-income countries.

In addition to being the largest contributor to GDP levels, services are also the largest contributor to GDP growth in South Asia. Figure 1.2 compares the sectoral contribution of service, industry, and agriculture

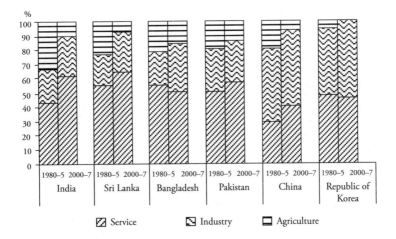

FIGURE 1.2   **Contribution of Services to GDP Growth in South Asia (1980–5, 2000–7)**

Source: World Bank (2008a).

to GDP growth in South Asian countries with that of China and Korea for the period 1980–5 and 2000–7. The contribution of services to GDP growth in South Asia is twice that of industry. The contribution of services to GDP growth has also increased over time in India, Sri Lanka, and Pakistan. In China, the contribution of industry to GDP growth is much higher than the contribution of services to GDP growth.

The manufacturing sector presents a contrasting picture. South Asia's manufacturing sector has remained small, despite several policy efforts to unshackle the sector (Rajan 2006). South Asia's share of manufacturing in GDP was only 16 per cent (in 2005) compared to 31 per cent for East Asia. South Asia's share of service value added in GDP was 52 per cent (in 2005), compared to 41 per cent for East Asia.

The South Asian experience of growth in the twenty-first century is remarkable because it contradicts a seemingly iron law of development that has held true for almost 200 years since the start of the Industrial Revolution. This conventional wisdom says that industrialization is the only route to rapid economic development. It goes further to say that as a result of globalization the pace of development can be explosive. But the potential for explosive growth has until now been distinctive to manufacturing (see UNIDO 2009). This is no longer the case in the most recent years.

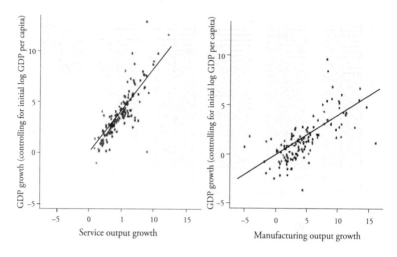

FIGURE 1.3   Relationship
between GDP Growth and
Service Value-added Growth
(2000–5)

FIGURE 1.4   Relationship
between GDP Growth and
Manufacturing Value-added
Growth (2000–5)

Source: Author's calculation using data from the World Bank (2008a).
Notes: Each point in the chart corresponds to five-year growth during 2000–5 for a specific country. GDP growth rates control for level of initial income per capita. All values are in constant 2000 US$. Growth rates are compounded annual averages. The sample consists of 134 countries.

Figures 1.3 and 1.4 plot the relationship between GDP growth on the y-axis and manufacturing growth and service output growth on the x-axis for 134 countries, controlling for initial GDP per capita. As expected, both sectors are positively associated with GDP growth. But the relationship between GDP growth and service output growth is steeper in comparison to the relationship between GDP growth and manufacturing output growth. Clearly, manufacturing is not the only route to development as assumed by conventional development economics. In particular, South Asia's development experience has shown that service-led growth is an alternative route to development.

A cross-country growth regression shows that both the service and manufacturing sectors are important to GDP growth, but that the service sector has a stronger association with overall growth than the manufacturing sector. Table 1.1 reports the cross-country estimate of

TABLE 1.1   Contribution of Manufacturing
and Service Growth to GDP Growth

	GDP Growth (2000–5)
Manufacturing output growth	0.21***
	(0.05)
Service output growth	0.63***
	(0.09)
Controlling for initial GDP per capita	Yes
Test manufacturing growth = service growth	10.41***
F-stat	
Country observations	134

Source: World Bank (2008a).
Note: Dependent variable is GDP growth. *** represents significance at 1%.

GDP growth against manufacturing value-added growth and service value-added growth, controlling for initial real GDP per capita. The coefficients on both manufacturing and service output are statistically significant. But the coefficient on service output is nearly double the coefficient on manufacturing output. Thus, the service sector is more important for GDP growth. A statistical test to examine the null hypothesis that the coefficients on service and manufacturing output are not different from each other is rejected.

The unconventional growth patterns of South Asia have attracted a lot of attention and have been hotly debated and discussed in the context of India's growth spurt.[2] Some have labelled India's growth pattern as idiosyncratic and unique (Kocchar et al. 2006), while others have suggested that South Asia should not give up its capabilities in the service sector 'in a blind attempt to follow the East Asian path of unskilled, labor-intensive, manufacturing' (Rajan 2006: 52).

The more important question, however, is not whether South Asian growth patterns are idiosyncratic and paradoxical, but how robust and sustainable is South Asia's service-led growth. This is the focus of this chapter.

This chapter compares the growth patterns in Bangladesh, India, Pakistan, and Sri Lanka, with 100 other developing and developed

[2]See Bosworth et al. (2007). Some have called India's growth pattern a 'paradox' (Banerjee 2006), others have labelled it 'idiosyncratic' (Kochhar et al. 2006), and there is emerging consensus that India's growth is a service revolution (Banga 2005; Gordon and Gupta 2004).

countries over the last quarter century. The focus is on comparing growth patterns in South Asia with East Asia, with an emphasis on distilling stylized facts on growth, export, job creation, and poverty reduction rather than identifying fundamental causes of growth and poverty reduction. This chapter addresses four questions:

1. First, how different are the growth patterns in South Asia from that of East Asia? Are these growth patterns converging or diverging?
2. Second, in what ways is South Asia's export performance distinctive?
3. Third, how pro-poor is service-led growth? Have services, manufacturing, or agriculture contributed more to job creation, poverty reduction, and gender equality?
4. Finally, can service-led growth and service exports be sustained in the face of institutional bottlenecks and the global downturn?

The rest of the chapter is organized as follows. The first section discusses the factors behind the globalization of services in the past two decades. It compares the similarities and differences between the globalization of services and the globalization of manufacturing. The second section examines the contribution of services and manufacturing sectors to GDP growth in South Asia and East Asia, and the third section analyses South Asia's export growth patterns. The fourth section explores the contribution of service-led growth to poverty reduction. The fifth section examines factors that encouraged service-led growth in South Asia, and the last section provides a conclusion with policy messages for latecomers to development.

South Asia's experience offers hope that globalization of services can indeed be a force for development in many more countries. The marginalization of Africa during a period when China and other East Asian countries grew rapidly led some to wonder if latecomers to development were doomed to failure. The process of globalization in the late twentieth century led to a divergence in incomes between those who industrialized and broke into global markets and a 'bottom billion' of people in some sixty countries where incomes stagnated for twenty years (Collier 2007). It seemed as if the 'bottom billion' would have to wait their turn for development, until giant industrializers like China became rich and uncompetitive in labour-intensive manufacturing.

The promise of the services revolution is that countries do not need to wait to get started with rapid development. There is a new boat that development latecomers can take. The globalization of service exports provides alternative opportunities for developing countries to find niches beyond manufacturing where they can specialize, scale up, and achieve explosive growth, just like the industrializers. It suggests that industrialization is *not the only* route to economic development.

THE SERVICES REVOLUTION

What contributes to growth, *how* growth takes place, and *where* it takes place, have been extensively discussed in recent empirical literature on endogenous growth, economic geography, trade, industrial organization, and urban economics (Duranton and Puga 2004; Fujita et al. 2001; Hausmann et al. 2005a; Henderson 2003; Pack and Westphal 1986; Stewart and Ghani 1991; Wolfl 2005; Young 1991). There is strong evidence that higher economic density/population density, low distance/low transportation costs, and less division/more trade—popularly labelled as the 3Ds in the World Development Report (WDR) 2009 (World Bank 2009a)—contribute to a virtuous cycle of growth, with initial growth leading to more growth. However, the 3Ds apply more to goods and less to services. The 3Ds fail to capture important differences in the characteristics of services and goods, and how these differences could potentially impact *what, how,* and *where* services grow.

The 3Ts—Technology, Transportability, and Tradability

The service sector is a latecomer to globalization. This is because services are difficult to transport and store. They are bound by 'time' and 'proximity' (for example, eating in a restaurant and getting a haircut). They are difficult to measure, monitor, and tax (Deardorff and Stern 2006; Griliches 1992). Services thus entail a higher 'cost of transaction', and often require face-to-face interaction. These characteristics tend to reduce the relevance of the 3Ds in explaining service growth dynamics, and increase the importance of 3Ts—technology, transportability, and tradability.

Technology, in particular information and communication technology (ICT), has 'disembodied' and 'splintered' services (Bhagwati 1984a, 1984b, 1987; Bhagwati et al. 2004). Personal services, which required face-to-face transactions, have been transformed into impersonal services which can be delivered electronically over long distances with little or no degradation in quality. The location, proximity, and time requirements that inhibited service trade earlier are made redundant by technology. Technology has also reduced the cost of trading or 'cost of transaction', as services can be more easily measured, exchanged, and outsourced.[3] The second T, transport, has benefitted services as cost of transporting services has come down. A key difference between globalization of services and globalization of goods is the means by which services are traded. Whereas imported goods arrive by ship, air, and road, globally traded services are often delivered using telephone lines or the internet.

Services can now be easily transported internationally through satellite and telecom networks. This is most visible in the speed with which international exchange of business services has increased. Transportation of goods has become cheaper in the past eighty years, but the cost of transporting services that could be digitized has fallen even more dramatically. Telephones and the internet have contributed to global supply chains being formed in services, just as they have been formed in manufactured goods, and enabled service firms and workers to benefit from specialization and economies of scale (Blinder 2006; Dasgupta and Singh 2000, 2005; Dossani and Kenney 2004).[4]

The third T, tradability, refers to the fact that unlike goods, many modern services face few government barriers when they are moved from one country to another. There are no borders, customs, or tariffs on the international exchange of most modern impersonal service trade.[5] Services are more widely traded thanks to a more liberal trade regime in services. The 3Ts have made more services tradable now.

[3]Google is an example of increased tangibility of advertisement service products, as its 'pay-per-click' business model has made advertisement service tangible.

[4]The IT software enabled technological unbundling of complex service processes (which codifies, standardizes, and digitizes knowledge) allowed division of certain services into components requiring different levels of skills and interactivity, thereby allowing certain portions of the erstwhile non-tradable services to be splintered into smaller jobs and farmed to outside providers for enhanced efficiency and exploring new opportunities for supply-chain management in services.

[5]United States Schedule of Specific Commitments under the General Agreement on Trade in Services (GATS) shows that there are no 'tariff' barriers *per se* on trade in modern impersonal services. Pricing and tax related measures may apply, but there are no 'at the border' tariffs, because modern impersonal services delivered electronically are difficult to monitor, especially mode 1 (cross-border) flow of services. Traditional services (modes 2, 3, 4—see Chapter 1 for details) might have a tariff component, or a regulatory related payment that can be considered to be equivalent to a tariff. For example, in air transport services, foreign owned freight aircraft might have to pay a higher airport fee, and the difference between airport fees for foreign and domestic providers can be said to be a tariff equivalent.

The world is in the early stage of the third industrial revolution—the information age (Blinder 2006). The internet age will continue to transform personal services into impersonal services. The 3Ts are contributing to the globalization of services at a dizzying pace. The range of business processes that can be globalized and digitized is constantly expanding: processing insurance claims; desktop publishing; the remote management and maintenance of information technology (IT) networks; compiling audits; completing tax returns; transcribing medical records; and financial research and analysis. The list of possible activities is almost endless.

BOX 1.1   Growth of the Global IT Service Industry in India

Half a century ago most firms kept their management offices close to their production locations and factories. Reductions in transport and communication costs have now greatly facilitated managing production from a distance. Headquarters are increasingly co-locating with other headquarters to share business services, as business services tend to exhibit *greater* economies of agglomeration, are less land intensive, employ high skilled employees valuing amenities, and are located in larger cities. Industrial production facilities increasingly co-locate with other production plants in smaller and more specialized towns and not in big cities. This partly explains why small towns have grown faster in China than in India, as China has followed manufacturing-led growth which benefits from production being shifted away from large cities into small towns. The urbanization pattern in India is different as India has relied more on service-led growth.

Most ICT service firms in India provide support to global business services. They, in turn, are concentrated in cities. Bangalore is an example of this. There are other emerging cities (for example, Hyderabad) where service export has exploded.

Bangalore is a concentrated service centre, as it accounts for about one-third of India's software exports and nearly one-third of total employment in IT services and business processing services. The IT firms in Bangalore have built huge campuses, some of which are as modern and efficient as anything in Silicon Valley. Abundance of high skilled labour and firms in Bangalore has attracted even more high skilled workers and more firms to the city. The spectrum of providing business service support from Bangalore is wide ranging from low-skill functions (for example, data mining and call centres) to high-skill functions (for example, accounting support and software programming).

Service firms and workers are more productive in concentrated markets (see Deardorff 1985, 2001; Deardorff and Stern 2006; Duranton and Puga 2005; Puga 1999, 2002) such as Bangalore because:

- sellers can cluster within a reasonable distance, but both buyers and sellers in ICT do not have to cluster within a reasonable distance, as long-distance infrastructure allows the benefits of such an agglomeration to be reaped;
- concentration allows for a more efficient sharing of local infrastructure;
- a thick market allows for a better matching between employees and employers; and
- a larger market facilitates networking, learning, and internalization of knowledge spillovers.

Services are now a high productivity area. Service firms and service workers tend to cluster to take advantage of scale economies and externalities, just like the manufacturing sector. They tend to be geographically concentrated, for example, finance in New York and Mumbai, insurance in Hartford, IT services in Silicon Valley and in Bangalore in India (Box 1.1). Clustering in services can potentially be more persistent and concentrated as services are less land intensive and they benefit more from knowledge spillovers. A large-scale call centre in India is run more like a factory, reaping economies of scale. The contracting for services from specialist providers is a way to achieve economies of scale and specialization in providing services. All in all, technological change has digitalized commerce, and made services tangible, transportable, and tradable. So, are there some services which are benefitting more than the others from the 3Ts?

Modern and Traditional Services

Services can be divided into two broad categories—modern impersonal services and traditional personal services. Modern impersonal services include what Baumol called in 1985 'progressive impersonal services'. The use of the 3Ts has enabled personal services to be delivered impersonally and electronically. These include communication, banking, insurance, and business related services. These services take advantage of ICT, globalization, and scale economies and benefit from higher productivity growth rates. The definition of modern services can change as ICT enables traditional personal services to be delivered electronically. For example, medical services (transcription, radiology) have the potential of being globalized. E-government initiatives can be outsourced. Modern impersonal services have experienced rapid growth because they are more intensive users of ICT capital equipment, which has made modern services more dynamic.

Traditional personal services include what Baumol (1985) has called 'stagnant personal services' such as trade, hotels, restaurants, beauty shops, barbers, education, and health, which often require face-to-face interaction, and where use of ICT is limited. Traditional services also include 'stagnant impersonal services' such as transport, government, and public administration services. Stagnant personal and stagnant impersonal services benefit less from ICT and technological changes, although there is scope to improve their productivity (for example, increased use of ICT in retail and wholesale trade and government services) with the use of technology. In general, traditional personal services have benefitted less from the 3Ts. They have not grown as rapidly as modern impersonal services.

As a result of the 3Ts, services have become the fastest growing sector in global trade. Since the 1980s, global trade in services has grown faster than global trade in merchandise goods (see WTO 2009). More interestingly, developing countries appear to be accessing these forces of globalization more than developed countries. Figure 1.5 shows service exports as a share of service value added for developing and developed countries, over the period 1985–2005. What stands out is that this ratio has increased much *faster* for developing countries than for developed countries. This suggests that developing countries are focusing on the production of services which can be traded. An example of this is the IT and IT-enabled services (ITES) sector in India which is mostly export driven, with little domestic market.

A disaggregation of global service exports into *modern impersonal service* exports (computer and information services, financial services, business services, and communication) and *traditional personal service* exports (remittances from migrants, travel and transport) shows that the former is growing much faster than the latter, in both developing and developed countries. It is also striking that modern service exports from developing countries have grown much faster than those from developed countries. This is despite the fact that many modern services are skill intensive.

South Asia, in particular, is a global leader in service exports, having experienced an exponential growth after starting from a low base. The

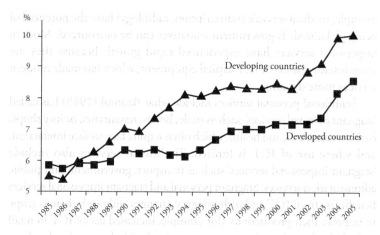

FIGURE 1.5   Service Exports as a Share of Total Services Value Added
(*percentage*)

Source: World Bank (2008a).
Note: Developing countries are defined as middle and low-income countries.
Developed countries are high-income OECD countries.

pace at which the share of service exports has grown in South Asia has
exceeded the growth rate in the share of service exports and goods exports
from East Asia during the last decade (Figure 1.6). Global trade in
services has increased productivity and enabled service-led growth to be
sustained in South Asia over the last two decades. The shift of resources
from low productivity (agriculture and some manufacturing goods in
South Asia) to high productivity (modern and impersonal services that
can take advantage of technology) has been a key driver of accelerated
growth in South Asia.

ARE SERVICES AN ENGINE OF GROWTH?

This section examines four different aspects of service-led growth in South
Asia. First, how distinctive is South Asia's service-led growth? Second, are
growth patterns in South Asia and East Asia converging or diverging?
Third, which types of services are driving service growth—modern
impersonal services or traditional personal services? Fourth, what has
been the contribution of services to productivity growth?

There are two distinctive features of South Asia's growth pattern. First,
South Asian countries have not followed the traditional development path

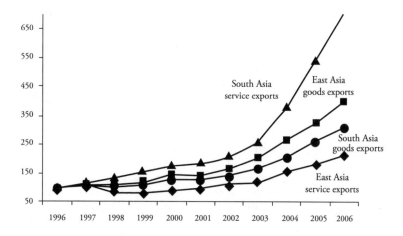

Source: IMF (2008).

FIGURE 1.6   Service and Goods Exports in South Asia and East Asia
(*service and good exports, 1996 = 100*)

Notes: Exports are in current US$ terms. East Asia includes developing countries such as Cambodia, China, Indonesia, Malaysia, the Phillipines, Thailand, and Vietnam. South Asia includes Bangladesh, India, Maldives, Nepal, Pakistan, and Sri Lanka.

of 'agriculture to manufacturing to services'. The second feature of the region is that the growth rate in service value added has far exceeded the growth rate in GDP during the last decade for the region as a whole. The decadal growth in service output for South Asia is significantly higher than the growth rates in other developing countries, developed counties, and the world average.

How big is the service sector in South Asia? We can check whether South Asia's share of services in GDP is too big or too small compared to other developing and developed countries by regressing the service share of GDP on the level of per capita income, non-linearities in development (captured by the square of per capita income), and country size (proxied for by land area), and including dummy variables for the different South Asian countries. These regressions are similar to the ones reported in Kochhar et al. (2006). We report these regressions for 1981, 1991, and 2005 in Table 1.2.

In 1981, India had a negative coefficient when one compares its share of services in GDP to other developing and developed economies, but it was not a significant outlier. The other South Asian countries had a

TABLE 1.2   South Asia and China in the Cross Section: Shares
of Manufacturing and Services in GDP

	Panel A					
	Share of Output Services			Share of Output Manufacturing		
	1981	1991	2005	1981	1991	2005
Log GDP per capita	33.20*	10.86	24.20**	29.74***	33.70***	18.80***
	(19.92)	(12.74)	(12.00)	(12.42)	(10.45)	(6.89)
Log GDP per capita^2	−4.00	0.32	−1.60	−3.74**	−4.53***	−2.38**
	(3.10)	(1.92)	(1.77)	(1.91)	(1.58)	(1.03)
India indicator	−0.58	4.77***	5.80***	6.73***	2.91***	3.21***
	(2.06)	(1.59)	(1.52)	(1.94)	(1.23)	(0.78)
China indicator	−16.67***	−6.72**	−9.59***	24.75***	18.04***	18.51***
	(4.96)	(3.52)	(3.41)	(5.86)	(2.88)	(1.52)
Bangladesh indicator	6.48***	8.49***	7.35***	5.93***	1.76*	5.11***
	(1.77)	(1.49)	(1.43)	(1.15)	(1.01)	(0.73)
Pakistan indicator	3.40***	6.28***	3.64***	4.86***	2.69***	6.02***
	(1.31)	(1.22)	(1.29)	(0.85)	(0.95)	(0.73)
Sri Lanka indicator	−0.46	3.81***	6.57***	5.27***	−0.47	5.91***
	(1.25)	(1.27)	(1.34)	(0.85)	(1.03)	(0.83)
Control for size	Yes	Yes	Yes	Yes	Yes	Yes
Test India=China, F-value		20.50***	39.08***	19.03***	58.80***	210.06***
Observations	125	158	161	100	136	155

	Panel B			
	Change in Share of Output in Services		Change in Share of Output in Manufacturing	
	1981–2005	1991–2005	1981–2005	1991–2005
	(1)	(7)	(2)	(4)
Log initial GDP per capita	6.94***	1.45	−2.77**	−0.78
	(1.52)	(1.28)	(1.32)	(0.83)
Average annual GDP growth	−0.11	−1.46***	0.57	0.80***
	(0.66)	(0.33)	(0.54)	(0.25)
India indicator	12.35***	8.60***	−3.51**	0.23
	(2.42)	(1.60)	(1.72)	(1.04)
China indicator	19.21***	12.79***	−10.30***	−2.20
	(4.68)	(2.38)	(3.80)	(1.78)
Bangladesh indicator	5.14***	3.89***	0.93	4.11***
	(2.06)	(1.56)	(1.27)	(0.94)
Pakistan indicator	3.63**	0.12	1.80	3.34***
	(1.96)	(1.29)	(1.28)	(0.75)

(contd...)

(Table 1.2 contd...)

	Panel B			
	Change in Share of Output in Services		Change in Share of Output in Manufacturing	
	1981–2005	1991–2005	1981–2005	1991–2005
	(1)	(7)	(2)	(4)
Sri Lanka indicator	11.53***	8.49***	2.22**	6.27***
	(1.70)	(1.22)	(1.05)	(0.73)
Observations	113	145	88	122

Notes: Robust standard errors are reported in paranthesis.
*** represents significance at 1%, ** at 5%, and * at 10%.
Country size is measured by area in square kilometres.

larger relative size of services in GDP in 1981. Both Bangladesh and Pakistan were large significant positive outliers in 1981 compared to the norm. China had an unusually small share of the service sector in GDP in 1981.

By 1991, India had become a significant positive outlier in its share of service output in GDP, compared to the norm. China remained a negative outlier, but less so in 1991 (6.7 percentage points below the norm) compared to 1981 (16.7 percentage points below the norm). The other South Asian counties remained significant positive outliers compared to the norm in 1991.

By 2005, India and other South Asian countries had emerged as even bigger positive outliers compared to the norm, while China remained a negative outlier. Thus, a divergence in growth pattern can be clearly seen between India, on the one hand, and China, on the other. South Asia has indeed witnessed a service-led growth which is very different from the manufacturing-led growth in China.

What about the manufacturing sector? Is South Asia a huge negative outlier in manufacturing compared to the norm? Table 1.2 reports similar regressions for the manufacturing sector as well. The regression results show that compared to the norm, China was a massive positive outlier in manufacturing in 1981. Its share of manufacturing in GDP was 24 percentage points greater than the norm, controlling for other factors. Bangladesh, India, Pakistan, and Sri Lanka were also significant positive outliers in manufacturing in 1981. But they were small outliers compared to China. By 1991 and 2005, South Asia had become less of an outlier compared to the norm. While remaining a large positive outlier compared to the norm, China's share of manufacturing in GDP dropped to 18.5 percentage points above the norm in 2005.

Are Service-led and Manufacturing-led Growth Converging?

As business conditions change, the distinction between services and manufacturing is becoming increasingly blurred. This blurring between manufacturing and services would suggest that growth patterns in South Asia and East Asia should be converging. The manufacturing sector is taking on characteristics of the service sector, with a growing share of service occupations and more revenues being derived from services, whereas services are becoming more like manufacturing as they have a growing impact on other sectors of the economy (OECD 2005). Firms' business models are evolving from 'make it, sell it' to 'make it, sell it, and service it'. An example of this is Rolls Royce in the UK, which traditionally relied on manufacturing jet engine goods, but is now as much a service firm, as it makes more profit from service, repair, and maintenance. Will India's 'idiosyncratic' growth pattern finally turn out to be no different from that of China, as India catches up in manufacturing, and China catches up with India in services?

South Asia and East Asia indeed appear to be converging in their growth patterns. The cross-country regression results for changes in sectoral shares of service in GDP for the periods 1981–2005 and 1991–2005 are reported in Table 1.2. China's share of service sector in GDP has increased at a more dramatic pace compared to the norm. It increased by 19 percentage points more than the norm during the period 1981–2005, and 12.79 percentage points more than the norm during the period 1991–2005. India has also experienced rapid growth in service share, but its growth is less dramatic. India's service share in GDP increased by 12 percentage points compared to other countries during the period 1981–2005, and 8.6 percentage points more than the other countries during the period 1991– 2005.

China's service sector started from a small base, and it has therefore experienced a faster growth rate. Bangladesh, Pakistan, and Sri Lanka are also positive outliers in changes of service share in GDP compared to the norm, but they have grown at a slower rate than India and China. The more rapid growth rate in China compared to India would suggest that the growth patterns in China and India are indeed converging over time.

Their growth patterns are also converging when we compare the change in share of manufacturing in GDP. In China, this has grown at a significant negative rate compared to the norm. India has also experienced a negative growth rate in its share of manufacturing in GDP compared to the norm, but less so than China. While India remains the laggard in manufacturing, Bangladesh and Pakistan have performed well in manufacturing compared to the norm.

In conclusion, the cross-country regressions on sectoral growth patterns suggest that South Asia has experienced service-led growth and East Asia has experienced manufacturing-led growth over the last three decades. Service is a large sector in South Asia compared to the norm after controlling for the stage of development. It is not only India but other South Asian countries that are large positive outliers in service when we compare their share of service value added in GDP with the rest of the world. But their growth patterns are converging. The growth in share of service output in GDP has increased faster in China compared to the norm. Thus, India and China appear to be converging when we compare the growth in *size* of service share in GDP.[6] More importantly, India has experienced a rapid growth in services despite a small manufacturing sector. This suggests that manufacturing is not a pre-requisite to services-led growth.

Which Services are Growing Faster?

Has growth in modern impersonal services outperformed growth in traditional personal services in South Asia? Figure 1.7 compares the growth in modern impersonal service output and traditional personal service output. It shows that the 3Ts have enabled much faster growth in modern service output.[7] Modern impersonal service output, which includes business service, communication, banking, and insurance, has seen an average annual growth rate of more than 10 per cent per annum in Bangladesh, India, and Sri Lanka during the period 2000–6. Pakistan and Nepal have experienced lower growth rates in modern service output. Traditional personal services, which include migration and remittances, tourism, and transport, have grown at a slightly lower growth rate.

[6]What are the limits to either pattern of growth? The differences in growth patterns can persist because of hysteresis and specialization, and because services are generally more 'independent' than the manufacturing sector (Pilat and Wolfl 2005). Services can thrive, even if the manufacturing sector remains stagnant, if service growth depends on export rather than domestic markets. But a dynamic manufacturing sector will be difficult to sustain if the services that support modern manufacturing enterprises (for example, telecom, banking, and transport) are not well developed.

[7]Unlike India, China has seen a faster growth in traditional services. In the recently approved Eleventh Five Year Plan (2006–10), 'Promoting Modern Services Industry' has been given a prominent position for the first time. This emphasis on services confirms China's determination to expand from traditional into modern services.

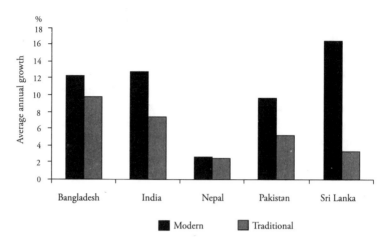

FIGURE 1.7   Modern and Traditional Service Outputs in
South Asia (2000–6)
(*average annual growth, per cent*)

Sources: India—CSO-India Stats; Pakistan—1975–2004: *Handbook of Statistics on Pakistan Economy 2005*; Nepal—*Statistical Yearbook of Nepal 2005* and *Economic Report Nepal Rastra Bank 2005/2006*; Sri Lanka—Economic and Social Statistics of Sri Lanka.

Notes: Modern services include banking, insurance, financial, and communication-related services. Traditional services include trade, hotels and restaurants, personal, cultural and recreational, community and social, transportation, storage, real estate dwelling, and government and public administration services. In the case of Nepal and Bangladesh, where national accounts data has transportation, storage, and communication as one category, this service category has been included under traditional services.

In OECD economies, several modern impersonal service industries are characterized by strong productivity growth. These growth rates are comparable to some high-growth industries within manufacturing. Moreover, modern services have consistently shown strong positive growth rates over the past twenty years. High productivity growth rates in services are attributed to trade, increasing returns to scale, strong uptake of ICT equipment, and competitive pressures (Baily and Gordon 1988; Triplett and Bosworth 2004).

Table 1.3 reports total factor productivity (TFP) growth rates for China and India for different sectors and for different periods (Bosworth and Collins 2008). India has experienced much higher TFP growth rates in the service sector compared to the manufacturing and agricultural

TABLE 1.3 Sources of Growth in Output per Worker in India and China: Total Economy and Major Sectors (1980–2006)

Component	Total Economy				Agriculture				Industry				Services			
	1980–90	1990–2000	2000–6	1980–2006	1980–90	1990–2000	2000–6	1980–2006	1980–90	1990–2000	2000–6	1980–2006	1980–90	1990–2000	2000–6	1980–2006
India																
Output per worker	3.5	4.1	4.5	4.0	2.2	1.3	1.4	1.6	3.4	3.3	2.7	3.1	2.8	4.9	4.6	4.1
Contribution of capital	1.1	1.8	2	1.6	0.2	0.5	0.5	0.4	1.5	2.4	0.9	1.6	0.4	1.3	2.3	1.3
Contribution of education	0.3	0.4	0.4	0.4	0.3	0.3	0.4	0.3	0.3	0.4	0.2	0.3	0.3	0.4	0.4	0.4
Contribution of land	-0.1	0	-0.1	-0.1	-0.1	-0.1	-0.4	-0.2	0.0	0.0	0.0	0.0	0.0	0.0	0.0	0.0
TFP	2.2	1.8	2.1	2.0	1.9	0.7	0.9	1.2	1.5	0.6	1.6	1.2	2.1	3.1	1.9	2.4
China*																
Output per worker	5.5	8.9	9.0	7.8	4.7	4.6	4.2	4.5	2.7	10.2	10.4	7.8	5.5	4.7	6.0	5.4
Contribution of capital	2.4	3.8	4.2	3.5	1.8	2.2	1.7	1.9	1.5	2.8	3.4	2.6	1.8	3.4	3.8	3.0
Contribution of education	0.4	0.3	0.3	0.0	0.3	0.2	0.2	0.3	0.4	0.3	0.3	0.3	0.4	0.3	0.3	0.3
Contribution of land	-0.1	0.1	0.0	0.3	-0.3	0.3	0.0	0.0	0.0	0.0	0.0	0.0	0.0	0.0	0.0	0.0
TFP	2.7	4.5	4.4	3.9	2.9	1.8	2.2	2.3	0.8	6.9	6.4	4.7	3.2	1.1	1.8	2.0

Source: Bosworth and Collins (2008).

Note: * Time periods used for China end at 2004.

sectors. India's TFP growth rate in the service sector has increased at twice the rate compared to industry. India has also performed better than China when we compare its TFP growth rates in the service sector with that of China. China has experienced a much higher productivity growth rate in manufacturing compared to India.

Figure 1.8 compares the contribution of service, industry, agriculture, and resource reallocation to national labour productivity growth rates for the 1990s and 2000–6 for China, India, Bangladesh, Pakistan, Sri Lanka, and USA. It shows that the sectoral contribution of the service sector to aggregate labour productivity growth has increased over time in India, Bangladesh, Pakistan, and Sri Lanka. The contribution of services to national labour productivity growth is far greater than the contribution of industrial labour productivity growth in South Asia. China's labour productivity growth pattern is different. In China, industrial labour productivity has contributed more to aggregate labour productivity growth, and its contribution

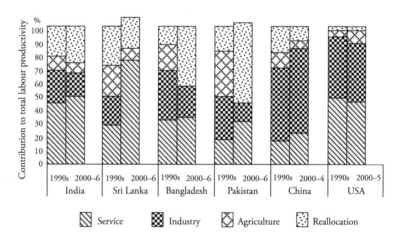

FIGURE 1.8   Contribution of the Service Sector to National Labour
Productivity in South Asia, China, and USA (1990–2006)

Source: World Bank (2008a).
Note: Labour productivity is calculated as average annual growth in real output per worker. The contribution from resource reallocation is calculated by subtracting each sector's growth rate, weighted by the sector's share in value added at the outset of each sub-period from the total economy's growth rate. The figure is restricted to only positive contributions to labour productivity growth.

has increased over time. In the US, the contribution of sectoral labour productivity growth rates to the national labour productivity growth rate is evenly balanced across sectors.

A striking feature of Figure 1.8 is that the increase in national labour productivity growth rate from the reallocation of labour across sectors is much higher in South Asia compared to China and the US. This is expected as agriculture still accounts for a large share of the labour force in South Asia. Labour productivity in agriculture is low. Given the large size of the agricultural sector in South Asia, there is huge scope for sustaining a service-led growth in the region, as resources reallocate from low productivity to high productivity sectors.

A comparison of cross-country regression results in growth rates in total labour productivity, service labour productivity, and industrial labour productivity further confirms the miracle of service-led growth in South Asia and manufacturing-led growth in East Asia. Table 1.4 shows the results of cross-country regressions in growth in total labour productivity, service labour productivity, and industrial labour productivity for 100 countries, controlling for initial GDP per capita, and average annual GDP growth rate for the period 1991–2005.

From the cross-country regression results it is clear that service is not a stagnant sector. Column 1 in Table 1.4 reports cross-country results of growth in national labour productivity regressed on initial GDP per capita to control for stage of development, and average annual growth rate in agriculture, manufacturing, and service output. Agricultural output growth has a negative and significant coefficient. The coefficients on growth in manufacturing output and service output are both positive and significant. However, the size of the coefficient on service output growth is more than double compared to the coefficient on manufacturing output growth. The larger coefficient on service output growth compared to manufacturing output growth would suggest that service is a bigger source of labour productivity growth.

Column 2 in Table 1.4 shows the coefficients on country indicators for the same regressions. China has experienced a much higher total labour productivity growth rate compared to other developing and developed countries. India is also a positive outlier in the total labour productivity growth rate as compared to the norm, but is less of an outlier compared to China. The other South Asian countries including Bangladesh and Sri Lanka are also significant positive outliers on national labour productivity growth compared to the norm. Pakistan is an exception in South Asia, as it has a significant negative coefficient.

Column 6 in Table 1.4 shows the results for growth in industrial labour productivity. The lack of availability of data on industrial employment has reduced the number of country observations dramatically, and we limit country indicators to China and India. We use industrial labour productivity growth in the regression as data on manufacturing employment is not available. When we compare their industrial labour

TABLE 1.4   India and China in the Cross Section: Labour Productivity (1991, 2005)

	Growth in Total Labour Productivity		Growth in Services Labour Productivity		Growth in Industrial Labour Productivity	
	(1)	(2)	(3)	(4)	(5)	(6)
Log initial GDP	0.0004	0.001	0.007***	0.009***	0.01***	0.01***
per capita	(0.002)	(0.002)	(0.002)	(0.004)	(0.003)	(0.004)
Average annual			0.60***	0.45***	0.81***	0.51***
GDP growth			(0.10)	(0.28)	(0.20)	(0.17)
Average annual growth						
in agricultural output	−0.24**	−0.22**				
	(0.10)	(0.10)				
Average annual growth						
in manufacturing output	0.18***	0.16***				
	(0.05)	(0.06)				
Average annual growth						
in services output	0.48***	0.45***				
	(0.07)	(0.07)				
India indicator		0.009***		0.03***		0.01*
		(0.003)		(0.006)		(0.006)
China indicator		0.03***		0.02***		0.06**
		(0.004)		(0.01)		(0.01)
Bangladesh indicator		0.009***				
		(0.002)				
Pakistan indicator		−0.008***				
		(0.002)				
Sri Lanka indicator		0.004*				
		(0.002)				
Observations	101	101	44	44	44	44

Notes: Robust standard errors are reported in paranthesis.
*** represents significance at 1%, ** at 5%, and * at 10%.
Country size is measured by area in square kilometres.

productivity growth with other countries, and control for stage of development and average annual GDP growth, the coefficient on the China indicator is positive and significant. This is consistent with China being a global power house in manufacturing. The coefficient on the India indicator is also positive but small.

The results for growth in service labour productivity are reported in columns 3 and 4 in Table 1.4. Once again, lack of data availability has limited the use of country indictors to China and India. When we compare their service labour productivity growth with other countries, and control for stage of development and average annual GDP growth, the coefficient on the India indicator is positive and significant. This is consistent with India emerging as a global power house in services. The coefficient on the China indicator is also positive.

Figure 1.9 plots service labour productivity against industrial labour productivity, after controlling for initial GDP per capita and GDP growth. It shows that there is as much potential for developing countries to gain from service-led growth as they have from following a manufacturing-led growth. India is way above the line and it shows much higher labour productivity in the service sector as compared to industry. China shows much higher labour productivity in industry compared to services. There are two tipping points that are driving higher service labour productivity growth rates. First, low-income countries that have the benefit of low wage rates, like India, are catching up with the global production possibility frontier in services. Second, high-income countries like Singapore, Sweden, United Kingdom, and United States are pushing the global production possibility frontier in services through innovation.

To summarize, GDP growth in South Asia has benefitted from an expanding service sector which, in turn, has benefitted from higher labour productivity growth rates. In essence, the service sector in South Asia has behaved like the manufacturing sector in East Asia.

There is as much scope for catch-up through productivity growth in services as there is in manufacturing. As the service sector is much larger in relative size than manufacturing, both regionally and globally, heeding the needs of services growth is important for policymakers.

Because of tradability, the demand curve for many services has become much more elastic. This permits services to be a source of sustained growth (absent this, growth is choked off by declining prices when the demand curve slopes down). The demand for services increases disproportionately with increasing income. Services have huge potential for productivity gains because of trade, income elasticity, economies of

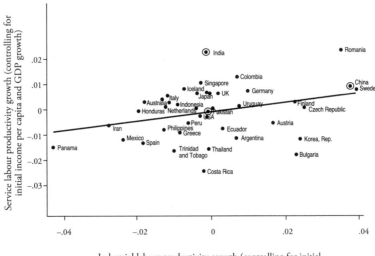

FIGURE 1.9   Comparing Service Labour Productivity Growth and Manufacturing Labour Productivity Growth (1991–2005)

Note: The vertical axis is growth in service labour productivity after controlling for initial income per capita and GDP growth whereas the horizontal axis is industrial labour productivity growth controlled for initial income per capita and GDP growth, for the time period 1991–2005. The line represents a linear regression line.

scale and specialization, and externalities from learning, networking, and knowledge spillovers.

HOW DISTINCTIVE IS SOUTH ASIA'S EXPORT PATTERN?

A distinctive feature of South Asia is that it is emerging as a major service exporter. Modern impersonal service export is growing faster than traditional personal service export in all South Asian countries. India has the highest decadal growth rate in modern service export (Figure 1.10).[8]

[8]Trade in services takes place through four main channels, and the World Trade Organization (WTO) distinguishes four different modes of services delivery. These include cross-border trade in services such as IT and ITES exports (mode 1), consumption abroad such as tourism (mode 2), commercial presence through foreign direct investments (mode 3), and movement of natural persons which brings in remittances (mode 4). Mode 1

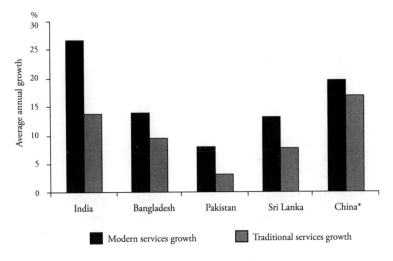

FIGURE 1.10   **Average Annual Growth in Modern and Traditional Service Exports (1995–2005)**
(*percentage*)

Source: IMF (2008).

Note: Modern services include exports in telecommunications, computer and information services, other business services, financial services, insurance, royalties, and license fees. Traditional services include travel, transportation, construction, and personal, cultural, and recreational service exports. * Data for China is from 1995 to 2007.

Figure 1.11 compares the share of IT and ITES, the fastest growing modern impersonal services, in total service exports, against real GDP per capita for South Asia, East Asia, and OECD countries. We see that India is a huge outlier as its service exports mainly consist of IT/ITES exports. The export patterns for other South Asian countries are also dominated by modern service exports, compared to China for example. The share of IT and ITES exports in total service exports for South Asia resembles the export patterns of more developed economies like USA. This is remarkable given that South Asia is still at an early stage of development.

---

is equivalent to modern impersonal service export. Modes 2,3, and 4 are equivalent to traditional personal service export. The WTO estimates that the shares of modes 1, 2, 3, and 4 in global trade in service are 28, 14, 57, and 1 per cent, respectively. The share of mode 1 is on the rise compared to other modes of delivery. Remittances are not counted as exports in Balance of Payments statistics (they are reported separately). Remittances are only a small portion of the value added by immigrants abroad—their full earnings from providing services are not counted in a country's exports.

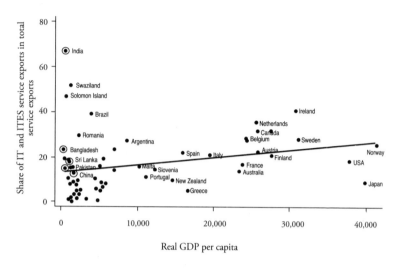

FIGURE 1.11   IT and ITES Exports as a Ratio
of Total Service Exports (2006)

Source: IMF (2008).
Note: IT and ITES are measured by adding computer and information services plus
the miscellaneous business services category in the Balance of Payments.

Table 1.5 reports cross-country level regression results for the share
of total service exports in total exports of goods and services, and the
share of modern impersonal service export (IT and ITES exports) in
total exports. In 1982, the South Asian countries were negative outliers
when we compare the share of their service export in total exports with
other countries, and control for stage of development, non-linearities in
development, and country size. Only India had a positive coefficient, but
it was not significantly different from zero. In 2006, India was a significant
and large positive outlier. Its share of service export in total exports was
18.38 percentage points greater than the norm. China also had a positive
coefficient but it was not significantly different from zero.

Modern impersonal service exports include a good measure of IT
and ITES. Cross-country data for IT exports is available only from 2000
onwards. In 2000, India stands out as a significant and positive outlier
when we compare its share of IT and ITES exports in total exports of
goods and services with the rest of the world, and control for real GDP per
capita and non-linearities in development (see Table 1.5). The other South
Asian countries including Pakistan and Sri Lanka also have significant

TABLE 1.5   South Asia in the Cross Section—Share of Service Exports and Modern Service Exports (Computer and Information Service Exports) in Total Exports of Goods and Services

	Panel A							
	Share of Service Exports in Total Exports				Share of Computer, Information Services			
	1982	1982	2006	2006	2000	2000	2006	2006
Log GDP per capita	−7.2	−9.3	−1.41	−3.01	−2.01**	−1.94*	−3.17*	−3.21*
	(27.09)	(29.95)	(26.37)	(27.1)	(1.06)	(1.08)	(1.90)	(1.89)
Log GDP per capita^2	0.83	1.1	0.59	0.81	0.35**	0.35**	0.53*	0.57*
	(3.94)	(4.3)	(3.82)	(3.9)	(0.18)	(0.18)	(0.30)	(0.30)
India indicator		0.87		18.3***		7.98***		14.74***
		(4.73)		(3.3)		(0.09)		(0.16)
China indicator		−1.37		8.03		0.38		0.68*
		(7.6)		(8.4)		(0.28)		(0.41)
Bangladesh indicator		−6.3		−17.6***		0.04***		0.10
		(4.4)		(2.8)		(0.01)		(0.07)
Pakistan indicator		−1.1		−9.2***		0.25***		0.34***
		(3.2)		(2.5)		(0.04)		(0.09)
Sri Lanka indicator		−5.1*		−9.7***		−0.0004		0.99***
		(2.7)		(2.6)		(0.04)		(0.09)
Control for size	Yes	Yes	Yes	Yes	Yes	Yes	Yes	Yes
Observations	109	109	125	125	137	137	116	116

	Panel B			
	Change in Share of Service Exports 1982–2006		Change in Share of Computer, Info. Services 2000–6	
	(1)	(2)	(3)	(4)
Log initial GDP per capita	1.40	1.27	0.20	0.28**
	(2.73)	(3.09)	(0.14)	(0.14)
Average annual GDP growth	−0.69	−0.77	5.73	4.01
	(0.71)	(0.87)	(3.77)	(0.20)
India indicator		14.9***		6.59***
		(4.95)		(0.09)
China indicator		2.44		−0.22
		(7.48)		(0.17)
Bangladesh indicator		−11.61***		0.11
		(4.51)		(0.08)
Pakistan indicator		−8.27**		0.08
		(4.11)⁻		(0.06)

(contd...)

(Table 1.5 contd...)

	Panel B		
	Change in Share of Service Exports 1982–2006		Change in Share of Computer, Info. Services 2000–6
	(1)	(2)	(3)	(4)
Sri Lanka indicator		–3.45		1.00***
		(3.70)		(0.05)
Observations	93	93	94	94

Notes: Robust standard errors are reported in paranthesis.
*** represents significance at 1%, ** at 5%, and * at 10%.
Country size is measured by area in square kilometres.

positive coefficients. Bangladesh is the only country in South Asia whose modern service export is no different than the norm.

How important are traditional service exports to South Asia? The movement of natural persons which brings in remittances (mode 4 according to WTO) is an important component of traditional personal service export from South Asia. However, remittances are not counted as exports in Balance of Payments statistics (they are reported separately).

It is estimated that over 22 million people, or 1.5 per cent of the South Asian population, live outside their country of birth. Intra-regional migration (34.5 per cent) covers the largest share of international migration movement in South Asia, while high-income non-OECD countries (25.3 per cent) and high-income OECD countries (20.3 per cent) are the second and third largest destinations, respectively. Bangladesh–India and India–United Arab Emirates are the top two migration corridors in the region. Remittances have become increasingly prominent in South Asia.

Table 1.6 shows that South Asian countries were significant and positive outliers when we compare their remittances as a ratio of GDP with the rest of the world, and control for stage of development, country size, and non-linearities in development. India, Bangladesh, Pakistan, and Sri Lanka were all significant positive outliers compared to the norm in 1982. China was not a significant outlier compared to the norm. Thus remittances are an important source of service export for South Asia. However, its importance as a source of foreign exchange earnings has declined over time in India and Pakistan. Bangladesh, Sri Lanka, and Nepal remained significant and positive outliers in 2005, when

TABLE 1.6   South Asia and China in the Cross Section on Traditional
Service Export Remittances as a Ratio of GDP and Imports

| | Panel A | | | |
| | Share of Remittances in GDP | | Share of Remittances in Imports | |
	1982	2006	1982	2006
Log GDP per capita	0.18**	0.07	0.36**	0.25***
	(0.07)	(0.08)	(0.16)	(0.13)
Log GDP per capita^2	−0.02**	−0.01	−0.05**	−0.04**
	(0.01)	(0.01)	(0.02)	(0.01)
India indicator	0.02***	−0.02**	0.16***	0.02*
	(0.009)	(0.008)	(0.02)	(0.01)
China indicator	0.03	−0.008	0.07**	−0.02
	(0.01)	(0.01)	(0.03)	(0.02)
Bangladesh indicator	0.03***	0.02*	0.20***	0.22***
	(0.008)	(0.01)	(0.02)	(0.01)
Pakistan indicator	0.08***	−0.01*	0.37***	0.04***
	(0.006)	(0.009)	(0.01)	(0.01)
Sri Lanka indicator	0.05***	0.01**	0.11***	0.07***
	(0.006)	(0.008)	(0.01)	(0.02)
Nepal indicator		0.08***		0.34***
		(0.01)		(0.02)
Control for size	Yes	Yes	Yes	Yes
Observations	97	114	99	114

| | Panel B | |
	Change in Share of Remittances in GDP 1982–2006 (1)	Change in Share of Remittances in Imports 1982–2005 (2)
Log initial GDP per capita	−0.03***	−0.04**
	(0.01)	(0.01)
Average annual GDP growth	−1.49***	−0.009**
	(0.40)	(0.004)
India indicator	−0.002	−0.10***
	(0.01)	(0.03)
China indicator	0.04	0.001
	(0.02)	(0.06)
Bangladesh indicator	0.02	0.04
	(0.01)	(0.02)
Pakistan indicator	−0.06***	−0.30***
	(0.01)	(0.02)

(contd...)

(Table 1.6 contd...)

	Panel B	
	Change in Share of Remittances in GDP 1982–2006	Change in Share of Remittances in Imports 1982–2005
	(1)	(2)
Sri Lanka indicator	–0.01	0.01
	(0.01)	(0.03)
Observations	53	58

Notes: Robust standard errors are reported in paranthesis.
*** represents significance at 1%, ** at 5%, and * at 10%.
Country size is measured by area in square kilometres.

we compare their share of remittances in GDP with more than 100 countries. These results hold when we compare their remittances as a ratio of imports. Bangladesh, Sri Lanka, and Nepal are major exporters of man-made traditional personal service exports.

The other traditional services include tourism and transport. However, they are not as important for South Asia. Table 1.7 reports the share of transport service export in total exports and the share of travel service export in total exports. India's coefficient on transportation services is no different than the norm. Its coefficient on travel service was negative in 2006.

Do Exports Matter?

Although modern impersonal service exports have grown rapidly, their overall size as a share of GDP is small. The small size of service export and the knowledge intensive nature of service export have raised doubts about the viability of service export-led growth. What is more important—how much you export or what you export—is a subject much debated in the growth literature (Hausmann et al. 2005b).

There is increasing evidence that countries that specialize in the types of goods that rich countries export are likely to grow faster than countries that specialize in goods that low-income countries export. That is, specializing in knowledge service exports may sustain higher growth rates than specializing in low skill goods. South Asia's IT and ITES exports have more in common with exports of developed countries[9] than

---

[9]The share of a country's IT exports to total exports is highly correlated with its per capita GDP.

TABLE 1.7   South Asia and China in the Cross Section: Share of Transport and Travel Service Exports in Total Exports of Goods and Services

	Share of Transportation Service Exports				Share of Travel Service Exports			
	1991	1991	2006	2006	1991	1991	2006	2006
Log GDP per capita	−0.08	−0.08	0.008	0.008	0.45***	0.45***	0.54***	0.54***
	(0.13)	(0.13)	(0.07)	(0.07)	(0.14)	(0.14)	(0.17)	(0.17)
Log GDP per capita^2	0.01	0.01	−0.0004	−0.0003	−0.06***	−0.06***	−0.07***	−0.07***
	(0.01)	(0.01)	(0.01)	(0.01)	(0.02)	(0.02)	(0.02)	(0.02)
India indicator		−0.01		−0.007		0.05***		−0.05***
		(0.01)		(0.008)		(0.01)		(0.01)
China indicator		−0.003		−0.001		0.10**		−0.007
		(0.01)		(0.01)		(0.05)		(0.03)
Control for size	Yes	Yes	Yes	Yes	Yes	Yes	Yes	Yes
Observations	134	134	142	142	134	134	142	142

	Change in Share of Transportation Service Exports 1991–2006		Change in Share of Travel Service Exports 1991–2006	
	(5)	(6)	(7)	(8)
Log initial GDP per capita	0.008	0.008	−0.04***	−0.04***
	(0.008)	(0.008)	(0.01)	(0.01)
Average annual GDP growth	−0.10	−0.10	−0.62*	−0.61**
	(0.12)	(−0.13)	(0.32)	(0.33)
India indicator		0.01		−0.07***
		(0.009)		(0.02)
China indicator		0.007		−0.01
		(0.01)		(0.02)
Observations	114	114	114	114

Notes: Robust standard errors are reported in paranthesis.
*** represents significance at 1%, ** at 5%, and * at 10%.
Country size is measured by area in square kilometres.

with the export of East Asia and other developing countries. India and other South Asian countries have a ratio on IT service exports to total exports which is much higher than what would be predicted based on their income levels. This bodes well for sustaining the service export-led growth in South Asia.

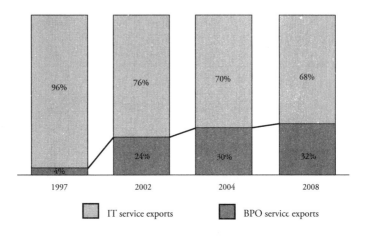

FIGURE 1.12   India's Spillover from Skill Intensive (IT)
to Less Skill Intensive Service Exports (BPO)

Sources: NASSCOM. For 1997, 2002, the World Bank staff estimates are from
Mattoo and Mishra (2004). For later years the World Bank staff estimates are from
NASSCOM (2008).

Notes: Business Process Outsourcing (BPO) services comprise data entry, data
conversions, medical transcriptions, insurance claims, call centres, database services,
etc. Information Technology Services (ITS) include custom application development,
application outsourcing, packaged software installation and support, network
infrastructure management, IT training and education, and network consulting
and integration.

The 'spillover' effects of ICT exports on the domestic economy can be
immense. First, it can lead to the development of other export-oriented
service industries, creating more jobs. This can be most clearly seen in the
case of India, which began with skill intensive software exports (custom
application development, packaged software installation, network
infrastructure management, and network consulting integration) and
has now expanded to less skill intensive service exports such as BPO
(Figure 1.12).

The spillover effects of the rapidly expanding modern service sectors
are also being felt across countries. Service exports have expanded from
India to other countries in the region; ITES and BPO services are
becoming a focus in Bangladesh, Sri Lanka, and Pakistan as they try to
enter or establish themselves in particular segments of the BPO space
such as in transcriptions, data entry and conversion, and call centres.

How Vulnerable are Service Exports to the Global Economic Downturn?

The sustainability of service-led growth will depend on both global factors beyond South Asia's control (for example, the global financial crisis and economic downturn, and the potential threat of protectionism) as well as the ability of South Asian countries to take advantage of the opportunities arising from the increasing globalization of services.

How volatile is service trade compared to goods trade? Figure 1.13 shows annual growth in GDP, goods import, and service import for USA. The figure shows that growth in both goods imports and services imports turned negative during the last two economic downturns in USA in 1991 and 2001. However, the decline in service imports was less than the decline in goods imports. This continues to be true of the current global crisis as well.

There are several reasons why modern service exports are likely to be relatively resilient to any downturn. First, modern service IT exporting firms require less trade credit, and hence they are less likely to be affected by the global credit crunch. Several global IT companies like Infosys and TCS have sufficient cash reserves on hand, and no debt. Service firms also do not suffer from inventory-driven collapses of demand, since most high-tech services cannot be stored.

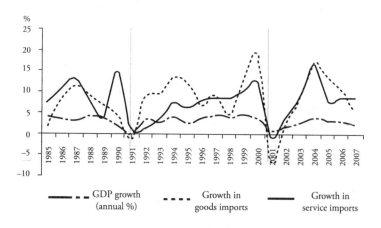

FIGURE 1.13   Volatility of Services as Compared to Goods, USA
(*per cent*)

Source: World Bank (2008a).

TABLE 1.8　Investment in Manufacturing as Compared to Services

Average Manufacturing Growth	1995–2007	Average Service Growth	1995–2007
Investment (as ratio of GDP)	0.74***	Investment (as ratio of GDP)	0.16***
Initial GDP per capita	0.000	Initial GDP per capita	0.000
Openness (trade as % of GDP)	0.01	Openness (trade as % of GDP)	0.003
Credit (% of GDP)	–0.08***	Credit (% of GDP)	–0.01
Population growth	0.94**	Population growth	0.04
Control for size	Yes	Control for size	Yes
Observations	157	Observations	161

Source: World Bank (2008a).
Notes: Robust standard errors are reported in parenthesis.
*** Represents significance at 1%, ** at 5%, and * at 10%.
Country size is measured by area in square kilometres.

Some evidence for this is provided by the cross-country regressions in Table 1.8, where manufacturing and service growth over 1995–2007 is regressed on investment (as a percentage of GDP), financial development (proxied for by percentage of domestic credit provided by banks), openness (proxied for ratio of exports and imports to GDP), initial level of development (proxied for by initial GDP per capita), and demographic features (proxied for by population growth). We see that growth in manufacturing and service both depend positively on the investment rate. However, the interesting and striking feature is that the coefficient on investment rate is much higher for manufacturing than for services. It suggests that manufacturing growth is much more dependent on the investment rate than service growth.

Traditional service exports such as migration and remittances, although not immune to the global financial crisis, are also much less volatile compared to other capital inflows such as portfolio and FDI inflows. Figure 1.14 shows that the bulk of capital inflows into the South Asian economy consist of remittances followed by FDI in 2007, both relatively stable forms of capital flows.[10] While remittances amount to almost 6 per cent of GDP, FDI inflows amount to one-third of this. Portfolio and other investment inflows only account for a small portion.

[10]Countries included in this average are India, Pakistan, Sri Lanka, and Bangladesh.

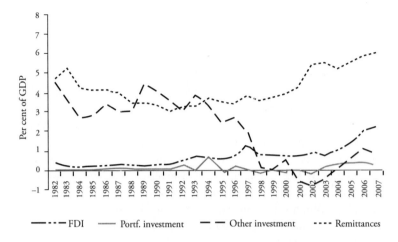

FIGURE 1.14   Capital Inflows into South Asia

Source: IMF, International Financial Statistics, and the World Bank staff estimates.

During the period 1982–2007 remittances were significantly less volatile than the other types of inflow.

In conclusion, there are many reasons to believe that the service sector will continue to be an engine of growth in South Asia:

1. First, South Asia has a large agricultural sector with low productivity. The reallocation of labour from low productivity to high productivity modern service sectors will sustain growth for a long time. The scope for this reallocation is bigger for South Asia compared to East Asia, given the large size of its agricultural sector.

2. Second, the conventional wisdom that manufacturing is dynamic and services are stagnant is no longer valid. The dynamism of services has strengthened because of the 3Ts. TFP growth in services is higher than manufacturing in India. Modern impersonal services reflect the same scope for economies of scale and specialization that we have found in manufacturing.

3. Third, despite the global financial crisis, there remains huge potential for growth in South Asia through catch-up. There is a huge gap in labour productivity, for example, between India and USA. The global financial crisis has not diminished the benefits of technological spillovers, as the stock of knowledge in USA and other advanced economies has not been diminished by the global crisis.

IS SERVICE-LED GROWTH PRO-POOR?

Growth is inclusive when it reduces poverty, creates jobs, and reduces gender inequality. These features of economic growth are also popularly known as pro-poor growth.

There are different meanings attached to pro-poor and inclusive growth in the academic literature and policy debates (McKay and Aryeetey 2004). This debate revolves around a distinction between the absolute and relative concepts of inclusive and pro-poor growth. The absolute concept is that growth is inclusive and pro-poor when it reduces poverty (see Ravallion 2001). The relative concept of pro-poor growth focuses on job creation, and reduction in inequality and gender inequality. Job creation and reduction in gender inequality are better measures than income inequality, as the growth dynamic changes from 'race to the bottom' to 'race to the top'.

It is well known that rapid growth has contributed to poverty reduction in South Asia (Ghani and Ahmed 2009). However, what is less well known is how differences in growth patterns impact the pace of poverty reduction. If the bulk of growth occurs in places and/or sectors of the economy where the poor are not concentrated, then poverty will not decline significantly. If service-led growth is more skill intensive than manufacturing-led growth, it is likely that the pace of job creation will be low. The geography of public spending, restrictions on factor mobility, and lack of market integration can also make it harder for people in lagging regions to escape poverty.

There are three reasons why conventional wisdom has considered service-led growth not to be pro-poor. First, conventional wisdom says that services are stagnant while manufacturing is dynamic and, therefore, developing countries should opt for the manufacturing sector. We have already shown that the service sector has a higher labour productivity compared to manufacturing for South Asia.

The second potential objection is that the service sector is more skill intensive compared to manufacturing. Since education is in limited supply in developing countries, it has been argued that service-led growth cannot be sustained. Table 1.9 compares the average years of schooling of employees in agriculture, industry, and services in Bangladesh, China, India, Korea, Nepal, Malaysia, Pakistan, Sri Lanka, and Thailand. Services are indeed the most skill intensive sector in South Asia, as measured by the average years of schooling of employees. In India, the average years of education for service employees is more than twice that for agriculture

TABLE 1.9   Educational Attainment by Sector of Employment
(2002–6)

Country	Literacy Rate (%)	Years of Schooling—Employed Persons			
		Total	Agriculture	Industry	Services
Bangladesh	44	4.4	2.9	4.6	6.3
India	61	4.7	3.2	5.2	7.9
Maldives	96	6.0	NA	NA	NA
Nepal	49	3.7	2.5	5.2	5.8
Pakistan	50	4.3	2.3	4.6	7.1
Sri Lanka	91	8.4	6.5	8.8	9.7
China	91	91.0	6.0		
Korea	98	11.4	7.3	12.1	11.3
Malaysia	89	9.6	5.9	9.6	10.6
Thailand	93	8.0	6.2	8.5	9.8

Source: Bosworth and Maertens (2009).

and is also much higher than it is in industry. Given that skills are a scarce resource in South Asia, will the limited supply of education (and unequal access to education)[11] put a brake on service-led growth and poverty reduction? Not so.

India's service-led growth story shows that the supply of education has increased in response to service-led growth. In particular, high school enrollment has increased in precisely those areas where IT-related growth was concentrated (Shastry 2008). Indeed, service-led growth has generated a virtuous circle of service growth and education growth, as higher wages for skilled workers has increased the rate of return to higher education, thus increasing the demand for education. This in turn has increased the supply of private education, and induced more service-led growth.

The third reason why services are considered not to be pro-poor is because service-led growth is likely to be geographically concentrated in large cities and leading regions. There is some evidence to support

[11]In India, a youngster from Maharashtra is 1.7 times more likely to attend tertiary education than a peer from Madhya Pradesh. An equitable expansion of secondary education is necessary for fundamental improvement in equity in tertiary education; in particular for low-income families, girls, Muslims, disadvantaged groups (SCs, STs, and OBCs), and rural areas. The inequality of participation in tertiary education risks jeopardizing a more inclusive Indian society (see Azam and Blom 2009).

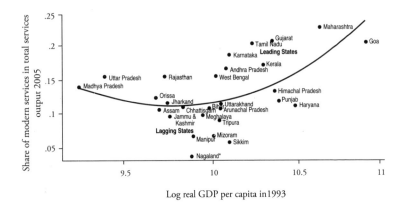

FIGURE 1.15   Concentration of Modern Tradable Services in the
Leading States of India (2005)

Sources: Authors' calculation based on the System of National Accounts, Planning
Commission of India, and World Bank (2007).
Notes: Modern services include banking, insurance, and telecommunication services.
Business service has been lumped together with real estate and ownership of dwellings,
so it has not been excluded in the modern services category.

this view. Figure 1.15 shows the share of modern tradable services in
total service value added for the leading and lagging states in India. The
leading states, with a higher per capita state level GDP, have a much
higher share of modern service output in their service value added. These
leading states have experienced accelerated growth and have benefitted
from the globalization of services, as they have the critical levels of skill
endowments and types of infrastructure that are important to service
export-led growth. The lagging regions have a smaller share of modern
tradable services in their service value added.

However, we should note that a geographically concentrated growth
pattern is not unique to service-led growth. It is also common to
manufacturing-led growth, as in East Asia (see World Bank 2009a).
Growth tends to concentrate in regions that are close to the market, so
that firms and workers can benefit from technology, factor mobility, trade,
and scale economies. Geographic concentration of economic activity has
long been identified as a region's export base (Krugman 1980, 1991;
Krugman and Venables 1995). In China, manufacturing economic
activity is concentrated in the leading coastal regions and has helped
sustain long-run growth and reduce poverty. Likewise, geographically

concentrated growth should also help sustain a service-led growth in South Asia and reduce poverty (see World Bank 2009b).

What is the Contribution of Service Growth to Poverty Reduction?

We find that growth in the service sector is more correlated with poverty reduction than growth in agriculture and manufacturing for a sample of fifty developing countries. Figure 1.16 shows the relationship between the change in poverty in the 1990s (on the y-axis) and growth in the agricultural, manufacturing, and service sectors (on the x-axis), after controlling for the initial level of poverty. We see that the change in poverty is negatively related to growth in both the service and manufacturing sectors, that is, higher growth rates in either of these sectors is associated with a higher reduction in poverty. It is interesting to note that the slope for the service sector growth is steeper than for manufacturing, suggesting that service sector growth is associated with a faster reduction in poverty. On the other hand, agricultural growth is associated with increases in the poverty level.

We document these relationships using regressions in Table 1.10. While these regressions do not necessarily establish a causal relationship, this is an interesting stylized fact to keep in mind. There could of course be reverse causality in the sense that service growth picks up in those areas where, for other reasons, poverty is declining rapidly. However, these results do rule out the possibility that a focus on the service sector might slow down overall growth. In particular, it is especially interesting that growth in manufacturing and agriculture do not show a statistically

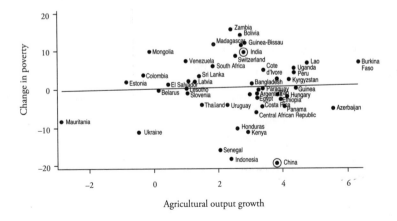

Agricultural output growth

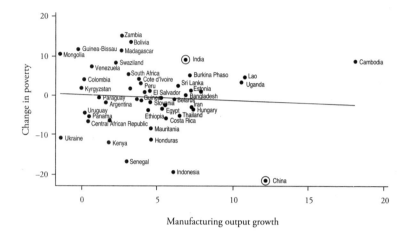

FIGURE 1.16   Cross-country Evidence on Growth Patterns and
Poverty Reduction

Source: World Bank, *World Development Indicators* (2009); Povcalnet, World Bank
(2008).
Note: Change in poverty (1991–2005) after controlling for initial level of poverty, and
growth in agricultural output, manufacturing output, and service output. For more
information on the regression, please see Poverty Regression, Table 1.10 column (1).
Poverty is defined as percentage of population below US$1 (PPP) per day.
*** Represents significance at 1%, ** at 5%, and * at 10%.
Country size is measured by area in square kilometres.

TABLE 1.10   South Asia and China in the Cross Section:
Change in Poverty Headcount (1990–2005)

	(1)	(2)	(3)	(4)	Sectoral Output Growth Weighted by Initial Share of Sector in GDP (5)	(6)
Log GDP per			9.99***	9.82***	14.59***	13.87***
capita initial			(3.07)	(3.36)	(3.84)	(4.26)
Initial level of poverty	−0.17*	−0.17*				
	(0.08)	(0.09)				
Growth in agriculture	0.55	0.58	0.51	0.55	0.02	0.02
output	(0.97)	(1.04)	(0.91)	(0.97)	(0.02)	(0.02)
Growth in manu-	−0.06	0.08	−0.01	0.11	−0.03	0.001
facturing output	(0.46)	(0.44)	(0.54)	(0.53)	(0.02)	(0.02)
Growth in services	−2.30***	−2.11**	−1.92**	−1.74*	−0.02**	−0.04***
output	(0.86)	(0.89)	(0.88)	(0.91)	(0.01)	(0.01)
India indicator		9.44**		8.83**		10.63***
		(4.22)		(3.71)		(3.64)
China indicator		−24.48***		−23.01***		−27.51***
		(5.48)		(5.35)		(8.84)
Bangladesh indicator		−3.99		−4.24		−2.06
		(4.19)		(3.24)		(3.72)
Sri Lanka indicator		4.51**		7.76***		9.25***
		(1.98)		(2.35)		(2.58)
Control for time period	Yes	Yes	Yes	Yes	Yes	Yes
Observations	50	50	50	50	50	50

Notes: Robust standard errors are reported in paranthesis.
*** represents significance at 1%, ** at 5%, and * at 10%.
Country size is measured by area in square kilometres.

significant correlation with poverty reduction in the 1990s. Another interesting stylized fact is that, even after accounting for faster service sector growth, India is reducing poverty at a slower pace than other countries. Sri Lanka also lags behind the norm, while China has achieved poverty reduction at a faster-than-normal pace.[12]

We observe a similar relationship between service sector growth and poverty reduction within India using state level data (Figure 1.17). We note that Andhra Pradesh, which has made special efforts to attract IT

[12]These results do not change whether we use weighted or unweighted sectoral growth rates, and control for initial stage of development either using initial real GDP per capita or initial poverty rate.

investment to the state, has also achieved one of the most impressive rates of poverty reduction. Box 1.2 documents these relationships using regressions similar to the cross-country regressions reported earlier.

While these associations between service-led growth and poverty reduction are important, it is useful to consider how service-led growth might translate into lower poverty levels. We now turn to examining the

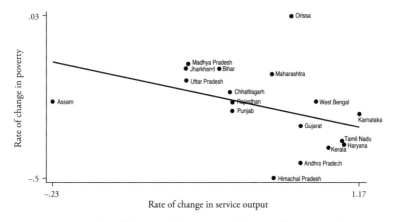

FIGURE 1.17   Change in Poverty and Service Outputs at the
State Level in India (1994–2005)

Source: Planning Commission of India.

BOX 1.2   The Role of Services in Poverty Reduction in India

Growth in the service sector has been associated with reduction in poverty. Economic literature on poverty and growth has shown that geographical and sectoral composition of growth matters for poverty reduction. But not a single growth pattern maximizes poverty alleviation in all circumstances. Initial conditions, including the macroeconomic environment, state of human development, and the quality of institutions and legislation also have an important influence in the dynamics of poverty.

Services have played an essential, though not uniform, role in the rapid development and the reduction of poverty in South Asia. Growth in the service sector in Indonesia, in particular in the urban service sector, has recently proven to be the most beneficial for the poor.

The contribution of the service sector to poverty reduction can be examined using a simple specification for a panel of Indian state data from 1994 to 2005.

$$P_{it} = \beta_0 + \beta_1 S_{1it} y_{1it} + \beta_2 S_{2it} y_{2it} + \beta_3 S_{3it} y_{3it} + u_{it}$$

where i denotes the state and t the year; P_{it} is the growth rate of the poverty ratio; $s_{jit} = Y_{jit}/Y_{it}$ denotes the output share of the sector; and y_{jit} is the growth rate of the sector. β measure sectoral contribution to poverty rate alleviation. Poverty is calculated using the official headcount ratio by the Planning Commission for the periods 1993–4, 1999–2000, and 2004–5. GDP data are provided by the World Bank country regional office. A state fixed effect control is included.

Our results show that trend growth in the service sector among Indian states is associated with a decrease in the trend of the headcount poverty rate of almost 1.5 points during the sample period. In fact, the service sector is the only sector showing a statistically significant association with poverty reduction. Similar results are found when differentiating into rural and urban poverty. Service sector growth is also strongly associated with a reduction in rural and urban poverty rates. However, some precaution should be taken since the comparability of the figures of some of the official consumer expenditure surveys by the National Sample Survey Organisation (especially results in 1999–2000) has been contested by some academics.

Some states like Karnataka, Tamil Nadu, Andhra Pradesh, and West Bengal have experienced a significant decrease in urban poverty that may be associated with an increase in their service sector share (probably due to the attraction of a significant bulk of IT investment that translated into an increase in urban employment). On the contrary other states like Orissa have experienced a weaker service sector performance and a more disappointing record of poverty alleviation.

Sector Growth	Change in poverty rate	Change in rural poverty rate	Change in urban poverty rate
Agriculture	0.285 [0.429]	0.137 [0.613]	0.009 [0.427]
Industrial	0.159 [0.198]	0.132 [0.283]	–0.147 [0.197]
Services	–1.458** [0.442]	–1.522* [0.632]	–1.055* [0.440]
R-squared	0.488	0.313	0.458

+ significant at 10%; * significant at 5%; ** significant at 1%
States included: Andhra Pradesh, Assam, Bihar, Chhattisgarh, Gujarat, Haryana, Himachal Pradesh, Jharkhand, Karnataka, Kerala, Madhya Pradesh, Maharashtra, Orissa, Punjab, Rajasthan, Tamil Nadu, Uttar Pradesh, Uttaranchal, West Bengal.
Source: Pilar Garcia Martinez (World Bank).

role of the service sector in job creation and wage growth. For services to be a sustainable source of growth, they must generate productive jobs to absorb the young and growing South Asian workforce. More than 150 million people will enter the prime working age population over the next decade. Labour supply growth is 2.3 per cent per annum in South Asia, above the global average of 1.8 per cent.

Job Creation

There is evidence that the service sector has created the largest number of jobs in South Asia in recent years (Figure 1.18). The effect is not uniform across countries: for India and Pakistan, the service sector has created jobs at a faster pace than agriculture or industry, while for Bangladesh and Sri Lanka, job creation in services is substantially higher than in agriculture, but somewhat slower than in the manufacturing sector. A recent World Bank study on India also reported faster changes in employment away from agriculture to construction and trade, hotels and restaurants, and transport and communications (World Bank 2008).

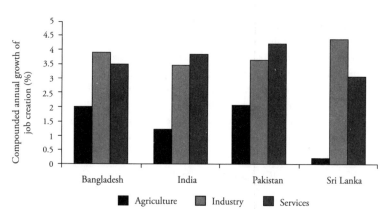

FIGURE 1.18   Job Creation Rates in Agriculture, Industry, and Service Sectors (1990–2006)

Sources: International Labour Organization (ILO) (2008). Bangladesh—Labour Force Surveys, in *Key Findings of Labour Force Survey and Statistical Yearbook*, various editions. India—Sivasubramaniam, *The Sources of Economic Growth in India: 1950–1 to 1999–2000* for earlier years, and Bosworth et al. (2007) for the more recent period. Pakistan—LABOURSTAT, ILO (2008) and *Handbook of Statistics on Pakistan Economy*. Sri Lanka—up to 1989 Key Indicators for the Labor Market (KILM), from 1990 onwards *Labour Survey Reports*, various editions.

There is some concern that service sector growth in India has been geared more towards 'high-tech' and modern services which employ fewer people than 'low-tech' and traditional services. It is difficult to generalize whether modern and impersonal services are more skill intensive compared to traditional and personal services (see Blinder 2006). Feenstra and Hanson (1996) have argued that developed countries typically outsource production of less skill intensive intermediate goods to developing countries. However, these intermediate goods are relatively more skill intensive in developing countries. Hence, globalization and outsourcing increase the relative demand for skilled labour in both developed and developing countries, thereby increasing the skill premium.

We find that consistent with the greater role of growth and productivity increases in modern services compared to traditional services, the modern service sector created jobs faster than the traditional sector over the past two decades (Figure 1.19). More encouragingly, the job creation rates are faster than the rate of growth of the labour force as a whole. If this trend can be sustained, then service growth can help to absorb a larger proportion of the growing workforce.

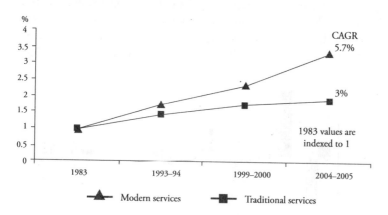

FIGURE 1.19   Job Creation in the Modern and Traditional Service Sectors in India

Source: National Sample Survey Organisation (NSSO), various years.
Notes: Traditional services employment encompass the following sectors: trade, hotels and restaurants; transport, storage, and communications; personal, business, and cultural services. Modern services include financial, insurance, real estate, and business services. Compounded annual growth is calculated for 1983–2005.

In addition to direct job creation, some estimates suggest that the indirect effects of a growing service sector can be larger than the direct effects. For instance, India's IT industry association NASSCOM estimates that for every job created in the IT sector, four additional jobs are created in the rest of the economy due to high levels of consumption spending by professionals employed in this sector (NASSCOM and CRISIL 2007).

We should note further that wage growth has been higher in the service sector than in manufacturing and agriculture in recent years (see Figure 1.20 for India). This suggests that the indirect channels stimulated by higher consumption are more likely to operate, since the service sector is creating high-wage jobs.

How does South Asia compare with other developing countries in the rate of service job creation? Table 1.11 reports cross-country level regressions on share of employment in the service and manufacturing sectors in total employment for 1991 and 2005. In 1991, India was a significant negative outlier, when we control for stage of development, non-linearities in development, and country size. It became an even bigger negative outlier in 2005. The share of service sector employment in total employment for India is some 19 percentage points below the norm, controlling for other factors. China is an even bigger negative outlier compared to the norm.

The results of cross-country level regressions on industrial employment show that India was a positive outlier in 1991, however, the coefficient on India was not statistically significant. China was an even bigger

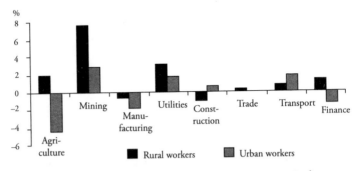

FIGURE 1.20   Growth in Average Daily Earnings in India
(1999–2000/2004–5)

Source: Kundu and Mohanan (2009).
Note: Agriculture includes agriculture, forestry and fishing; mining includes mining and quarrying; utilities includes electricity, gas, and water supply; trade includes trade, and hotels and restaurants; transport includes transport, storage, and communications; finance includes financial intermediation, real estate, and business.

TABLE 1.11   India and China in the Cross Section: Employment
Shares of Industry and Services in Total Employment (1991, 2005)

| | Panel A | | | |
| | Share of Employment in Service | | Share of Employment in Industry | |
	1991	2005	1991	2005
Log GDP per capita	22.5	25.8	64.5*	68.7***
	(32.8)	(21.4)	(34.9)	(15.6)
Log GDP per capita^2	–0.76	–1.2	–8.04*	–8.8***
	(4.4)	(2.9)	(4.6)	(2.0)
India indicator	–14.2**	–19.2***	4.4	3.6*
	(7.1)	(3.2)	(6.6)	(1.9)
China indicator	–25.3**	–23.7***	13.2**	5.1***
	(6.7)	(3.5)	(5.4)	(1.6)
Pakistan indicator	–2.5	–7.2**	2.7	4.5**
	(5.5)	(3.0)	(4.9)	(1.9)
Control for size	Yes	Yes	Yes	Yes
Observations	56	57	56	57

| | Panel B | |
| | Change in Share of Employment in Services | Change in Share of Employment in Industry |
(1991–2005)	(1)	(2)
Log initial GDP per capita	–0.29	–2.7
	(2.1)	(1.7)
Average annual GDP growth	–98.8	15.9
	(110.6)	(85.1)
India indicator	–1.02	3.2
	(3.1)	(2.2)
China indicator	10.1	2.4
	(6.4)	(4.8)
Pakistan indicator	–4.3*	1.6
	(2.4)	(1.8)
Observations	57	57

Notes: Robust standard errors are reported in paranthesis.
*** represents significance at 1%, ** at 5%, and * at 10%.
Country size is measured by area in square kilometres.

outlier compared to the norm and controlling for other factors. In 2005,
China and India were less of outliers. The cross-country regressions
on change in share of industrial employment in total employment are
also reported in Table 1.11. Both China and India have experienced a
significantly higher increase in the share of industrial employment in

total employment over the period 1991–2005, but the coefficients are not statistically significant.

In summary, South Asia has done well in promoting pro-poor growth, though there are some points of concern regarding the job growth picture. One is that the rate of job creation is slow compared to other developing countries. This may partially account for the fact that South Asia is slower at reducing poverty compared to other developing countries. The other potential concern is that the newly created service jobs are geographically clustered. Because the service sector is more skill intensive than manufacturing and agriculture, clusters tend to occur in the more developed states, for instance, Tamil Nadu and Maharashtra in India.

Female Participation in Employment

Labour markets are the main channels through which economic growth is distributed across the population. In this context, we should note that South Asia suffers from one of the lowest female participation rates in the labour force in the world, and the rapidly increasing service sector will be able to tap into a potentially large female labour force.

Figure 1.21 shows that high employment in services goes hand in hand with high employment for women. It shows that countries with a

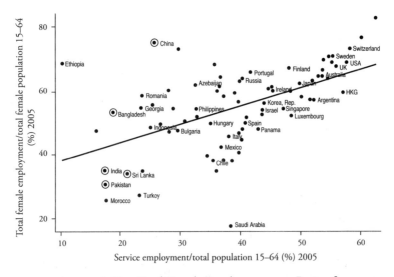

FIGURE 1.21   Total Female Employment as a Ratio of
Total Female Population (Age 15–64)

Source: The World Bank (2008a).

high share of the population employed in services tend to have the highest participation of women in the labour market. In India, women make up 30 per cent of the IT services and ITES workforce—a much higher rate of female participation than in the service sector in general. In Ireland, 70 per cent of call centre employees are women. Women account for 65 per cent of the total professional and technical workers in IT and ITES in the Philippines (Dongier and Sudan 2009). The growth of services is key to enhancing female labour force participation, by providing the kind of jobs that are needed to attract new worker groups, such as part-timers.

Table 1.12 reports cross-country regressions on the female labour force as a share of the total labour force. Compared to the norm, all South Asian countries are negative outliers. They were huge negative outliers in 1982. They were less of outliers in 2006, but still remained well below

TABLE 1.12   South Asia and China in the Cross Section: Female Labour Force as a Share of Total Labour Force (1982, 2006)

	Panel A			
	Labour Force, Female (% of total labour force)			
	1982	1982	2006	2006
Log GDP per capita	–44.34***	–47.94***	–30.51***	–30.63***
	(15.15)	(15.58)	(5.96)	(6.19)
Log GDP per capita^2	6.10***	6.58***	4.54***	4.52***
	(2.36)	(2.43)	(0.86)	(0.89)
India indicator		–14.86***		–12.81***
		(1.47)		(0.91)
China indicator		0.75		2.96
		(3.79)		(2.08)
Bangladesh indicator		–2.78**		–4.62***
		(1.19)		(0.72)
Pakistan indicator		–17.95***		–13.03***
		(0.89)		(0.72)
Sri Lanka indicator		–7.59***		–6.94***
		(0.91)		(0.77)
Thailand indicator		11.29***		7.98***
		(1.15)		(0.83)
Control for size	Yes	Yes	Yes	Yes
Observations	142	142	162	162

Notes: Robust standard errors are reported in paranthesis.
*** represents significance at 1%, ** at 5%, and * at 10%.
Country size is measured by area in square kilometres.
End data for China is 2005 instead of 2006 as manufacturing value-added data is unavailable for 2006.

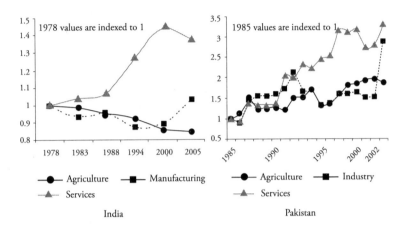

FIGURE 1.22   Female Labour Force Participation by
Sector in India and Pakistan

Sources: India—National Sample Survey (NSS), respective years. Pakistan—Labour
Force Survey and KILM, ILO (2008).
Note: For India, service sector employment includes trade, restaurant, transport
and communications, and other services category. The figure represents the sum of
employment figures for rural and urban areas. For India, the female employment is
reported as the number of females employed per 1,000 employed persons.

the norm. China and Thailand are positive outliers. The relatively low
rate of female participation suggests that South Asia still has a lot of
underutilized labour resources that it can tap to expand the service and
manufacturing sectors.

In this regard, it is encouraging to see that female labour force
participation has increased greatly in the service sector in South Asia
(Figure 1.22). Over the last three decades, the largest growth in female
labour force participation has been in the service sector, for both India
and Pakistan, while participation levels in agriculture and industry have
remained steady or fallen. Overall, these trends suggest that the service
sector has a considerable potential to generate jobs on a large scale, and to
provide employment opportunities for women, currently an underutilized
labour resource in South Asian countries.

An additional benefit of service-led growth for South Asia is that
its environmental impact would be less dramatic, allowing time for
income effects (favouring a clean environment) to work their way
through to environmental regulations. Service-led industrialization

may also avoid problems that come from natural resource export paths of development.

WHAT EXPLAINS SOUTH ASIA'S SERVICE-LED GROWTH?

The 3Ts—technology, transportability, and tradability—have enabled rapid globalization of services, and for South Asia to benefit from it. However, the 3Ts are common to all countries in the world. Why has South Asia grasped this opportunity while East Asia has gone for manufacturing? Was this a matter of luck and hysteresis, for example, East Asia was an early integrator into the global economy and got 'locked' into manufacturing? Was South Asia lucky in being a latecomer to development, as it has benefitted from the late globalization of services?[13] Or, did South Asia pursue policies and develop institutions to make this happen? Has India adopted pro-growth policies in the service sector, just like China adopted pro-growth policies towards manufacturing?

Growth is an outcome of complex interactions between market integration, institutions, education, infrastructure, geography, and leadership (see Growth Commission Report 2008; for South Asia, see World Bank 2009b [forthcoming]). Growth has common characteristics such as sound economic management, high rates of saving and investment, trade liberalization to tap into global markets, rapid technological adaptation and learning, and, above all, resource mobility away from low productivity and into high productivity areas. These policies are important to both service-led and manufacturing-led growth.

India's emergence as an exporter of modern impersonal services has resulted from a combination of factors, including:

1. market integration;
2. availability of education and skilled labour force—scalability, depth, and quality of the talent pool;
3. better institutions that impacted day-to-day running of the service business; and
4. improved availability and quality of infrastructure supportive of service growth.

[13]China and other East Asian countries were early participants in global integration and they benefitted from early globalization of manufacturing. India and other South Asian countries are latecomers to global integration, and they are benefitting from late globalization of services. The differences in the timing of globalization of manufacturing and services partly explain the differences in the growth patterns of East Asia and South Asia.

Market Integration

South Asia is not as well integrated in goods trade with the global economy as East Asia, but it has adopted more liberal policies towards the service sector (see Ghani and Ahmed 2009). All South Asian countries are more open to trade in services than they were two decades ago. Liberalized services like business and telecommunication services have attracted significant domestic and foreign investment. In India, a majority of the FDI inflows are concentrated in the service sector, and in particular in modern impersonal services (see Gordon and Gupta 2004; World Bank 2008b).

Public–private partnerships (PPP) are common in IT and ITES business. Government and IT firms routinely work together to address resource constraints. In the area of skill development, for example, NASSCOM—the industry association in India representing more than 1,200 IT companies—has created standards for competency assessment that are now also being used by state training institutions. The Indian diaspora has also played an important role in fostering the country's IT-BPO industry. It provided the contacts and networks that facilitated access to senior executives of major foreign companies who might otherwise not have considered investing in India as an IT-BPO destination in the early years.

The dramatic success of modern service exports from India illustrates the importance of education which has depth and talent, and which can be easily scaled up. India has benefitted from the globalization of services because it has a large number of highly skilled graduates. India has earned a strong reputation for its Indian Institutes of Technology (IITs) and the English language ability of IIT graduates.

Education

India's education system differs from the rest of the world. India spends more on tertiary education. Table 1.13 compares the ratio of public expenditure on tertiary education per student to public expenditure on primary education per student for a group of countries. India spends six times more on tertiary education per student compared to primary education.

This ratio is high when one compares it to Ireland, Israel, Mexico, South Africa, Kenya, USA, and the Philippines. Malaysia is the only country where the ratio of public expenditure on tertiary education to primary education per student is above six.

TABLE 1.13   Ratio of Public Expenditure
on Tertiary Education to Primary
Education per Student

	2000	2005
India	6.25	6.64
USA*	1.51	1.13
Ireland	2.75	1.69
Mexico*	4.09	2.75
Israel**	1.49	1.15
Kenya	9.24	4.89
Malaysia**	6.50	4.89
South Africa	3.97	3.51
Philippines	1.20	1.34

Source: World Bank (2008a).
Note: * 1999; ** 2004.

TABLE 1.14   Cross-country Regression: Public Expenditure on Tertiary
Education per Student

	Panel A	
	2000	2005
Log GDP per capita	–1.10*	–1.97***
	(0.63)	(0.70)
Log GDP per capita^2	0.25***	0.39***
	(0.08)	(0.09)
India indicator	2.48*	2.59**
	(1.47)	(1.23)
USA indicator	0.54	0.40
	(0.38)	(0.32)
Control for population	Yes	Yes
Observations	62	64

Notes: Robust standard errors are reported in paranthesis.
*** represents significance at 1%, ** at 5%, and * at 10%.
Country size is measured by area in square kilometres.

Cross-country regressions in Table 1.14 verify that India is an outlier
in tertiary education spending. The table shows public expenditure on
tertiary education per student for a group of sixty countries, controlling
for initial GDP per capita, stage of development, and country size
(measured by country population). The coefficient on the India country
indicator was significant in 2000. The coefficient on India was more than
2 percentage points above the norm, one of the highest in the sample. It

was statistically different from zero. The coefficient on China was also positive and statistically significant in 1999. But its coefficient was small in comparison to the coefficient on the India country indicator. The coefficient on USA was not significantly different from zero.

In 2005, India was again a large positive outlier and its coefficient was significantly different from zero. India's public expenditure on tertiary education per student is more than 2 percentage points above the norm. Data on China is not available for 2000 or 2005, and therefore the country indicator for China is excluded. The coefficient on USA is not different from zero.

Limitations to growth in modern impersonal services are mostly on the supply side, and in particular the availability of employees with education and skills that meet the requirements of the global service market. The globalizing market for skills, however, allows developing countries to take advantage of their cost advantage in terms of labour and to make investments in expanding the skills of their labour forces in order to make them suitable for employment in the fast-growing global IT and ITES industries. Locations with comparatively large talent pools will have an advantage in attracting IT services and ITES companies because large companies prefer to source services from locations where scalability is feasible.

Institutions

The institutions that affect day-to-day functioning of service firms in India are far more business friendly compared to institutions that impact goods. For example, the Telecommunications Regulatory Authority of India (TRAI), which impacts the electronic delivery of service, has performed better than institutions affecting trade in goods (roads authority, port authority, customs, and product quality certification). The IT service industry was declared an 'essential services industry' in some states in India, allowing '365 x 24 x 7' operations, which was otherwise prohibited by restrictive labour laws in the country.

There is emerging literature on the importance of institutions to growth and development (Acemoglu and Johnson 2005). This relationship has been examined in detail for the South Asian countries at the macro and micro levels, distinguishing between the two key dimensions of institutional performance—property rights institutions and contracting institutions (see Ahmed and Ghani 2007, chapter 4 by Fernandes and Kraay). We have found evidence that property rights institutions matter more for economic growth than contracting institutions.

However, since services differ in characteristics from goods, it is not clear which institutions matter more for service-led growth. We examine the role of property rights institutions and contracting institutions in service-led growth at the sub-national level in South Asia, using the World Bank Doing Business indicators and enterprise surveys. A drawback of these surveys is that they are largely focused on goods and ignore services.

The term property right institutions refers to an owner's right to use a good or service for consumption and/or income generation. There are four different ways by which property rights affect economic activity (see Beasley and Ghattak 2009). The first is expropriation risk—insecure property rights imply that individuals may fail to realize the fruits of their investment and efforts in producing goods and services. Second, poor property rights lead to high costs that firms and individuals have to incur to defend their property, which can be unproductive. The third is failure to facilitate gains from trade—a productive economy requires that assets be used by those who can do so most productively, and improvements in property rights facilitate this. The fourth is the use of property in supporting other transactions.

We have proxied property rights institutions in South Asia by the time taken to register a property, using the World Bank's Doing Business Surveys. Figure 1.23 shows that there is a negative association between time taken to register a property and state level service output per capita. Sub-national data for Bangladesh and India suggest that Bangladesh is weak in property rights institutions and India is strong. There is variation in property rights institutions within India. Bihar and Orissa have weak property rights institutions compared to Andhra Pradesh and Karnataka. There is a clear negative association between property rights institutions and service output per capita. States that have experienced higher service-led growth also have stronger property rights institutions, as measured by the administrative dimension of property rights, which is weaker in low-income states. A measure of contracting institutions is time spent dealing with government officials. Figure 1.24 plots the relationship between this indicator and state level service output per capita. It shows a negative association.

These plots say nothing about the direction of causation. It is possible that growth in services output induces a switch to improved property rights, as opposed to property rights and contracting institutions facilitating faster service output growth.

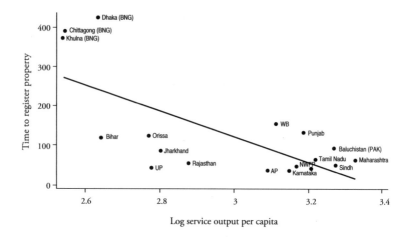

FIGURE 1.23   **Property Rights Institutions and Service Output
per Capita in South Asia**

Source: Doing Business Firm Level Surveys, 2007 and 2006. These firm level surveys
were done at the state level in leading and lagging regions of South Asia (Bangladesh,
India, Pakistan, Sri Lanka).
Notes: The vertical axis variable is defined as time (days) spent to register property. The
horizontal axis is gross state service output per capita from 2006 for India and Pakistan
in 2000 international US$ PPP terms. Since service output data for Bangladesh was
unavailable, we used gross state domestic product per capita terms for 2004.

An important institution to explore is the impact of labour laws on
growth. It has been widely recognized that restrictive labour laws in South
Asia are associated with its small manufacturing sector. Figure 1.25 plots
data from firm level surveys on labour regulations as an obstacle to doing
business in South Asia on the vertical axis with log real service output per
capita on the x-axis. Clearly, there is no negative realtionship between
the two. This may reflect the fact that restrictive labour laws apply more
to the manufacturing and less to the service sector. This paradox is worth
exploring in future work.

Infrastructure

South Asia is well known for its poor infrastructure. But the infrastructure
that matters to modern impersonal service trade is in a better shape.
Manufacturing relies on hard infrastructure for transportation of
goods—ports, roads, ships, air, and customs. Services rely on telephone
lines and the internet for electronic delivery. So, what matters for services

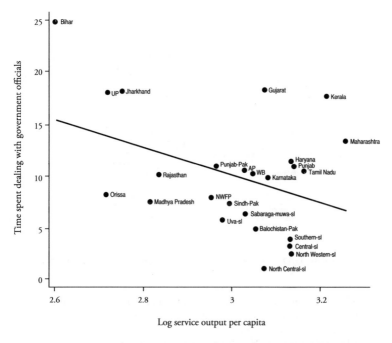

FIGURE 1.24   Contracting Institutions and Service Output per Capita

Source: Enterprise Survey, World Bank (2008) Available at http://www.enterprisesurveys.org/, accessed in February 2009.

Notes: The vertical axis variable is defined as average percentage of firms' senior management's time spent dealing with government regulations in the region/state. The horizontal axis is gross state service output per capita in 2000 international US$ PPP terms. The data for India is from 2005, for Sri Lanka from 2004, and for Pakistan from 2002.

are the availability, quality, and reliability of telecommunications, including broadband. Competitive broadband telecommunications markets are a particularly critical factor for the growth of trade in IT services and ITES.

India has experienced a telecom revolution. The sector has experienced major investment and competition, and this has improved electronic delivery of services tremendously. Technological change has favoured the tradability of modern impersonal services (IT and business) which can be digitized and delivered long distance, relative to traditional personal services (tourism and trade) which can only be delivered in person and face poor infrastructure.

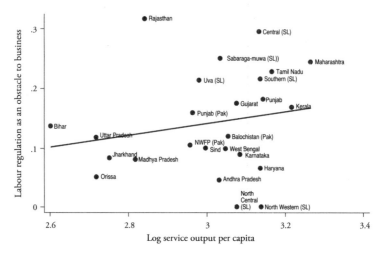

FIGURE 1.25   Impact of Restrictive Labour Laws on Service
Growth in South Asia

Source: Doing Business Firm Level Surveys, 2007 and 2006. These firm level surveys were done at the state level in leading and lagging regions of South Asia (Bangladesh, India, Pakistan, and Sri Lanka).

Notes: The vertical axis variable is defined as average share of firms in the region/state reporting labour regulation as an obstacle to their business. The horizontal axis is gross state service output per capita. It is in 2000 international US$ PPP terms. The data is from 2005 for India, from 2002 for Pakistan, and from 2004 for Sri Lanka.

The Software Technology Parks of India (STPI) initiative launched by the Indian government in 1991 to overcome infrastructural and procedural constraints by providing data communication facilities, office space, and 'single window' statutory services was extremely beneficial. The technology parks proved essential to the growth of the industry given the broader context of deficient infrastructure and bureaucratic red tape. India's telecommunications policies of 1994 and 1999 allowed private sector investments into the sector and cleared the path for the establishment of alternative international gateways that were also critical to the development of the IT services and ITES industries.[14]

[14]In countries with unreliable public infrastructure, companies look for customized facilities such as IT parks—with modern office space, high-speed broadband links, reliable power supply (including backup supply), security services, and ancillary infrastructure including banks, travel desks, restaurants, transportation systems, and hotel accommodation for visiting executives (see Dongier and Sudan 2009). They also look for availability of land and business-friendly procedures such as quick building clearances

CONCLUSION

Until fairly recently, global trade in services was not possible because services, unlike goods, are more difficult to trade, transport, and store. However, the 3Ts—technology, transportability, and tradability—have permitted significant product divisibility and tradability in services. Within the service sector, modern impersonal services (business service, telecom, and insurance and banking) have benefitted more from the 3Ts than traditional personal services (trade, hotel, restaurant, beauty shops, barbers, transport, and public administration services). The number of services that can be produced and traded is constantly expanding—processing insurance claims; call centres; desktop publishing; the remote management and maintenance of IT networks; compiling audits; completing tax returns; transcribing medical records; health records; and financial research and analysis. The 3Ts have unleashed the next industrial revolution—the information and internet age.

Service is the fastest growing sector in global trade. Since the 1980s, world service trade has grown more rapidly than merchandise trade. The share of service trade in service value added has increased at a much faster rate in developing countries as compared to the developed countries. Globalization of services has enabled developing countries to tap into services as a source of growth. In particular, trade in modern impersonal services has grown more rapidly compared to trade in traditional personal services.

In this context, this chapter set out to examine four questions: how different are the growth patterns in South Asia from that of East Asia, in what ways is South Asia's export performance distinctive, how pro-poor service-led growth is, and how service-led growth and service exports can be sustained in the face of institutional bottlenecks and the global downturn.

South Asia has experienced a remarkable service-led growth in the past two decades. The service sector now accounts for more than 50 per cent of GDP in all South Asian countries, a pattern of growth distinctly different from those of East Asian countries, where manufacturing has played a much bigger role.

South Asia's growth experience shows that services are dynamic, with TFP approaching a healthy 2 per cent annually. India's TFP growth rate in the service sector has increased at twice the rate of TFP growth in

---

for real estate development. The availability of international airports with good flight connections near IT/ITES locations is also an important factor.

industry. India has outperformed China in services when we compare their TFP growth rates in services. Service labour productivity growth is much higher in South Asia as compared to manufacturing labour productivity growth. This leads us to revise the old view that services are low productivity growth areas, without the dynamic externalities often attributed to manufacturing.

We found that South Asia's export pattern is distinctive in terms of focusing on services. In particular, India is a significant outlier because its service exports are geared primarily towards IT and ITES exports, which is usually associated with high-income countries. Given the lower dependence of the service sector on heavy investments, and its relative resilience to previous economic downturns, we expect this pattern of exports to be relatively more stable in the face of the current global economic downturn compared to a pattern of manufacturing-led exports.

Services growth has contributed more than manufacturing and agricultural growth to poverty reduction globally and regionally. Cross-country evidence from some fifty developing countries suggests that growth in the service sector is more correlated to poverty reduction than growth in manufacturing. Trend growth in the service sector among Indian states is associated with a decrease in the trend of the headcount poverty rate of almost 1.5 points. Some states in India like Karnataka, Tamil Nadu, and Andhra Pradesh have experienced a significant decrease in urban poverty that may be associated with an increase in their service sector share.

We also found that the service sector has created the largest number of jobs in South Asia over the past decade, that in many cases these jobs have seen high wage growth, and that services are the largest source of increasing female labour force participation. These, together with the observed high contribution of services to overall labour productivity, augur well for service-led growth to be pro-poor.

The sustainability of service-led growth will depend on both global factors beyond South Asia's control as well as the ability of South Asian countries to take advantage of the opportunities arising from the increasing globalization of services, and political support for a growth strategy that may be more geographically concentrated (in leading and not lagging regions, in urban areas and not rural areas, and in large cities and not in small towns) than manufacturing.

To ensure that service-led growth is sustained and the benefits of service-led growth are widely shared, policymakers in South Asia will need to focus on three priorities:

1. First, the solution to geographical concentration and clustering of services is not relocation of production but market integration within the country, across countries, and globally. People outside the tradable services hubs have to be able to take advantage of the jobs and opportunities available in these hubs. In order to ensure this, impediments to people's mobility, and mobility of capital and ideas, have to be removed.

2. Second, given that the skill requirements in services are higher than in manufacturing, investing in education is of paramount importance. Without good education, people will simply not be able to benefit from the developments in the tradable services sector as they will not be able to perform the tasks required. Rapidly growing services and education can become a virtuous circle in South Asia, as tradable services have increased demand for skilled workers and return to education.

3. Third, South Asia will need to invest more in infrastructure, without which market integration and connectivity cannot be achieved. Maintaining and upgrading both the quantity and quality of its communication infrastructure, electricity provision, and air transportation is crucial for ensuring the possibility of engaging in trade in the first place. Given the large fixed costs associated with establishing the necessary infrastructure to be able to trade in services, and given the positive externalities that can be reaped to a much greater extent in an agglomerated service hub, focusing on a few locations will likely be most successful. Continued improvements in the institutional environment related to property rights protection and contracting will also help to encourage service-led growth.

South Asia's experience shows that latecomers to development are not doomed to failure and the 'bottom billion' have not missed the boat. Globalization of services provides many more opportunities for developing countries to find niches, beyond manufacturing, where they can dominate. South Asia's experience also shows that industrialization is not the *only* route to economic development.

Each country should try its best to capture the opportunities opened to it no matter whether they come from service or manufacturing. However, when an opportunity arises, whether a country has the ability to capture it may depend on its relative strength. India's growth in service-led and China's growth in manufacturing-led may reflect, among others, their relative strength in education and infrastructure, and the timing of the globalization of services.

ANNEXURE 1A   LIST OF VARIABLES, DATA DESCRIPTION, AND SOURCES

Country size	Country area in square kilometres	World Bank 2008, WDI
Employment share	Employment in agriculture, manufacturing, industry, and services in per cent of total employment	World Bank 2008, WDI; Sivasubramaniam 2007 for India; Bosworth and Collins 2007 for China
Expenditure on tertiary education per capita (% of GDP)	Public expenditure per student is the public current spending on education divided by the total number of students by level, as a percentage of GDP per capita.	UNESCO 2008
Expected years of schooling	Expected years of schooling is the number of years a child of school entrance age is expected to spend, at school, or university, including years spent on repetition.	UNESCO 2008
Female employment (% of labour force)	Female labour force as a percentage of the total shows the extent to which women are active in the labour force.	ILO; WDI 2008
Financial services	Financial services cover financial intermediary and auxiliary services (except those of insurance enterprises and pension funds) conducted between residents and non-residents.	IMF 2008, Balance of Payments
Goods exports	Goods exports refer to all movable goods (including non-monetary gold) involved in a change of ownership from residents to non-residents. Forms of processed goods, repairs on goods, and goods procured in ports by carriers.	IMF 2008, Balance of Payments
Insurance services	Insurance services cover the provision of various types of insurance to non-residents by trade in services by service-category and country resident insurance enterprises, and vice versa.	IMF, Balance of Payments

(contd...)

(Annexure 1A contd...)

IT services	ITS like custom application development, application outsourcing, packaged software installation and support, network infrastructure management, IT training and education, network consulting and integration.	NASSCOM 2008
Industrial labour productivity	Value added by industry (at constant 2000 US$) divided by total employment in the industrial sector.	World Bank 2008, WDI; Sivasubramaniam 2007 for India; IMF 2008, Balance of Payments; Bosworth and Collins 2007 for China
Log GDP per capita	Natural log of GDP per capita, which is measured in constant 2000 US$.	Planning Commission of India 2007 for subnational; World Bank 2008, WDI
Personal, cultural, and recreational services	(i) audiovisual and related service and (ii) other personal, cultural, and recreational services.	IMF 2008, Balance of Payments
Poverty headcount (% of population)	Poverty is defined as percentage of population below $1 (PPP) per day.	MDG Indicators 2008, World Bank
Service exports	Services refer to economic output of intangible commodities that may be produced, transferred, and consumed at the same time.	IMF 2008, Balance of Payments
Service labour productivity	Value added by services (at constant 2000 US$) divided by total employment in the tertiary sector.	World Bank 2008, WDI; Sivasubramaniam 2007 for India; IMF 2008, Balance of Payment; Bosworth and Collins 2007 for China
Total employment by sector	For total number in the age group 15+ employed in agriculture, manufacturing. industry, and services for India and China, we use Bosworth and Collins.	ILO 2008, KILM; WDI 2008

(contd...)

(Annexure 1A contd...)

Transportation services	Transportation covers all transportation (sea, air, and others including land, internal waterway, space, and pipeline) services that involve the carriage of passengers, the movement of goods (freight), retails (charters) of carriers with crew, and related supporting and auxiliary services.	IMF 2008, Balance of Payments
Travel services	Travel covers primarily the goods and services acquired from an economy by travellers during visits of less than one year in that economy.	IMF 2008, Balance of Payments
Value added	Value added in agriculture, manufacturing, industry, and services in constant 2000 US$.	World Bank 2008, WDI
Value-added share	Value added in agriculture, manufacturing, industry, and services in per cent of GDP.	World Bank 2008, WDI
Worker remittances (net)	Worker's remittances are current transfers by migrants who are employed or intend to remain employed for more than a year in another economy in which they are considered residents. Some developing countries classify workers' remittances as a factor income receipt.	IMF 2008, Balance of Payments

REFERENCES

Acemoglu, D. and S. Johnson. 2005. 'Unbundling Institutions', MIT Working Paper 03–29, Massachusetts Institute of Technology, Cambridge, MA.

Ahmed, S. and Ejaz Ghani (eds). 2007. *South Asia: Growth and Regional Integration*. New Delhi: Macmillan Press.

————. 2008. 'Making Regional Cooperation Work for South Asia's Poor', Policy Research Working Paper 4736, World Bank, Washington, D.C.

Azam, M. and A. Blom. 2009. 'Progress in Participation in Tertiary Education in India from 1983 to 2004', Policy Research Working Paper 4793, World Bank, Washington, D.C.

Baily, M.N. and R. Gordon. 1988. 'The Productivity Slowdown, Measurement Issues, and the Explosion of Computer Power', *Brookings Papers on Economic Activity*, 2: 347–420.

Banerjee, A. 2006. 'The Paradox Indian Growth: A Comment on Kochhar et al.', *Journal of Monetary Economics*, 53(5): 1021–6.

Banga, Rashmi. 2005. 'Critical Issues in India's Service-led Growth', ICRIER Working Paper 171, Indian Council for Research on International Economic Relations, New Delhi.

Baumol, William J. 1967. 'Macroeconomics of Unbalanced Growth: the Anatomy of Urban Crisis', *American Economic Review*, 57(3): 415–26.

Baumol, William J. 1985. 'Productivity Growth and the Service Sector', in R.P. Inman (ed.), *Managing the Service Sector: Prospects and Problems*. Cambridge: Cambridge University Press.

Baumol, William J., Sue Anne Batey Blackman, and Edward N. Wolff. 1985. 'Unbalanced Growth Revisited: Asymptotic Stagnancy and New Evidence', *American Economic Review*, 75(4): 806–17.

Beasley, T. and M. Ghattak. 2009. 'Property Rights and Economic Development', in Dani Rodrik and Mark Rosenzweig (eds), *Handbook of Development Economics*, vol. 5. Amsterdam: North Holland (forthcoming).

Bhagwati, Jagdish. 1984a. 'Splintering and Disembodiment of Services and Developing Nations', *The World Economy*, 7: 133–44.

———. 1984b. 'Why are Services Cheaper in Poor Countries?', *Economic Journal*, 94: 279–86.

———. 1987. 'Trade in Services and Multilateral Trade Negotiations', *World Bank Economic Review*, 1: 549–69.

Bhagwati, Jagdish, A. Panagariya, and T.N. Srinivasan. 2004. 'The Muddles Over Outsourcing', *Journal of Economic Perspectives*, 18(4): 93–114.

Blinder, Alan S. 2006. 'Offshoring: The Next Industrial Revolution?', *Foreign Affairs*, 85(2): 113–28.

Bosworth, Barry and Susan M. Collins. 2008. 'Accounting for Growth—Comparing China and India', *Journal of Economic Perspectives*, 22(1): 45–66.

Bosworth, B. and A. Maertens. 2009. 'The Role of the Service Sector in South Asia in Economic Growth and Employment Generation', in *Service-led Growth in South Asia*. Washington, D.C.: World Bank (forthcoming).

Bosworth, Barry, Susan Collins, and Arvind Virmani. 2007. 'Sources of Growth in the Indian Economy', in *India Policy Forum*. Washington, D.C.: Brookings. Available at http://www.brookings.edu/papers/2006/0715globaleconomics_bosworth.aspx, accessed in February 2009.

Collier, P. 2007. *The Bottom Billion: Why the Poorest Countries are Failing and What Can Be Done about It*. New York: Oxford University Press.

Dasgupta, Sukti and Ajit Singh. 2000. 'Manufacturing, Services and Premature De-industrialization in Developing Countries: A Kaldorian Empirical Analysis', paper presented at the World Institute for Development Economics Research Jubilee Conference, Helsinki.

———. 2005. 'Will Services be the New Engine of Economic Growth in India?', Working Paper 310, Centre for Business Research, University of Cambridge, Cambridge.

Deardorff, Alan. 1985. 'Comparative Advantage and International Trade and Investment in Services', in Robert Stern (ed.), *Trade and Investment in Services: Canada-US Perspectives*. Toronto: University of Toronto Press.

_____. 2001. 'International Provision of Trade Services, Trade and Fragmentation', *Review of International Economics*, 9: 233–48.

Deardorff, Alan and Robert Stern. 2006. 'Empirical Analysis of Barriers to International Services Transactions and the Consequences of Liberalization', in R. Stern, A. Mattoo, and G. Zannini (eds), *A Handbook on International Trade in Services*. Oxford: Oxford University Press.

Dongier, Philippe and Randeep Sudan. 2009. 'Realizing the Opportunities Presented by the Global Trade in IT-Based Services', *Information and Communications for Development 2009: Extending Reach and Increasing Impact*, pp. 103–22. Washington, D.C.: World Bank.

Dossani, Rafiq and Martin Kenney. 2004. 'The Next Wave of Globalization? Exploring the Relocation of Service Provision to India', Working Paper 156, Berkeley Roundtable on the International Economy Economic Council of Canada (1991), Employment in the Service Sector, Minister of Supply and Services, Canada, Ottawa.

Duranton, Gilles and Diego Puga. 2004. 'Micro-foundations of Urban Agglomeration Economies', in Vernon Henderson and Jacques-Francois Thisse (eds), *Handbook of Regional and Urban Economics*, vol. 4, pp. 2063–117. Amsterdam: North-Holland.

_____. 2005. 'From Pectoral to Functional Urban Specialization', *Journal of Urban Economics*, 57(2): 343–70.

Feenstra, Robert C. and Gordon Hanson. 1996. 'Global Outsourcing and Wage Inequality', *American Economic Review*, 86(2): 240–5.

Fujita, M., P. Krugman and A.J. Venables. 2001. *The Spatial Economy: Cities, Regions, and International Trade*. Cambridge, M.A.: MIT Press.

Ghani, E. and S. Ahmed. 2009. *Accelerating Growth and Job Creation*. New Delhi: Oxford University Press.

Gordon, James and Poonam Gupta. 2004. 'Understanding India's Services Revolution', International Monetary Fund Working Paper WP/04/171, IMF, Washington, D.C., September.

Growth Commission Report. 2008. *Strategies for Sustained Growth and Inclusive Development*. Washington, D.C.: Commission on Growth and Development, World Bank.

Griliches, Zvi (ed.). 1992. 'Output Measurement in the Services Sectors', *NBER Studies in Income and Wealth*. Chicago: University of Chicago Press.

Hausmann, Ricardo, Dani Rodik, and Andres Velasco. 2005a. 'Growth Diagnostics', Working Paper, Kennedy School of Government, Harvard University, Cambridge, M.A.

Hausmann, Ricardo, Jason Hwang, and Dani Rodrik. 2005b. 'What You Export

Matters', NBER Working Paper 11905, National Bureau of Economic Research, Cambridge, M.A.

Henderson, J. Vernon. 2003. 'The Urbanization Process and Economic Growth: The So What Question', *Journal of Economic Growth*, 8(1): 47–71.

International Labour Organization (ILO). 2008. *Key Indicators of the Labor Market (KILM)*. Geneva: ILO.

International Monetary Fund (IMF). 2008. *Balance of Payments Statistical Yearbook*. Washington, D.C.: IMF.

Kochhar, Kalpana, Utsav Kumar, Raghuram Rajan, Arvind Subramanian, and Ioannis Tokatlidis. 2006. 'India's Pattern of Development: What Happened, What Follows?', IMF Working Paper WP/06/22, IMF, Washington, D.C.

Krugman, Paul R. 1980. 'Scale Economies, Product Differentiation, and the Pattern of Trade', *American Economic Review*, 70(5): 950–9.

──────. 1991. 'Increasing Returns and Economic Geography', *Journal of Political Economy*, 99(3): 484–99.

Krugman, Paul R. and Anthony J. Venables. 1995. 'Globalization and the Inequality of Nations', *Quarterly Journal of Economics*, 110(4): 857–80.

Kundu, Amitabh and P.C. Mohanan. 2009. 'Poverty and Inequality Outcomes of Economic Growth in India: Focus on Employment Pattern during the Period of Structural Adjustment', presentation at the OECD Seminar on 'Employment Outcomes and Inequality: New Evidence, Links and Policy Responses in Brazil, China and India'. Available at http://www.oecd.org/dataoecd/60/42/42560797.pdf, accessed in May 2009.

Mattoo, A. and D. Mishra. 2004. *Sustaining India's Services Revolution*. Washington, D.C.: World Bank.

McKay, Andrew and Ernest Aryeetey. 2004. 'Operationalising Pro-poor Growth', *A Country Case Study on Ghana*. Washington, D.C.: A joint initiative of AFD, BMZ (GTZ, KfW Development Bank), DFID, and the World Bank.

NASSCOM and CRISIL. 2007. 'The Rising Tide: Output and Employment Linkages of IT-ITES'. Available at http://www.nasscom.in/upload/51269/NASSCOM_CRISIL.pdf.

Organisation for Economic Co-operation and Development (OECD). 2001. *Measuring Productivity—OECD Manual, Measurement of Aggregate and Industry-Level Productivity Growth*. Paris: OECD.

──────. 2005. *The Service Economy in OECD Countries: Enhancing the Performance of the Services Sector*. Paris: OECD.

Pack, Howard. 2008. 'Should South Asia Emulate East Asian Tigers?', in Ejaz Ghani and Sadiq Ahmed (eds), *Accelerating Growth and Creating Jobs in South Asia*. Washington, D.C.: World Bank.

Pack, Howard and Larry Westphal. 1986. 'Industrial Strategy and Technological Change: Theory versus Reality', *Journal of Development Economics*, 22: 87–128.

Pilat, Dirk and Anita Wolfl. 2005. 'Measuring the Interaction between Manufacturing and Services', OECD Science Technology and Industry Working Papers 2005/5, OECD, Paris.

Puga, Diego. 1999. 'The Rise and Fall of Regional Inequalities', *European Economic Review*, 43(2): 303–34.

————. 2002. 'European Regional Policy in Light of Recent Location Theories', *Journal of Economic Geography*, 2(4): 372–406.

Rajan, Raghuram, G. 2006. 'India: The Past and Its Future', *Asian Development Review*, 23(2): 36–52.

Ravallion, M. 2001. 'Growth, Inequities and Poverty—Looking Beyond Averages', *World Development*, 29(11): 1803–15.

Shastry, G.K. 2008. 'Human Capital Response to Globalization: Education and Information Technology in India', University of Virginia. Available at http://ssrn.com/abstract=1334684, accessed in February 2009.

Stewart, F. and E. Ghani. 1991. 'How Significant are Externalities for Development?', *World Development*, 19(6): 569–94.

Triplett, Jack E. and Barry P. Bosworth. 2004. *Productivity in the US Services Sector: New Sources of Economic Growth*. Washington, D.C.: Brookings Institution Press.

United Nations Education Scientific and Cultural Organization (UNESCO). 2008. Institute for Statistics. UNESCO, Montreal.

United Nations Industrial Development Organization (UNIDO). 2009. *Breaking In and Moving Up: New Industrial Challenges for the Bottom Billion and the Middle Income Countries*, Industrial Development Report. Vienna: UNIDO.

Wolfl, A. 2005. 'The Service Economy in OECD Countries', OECD Science Technology and Industry Working Paper 2005/3, OECD, Paris.

World Bank. 2008. 'India's Employment Challenges—Creating Jobs, Helping Workers', Report Number 35772-IN.

————. 2008a. *World Development Indicators*. Washington, D.C.: World Bank.

————. 2008b. *Accelerating Growth and Creating Jobs in South Asia*. New Delhi: Oxford University Press.

————. 2009a. *Reshaping Economic Geography*. Washington, D.C.: World Bank.

————. 2009b. *Bottom Half Billion in South Asia*. Washington, D.C.: World Bank (forthcoming).

World Trade Organization (WTO). 2009. *Opening Markets for Trade in Services: Countries and Sectors in Bilateral and WTO Negotiations*. Geneva: WTO.

Young, A. 1991. 'Learning by Doing and the Dynamic Effects of International Trade', *Quarterly Journal of Economics*, 106: 369–405.

2

Economic Growth and Employment Generation
The Role of the Service Sector

Barry Bosworth and Annemie Maertens[#]

The services sector is a substantial and growing component of South Asian economies. In 2006, output of services exceeded 50 per cent of Gross Domestic Product (GDP) in India, Pakistan, Sri Lanka, Bangladesh, and Maldives, and it is a growing share in every country. For the region as a whole, agriculture has declined sharply over the past quarter century to less than 20 per cent of GDP from 37 per cent in 1980 (Figure 2.1). While the share of industry has grown only modestly to 27 per cent, services have expanded from 39 per cent of GDP in 1980 to 54 per cent in 2005. In this respect, South Asia contrasts with the high-growth developing economies of East Asia where industry has played a more dominant role in the early stages of economic development. As shown in Figure 2.1, the shares of agriculture, industry, and services in East Asia are 13, 46, and 41 per cent, respectively. South Asia has a larger services sector despite being at a substantially earlier stage of its economic development.

This chapter focuses on the performance of the service sector in the economies of South Asia. Driven by the recent performance of India, the emergence of dynamic new services industries, particularly those affected by information technology (IT), is seen as offering a powerful new approach to economic development as an alternative to the traditional

[#]Aaron Flaaen of the Brookings Institution provided expert research assistance.

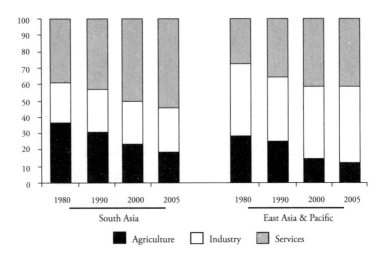

FIGURE 2.1   Structure of GDP: South Asia versus East Asia

Source: World Bank (2008).

path from agriculture to manufacturing with services emerging only in the later stages.

We highlight two aspects of growth in services, the contribution to improvements in productivity, and job creation. First, except for Bangladesh and Bhutan, the service sector has a higher level of output per worker than industry—a sharp contrast with East Asia. Second, for the four large economies of Bangladesh, India, Pakistan, and Sri Lanka, services contribute the largest share of growth in overall output per worker over the period of 2000–6. On the employment side, services have been the major source of job growth since 1990 in both India and Pakistan.

However, it is important to remember that the services industries are far less dominant when viewed from the perspective of the distribution of employment. Even though agriculture has declined to less than a fifth of GDP in the region, it still accounts for nearly half of the total employment; and services, with more than half of the GDP, employ less than a third of the workforce (Figure 2.2). In fact, East Asia, with a smaller share of its GDP in services, has a substantially larger share of its employment in the sector. While it is difficult to obtain historical data on employment by sector for South Asian countries, it is evident that the changes in sector distribution have been much less than those

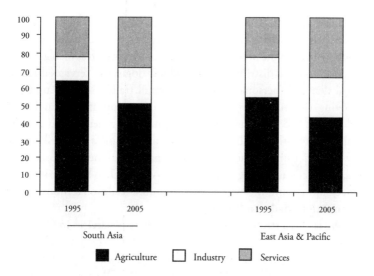

FIGURE 2.2   Structure of Employment: South Asia versus East Asia

Source: Global Employment Trends, ILO (2008).

for output. In part, this reflects the residual nature of employment in agriculture in low-income countries where a substantial number of workers are underemployed; but it also is the result of higher levels of labour productivity (output per worker) in industry and services.

The discordance between changes in the services' share in GDP and its share in employment has attracted attention and created worries. Given the increasing importance of the service sector in the GDP and perceptions of its limited ability to absorb labour, is South Asia's growth of a job-less nature? And given the large supplies of unskilled workers, will this lack of employment generation have a negative impact on poverty rates in the region? Nor is it evident that the expansion of the share of services in GDP should be interpreted as a completely positive development. Some observers have argued that it is more a reflection of the under-performance of the industrial sector where regulatory barriers and other factors have constrained growth.

Services comprise a diverse set of industries which render generalizations difficult. They differ from goods in that they cannot be stored and must in general be consumed at time of purchase. We adopt a standard national accounts definition of the boundary between goods and services that allocates mining, manufacturing, construction, natural gas, electricity, and water to the industrial sector.[1] Services-based activities include assisting in the production of other products such as managing the transportation and distribution of products (logistics), services directed to final demand (personal services and retail trade), services aimed at improving the quality of other inputs (education and research and development [R&D]), and services designed as a general infrastructure of inputs into other industries (finance and business services). Some analysts, in focusing on the remarkable expansion of the service sector in India, also prefer to distinguish modern services such as business services, finance, and communications, from the more traditional industries of transportation, trade, and personal services.

There is also a strong tendency for the share of services in GDP and employment to rise with increasing incomes. Thus, the share of services averages over 70 per cent of GDP in the high-income Organisation for Economic Co-operation and Development (OECD) countries, whereas it represents only 45 per cent for the least developed countries. Two explanations have been given for the positive association of services with income. On the demand side, it is noted that services tend to have a higher income elasticity. However, the assumption of a low elasticity of demand for goods is strongly influenced by the inclusion of food whose income elasticity is low compared to durable goods. In contrast, restaurant meals, for which expenditures typically rise with income, are classified as part of the service sector. Outside of food, income elasticities for aggregate goods and services seem similar. On the supply side, Baumol (1967) argued that the rising share reflects limited opportunities to raise productivity in many service producing industries. Wage increases equal to those in goods production, combined with lower productivity growth, raise nominal costs in services at a faster rate. The result is a rising share of nominal GDP being allocated to the production of services, and a belief that the slow productivity growth in services is a drag on the performance of the overall economy.

The whole debate is confounded by difficulties of measuring the price and output of services. Many countries produce their service-industry statistics by deflating nominal output with a measure of the price of the inputs ruling out productivity growth by assumption, or by simply

[1]The national accounts of some countries assign electric, gas, and water utilities to the service sector. We follow the practice of the World Development Indicators (WDI) and put utilities in the industrial sector.

assuming that service prices rise in line with the overall consumer price index.[2] In USA, where significant efforts have been made to improve the measurement of service prices and output, rates of improvement in labour productivity seem roughly similar in the goods and services-producing sectors. Recent advancements in IT have had a greater impact on the provision of services, accelerating productivity growth in that sector. There is considerable variation across industries within each grouping, however, making it hard to draw definitive conclusions (Triplett and Bosworth 2004).

The first goal of this chapter is to review the evidence on some of these issues. Have services been a dominant source of growth in the South Asian economies, as argued in many discussions on India's recent growth or has the sector been plagued with low productivity growth, as is often claimed? We examine the performance of the service sector in the eight countries that make up the region in terms of their contribution to the growth of GDP and employment. We can compare the growth in services, both relative to that of agriculture and industry and differences in economic structures across the region. Second, for some of the countries we have sufficient data to examine the performance of productivity across the three major sectors of the economy.

The first section gives an overview of the basic economic structure in terms of GDP and employment of the eight South Asian countries: Afghanistan, Bangladesh, Bhutan, India, Maldives, Nepal, Pakistan, and Sri Lanka. In the second section we calculate the growth rates of output, employment, and output per worker by sector for all economies except for Afghanistan and Bhutan. In addition, we present the results of a growth accounting exercise—also by sector—for India and Pakistan. In the third section we look at the contribution of growth in individual sectors versus reallocation effects to overall economic growth in Bangladesh, India, Pakistan, and Sri Lanka. The fourth section examines the performance within the different industries of the service sector. Due to data limitations we focus on the larger economies of Bangladesh, India, Pakistan, and Sri Lanka. In the fifth section we present our results using survey data to measure the educational attainment of workers in the service sector relative to the rest of the economy. The sixth section briefly discusses trade and foreign direct investment (FDI) in the service sector in South Asia. The last section provides a conclusion.

---

[2]A number of the difficulties surrounding the measurement of services were highlighted in Griliches (1992).

BASIC ECONOMIC STRUCTURE

The eight countries that comprise the South Asian region vary enormously in the size of their populations and economies. India, with a population of 1.1 billion, accounts for 75 per cent of the region's population and 77 per cent of the GDP. In contrast, both Bhutan and Maldives have populations of only 6,00,000 and 3,00,000, respectively. Most of the data on output of services industries are derived from the national accounts of the individual countries, but for convenience we have relied on the data as republished in the WDI database.

Information on employment is much more incomplete since it is often limited to decennial censuses, but some of the countries are beginning to undertake labour force surveys (LFS) on a more frequent basis. That information was obtained from various statistical yearbooks, the websites of the national statistical agencies, and the online databanks of the International Labour Organization (ILO).[3] Some basic characteristics for each of the eight countries are summarized in Table 2.1.

Afghanistan has only recently restarted its national statistical system after it was disrupted during the years of Taliban control. The 2005 estimate, based on a 2003 census, put the population at about 25 million, similar in size to Nepal. Data on GDP and its structure are available since 2002, and estimates of employment by major industry are available for a similar period.[4] It is the most agrarian economy in the region based on the share of GDP and employment in the agricultural sector. Seventy per cent of the workforce is in agriculture and a miniscule 5 per cent of the workers are employed in industry. The service sector is rudimentary and largely limited to trade and transportation. Afghanistan did not participate in the 2005 international price comparison project aimed at measuring comparable standards of living, but its income per capita is at or below that of Bangladesh and Nepal.

Bangladesh is the third largest country in the region behind India and Pakistan in terms of population (137 million), but average income per capita is significantly below the other two. The structure of the three

---

[3]Statistical issues are discussed in more detail in a later section of this chapter.

[4]Basic economic data is available in International Monetary Fund (IMF) (2008). During 1978–95 the national accounts were compiled on the basis of Gross Material Product, which differs from the concept of GDP primarily in the service sector. The United Nations and the Asian Development Bank (ADB) provide estimates for the years prior to 2002 by pulling together data from a variety of different sources, but they are not fully converted to a GDP basis.

TABLE 2.1   Summary Statistics of South Asian Economies (2005)

	Afghanistan	Bangladesh	Bhutan	India	Maldives	Nepal	Pakistan	Sri Lanka	Total: South Asia
GDP (current USD, billion)	6.8	61.2	0.8	778.7	0.7	8.7	118.4	24	**999.3**
GDP per Capita (PPP current intl dollars)	NA	1,268	3,694	2,126	4,017	1,081	2,396	3,481	2,074
Total population (million)	25	137	0.6	1,101	0.3	25	154	20	**1,463**
Trade share of GDP	68.08	39.63	81.95	44.72	172.12	48.68	35.21	79.60	**44.58**
Sector share of GDP									
Agriculture	42	20	24	20	10	37	21	17	**20**
Industry	22	27	37	30	17	17	27	26	**29**
Services	35	53	39	50	73	49	51	57	**50**
Sector share of employment									
Agriculture	70	48	44	56	12	66	43	30	**54**
Industry	5	15	17	18	25	13	21	26	**18**
Services	26	37	39	26	63	20	36	43	**28**

Source: World Bank, '2005 International Comparison Project, Preliminary Results' (2007a) and individual country statistical agencies.

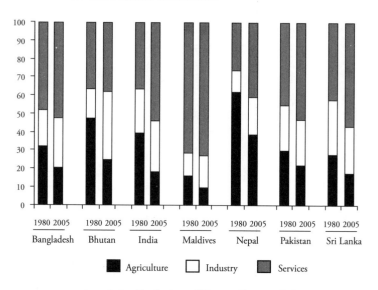

FIGURE 2.3   Evolution of Sector Shares of GDP,
South Asia (1980–2005)

Source: World Bank (2008).

economies is highly similar, however, with slightly more than 50 per cent of GDP originating in services. Bangladesh's overall economic growth rate has been only slightly below that of India over the past decade. As shown in Figure 2.3, the services share of the Bangladesh economy has grown modestly over the past quarter century, from 48 per cent of GDP in 1980 to 53 per cent in 2005. The country's growth, however, has been concentrated in manufacturing. There has been a large shift of employment out of agriculture into both industry and services, but, at 37 per cent of the total in 2005, services employment was more than twice that of industry.

Bhutan is a very small country with a reported population of only about 6,00,000. However, the government's estimate of the population is limited to those who are official citizens, and it is not fully consistent with earlier estimates. National accounts are also limited, but they do reflect the strong growth of GDP over the last decade, averaging 8 per cent annually, driven chiefly by an increased production of hydroelectric power. The estimated share of services in GDP has remained constant since 1980 at 38 per cent, but there has been a large change in the allocation between agriculture and industry. In 1980, Bhutan was primarily an agrarian society with agriculture accounting for 94 per cent of the workforce, but the ratio declined to less than 50 per cent in 2005. Employment has grown considerably in both industry and services, which conflicts somewhat with the suggestion of the national accounts that the growth has been concentrated in industry.[5] Bhutan also has a surprisingly high ratio of trade to GDP for a landlocked country, much of it associated with the development and sale of electric power. In addition, much of the labour for the hydroelectric projects has been supplied by emigrants from India.

India, the largest country in South Asia, clearly dominates the overall figures. GDP growth has averaged 6.7 per cent over the past decade. The well-publicized service sector does indeed display a strong performance in both the GDP and employment data. Figure 2.3 demonstrates that the decline in the share of agriculture in GDP from 39 per cent in 1980 to 18 per cent in 2005 has been largely absorbed by an increase in the share of services, from 37 per cent in 1980 to 54 per cent in 2005. In terms of employment, agriculture represented 70 per cent of the employed labour force in 1980 and 56 per cent in 2005, while the share of the service sector increased from 17 to 26 per cent. However, it is also important to note that the employment data are based on primary employment as reported in household surveys, although it is well known that many household members have multiple jobs. Thus, the sector assignment of employment may not be completely representative. Estimates of employment are only available from quinquennial surveys and the last available number is from 2004–5.

Maldives is an extremely small island-based economy with a population of only 3,00,000. With a land area of less than 300 square kilometres, it is very densely populated. As a result of the limited land area, agriculture constitutes a modest proportion of the economy, and while there is some fisheries production, the bulk of the economy is devoted to services. The service sector has exceeded 70 per cent of GDP throughout the post-1980 period and the share devoted to agriculture and fisheries has declined to only 10 per cent of GDP. The service sector is also the major employer, accounting for 63 per cent of the total employment. It has a very large ratio of trade to GDP consistent with its emphasis on tourism and the need to import most basic commodities. Maldives also

[5]The employment estimates for 1980 and 1990 were obtained from earlier publications of the ILO, but they are no longer included in the public data files of the ILO.

has the highest level of income per capita in the region and the fastest rate of GDP growth over the past decade.

Nepal has a highly agrarian economy, second only to Afghanistan among the South Asian countries, even though employment in agriculture had declined from 91 per cent of the total in the 1981 census to 66 per cent in 2001. Together with Afghanistan, it is the poorest country in the region. Insurgency and political unrest have limited growth over the past decade to an average of less than 4 per cent annually. It is a landlocked country and the dominant portion of its trade is with India. The share of services in the GDP has grown from 30 to 48 per cent over the period 1980–2005.

Pakistan is the second largest economy in the region, yet it is still only about one-sixth the size of India. The structure resembles that of India's with nearly identical shares of the three major sectors in GDP. However, the transition out of agriculture into services, after initially exceeding that of India, has slowed since 1980: the share of services in GDP grew from 46 per cent in 1980 to 53 per cent in 2005. From an employment perspective, the shift toward services is more pronounced, with an increase in the share from 27 per cent in 1980 to 36 per cent in 2005. Agriculture employment fell from 53 to 43 per cent of the total and the share employed in industry has remained unchanged. In the 2005 PPP study, Pakistan is reported to have an average income per capita marginally above that of India, although growth in GDP has been markedly less.

Among the larger economies, Sri Lanka has the highest income per capita, but growth has been held down by a long-running civil conflict. It also has the most extensive service sector, accounting for well over 50 per cent of GDP, and the share of the workforce in services is substantially above that of the other countries in the region, except for Maldives. As shown in Figure 2.3, the transition out of agriculture into services has also occurred at a fairly rapid pace, but Sri Lanka is the only country to have experienced a decline over the 1980 to 2005 period in the industry share of GDP.

GROWTH IN OUTPUT AND PRODUCTIVITY

All the countries of the region have national accounts from which we can measure output growth in the overall economy, and the contributions of the three major sectors. However, the quality of the national accounts data is highly variable and several of the countries lack sources of information on the size and sector allocation of the workforce, limiting the ability to measure labour productivity and other indicators of economic performance. These statistical problems are most severe in the service-producing industries and they arise largely because of the lack of basic survey information on the enterprises in these industries that could be used in the construction of national accounts.

Measures of the economic performance of the service sector are under-represented in the statistical systems of most countries for several reasons. First, attitudes toward the production of services were strongly influenced in the early stages of industrialization, when the focus was on the need to increase the production of food and other material necessities of life. Second, as few services were historically tradable across national borders, they could not be used to finance the purchase of advanced capital equipment and other products that were unavailable in the domestic economy. Both these factors led to an early emphasis on the goods-producing sector. In addition, there are unique difficulties in measuring the output of some service-producing industries. For some intangibles, it is hard to define a unit of output and its price. Finally, services are often produced in the informal sector within small enterprises that can be difficult to capture in statistical reporting systems. The result is that many countries undertake extensive annual surveys of enterprises in manufacturing and they have large statistical bureaucracies charged with gathering information on the production of agricultural commodities; but no such reporting system exists for service-producing enterprises.

India, Pakistan, and Sri Lanka have large statistical programmes that produce much of the essential information needed for evaluating the economic performance at the sector level. The national accounts have estimates of value added by industry covering several decades and we can construct annual measures back to 1980. However, the incomplete coverage of the informal sector results in considerable reliance on interpolation and extrapolation of estimates for services. The employment data were obtained from periodic population censuses or LFSs of households and interpolated and extrapolated for other years. Information on the allocation of capital among sectors or major industries is available only for India and Pakistan.[6]

For the other countries, the data are more restricted. Credible estimates of output and employment in Afghanistan are available only since 2002, and there are no meaningful measures of employment in

---

[6]Since 2000, these data are also available for Nepal.

Bhutan beyond the 2005 population census. Bangladesh has conducted periodic LFSs dating back to the early 1980s, but their structure has varied over time. Population censuses are available for Maldives at about five-year intervals and we have the data beginning in 1990, but large portions of the workforce have no identified industry of employment. There are three census estimates of employment for Nepal, but they imply an extraordinary 20 per cent annual rate of growth within the industry sector. For some countries, we also had access to individual household datasets for recent surveys. They provided additional information on the educational attainment of the workforce within the major industries.[7] Summary measures of annual rates of growth in output, employment, and labour productivity are reported in Table 2.2 for the overall economy, agriculture, industry, and services. It includes data for six countries but excludes Afghanistan and Bhutan due to the severity of data constraints in these countries.

Bangladesh

The economy has achieved strong growth in recent years, and in general the economy has done much better than would have been anticipated at the time of the country's creation, given the severe poverty and lack of any significant natural resources. In fact, Bangladesh's growth in agriculture and industry has consistently exceeded that of India since 1990. Output growth has also been strong in the service sector, even if not at the exceptional rates in India. Most notable, growth in Bangladesh has been employment intensive with a strong expansion of jobs in both industry and services. The improvement in labour productivity, while significant in recent years, accounts for less than a third of the overall growth and a fifth of the growth in services. There are no available measures of the capital stock at the sector level, but the overall investment rate, averaging about 25 per cent of GDP over the last decade, suggests a modest contribution of capital to growth.

India

The emphasis on services as the driving source of India's growth acceleration is very evident in the sector calculations of Table 2.2. At the level of the total economy, the growth averaged 7.5 per cent annually in 2000–6, compared to 5.7 per cent in the 1990s. The expansion of agricultural output slowed in the 1990s and has accelerated modestly

---

[7]The data sources are discussed more fully in Annexure 2A.1.

TABLE 2.2   Rates of Growth, Total Economy, and Major Sectors, South Asian Countries (1980–2006)

(average annual percentage rate of change)

Component	Total Economy			Agriculture			Industry			Services			Reallocation		
	1980–90	1990–2000	2000–6	1980–90	1990–2000	2000–6	1980–90	1990–2000	2000–6	1980–90	1990–2000	2000–6	1980–90	1990–2000	2000–6
Bangladesh															
Real output growth	3.7	4.7	5.6	2.5	3.2	2.8	5.8	6.9	7.8	3.7	4.5	5.8			
Employment	2.8	1.9	4.0	1.1	1.4	2.9	6.2	2.1	6.2	4.9	2.6	4.7			
Output per worker	0.9	2.7	1.6	1.3	1.8	0.0	-0.4	4.7	1.5	-1.1	1.8	1.1	1.0	0.3	0.7
India															
Real output growth	5.5	5.7	7.5	3.4	2.2	2.9	7.1	5.5	8.1	6.5	8.4	9.3			
Employment	2.0	1.6	2.9	1.2	0.8	1.6	3.6	2.2	5.2	3.6	3.4	4.4			
Output per worker	3.5	4.1	4.5	2.2	1.3	1.4	3.4	3.3	2.7	2.8	4.9	4.6	0.8	0.9	1.2
Maldives															
Real output growth	11.5	7.9	6.7	11.0	1.9	6.8	11.4	9.3	9.4	11.7	8.6	6.2			
Employment	N/A	4.4	4.2	N/A	-1.8	1.1	N/A	2.7	8.5	N/A	4.8	7.3			
Output per worker	N/A	3.3	2.5	N/A	3.8	5.6	N/A	6.4	0.8	N/A	3.6	-1.0	N/A	N/A	N/A
Nepal															
Real output growth	4.7	5.0	3.3	4.6	2.4	3.6	8.1	7.8	2.6	3.5	6.5	3.5			
Employment	0.7	1.8	1.9	-0.5	-0.1	-0.1	19.1	19.5	17.7	7.9	4.6	4.2			
Output per worker	4.0	3.1	1.4	5.1	2.5	3.7	-9.2	-9.8	-12.8	-4.0	1.9	-0.7	4.2	2.4	2.6

(contd...)

Table 2.2 (contd...)

Component	Total Economy 1980–90	Total Economy 1990–2000	Total Economy 2000–6	Agriculture 1980–90	Agriculture 1990–2000	Agriculture 2000–6	Industry 1980–90	Industry 1990–2000	Industry 2000–6	Services 1980–90	Services 1990–2000	Services 2000–6	Reallocation 1980–90	Reallocation 1990–2000	Reallocation 2000–6
Pakistan															
Real output growth	6.1	4.4	5.4	4.0	4.4	2.1	7.7	4.2	7.3	6.6	4.5	6.1			
Employment	2.0	2.1	4.1	1.8	1.6	2.2	1.8	1.2	6.6	2.8	3.7	5.3			
Output per worker	4.0	2.2	1.3	2.2	2.8	-0.2	5.8	2.9	0.7	3.7	0.8	0.8	0.3	0.4	0.8
Sri Lanka															
Real output growth	4.2	5.1	3.8	2.8	1.9	0.8	4.5	6.8	3.5	4.9	5.8	5.1			
Employment	1.4	2.3	2.0	1.7	-0.4	0.1	1.1	4.3	4.0	1.2	4.1	2.4			
Output per worker	2.7	2.8	1.8	1.1	2.2	0.7	3.4	2.3	-0.5	3.7	1.7	2.6	0.0	0.8	0.4

Source: Constructed by the authors from the data and sources listed in Annexure 2A.1.

in recent years. However, growth has been strong in both industry and services. Output growth in industry has recovered from a slowdown in the 1990s and has averaged 8 per cent annually after 2000 with two-thirds of the growth being reflected in employment gains.

Services output has accelerated to an average of more than 9 per cent per year with about half of the growth in employment and half in improvements in labour productivity. In recent years, the industry and service sectors have been strong sources of job growth in India. It is also notable that the employment gains in these sectors have been smaller than those of Bangladesh.

The Central Statistical Office of India produces estimates of the capital stock by industry, and we can obtain measures of the educational attainment of the workforce from the quinquennial household surveys. This added information enables us to construct more complete growth accounts that show the contribution of physical capital, education, and total factor productivity (TFP) to the growth of labour productivity in each of the three sectors.[8]

The results of the growth accounting exercise are shown in the top panel of Table 2.3. At the level of the total economy, increased capital per worker and improvements in educational attainment account for significant portions of the gains in labour productivity. However, improvements in TFP are also a substantial contributor to growth, a finding that contrasts with the findings in other regions at comparable stages of development (Young 1995). The sector detail indicates that the contribution of both increased capital per worker and TFP are concentrated in services. Also, the contribution of improvements in educational attainment, while it is most substantial for services, is small compared to the gains in some of the high-growth economies of East Asia, an issue that we return to later.

Maldives

Maldives is also a services-based economy, but its emphasis on tourism implies a much different role than it does in India. We have data on the structure of output and employment beginning in 1990. Agriculture and fisheries along with industry show strong rates of growth in recent years, but they represent very small shares of the overall economy. The growth of services GDP has slowed, but it continues to average more

---

[8]More complete explanations of the methodology are provided in Bosworth et al. (2007).

than 6 per cent per year. Consistent with the emphasis on tourism, the service sector has had little or no growth in labour productivity. However, we have limited confidence in the estimates of productivity at the sector level because a very large number of persons are not assigned to any specific industry in the population censuses. In the 2000 census, 17 per cent of the workforce had no specific industry, compared to 2–3 per cent in 1995 and 2006.

Nepal

The economy has grown slowly in recent years despite a surge in neighbouring India with which Nepal is closely linked. In particular, insurgency has held back the growth in tourism, but growth has also slowed in industry relative to the 1990s. Information on employment changes is severely limited. Population censuses were undertaken in 1981, 1991, and 2001, but the first two did not use international standards for defining employment status or industry. As a result, it is difficult to interpret the changes between census years. In addition, large numbers of persons are employed in very small rural enterprises that are not well reported in the statistics. These statistical problems dominate the extremely rapid rate of reported employment growth in industry (shown in Table 2.3), and result in an implied large decline in labour productivity. An LFS was completed in 1998–9 that indicated a level of employment in industry consistent with the 2001 census, but a much higher level of agricultural employment. A second round of the LFS was undertaken in 2008, but until it is available there is no means of estimating changes in employment over time.

Pakistan

Overall growth averaged 5.4 per cent annually in the 2000–6 period, held down by weak growth in agriculture, but output growth exceeded 7 per cent in industry and 6 per cent in services. In contrast to India, large portions of the growth have been reflected in increased employment rather than in productivity gains. In the most recent period, labour productivity has declined in agriculture and grown at less than 1 per cent per year in industry and services. Pakistan has conducted an LFS on an annual basis since 1980, and the estimates of employment growth by sector should be quite reliable.

Sufficient information on capital investment is available for Pakistan to allow us to construct more complete growth accounts, comparable to those for India. They are shown in the lower panel of Table 2.3. The most

TABLE 2.3   Sources of Growth in Output per Worker in India and Pakistan: Total Economy and Major Sectors (1980–2006)

(average annual percentage rate of change)

Component	Total Economy 1980–90	Total Economy 1990–2000	Total Economy 2000–6	Agriculture 1980–90	Agriculture 1990–2000	Agriculture 2000–6	Industry 1980–90	Industry 1990–2000	Industry 2000–6	Services 1980–90	Services 1990–2000	Services 2000–6
India												
Output per worker	3.5	4.1	4.5	2.2	1.3	1.4	3.4	3.3	2.7	2.8	4.9	4.6
Contribution of capital	1.1	1.8	2.0	0.2	0.5	0.5	1.5	2.4	0.9	0.4	1.3	2.3
Contribution of education	0.3	0.4	0.4	0.3	0.3	0.4	0.3	0.4	0.2	0.3	0.4	0.4
Contribution of land	-0.1	0.0	-0.1	-0.1	-0.1	-0.4	0.0	0.0	0.0	0.0	0.0	0.0
TFP	2.2	1.8	2.1	1.9	0.7	0.9	1.5	0.6	1.6	2.1	3.1	1.9
Pakistan												
Output per worker	4.0	2.2	1.3	2.2	2.8	-0.2	5.8	2.9	0.7	3.7	0.8	0.8
Contribution of capital	1.4	1.2	-0.1	1.3	1.1	0.1	1.2	1.9	-1.1	1.5	0.6	-0.6
Contribution of education	0.9	-0.2	0.3	0.8	-0.2	0.2	0.9	-0.2	0.3	0.9	-0.2	0.4
Contribution of land	-0.1	-0.1	-0.1	-0.4	-0.3	-0.6	0.0	0.0	0.0	0.0	0.0	0.0
TFP	1.8	1.3	1.2	0.6	2.1	0.1	3.6	1.2	1.5	1.2	0.4	1.0

Source: Constructed by the authors from the data and sources listed in Annexure 2A.1.

striking feature is the very modest contribution of capital accumulation to Pakistan's growth.

While we previously noted the low rate of improvement in labour productivity, it is all attributable to gains in TFP because the contribution of capital per worker has generally been negative across the three sectors during 2000–6. Gains in TFP within the industrial sector are above or comparable to those in India, but rates of improvement are markedly lower in services.

Sri Lanka

The economy has performed poorly in the post-2000 period under pressures of continued social conflict, and the overall growth of GDP has been below the average for the region. However, much of the growth slowdown is the result of limited gains in agriculture, and the expansion of the service sector has remained at or above 5 per cent per year. Within services, the growth has been equally divided between increases in employment and labour productivity. There are reasonably good statistics covering the national accounts and employment in Sri Lanka, but no information is available on the sector distribution of capital.

It is important to note that this growth accounting exercise does not explicitly allow for economies of scale, and as such these are subsumed within an overall residual of TFP. The service sector is traditionally known as a sector in which there are limited opportunities for within-firm economies of scale. This is due to the heterogeneity and simultaneity (where the consumer is involved in creating the service) which makes it more difficult to achieve scale economies. However, several sub-sectors of the service sector these days are run more like a factory. For instance a large-scale call centre or IT organization, exploiting economies of scale (Singh 2006). And of course, traditional infrastructural services like electricity, gas, and water supply that are often government monopolies also have scale economies.

Several empirical studies have examined economies of scale in traditional service sectors like electricity supply, transportation services, and postal services, and in non-traditional service sectors like marketing, telecommunication, health, and insurance. Most of these studies conclude that significant economies of scales exist. None of these studies have, however, looked at any of the service industries in South Asia.[9]

[9] In order to investigate whether the service sector exhibits economies of scale at the firm level, one would need a micro-level firm level dataset. Assuming a two factor Cobb

LABOUR PRODUCTIVITY AND REALLOCATION EFFECTS

Output growth can be generated from the reallocation of resources into higher productivity activities as well as from productivity gains within sectors. Indeed, this reallocation effect is potentially a very important source of growth for economies in which a large share of labour is initially underutilized in agriculture. We now examine the dimension of the sources of growth in some of the South Asian economies. Our first step is to examine sector differences in labour productivity. We then decompose aggregate growth in output per worker into the contributions from each sector and a residual, which can be interpreted as the effects from resource reallocation.

Table 2.4 shows the level of output per worker across the three major sectors of each country in 2005. We use PPP exchange rates from the recently completed international comparison project to construct measures that are roughly comparable across the countries of the region.[10] First, Table 2.4 provides a comparison of the cross-national performance of labour productivity. They are, of course, similar in relative magnitudes to the measures of GDP per capita shown in Table 2.1, differing only because of variations in the proportion of the total population that is employed. Pakistan, for example, reports a very low labour force participation rate for women; this raises the level of GDP per worker well above that of India.

Second, Table 2.4 highlights the substantial sectoral differences in labour productivity within the individual economies. Except for Maldives and Nepal, labour productivity is much higher in industry and services

---

Douglas production function, the most basic specification could test the following null-hypothesis H_o: $\alpha + \beta > 1$.

$$\ln y_i = \alpha \ln K_i + \beta \ln L_i + \varepsilon_i \qquad (2.1)$$

with y_i firm-level output, K_i firm-level capital, and L_i firm-level labour.

One could run regression (2.1) on a per-sector basis (agriculture, industry, and service) or a per sub-sector basis (within service industries) at different levels of aggregation. The suitable level of aggregation depends on the underlying hypothesis one wants to test and the structural assumptions on the error-term in specification (2.1).

[10]The PPP exchange rate is intended to apply only at the level of the total economy, but comparable sector measures do not exist. Within the region, the results are quite similar if the cross-country comparisons are based on market exchange rates. The one exception is Maldives where its small size dictates a very high degree of trade, and the PPP and market exchange rates are much closer than in the other countries. Afghanistan is excluded due to the lack of time-consistent data.

TABLE 2.4   South Asia Labour Productivity Levels by Sector (2005)

(PPP international dollars per worker)

	Total	Agriculture	Industry	Services	Ratio (3)/(2)	Ratio (4)/(2)
	(1)	(2)	(3)	(4)	(5)	(6)
Bangladesh	3,319	1,390	6,208	4,679	4.5	3.4
Bhutan	8,940	4,841	19,366	8,938	4.0	1.8
India	4,540	1,597	7,479	8,901	4.7	5.6
Maldives	10,271	8,474	7,533	12,790	0.9	1.5
Nepal	2,596	1,513	1,716	5,552	1.1	3.7
Pakistan	7,952	3,556	10,439	11,829	2.9	3.3
Sri Lanka	8,990	4,968	8,906	11,856	1.8	2.4
Addendum						
China*	7,230	2,021	14,853	9,608	7.4	4.8
Thailand	12,647	3,335	24,948	14,818	7.5	4.4
Malaysia**	30,593	17,544	49,270	25,439	2.8	1.5
Korea	40,013	17,199	60,012	34,556	3.5	2.0

Source: Same as that for Table 2.2 and the World Bank (2008).
Note: * Data for China is from 2004. ** The utilities industry in Malaysia is included in services rather than industry.

than in agriculture. India appears to have particularly large productivity differences, reflecting the magnitude of under-employment in rural areas. The differentials are less for Pakistan and Sri Lanka. As noted earlier, the level of labour productivity in Nepal seems unusually low, but it may reflect large numbers of workers engaged in household crafts. To our knowledge, no studies exist that try and explain the differences in labour productivity between the countries of South Asia. Applied macroeconomic cross-country studies traditionally explain differences in productivity levels and growth across countries by differences in political and economic institutions, and differences in culture, geographical locations, policies, and laws, while applied microeconomic studies, focusing on industry level or even firm level differences, use physical capital, education and health, land characteristics, and so on, as explanatory variables.

Note that five out of seven countries report higher labour productivity in the service sector as compared to the industry sector. Does this also mean that jobs in the service sector, on average, fetch higher wages and imply better working conditions? Few empirical studies have investigated this question. Abraham (2007) using National Sample Survey (NSS) data (from India) concludes that wage inequality is widening between the service sector and other sectors, but declining between the manufacturing and agriculture sectors. However, this does not imply any causality, or in other words, it does not mean that if one shifts one particular worker from the industry to the service sector, this worker would, on average, receive a higher wage. One would need to control for the selection of workers into the different sectors of the economy by taking into account education, work experience, ability, and other individual specific factors. Regarding the other aspects of job quality such as workers' rights and in general degree of formality, no studies to our knowledge have done a comprehensive comparison between sectors. According to Key Indicators of the Labour Market (KILM) the percentage of informal employment of total employment is 56 per cent in India, 73 per cent in Nepal, and 66 per cent in Pakistan.[11] One would need to match LFS data with the national definitions of informal/unorganized versus formal/organized employment in order to get an estimate of these percentages by the main economic sectors.

Third, let us compare the levels of labour productivity in South Asia with the rest of the world. The labour productivity of the economy as a whole in China is higher than in Nepal, Bangladesh, and India. In China, Malaysia, Thailand, and Korea, the industrial sector shows higher labour productivity than the service sector. As in South Asia, the labour productivity of the agricultural sector is much lower than the labour productivities in the industry/service sectors.

Fourth, we return to the discussion of labour laws and labour productivity. The link between labour productivity and labour laws is complex as at the firm level many decisions are involved and different laws affect different aspects of these decisions (Basu 2006). To our knowledge, no empirical studies exist on South Asia comparing the effects of a more stringent labour regulation on labour productivity in the industry versus the service sector. According to the 'Doing Business' employing workers indicator of the World Bank, the larger countries in South Asia, in terms of more stringent labour regulation, could be ranked as follows:

[11]This data is from KILM (ILO 2007), using the national definition. Figures are of 2000, apart for Nepal, which are for 1999.

1. Pakistan
2. India
3. Sri Lanka
4. Bangladesh

Looking at Table 2.4, it seems that it would be difficult to make a case for an inverse relation between labour productivity in either the service or industry sectors and the employer workers rank.

How much of the growth of labour productivity in each country can be attributed to the sectoral gains in output per worker? A simple measure of the contribution from each sector is simply the sector's growth rate (from Table 2.4) weighted by the sector's share in value added at the outset of each sub-period. The difference between total growth and the sum of sectoral contributions provides a (residual) measure of the effects due to resource reallocation. The decompositions of total productivity growth in 1990–2000 and 2000–6 are shown Figure 2.4. Note that Nepal has been excluded due to our concerns with employment statistics.

Only a small portion of Bangladesh's growth in overall labour productivity can be attributed to agriculture, and substantial gains were derived from industry and services, but the reallocation between low and high-productivity sectors was a major contributor in the second period.

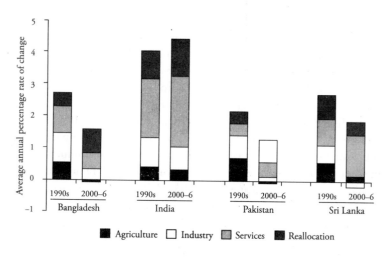

FIGURE 2.4   **Growth in Labour Productivity, Sector and Reallocation Effects (1990–2006)**

Source: Table 2.2.

The dominant role of services is clearly evident in India, but because of the large productivity differences across the sectors, it also had the largest reallocation gains. The pattern of growth between the two periods changed sharply in Pakistan, with a marked slowing of improvements in agriculture and industry, but the reallocation component expanded substantially in the second period. In Sri Lanka the gains in productivity were spread quite evenly across the four components during the 1990s, but productivity growth collapsed in agriculture and industry after 2000 and the reallocation term was of reduced importance.

COMPOSITION OF SERVICES

It is difficult to make meaningful cross-national comparisons of individual industries within services because the methods used to estimate services in national accounts are not always comparable. While all the countries profess to follow the guidelines of the international system of national accounts (SNA), the limited availability of primary source data—particularly in services—leads to significant differences in the actual construction of the accounts, and the smaller countries do not have the resources to undertake detailed estimates. In addition, the SNA industry groupings for services are not particularly useful because they often combine highly disparate activities. The degree of published details were increased with the 1993 SNA, but many countries are still in the process of conversion.

India provided the most detailed estimates for the service-producing industries, and it places special emphasis on developing estimates of employment and output in the large informal portion of the service sector. Household surveys are used to estimate employment by industry, and the estimates of employment are combined with measures of value added per worker obtained from a variety of enterprise surveys to construct the estimates of GDP at the industry level. The procedures are updated following the quinquennial household surveys. The methodology has also benefited from extensive outside evaluation. However, there is little information on which to base the estimates for years between the quinquennial surveys.[12] Pakistan uses a similar methodology, but the procedures are not updated in a regular cycle. Less information is available about the methodology used to construct the national accounts

---

[12]Using NSS and National Accounts data, Rangarajan et al. (2007) calculate employment elasticities of the different service sub-sectors. They conclude that the construction and finance and insurance sub-sectors have relatively high elasticities.

in the other countries of the region.[13] It is evident, however, that far less information is available for the construction of the GDP in services relative to that for goods. In addition, direct measures of sector-specific prices are seldom available, and several of the countries simply deflate nominal estimates of value added with the general consumer price index to obtain constant-price estimates.

In Figure 2.5, we show an allocation of value added in the service sector among the major industrial groups for the four large economies. In each case, wholesale and retail trade was the largest industry group, but the shares vary over a wide range, from 30 per cent in Bangladesh and India to 42 per cent in Sri Lanka. In large part, the difference is a reflection of methodology as Sri Lanka assigns margins on import and export trade to wholesale trade, raising the total, whereas the other countries leave much of the revenue with the industries producing the exports or using intermediate imports. In contrast, the shares of services accounted for by transportation and communications are very similar for all the countries. Bangladesh does not publish information on the rental income imputed to owned dwellings, which are treated in the national accounts as an investment that the household in turn rents to itself. Among the other countries, India does stand out for the magnitude of the cluster of industries grouped under the heading of finance and business services.[14] Comparisons of the final two categories of public administration and community services are distorted because the countries do not follow uniform procedures for allocating activities between the public and private sectors. Thus, the share devoted to community and personal services is unrealistically high for Bangladesh and too low for Sri Lanka.

The detailed estimates of GDP in services prepared as part of the Indian national accounts are particularly useful because they facilitate a division between traditional services (such as trade, transportation, and personal services) and modern service industries (communications, business services, finance, education, and healthcare) that are believed to be the drivers behind India's growth acceleration. While growth has been very rapid in the modern component within India—exceeding 10

[13]Much of what is known is the result of two workshops in 2000/1 on rebasing and linking of national account series that were sponsored by the ADB and the United Nations Economic and Social Commission for Asia and the Pacific. The country papers provide brief descriptions of each country's methodology. The papers are available at: http://www.adb.org/documents/books/reta5874/default.asp.

[14]As mentioned earlier, the estimate for Bangladesh is distorted by the inclusion of imputed income to owners of dwellings.

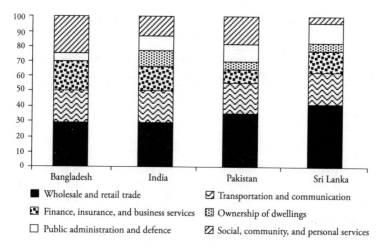

- ■ Wholesale and retail trade
- ☑ Finance, insurance, and business services
- □ Public administration and defence
- ☑ Transportation and communication
- ▦ Ownership of dwellings
- ☑ Social, community, and personal services

FIGURE 2.5   Composition of Services GDP by Country (2005–6)

Source: Authors' calculations and national accounts data from websites of national statistical agencies.

per cent per year in the last decade, it represents less than half of value added in the service sector, and it accounts for a relatively small portion of growth in the overall economy (see Bosworth et al. 2007). While the new service industries are an important part of the surge of economic activity in India, the detailed data highlight the fact that more is involved in India's growth acceleration than just the modern service industries.

THE ROLE OF EDUCATION

For several of the South Asian countries, we were able to obtain micro-data files from their LFSs. We used that data to tabulate educational attainment for workers in agriculture, industry, and services. The results are reported in Table 2.5 together with a measure of the overall literacy rate. First, except for Sri Lanka, overall levels of educational attainment are very low in the region, with average years of schooling of only 4–5 years. In fact, using the average literacy rate as an alternative measure of educational performance, South Asia averages 58 per cent, which is the lowest in any of the major geographic areas, falling substantially below 61 per cent for sub-Saharan Africa, and much below 91 per cent for East Asia.[15]

[15] The literacy rates for Afghanistan, Bhutan, and Maldives are 28, 60, and 96 per cent, respectively. Overall educational attainment in Maldives is still well below that of Sri Lanka, but for the younger generations it is quite comparable.

TABLE 2.5   Educational Attainment by Sector
of Employment (2002–5)

Country	Literacy Rate (%)	Years of Schooling—Employed Persons			
		Total	Agriculture	Industry	Services
Afghanistan	28	NA	NA	NA	NA
Bhutan	60	4.2	NA	NA	NA
Bangladesh	44	4.4	2.9	4.6	6.3
India	61	4.7	3.2	5.2	7.9
Maldives	96	6.0	NA	NA	NA
Nepal	49	3.7	2.5	5.2	5.8
Pakistan	50	4.3	2.3	4.6	7.1
Sri Lanka	91	8.4	6.5	8.8	9.7

Source: Authors' calculations.
Note: The years of data for individual countries are: Bangladesh (2005), India (2004), Nepal (2003), Pakistan (2004), and Sri Lanka (2002).

Educational requirements are substantially higher in the service sector. On average, the years of schooling are roughly 50 per cent higher in the service sector than for the economy as a whole and more than twice that for agriculture. Particularly in the 'modern service' industries, employment requires a minimum of a secondary level certificate and often a university-level degree. Even though India has a low general level of educational attainment, it has a small minority of persons with unusually high levels of schooling. The availability of such workers has been an important contributor to the expansion of business services in India, but their relative scarcity is beginning to be reflected in a widening of the wage premiums for secondary and university level graduates (Bosworth et al. 2007). These results suggest that improvements in educational attainment may be an important pre-requisite of growth in some service producing industries.

Psacharopoulus and Patrinos (2004) report an average return to additional schooling across countries of about 10 per cent both overall and for the sub-group of Asian economies.[16] However, there are some indications that the rates of return may be a bit lower in South Asia. A

---

[16]This analysis refers to 1990, and includes only a limited selection of South Asian countries. Note that there are two main methodological issues that can result in an overestimation of the returns to schooling; both have to do with selection. The first one is the fact that only wage workers were included; if the 'better abled' enter the labour market more easily, then this will lead to an overestimation of the coefficients. The second one is the lack of control of selection into the different levels of education, also, through the unobservable of ability, leading to an overestimation of returns to education.

series of papers on the returns to education in Pakistan and Bangladesh suggest returns in the range of 7 per cent.[17] A recent World Bank study looks at the return to education in Bangladesh, India, and Pakistan. It reports returns rising with the level of schooling (Riboud et al. 2007). They also separated the data by industry and found that returns to tertiary education were rising particularly rapidly in business services for India. In contrast, returns to tertiary education were flat or declining in Pakistan.

In summary, the most rapidly growing service-producing industries rely on relatively highly educated workers. Yet, it is this characteristic which is severely limited in most of South Asia. The region has a very low level of educational attainment, and recent rates of investment in education have led to rates of improvement that are less than those of other regions. Ribaud et al. (2007) examined levels of school attainment among persons aged 20–9 years, and concluded that at current levels of effort, the region's educational gap with East Asia will actually widen in future years. Therefore, an emphasis on services may not create jobs for the low-skilled workers who are most abundant in the region.

EXTERNAL SERVICES TRADE AND FOREIGN INVESTMENT

Total global trade in commercial services reached US$ 2.8 trillion in 2006; double that of ten years earlier (World Trade Organization, 2007). Technical innovations in telecommunications and the expanded opportunities that they create for cross-border trade in services have greatly increased interest in services trade as a source of growth and its potential for a major realignment of areas of comparative advantage. In earlier decades, many large corporations outsourced substantial portions of their services to specialty firms within their own country. Financial firms, for example, moved their backroom operations, call centres, and other processing activities to cheaper domestic locations. With improvements in telecommunications, those labour-intensive services can now effectively be outsourced across national borders.[18] Gordon

---

[17]The papers are Abbas and Foreman-Peck (2007), Razmi (2007) for Pakistan, and Asadullah (2005) for Bangladesh. These studies employ a somewhat better method, controlling for labour-market entry selection. They are also more recent (2000+).

[18]For a discussion of the link between technological changes in telecommunications and service exports from India, see the discussion in Gordon and Gupta (2004) and Dasgupta and Singh (2005). Bhagwati et al. (2004) provide a general framework that emphasizes the similarities between outsourcing of services and trade in goods.

and Gupta (2004), for example, estimate that the growth of IT-related service exports added about 0.6 per cent annually to the growth of GDP in India during the 1990s.

Table 2.6 shows the distribution of trade in services for the six countries for which we have data. The table highlights the extent to which India's trade is different from that of the other countries in the region. First, India accounts for 90 per cent of the region's total of commercial service exports, and 70 per cent of its receipts are from computer and related services. This category is less than a quarter of services exports for the other countries. Maldives has a substantial trade surplus from tourism, but all the other countries report service trade revenues that are a small share of GDP and they have significant deficits in services trade. In addition, only India reports that trade in services is a major contributor to growth. For the others, service exports are rising at the rate of GDP or less.

There are significant concerns, however, about the extent to which the individual countries capture services trade in their balance of payments statistics. The measurement of services trade is more difficult than that of goods because in many cases the service transactions cannot be tied to any physical movement across a national border. Instead, the transactions are defined in terms of the residence of the buyer and seller, but residence can be a vague and easily changed standard. In recent years, India, for example, has consistently reported a level of exports to the US in the category of business, professional, and technical services that is far larger than the imports reported by the US (see United States General Accountability Office 2004, 2005). The Indian balance of payments deviates from the US practice in two major respects. First, the earnings of Indian workers who reside in the US are included in India's service exports, but excluded in the US data if they intend to stay for more than one year. That activity is believed to represent about 40 per cent of India's total BPT exports. Second, India reports the internal sale of services to local affiliates of US firms as part of its exports. That is estimated to be about 30 per cent of the BPT total.[19] Since statistics on services trade have only recently become a focus of international attention, many of these measurement issues have not been fully resolved.

---

[19]Some of the issues for computer services are discussed from the Indian perspective in Reserve Bank of India (2005).

TABLE 2.6   2006 Services Trade by Type, South Asia

(in million US$)

	Bangladesh	India	Maldives	Nepal	Pakistan	Sri Lanka	South Asia
Credit	1,334	75,354	473	386	3,506	1,625	**82,678**
Transportation services	89	7,629	26	35	1,112	751	**9,641**
Travel services	80	8,934	434	128	255	410	**10,241**
Other services	1,165	58,791	13	223	2,139	464	**62,795**
Communications	62	2,191	0	35	157	68	**2,513**
Construction	22	403	0	0	31	29	**485**
Royalties and license fees	0	112	10	0	53	0	**175**
Finance and insurance	34	3,187	1	2	84	57	**3,365**
Computer and business services	312	52,384	0	52	552	288	**53,588**
Other services	734	515	3	134	1,262	21	**2,669**
Debit	−2,340	−63,537	−233	−493	−8,418	−2,394	**−77,416**
Transportation services	−1,608	−25,198	−115	−186	−3,027	−1,462	**−31,597**
Travel services	−140	−7,352	−78	−185	−1,545	−373	**−9,673**
Other services	−593	−30,987	−39	−121	−3,846	−558	**−36,146**
Communications	−12	−899	0	−4	−89	−49	**−1,053**
Construction	−1	−906	0	0	−58	−6	**−971**
Royalties and license fees	−5	−949	0	0	−106	0	**−1,060**
Finance and insurance	−195	−3,980	−9	−29	−257	−140	**−4,610**
Computer and other services	−150	−23,652	−25	−84	−3,009	−329	**−27,249**
Other services	−230	−601	−5	−5	−327	−35	**−1,202**
Addenda: Per cent of GDP							
Credit	2.15	8.31	51.71	4.79	2.72	6.03	**7.30**
Debit	−3.78	−7.01	−25.48	−6.12	−6.53	−8.88	**−6.83**
Balance	−1.62	1.30	26.23	−1.33	−3.81	−2.85	**0.46**

Source: IMF (2008).

TABLE 2.7   Stock of Inward FDI (1990 and 2006)

Country	Millions of dollars		Per cent of GDP		Services Share
	1990	2006	1990	2006	(%)
Afghanistan	12	27	0.3	0.3	
Bangladesh	706	4,133	2.2	6.3	30
Bhutan	2	28	0.7	2.8	30
India	1,657	50,680	0.5	5.7	50
Maldives	25	194	11.6	21.4	80
Nepal	12	120	0.3	1.5	50
Pakistan	1,892	14,753	3.6	11.4	70
Sri Lanka	679	2,927	8.5	10.9	60
South Asia	4,984	72,862	1.2	6.5	

Source: United Nations Conference on Trade and Development (UNCTAD 2004, 2007).
Note: The measures of the shares of FDI devoted to services are rough estimates from the 2004 report.

In addition to trade, FDI is an important medium by which external factors influence the development of the service-producing industries. Between 1990 and 2006, the stock of FDI increased fivefold within the developed economies and nearly sevenfold in the developing world. Investment in the developed countries now totals about US$ 7.5 trillion and US$ 2.5 trillion in the developing world. The relaxation of restrictions on FDI has also led to a substantial shift of FDI toward services, which now account for 60 per cent of the FDI in both developed and developing regions, compared to 50 per cent in 1990.

The distribution of FDI stocks among the South Asian economies is shown in Table 2.7. The volume of investment has grown at an explosive rate, increasing fifteenfold between 1990 and 2006; but the totals are dominated by the growth of FDI into India. Seventy per cent of the stock of FDI is in India and it is growing at three times the rate of the rest of the region.[20] However, as a share of GDP, FDI is substantial and growing in Bangladesh, Maldives, Pakistan, and Sri Lanka.

[20]The FDI stocks are likely to be understated because until 2000 India was unable to include retained earnings of foreign affiliates as called for under the IMF guidelines. It is a common problem for the other countries as well. Also, UNCTAD does not publish estimates of the industry distribution of the stock of FDI for India. The estimate of the share devoted to services may not be fully comparable to other countries.

Chakraborty and Nunnenkamp (2006) assembled data on FDI stocks in India by sector and report a rapid increase in the services share in the late 1990s. They were unable, however, to detect a positive causal relationship between services FDI and output, which they contrasted with a finding of a positive relationship for manufacturing. This is somewhat surprising in view of the claim that the growth of services in India is a product of outsourcing by developed country firms. It is consistent with the prior finding, however, that the growth of the service sector has been much broader than business services alone. An analysis of FDI in the four largest South Asian countries has been undertaken by Sahoo (2006), but without the sector-based detail of Chakraborty and Nunnenkamp (2006). He found a small but significant causal link between FDI and GDP growth.

CONCLUSION

The service sector has been a major source of economic growth in South Asia, but the extent of its contribution varies widely across the eight countries of the region. Over the past quarter century, the share of the service-producing industries in GDP has grown substantially, with the most notable increases in India, Pakistan, and Sri Lanka. Similarly, the share of services in total employment has expanded in the larger economies. However, the changes in employment are typically less dramatic than for output because services have also had the highest levels of labour productivity—the two exceptions being Bangladesh and Bhutan with higher productivity in industry. Thus, a part of the growth in services output has been accommodated by improved labour productivity rather than employment gains. The productivity differences between industry/services and agriculture are particularly large for India.

The emphasis on services as a driver of overall economic growth is most evident in India where the growth of output has been in the range of 8–10 per cent in recent years with about half taking the form of gains in employment and half in improvements in labour productivity. This contrasts with the experience of Bangladesh which has had relatively stronger growth in industry. Growth in Pakistan and Sri Lanka has been more balanced between industry and services but with notably smaller improvements in labour productivity.

The contribution of the service sector to total employment growth in the 1990s was 72 per cent in Afghanistan, 63 per cent in Bangladesh,

46 per cent in India, 53 per cent in Maldives, 42 per cent in Nepal, 53 per cent in Pakistan, and 61 per cent in Sri Lanka. The contribution of the industry sector to employment growth for the same period was negative for Afghanistan, Bangladesh, and Maldives, and 21 per cent for India, 63 per cent for Nepal, 24 per cent for Pakistan, and 37 per cent for Sri Lanka. [21] Even though these figures do not say anything about the future, if this trend continues, it seems that the service sector, despite its relatively low employment elasticity, 0.36 versus 0.57 in the rest of the world in the same period (Basu and Maertens 2007: Table 12), will be responsible for a major portion of job growth in South Asia.

Information on the composition of the industries within the service sector is limited and there are significant differences in the methods of compiling data. However, India does stand out for the importance of finance and business services, and those activities are not large in the other countries. Instead, the sector is dominated by the more traditional categories of wholesale and retail trade, transportation, and communications. Employment data at the industry level are not readily available but can be calculated from the LFSs of the respective countries.

The service sector consistently employs a disproportionate share of the most educated portion of the population. On average, years of schooling in service producing jobs are roughly 50 per cent higher than for the economy as a whole. In India and Pakistan, for example, average years of schooling in services exceed that of industry by 2–3 years. The emphasis on education requirements in modern service industries would seem to place South Asia at a disadvantage because, except for Sri Lanka, average levels of schooling are very low, and the gap with

[21]Sources (authors' calculation from): Afghanistan—Key Indicators ADB (1972–5 from the April 1977, 1976–8 from July 1980, 1978–85 from July 1990, 1986–90 from July 1992, 2001–4 from ADB 2007), for the statistics pertaining to the year 2000, the 2001 data were used, series from 1972 up to 2004; Bangladesh—WDI 2008 (from 1983 to 2000); Bhutan—KILM (third edn); India—data from Bosworth et al. (2007); Maldives—KILM (fourth edn); Nepal—KILM (fifth edn) (years taken—1961, 1971, 1981, 1991, and 2001); Pakistan—*Handbook of Statistics of the Pakistan Economy 2005* using population estimates of WDI 2008 (years used—1963, 1971, 1981, 1991, and 2001); Sri Lanka—KILM (fifth edn). Note that for Sri Lanka, the 1980s are calculated using data of the entire country (from 1981 to 1990) while the 1990s are calculated using data excluding the eastern and northern provinces (from 1991 to 2002).

other regions is increasing over time. Yet, available research finds rates of return to education equal to that in other regions, suggesting that the problems are largely on the supply side with a failure to provide adequate funding.

Finally, trade in services is substantial only for India. With the exception of tourism in Maldives, the other countries report significant deficits in services trade. India's exports are dominated by sales of computer and business services (call centres and back-office support). In recent years, FDI flows to the region have also increased at a rapid pace, mainly due to increased investment in India; yet, the overall magnitude of the flow—US$ 22 billion in 2006—is still low in comparison to that of other regions. There is a strong shift in the composition of FDI toward services, which now account for more than half of the inflow; but again much of that is due to the flow of funds into India, which accounted for 70 per cent of the total in 2006.

ANNEXURE 2A.1   SOURCES AND QUALITY OF DATA

Afghanistan

Output

Data on output for Afghanistan comes from SNA93 national accounts publications, but data is only available beginning in 2002. The United Nations (UN) has attempted to splice in data for earlier years; however since the earlier data is based on a Gross Material Product formulation, it leads to inconsistent results. Also, it appears that the official data excludes opium production, which, by some estimates, constitutes a substantial percentage of the economic output of the country.

Employment

Employment values for the total economy and three major sectors are taken from the KILM database of the ILO (see http://www.ilo.org/public/english/employment/strat/kilm/index.htm) for years 1980 and 1990. Estimates for 1986, 1988–9, and 2001–4 are taken from the ADB's 'Key Indicators' (see http://www.adb.org/Statistics/ki.asp).

Educational Attainment

Apart from sporadic values of gross enrollment rates provided by the World Bank, there is no available data for educational attainment for

Afghanistan. Average educational attainment values for the total economy are taken from Barro and Lee (2000).

Capital Stock

The WDI of the World Bank provide data on gross capital formation (at the total economy level only) but the first available year is 2002.

Bangladesh

Output

Output values are taken from WDI, 2008. Constant GDP data are chained 2000 values.

Employment

Data on employment comes from the LFS for a given year. There is, however, a substantial discontinuity in the LFS estimate for total employment in 1989, and this discontinuity appears to last through the 2000 iteration of the survey. It is our understanding that the discrepancy is a result in a change in the treatment of selected women's activities beginning in the 1989 survey, which essentially inflated the employment numbers during that period. Therefore, when corrected data was unavailable, we were forced to ignore employment values for this period in order to maintain consistency in our estimates. Consequently, employment data was built upon data from the LFSs of 1986, 1996, 2000, 2003, and 2005. The intervening years were interpolated and labour force is on a 15+ age basis.

Educational Attainment

Estimates of the average years of schooling by sector is taken from our calculations from the household income and expenditure surveys (HIES) of 2000 and 2005. As equivalent measures are not publicly provided by the Bangladesh Bureau of Statistics, we supplemented our calculations of educational attainment for the total economy with the estimates of Barro and Lee (2000).

Capital Stock

Estimates of gross fixed capital formation are available from WDI going back to 1980, however only at the level of the total economy.

Bhutan

Output

Output values are taken from WDI, 2008. Constant GDP data are chained 2000 values.

Employment

Employment by sector for 1980 and 1990 is provided by ILO's KILM database. More recent estimates from a 2005 LFS, and a 2007 living standards survey, however, appear to provide estimates that are inconsistent (substantially smaller) with the earlier values from ILO.

Educational Attainment

Apart from rough data on the distribution of the population by completed level of education, which is provided in the LFS of 2005, there are no sources of educational attainment data for Bhutan.

Capital Stock

Estimates of gross fixed capital formation are available from WDI going back to 1980, however only at the level of the total economy.

India

Output

Output data for India come from the National Income Accounts which are on a 1993 benchmark. More recent data is provided on a 1998 benchmark; however, since this data has not yet been linked backwards to previous years, we have simply linked the recent data to the 1993 basis. As a result, the summation of the three sectors in constant terms will not equal the aggregate value after the year 1993.

Employment

Indian employment data by sector is taken from Sivasubramaniam (2004) for earlier years, and from Bosworth et al. (2007) for the more recent period.

Educational Attainment

Estimates of educational attainment are calculated from the micro-data file of various rounds of the NSS of India.

Capital Stock

Estimates of the capital stock for the total economy and three major sectors come from the National Income Accounts of India.

Maldives

Output

We accessed data on value added by kind of economic activity for Maldives from the UN National Accounts Database (see http://unstats. un.org/unsd/snaama/SelectionCountry.asp). Also, the Ministry of Planning and National Development of the Republic of Maldives contains tables and charts of the census data from 1995, 2000, and 2006, as well as the actual micro-data from the 2000 Census. In addition, historical GDP data for 1984–2003 is available on their website (see http://www.planning.gov.mv/en/).

Employment

Employment data for the Republic of Maldives is calculated using data from the census, which has taken place every five years in recent history (1995, 2000, and 2006 [the 2005 census was pushed back due to the tsunami of December 2005]). However, sectoral allocation of employment is nearly impossible due to the result of a large percentage of employment listed as 'Don't Know'. Because the percentage of this group varies substantially by year (from 3.4 per cent of the total in 1995 to over 17 per cent in 2000), there is no basis upon which we can accurately distribute this residual employment into the three sectors. The age basis for 2006 is 15+ although previous year estimates are on a 12+ basis.

Educational Attainment

Tables from the censuses of 2000 and 2006 provide estimates of the educational attainment of the population, which we use to calculate average years of schooling, but at the level of the total economy only.

Capital Stock

Apart from limited data on gross fixed capital formation going back only to 1995, from WDI, there are no available estimates of the capital stock of Maldives.

Nepal

Output

The WDI contains data on output by sector on the SNA 1995 base for Nepal back to 1965. In addition, data on a revised basis for 2000–7 were obtained from the website of the central statistical office. The two series were linked by applying the growth rates of WDI 1995 base to the 2000–1 value provided in the new base. Rather than including the residual amount allocated to FISIM in the total value of GDP after 2000, we have defined aggregate GDP as the sum of the three components in the interest of consistency over time.

Employment

We have data on employment by industry based on census data for three years: 1981, 1991, and 2001. The estimates for 1981 and 2001 were obtained from the Statistical Yearbooks of 1991 and 2005, respectively, which are published by the Central Bureau of Statistics (CBS) (see http://www.cbs.gov.np/statistical_year_book.php). We obtained the 1991 Census values from the Economic Survey of 2000–1 provided by the Ministry of Finance Nepal (see http://www.mof.gov.np/publication/index.php). All values are on a 10+ age basis.

Educational Attainment

Our estimates on the average years of schooling for the total economy and the three sectors are limited to the years 1981, 1995, and 2003. We were able to use the micro-data of the 1995 and 2003 Nepal Living Standards Survey to estimate a weighted average of the years of schooling by industry. The *Population Monograph of Nepal 2003* also contains data on education attainment by age group for the census years of 1981, 1991, and 2001, but only at the level of the total economy. Thus, in order to obtain educational attainment estimates for the three sectors for 1981, we applied the sectoral proportions of average years of schooling from the 1995 Living Standards Survey estimates to our total economy estimate for the year 1981. The values of intervening years were interpolated, and the values are on a 15+ age basis.

Capital Stock

Estimates of gross fixed capital formation by major industry groups were provided by the CBS of Nepal for 2001–6. In addition, WDI provides gross fixed capital formation at the level of the total economy for the years 1975 to 2005. Thus, we used the growth rates of the capital stock implied by the WDI data for the pre-2001 years and linked them to the level given by CBS in 2001. To allocate the capital stock by the three major sectors in the years prior to 2001, we applied the fixed proportions from the 2001 values provided by CBS.

Pakistan

Output

Output values are taken from World Bank (2008). Constant GDP data are chained 2000 values.

Employment

Employment estimates for the total economy and three major sectors are obtained from ILO's LABORSTA Database (see http://laborsta.ilo.org/) for 1981–2002. These values are on a 10+ age basis. Distribution of employed persons by industry is given by the *Handbook of Statistics of Pakistan Economy* provided by the State Bank of Pakistan (2005, see http://www.sbp.org.pk/publications/index2.asp). For estimates of employment for the total economy, the 2004 value is 7.7 per cent of the labour force, and the intervening years are interpolated. Then, the sectoral distribution of employment estimates from the State Bank of Pakistan (2005) are applied to the measures of total employment to obtain estimates of employment by sector for the years 2003–6.

Educational Attainment

Average years of schooling are calculated from the LFS micro-data for the years 2002, 2004, and 2006. The growth rates of average years of schooling (at the level of the total economy only) for years prior to 2000 are taken from Barro and Lee (2000) and linked to the 2002 level calculated from the LFS micro-data of that year. Finally, in order to obtain educational attainment estimates for the three sectors for years prior to 2002, we applied the sectoral proportions to the total from the 2002 LFS estimates to the total economy estimates of prior years.

Capital Stock

There is no constant value investment data for Pakistan prior to 1981. Therefore, we used the aggregate price deflator from WDI on each of the three sectors to convert nominal investment to 1981 prices for the 1964–80 period. Data for 1981–2000 are adjusted to a 2000 benchmark revision by assuming discrepancy built up linearly after 1981. To achieve a common basis, the 1981-base data are converted to 2000 prices using the rate of price change in the WDI series between 1999 and 2000 to create an overlap. To convert the investment to capital stock, we used initial capital–output ratios from India in 1964 and altered the starting value to stabilize the long-term trend in capital to output. The initial capital to output ratios were: 1 for agriculture, 2.5 for industry, and 3 for services, and we utilized a 5 per cent geometric depreciation rate.

Sri Lanka

Output

Output values are taken from World Bank (2008). Constant GDP data are chained 2000 values.

Employment

Employment data for Sri Lanka for 1992–2006 come from the LFS of 2006 provided by the Department of Census and Statistics (see http://www.statistics.gov.lk/). The LFS of 2004 extends the series to include 1990 and 1991. Finally, employment estimates for 1981 and 1985 data come from ILO's KILM database (see http://www.ilo.org/public/english/employment/strat/kilm/index.htm). The intervening years are interpolated.

Educational Attainment

Years of schooling for the total economy and the three major sectors are obtained from calculations using the micro-data files of the LFS for Sri Lanka for years 1992–6 and 1998–2002. We obtained estimates for 1990–1, 1997, and 2003–6 from the LFS of 2006, but only at the level of the total economy.

Capital Stock

Estimates of gross fixed capital formation are available from WDI going back to 1960, however only at the level of the total economy. So, we can create a capital stock value for the total economy using an artificial beginning value (taken from a plausible capital–output ratio) and allowing for a 5 per cent geometric depreciation.

ANNEXURE 2A.2   THE SERVICE SECTOR

TABLE 2A.2.1   Characteristics of the Service Sectors
in Bangladesh (2005)

	Average Number of Years of Education	Average Earnings (Tk/month)	% of Workers in Formal Jobs	% of the Jobs
Trade, hotels, and restaurants	5.40	4,901	25.10	26.02
Transportation and communication	2.93	3,383	80.89	27.99
Financial intermediation, real estate, renting, and business services	7.99	5,709	56.05	11.13
Other services	9.23	4,953	86.56	34.85

Source: Authors' calculations from HIES 2005 survey.
Note: Persons younger than 15 years not included; and formal job defined as not self-employed.

TABLE 2A.2.2   Characteristics of the Service Sectors in India (2004)

	Average Number of Years of Education	Average Earnings* (Rs/week)	% of Workers in Formal Jobs*	% of the Jobs*
Education	13.03	1,319	81.67	12.32
Extra-territorial organizations	10.00	–	100.00	0.03
Financial intermediation	12.94	2,029	71.65	2.65
Real estate, renting, and business	11.85	1,326	42.64	3.80
Health and social work	11.32	1,237	68.70	3.44
Hotels and restaurants	6.23	616	34.00	4.85
Other community, social, and personal services	6.08	584	32.81	6.26
Private households with employed persons	3.02	341	100.00	3.21
Public administration and defence	10.59	1,556	98.85	10.71
Transport, storage, and communication	6.95	860	59.90	12.10
Wholesale and retail trade	7.91	525	23.62	40.64

Source: Authors' calculations from NSS Round 60.
Note: Persons younger than 15 years not included; *calculated with each worker-job as a data point instead of each worker; earnings per week include both full-time as well as part-time earnings of current activities.

TABLE 2A.2.3   Characteristics of the Service Sectors in Pakistan (2005–6)

	Average Number of Years of Education	Average Earnings (Rp/month)	% of Workers in Formal Jobs	% of the Jobs
Community, social, and personal services	10.52	6,956	76.67	62.49
Financing, insurance, real estate, and business services	11.50	14,747	55.13	3.67
Transport, storage, and communication	4.73	6,456	61.00	19.28
Wholesale and retail trade and restaurants and hotels	5.95	4,242	18.99	14.56

Source: Authors' calculations from LFS 2005–6.
Note: Persons younger than 15 years not included.

TABLE 2A.2.4   Characteristics of the Service Sectors in Maldives (2000)

	Average Number of Years of Education	Average Earnings (Rf/month)	% of Workers in Formal Jobs	% of the Jobs
Education	9.76	19,279	88.20	11.23
Extra-territorial organizations	10.93	6,539	86.21	0.17
Financial intermediation	10.01	10,793	95.19	1.08
Health and social work	9.55	25,529	87.86	3.77
Other community, social, and personal services	8.58	22,236	83.58	4.23
Private households with employed persons	7.15	13,225	91.85	2.06
Public administration and defence	9.29	19,611	99.37	25.77
Real estate, renting, and business activities	8.60	18,291	73.87	2.44
Hotels and restaurants	8.24	25,022	50.44	8.55
Transport, storage, and communication	8.75	21,618	78.49	20.78
Wholesale and retail trade	8.11	22,119	39.89	19.93

Source: Authors' calculations from Census 2000.
Note: Persons younger than 15 years not included.

TABLE 2A.2.5   Characteristics of the Service Sectors in Sri Lanka (2002)

	Average Number of Years of Education	Average Earnings (Rp/month)	% of Workers in Formal Jobs	% of the Jobs
Education	13.10	8,011	90.55	9.60
Extra-territorial organizations	9.52	6,166	88.00	0.57
Financial intermediation	12.03	10,006	82.17	6.36
Health and social work	11.41	7099	87.30	3.48
Hotels and restaurants	8.90	6,068	60.52	4.79
Other community, social, and personal services	9.52	5,403	57.89	4.09
Private households with employed persons	5.19	3,602	97.35	3.42
Public administration and defence	11.15	7,345	99.03	20.96
Transport, storage, and communication	8.75	5,669	60.17	13.66
Wholesale and retail trade	9.11	5,532	32.83	33.07

Source: Authors' calculations from LFS 2002.
Note: Persons younger than 15 years not included.

REFERENCES

Abbas, Qaisar and James Foreman-Peck. 2007. 'The Mincer Human Capital Model in Pakistan: Implications for Education Policy', Cardiff Economics Working Papers E2007/24.

Abraham, Vinoj. 2007. 'Growth and Inequality of Wages in India: Recent Trends and Patterns', *Indian Journal of Labour Economics*, 50(4): 927–41.

Asadullah, Mohammad Niaz. 2005. 'Returns to Education in Bangladesh', QEH Working Papers 130, Queen Elizabeth House, University of Oxford, Oxford.

Asian Development Bank. 2007. *Key Indicators* (various issues). Latest issue available at: http://www.adb.org/documents/books/key_indicators/, accessed in December 2008.

Barro, Robert J. and Jong-Wha Lee. 2000. 'International Data on Educational Attainment: Updates and Implications', CID Working Paper 042, Harvard University, Cambridge, M.A.

Basu, Kaushik. 2006. 'Labor Laws and Labor Welfare in the Context of the Indian Experience', in Alain de Janvry and Ravi Kanbur (eds), *Poverty, Inequality and Development: Essays in Honor of Erik Thorbecke*, Economic Studies in Inequality, Social Exclusion and Well-Being, pp. 183–204. New York: Springer.

Basu, Kaushik and Annemie Maertens. 2007. 'The Growth of Industry and Services in South Asia and Its Impact on Employment: Analysis and Policy', in *Can South Asia Achieve Double Digit Growth?*, pp. 81–140. Washington, D.C.: World Bank.

Baumol, William J. 1967. 'Macroeconomics of Unbalanced Growth: The Anatomy of Urban Crisis', *American Economic Review*, LVII(3): 415–26.

Bhagwati, Jagdish, Arvind Panagariya, and T. N. Srinivasan. 2004. 'The Muddles over Outsourcing', *Journal of Economic Perspectives*, 18(4): 93–114.

Bosworth, Barry, Susan M. Collins, and Arvind Virmani. 2007. 'Sources of Growth in the Indian Economy', *India Policy Forum*, 3: 1–69, NCAER and Brookings Institute.

Chakraborty, Chandana and Peter Nunnenkamp. 2006. 'Economic Reforms, Foreign Direct Investment and its Economic Effects in India', Working Paper 1272, The Kiel Institute for the World Economy, Germany, March.

Dasgupta, Sukti and Ajit Singh. 2005. 'Will Services be the New Engine of Economic Growth in India?', Centre for Business Research Working Paper 310, University of Cambridge, Cambridge, September.

Gordon, James and Poonam Gupta. 2004. 'Understanding India's Services Revolution', Working Paper WP/04/171, International Monetary Fund, Washington, D.C., September.

Griliches, Zvi (ed.). 1992. *Output Measurements in the Service Sector*, Chicago: University of Chicago Press.

Government of India. 2008. *SIA Newsletter*, XVI(9), Secretariat for Industrial Assistance, Ministry of Commerce and Industry.

International Labour Organization (ILO). 2007. *Key Indicators of the Labor Market* (third, fourth, and fifth edns). Geneva: ILO.

———. 2008. *Global Employment Trends 2008*. Geneva: ILO.

International Monetary Fund (IMF). 2008. *Balance of Payments and International Investment Position Manual* (sixth edn). Washington, D.C.: IMF.

Psacharopoulos, George and Harry Anthony Patrinos. 2004. 'Returns to Investment in Education: A Further Update', *Education Economics, Taylor and Francis Journals*, 12(2): 111–34.

Rangarajan, C., I. Kaul, and S. Seema. 2007. 'Revisiting Employment and Growth', *ICRA Bulletin—Money & Finance*, 3(2): 57–68.

Razmi, Arslan. 2007. 'Analyzing Pakistan's Economic Prospects in an Increasingly Integrated World: External Constraints on Sustainable Development', paper presented at the Inaugural Symposium on Pakistan, organized by the Institute of South Asian Studies (ISAS) at the National University of Singapore, 24–5 May.

Reserve Bank of India (Balance of Payments Statistics Division). 2005. 'Computer Services Exports from India: 2002–03', *Reserve Bank of India Bulletin*, September, pp. 821–9.

Riboud, Michelle, Yevgenia Savchenko, and Hong Tan. 2007. 'The Knowledge Economy and Education and Training in South Asia', Manuscript Human

Development Unit, South Asia Region, World Bank. Available at www.worldbank.org, accessed in December 2008.

Sahoo, Pravakar. 2006. 'Foreign Direct Investment in South Asia: Policy, Trends, Impact and Determinants', Asian Development Bank Institute Discussion Paper 56. Available at http://www.adbi.org/publications/, accessed in December 2008.

Singh, Nivirkar. 2006. 'Services-Led Industrialization in India: Assessment and Lessons', Department of Economics Working Paper 622, University of California, Santa Cruz.

Sivasubramaniam, S. 2004. *The Sources of Economic Growth in India 1950–1 to 1999–2000*. New Delhi: Oxford University Press.

State Bank of Pakistan. (various editions). *Handbook of Statistics on the Pakistan Economy*. Latest edition available at http://www.sbp.org.pk/.

Triplett, Jack and Barry Bosworth. 2004. *Productivity in the U.S. Services Sector: New Sources of Economic Growth*. Washington, D.C.: Brookings Institution.

United Nations Conference on Trade and Development (UNCTAD). 2004. *World Investment Report*. New York and Geneva: UNCTAD.

———. 2007. *World Investment Report*. New York and Geneva: UNCTAD.

United States General Accountability Office. 2004. 'International Trade: Current Government Data Provide Limited Insight into Offshoring of Services', Report to Congressional Committees, September. Available at http://www.gao.gov/new.items/d04932.pdf, accessed in December 2008.

———. 2005. 'International Trade: U.S. and India Data on Offshoring Show Significant Differences', Report to Congressional Committees, October. Available at http://www.gao.gov/new.items/d06116.pdf, accessed in December 2008.

United States General Accountability Office. 2004. 'International Trade: Current Government Data Provide Limited Insight into Offshoring of Services', Report to Congressional Committees, September. Available at http://www.gao.gov/new.items/d04932.pdf, accessed in December 2008.

World Bank. 2007a. '2005 International Comparison Program, Preliminary Results', December. Available at www.worldbank.org, accessed in December 2008.

———. 2007b. *World Investment Report*. New York and Geneva: World Bank.

———. 2008. *World Development Indicators*. Washington, D.C.: World Bank.

World Trade Organization. 2007. *International Trade Statistics, 2007*. Geneva. Available at http://www.wto.org/english/res_e/statis_e/its2007_e/its07_toc_e.htm, accessed in December 2008.

Young, Alwyn. 1995. 'The Tyranny of Numbers: Confronting the Statistical Realities of the East Asian Growth Experience', *Quarterly Journal of Economics*, 110(3): 641–80.

3

New Economic Geography and Services

Maarten Bosker and Harry Garretsen

The *World Development Report* (WDR) (World Bank 2008) focuses on the role and importance of economic geography in explaining the evolution of spatial differences in economic development across nations, regions, and even cities. It provides a careful discussion of the historical evolution of spatial inequalities in economic development and explains this evolution through the lenses of modern spatial economics. WDR's title 'Reshaping Economic Geography' hints at the possibility for active policy to influence spatial outcomes and, in particular, to improve the prospects for currently disadvantaged (lagging) regions.

This interest in economic geography can largely be attributed to the so-called new economic geography (NEG) literature that followed Paul Krugman's[1] seminal contribution in 1991. Economic geography focuses on explaining the distribution of economic activity at various spatial scales: across the globe (see, for example, Mayer 2008; Redding and Venables 2004), and also for developing countries (Amiti and Cameron 2007; Au and Henderson 2006; Bosker and Garretsen 2009; Hering and Poncet 2008).

[1]To a large extent, Krugman was awarded the Nobel Prize in economics in 2008 for his work on new economic geography.

From its inception, the NEG theory has mainly concerned itself with the manufacturing sector. In most NEG models all the action, in terms of predictions regarding the spatial distribution of economic activity, takes place in the manufacturing sector. As such, NEG is ideally suited to explain the recent move of manufacturing from the 'old' industrial countries to mainly South East Asia or in making predictions about the effect of the expansion of the European Union's (EU) common market to Eastern Europe on the distribution of economic activity in both the old and new member states. When it comes to the service sector (the main subject of this volume), economic geography theory has until recently (see our discussion of Robert-Nicoud 2008 later in this chapter) remained largely silent, and this is true for the tradable services sector in particular. The main role that services play in the standard NEG models (see, for example, Helpman 1998; or Hanson 2005) is in the form of non-tradable consumption goods (like housing, haircuts, or dining out in a restaurant). In standard NEG models, these non-tradables act as an additional spreading or agglomeration force. A spreading force as people are, for instance, attracted by cheap housing, creating an incentive to leave the centre of a dense city where housing—as well as haircuts and dining out—is relatively very expensive (London, Paris, Moscow, or Mumbai immediately come to mind). An agglomeration force as people are attracted to big cities' amenities (opera houses, museums, etc.) that cannot profitably be offered in smaller cities or towns. We provide a more extensive discussion on the relevance of economic geography for the non-tradable service sector later in this chapter.

Today, mainly due to developments in communication technology, it is possible to trade and outsource services to an ever expanding degree. The production of many services (software, call centres, and back-office maintenance) that traditionally were largely located in developed countries close to the final markets for these services, are nowadays outsourced to developing countries (Blinder 2006). The increased ease with which these services can be traded, has allowed firms to look for countries where these services can be produced at much lower (wage) costs. From a NEG perspective, the increased tradability of services could (but need not) favour the dispersion of these services from the core (developed) world to the periphery (developing world) insofar as firms outsource some of their routine tasks to the periphery in search of lower wage costs. South Asia in particular has become well known for its (ever increasing) share in the non-tradable services market. Its recent extraordinary growth rate (driven by India in particular) has largely been ascribed to its tradable service sector. As Chapter 1 of this volume suggests, this apparent service-led growth experience has been put in sharp contrast to the manufacturing-led growth experience of its East Asian neighbours.

The purpose of this chapter is to apply an NEG framework to the role of services as a driver of economic development. We spell out ways in which the main insights from NEG relate to services, particularly in South Asia. As Chapter 1 argues, compared to other developing economies, South Asia stands out for the very prominent position of the service sector in the development process. Still, within the region of South Asia there are vast differences when it comes to the relevance of the service sector. We use the NEG framework to better understand why the relevance of the service sector differs across South Asian countries with India dominating the other countries (see also Chapter 2 of this volume). Such spatial differences are also starkly present within India, with several cities dominating the rest of the country in terms of their ability to attract and sustain a competitive (and expanding) tradable service sector, and we explore the possible role of economic geography in explaining these differences.

This chapter is organized as follows. In the first section we briefly introduce and summarize the main building blocks of the NEG approach. The second section deals with the service sector from a NEG perspective. We first deal with non-tradable services and then turn our attention to tradable services. Throughout this section we use NEG as our point of reference and, wherever possible and useful, illustrate our main arguments with relevant data. The final section summarizes and concludes, while also discussing some policy implications.

KEY INGREDIENTS OF NEG

The NEG approach offers a general equilibrium framework for the analysis of the allocation of economic activity across space. It is a stylized fact that economic activity is distributed rather unevenly across space and this holds true at various levels of spatial aggregation (see World Bank 2008). At the international, national, and regional levels, a few agglomerations typically dominate the economic landscape. Starting with the first full-blown NEG model (Krugman 1991), an explanation of these agglomeration patterns is the main aim of NEG. Previous or competing location models of economic geography at least partially assumed as given what, according to Krugman and other NEG researchers, in effect had to be explained: the location choices of economic agents and the corresponding location outcomes (Fujita and Thisse 2009; Ottaviano and Thisse 2004).

To assess the relevance of NEG for South Asia in general, and for the role of services in the economy of South Asia in particular, it is useful to summarize NEG by what might be called its 'holy trinity': increasing returns to scale, trade costs, and factor mobility. Following Krugman (1991), NEG literature has produced a vast array of different models, but they can all basically be cast in terms of these three key ingredients. The first two ingredients are home to (most) modern location models (Fujita and Thisse 2002). Increasing returns ensure that firms want to concentrate their production whereas trade costs, broadly defined, ensure that footloose firms are not indifferent as to where they locate.

Typically in NEG models, there are both internal and external increasing returns to scale. In the case of internal scale economies, the average costs of producing a unit of output falls with the number of units produced by the firm (for example, fixed costs like headquarter services or research and development [R&D] and marketing outlays give rise to a downward sloping average costs curve at the firm level). Because of internal scale economies, the market structure is one of imperfect competition. For our present purposes, it is important to note that in NEG models there are also localized external scale economies, the average costs of producing a unit of output for the firm falls with the number of units produced by, for instance, the total industry or with the size of the market. If a firm resides in a location with many other (similar) firms the possibility of positive (knowledge and other input) spillovers increases. In NEG models, the external scale economies are typical such that the size of the market drives down average costs for a firm. As we will see later, and this is certainly relevant for services too, scale economies can be negative as well. One can think of congestion costs or high land rents that go along with the spatial concentration of firms and people.

Trade costs are broadly defined to include all costs to get a good or service from one place to the other, including not only transport costs and tariffs, but also less tangible costs associated with language, cultural, or institutional differences. They ensure that footloose firms are not indifferent to where they locate. Without geographical differences in factor endowments or other asymmetries in terms of the physical geography (climate, access to sea, etc.) between regions or countries it is difficult to come up with a useful model of economic geography that somehow does not contain both scale economies and trade costs.

The real innovation of Krugman (1991) is the addition of the third element, factor mobility (mobile firms and/or workers) to the other two ingredients. As explained in our companion paper on NEG and South Asia (Bosker and Garretsen 2008), with factor mobility entering the story, NEG models start to display cumulative causation: firms want to locate where there is a large market demand for their goods, and a region's demand for goods depends on the location decision of workers who in turn locate in a region where there is a large demand for labour which depends on the location decision of firms and vice versa.

Subsequent theoretical developments in NEG following the Krugman (1991) model are manifold but they all basically consist of variations on and extensions to the menu of agglomeration and spreading forces, a menu that thus revolves around the earlier mentioned trinity of increasing returns to scale, transport costs, and factor mobility. Changes in this menu may give rise to very different spatial outcomes than the core–periphery pattern predicted by the Krugman (1991) model. Generally speaking, the potential relevance of NEG depends very much on the case at hand. NEG models are flexible in the sense that depending on the menu of agglomeration and spreading forces, multiple spatial outcomes are possible (Helpman 1998; Krugman and Venables 1995; Puga 1999).

The crucial NEG element of factor mobility and the resulting possibility of cumulative causation, or, in other words, the interdependency between the location of demand and supply, can be summed up by the statement that mobile firms and workers *ceteris paribus* prefer locations with good market access, that is, they prefer to be located in or close to easily accessible (that is, incurring low trade costs) large markets. This is also the main NEG angle in the 2009 WDR. If anything, the question about the relevance of NEG is first and foremost a question about the empirical importance of market access.

The crucial role of market access has by now received broad empirical support at various different spatial scales (see, for example, Brakman et al. 2006; Breinlich 2006; Hanson 2005; Hering and Poncet 2008; Redding and Venables 2004), and this is aptly summarized in the WDR 2009 (Mayer 2008; World Bank 2008). In the case of South Asia, Bosker and Garretsen (2009) show that market access plays an important role in explaining the existing differences in economic development at different spatials. Box 3.1 briefly summarizes the main findings in that paper.

BOX 3.1   Market Access and Spatial Economic Development
in South Asia

In our companion paper (Bosker and Garretsen 2009), we deal with the
role of market access for South Asia and do so for various spatial scales.
Since in our view our conclusions in this paper are also relevant for the
service sector in South Asia we briefly restate our findings here:

1. At the national level, each of the South Asian countries
underutilizes its potential market access. Market access matters for GDP
per capita but it could matter a lot more if economic integration were
to be improved. This holds in particular within the South Asian region.
Trade and labour migration between South Asian countries is extremely
low compared to the other regions in the world.

2. Also at the sub-national level, market access, the key NEG
variable, matters. But it is above all national market access that seems to
be important. Within each South Asian country the regions with good
access to national markets (that is a low distance in WDR 2009 terms)
typically have a higher GDP per capita. The economic ties between
South Asian countries are on the other hand relatively underdeveloped;
South Asian countries 'undertrade' (confirming the evidence at the
international level).

3. Besides inter-regional interdependencies that are thought to
explain the observed spatial distribution of economic activity, also its
intra-regional distribution turns out to be relevant for the economic
prosperity of South Asia's regions. Regions that are more urbanized
(with the bulk of urban population usually concentrated in one large
city) are showing stronger economic performance than their more rural
counterparts.

The main take away point for South Asia is that market access is
indeed a useful concept to summarize the relevance of NEG models.

However, turning to the main focus of this chapter, Bosker and
Garretsen (see Box 3.1) do not deal explicitly with the South Asian
service sector, instead focusing on the overall performance of the South
Asian national (and sub-national) economies. Work on NEG and
tradable services (or tradable tasks) is still in its infancy, making a direct
link between NEG theory and the rise of (particular regions of) South
Asia on the world's markets for tradable services less clear cut (but not
impossible as we will see in the next section). Insofar as services play
a role in these (early) NEG models, it is in the guise of non-tradable
consumption goods (housing or other non-tradable services) that usually
act as a spreading force since increased agglomeration increases the prices

of these goods thereby providing an incentive to move from to more peripheral locations where these non-tradable services can be consumed at a much lower cost.

Notwithstanding the fact that there is no explicit role for the service sector in the standard NEG models mentioned earlier, we argue that a somewhat (extended) NEG perspective can be of real use to understand the observed (evolution of the) spatial differences within South Asia in terms of the importance of the service sector, and the tradable services sector in particular. Hereby we give a central role to NEG's trinity—increasing returns to scale, transport costs, and factor mobility—and ask ourselves how these three concepts are relevant for services. In doing so, we make an explicit distinction between the tradable and non-tradable service sectors. Also, data permitting, we illustrate our claims regarding the relevance of these three concepts for the case of South Asia.

NEG AND SERVICES

From Chapters 1 and 2 of this volume (see Table 3.1 for an overview), we know that services take up an increasingly larger slice of South Asian GDP (especially so in India and to a [much] lesser extent in Bangladesh, Sri Lanka, and Pakistan). India really stands out in these figures: the share of the trade in 'other services' in total GDP grew with 6 percentage points from 0.65 per cent in 1995 to 6.54 per cent in 2006. It leapt from being the South Asian country with the lowest share of 'other services' in GDP to the country with the highest share over the last decade. For a breakdown of exports in the category 'other services' see Table 3.3 (which in turn is based on Table 2.6 from Chapter 2 of this volume). In line with the classification in Chapters 1 and 2, the trade in transport and travel services corresponds to trade in traditional service exports whereas the trade in other services contains trade in modern, impersonal services.

In the other countries, the share of the 'other services' sector (and for that matter in the travel and transport service sectors as well) is rather stagnating (or in decline as in Nepal) and as of 2006 still constituted less than 2 per cent of the total GDP. Interestingly in Sri Lanka, it is mainly the transport services sector (that is, the major port hub at Colombo) that is of importance.

Table 3.1 not only shows the share of services in total GDP, but it also zooms in on three specific categories of services—transport, travel (tourism), and other services. We will abstract from the first two categories, as NEG has basically very little to say about the other two types of services (and also government services). NEG is basically

TABLE 3.1 Share of Export Services in Total GDP

Year	Bangladesh Transport	Bangladesh Travel	Bangladesh Other	India Transport	India Travel	India Other	Nepal Transport	Nepal Travel	Nepal Other	Pakistan Transport	Pakistan Travel	Pakistan Other	Sri Lanka Transport	Sri Lanka Travel	Sri Lanka Other
1995	0.19	0.07	1.59	0.53	0.72	0.65	1.26	4.03	10.14	1.37	0.18	1.51	2.57	1.73	1.98
1996	0.20	0.08	1.21	0.51	0.73	0.62	1.68	3.55	11.52	1.23	0.17	1.78	2.44	1.20	1.87
1997	0.21	0.15	1.26	0.47	0.70	1.04	1.12	2.96	13.52	1.32	0.17	1.12	2.58	1.38	1.84
1998	0.21	0.12	1.31	0.43	0.71	1.67	1.22	3.89	6.52	1.15	0.14	0.97	2.55	1.46	1.8
1999	0.21	0.11	1.39	0.41	0.67	2.14	1.11	3.44	8.46	1.18	0.12	0.88	2.58	1.74	1.84
2000	0.19	0.11	1.43	0.43	0.75	2.44	1.12	2.87	5.22	1.14	0.11	0.62	2.45	1.52	1.78
2001	0.15	0.10	1.35	0.43	0.67	2.53	0.79	2.39	3.7	1.13	0.12	0.76	2.44	1.35	4.82
2002	0.19	0.12	1.47	0.49	0.61	2.74	0.60	1.71	2.74	1.10	0.13	2.13	3.11	2.2	2.36
2003	0.14	0.11	1.70	0.50	0.74	2.73	0.57	3.15	2.16	1.00	0.15	2.41	3.08	2.42	2.23
2004	0.14	0.12	1.66	0.63	0.89	3.99	0.45	3.17	2.72	0.96	0.18	1.66	3.11	2.56	1.94
2005	0.19	0.12	1.78	0.71	0.93	5.29	0.40	1.61	2.65	0.98	0.17	2.21	2.86	1.82	1.86
2006	0.14	0.13	1.88	0.84	0.98	6.45	0.39	1.43	2.49	0.88	0.20	1.69	2.78	1.52	1.72
Δ (2006–1995) (ppt)	-0.05	0.06	0.29	0.31	0.26	5.8	-0.87	-2.60	-7.65	-0.49	0.02	0.18	0.21	-0.21	-0.3

Source: World Trade Indicators (2007); see also Table 3.3 and Table 2.6 in Chapter 2 for a breakdown of the category 'other services'.

concerned with the last category that contains both tradable (software programming, call centres, accounting, etc.), non-tradable (dental care, cinemas, restaurants, etc.), and government services that are also largely non-tradable. As such, we will discuss NEG's potential relevance for the non-tradable (sometimes also referred to as the traditional) and tradable (or modern) service sectors only.

Non-tradable Services

To some extent the growth in services is simply due to the growth in the (local) provision of non-tradable services as a result of increased local demand for these services. It is a stylized fact that when a nation's prosperity increases, its citizens spend an increasingly larger share of their incomes on services. As South Asians become wealthier this is expected to increase the relative importance of the non-tradable service sector (at the expense of agriculture and manufacturing). People will start buying some services that they previously did themselves (household cleaning, hairdressing, etc.) or start spending their money on, for example, entertainment (cinemas, eating out, operas, etc.). To what extent can economic geography be useful to explain the spatial distribution of such non-tradable services? We will argue that the answer to this question is likely to be 'very little'. Why this is so becomes apparent when considering the relevance of NEG's 'holy trinity' for the non-tradable service sector.

Compared to the manufacturing sector, internal scale economies are less important in the (non-tradable) service sector. Certainly, for non-tradable services, the very nature of services production implies that services production will (have to) be located close to demand. This is a direct consequence of the fact that trade or transport costs are effectively so high that they prevent consumption and production to be separated spatially. Virtually all non-tradable services are by definition 'non-tradable' because they have to be consumed on the spot. Dining out, going to the cinema, cleaning services, education, or a heart surgery are all consumed at the location where they are bought. This is the main reason why the NEG theory has in principle very little to say about the spatial distribution of services. Trade or transport costs are the vital ingredient of any NEG model. Given that transport costs for non-tradable services are in a sense so high that these services have to be consumed on the spot makes it very hard to come up with NEG-based predictions for this sector. The fact that scale economies are relatively less relevant for services also implies that the disadvantages of spatial concentration, the so-called diseconomies of scale (think of congestion), are also less relevant for services compared to the manufacturing sector.

As far as the non-tradable services are concerned factor mobility has only an indirect impact. If mobile (manufacturing) firms and workers end up being located in a few agglomerations or centres, these centres will *ceteris paribus* provide for a larger (and more varied) market for non-tradables. The number (and variety of) restaurants, cinemas, hairdressers, etc., is positively correlated with the size (in economic and population terms) of a location.

In an international context, and as a direct consequence of labour migration, factor (labour) mobility leads itself to a rather different service that is certainly relevant in the context of South Asia. The (temporary) migration of labour from South Asia to the rest of the world (see Chapter 5 of this volume for a more in-depth discussion) does not, however, really alter the agglomeration dynamics between the South Asian region and the rest of the world as long as the resulting flow of remittances (a service activity) is substantial enough to ensure that the expenditure or demand effects of this migration are limited or even non-existent. The effects will be limited in the sense that even though labour is now employed elsewhere because of out-migration, spending is (largely) not relocated outside South Asia. From NEG literature we know that in this case, labour migration will not have much impact.[2]

Does this mean that the non-tradable service sector is unimportant within the NEG framework? The answer must be affirmative to the extent that NEG has not much to say when it comes to the determinants of the supply or demand for these services precisely because of their non-tradable nature. This is, however, not to say that the non-tradable service sector is wholly unimportant from an NEG perspective. Certainly in the context of South Asia and other developing countries, non-tradable services can act as an important determinant of, or trigger for, the location of footloose activity. Most NEG models assume a level playing field (that is, with regions all identical *ex-ante*), and are subsequently concerned with the question: how can such an initial level playing field give rise to an uneven distribution of economic activity across regions in equilibrium? Now in reality such a level playing field is hard to imagine and it is *inter alia* the provision of high quality reliable non-tradable services that can lead footloose firms and/or workers to choose to locate

[2]For an elaboration of this point see, for instance, Baldwin et al. (2003), and the distinction therein between so-called footloose capital and footloose entrepreneur models.

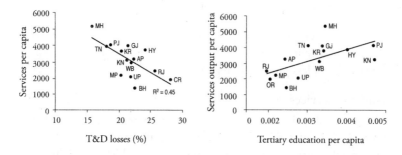

FIGURE 3.1(a)   Transmission and Distribution Losses of Electricity

FIGURE 3.1(b)   Tertiary Education

Source: Amin and Mattoo (2008).

in one place instead of the other (for example, Bangalore offering cheap real estate, exactly the important non-tradable service in the NEG model by Helpman 1998, and guaranteed bandwidth [not available in, for example, Delhi] were some of the alleged reasons for its initial attractiveness to foreign investors). Figure 3.1 illustrates this by showing that those Indian regions offering reliable electricity and good quality education are the regions attracting the highest services output per capita (Amin and Mattoo 2008).

Also, recent research (for example, Arnold et al. 2008 in the case of India) has shown that the provision of good quality services has substantial 'spillover' effects on the productivity of the manufacturing sector. High quality service inputs such as finance, communication, and transport are vital for a manufacturing firm's performance. As such they play an important role in attracting manufacturing firms, and can initiate or intensify a process of cumulative causation. The manufacturing firms become more productive, offering higher wages that attract people, which increases the demand for non-tradable services, etc.

When it comes to the non-tradable sector, the final conclusion is that NEG cannot tell us much about where and to what extent the non-tradable service sector will be important for economic development. Only indirectly, through its interaction with the manufacturing sector (or the tradable services sector) can the non-tradable service sector be of importance in explaining the observed spatial distribution of economic (both manufacturing and services) activity. The quality and quantity of non-tradable services provision by a location can either make it attract or repulse footloose economic activity. On the other hand, good quality non-tradable service provision can enhance a location's productivity level in footloose activity that can result in attracting more footloose economic activity than a less productive region.

Tradable Services

The conclusion in the previous sub-section regarding the relative unimportance of NEG forces in explaining the spatial distribution of non-tradable services changes radically when we shift our attention to the tradable service sector. Given the key role of trade costs (broadly defined) in NEG, this makes tradable services a much more interesting type of service for our present purposes.

Within the tradable service sector, we can make a further distinction between nationally traded and internationally traded services. Market access remains a very relevant concept for services that are tradable and bought by South Asian consumers outside the location where these services are produced. Just like with manufacturing goods, the South Asian regions or cities with high market access, that is, a large market for services, would then *ceteris paribus* be preferred locations for firms (like banks and insurance companies) that produce tradable services for the South Asian market. Chapter 7 of this volume argues specifically for the case of telecommunications in South Asia. It advocates that a further reduction of trade costs broadly defined (that is, a fall in transport and communication costs) could not only stimulate services activities per se but also the agglomeration of services activity. When it comes to the demand for tradable services within South Asia, the general conclusions mentioned in Box 3.1 are also relevant for that part of the tradable service sector that produces for the local, that is, internal South Asian (or Indian) market.

However, as shown by Table 3.2, a bulk of the tradable services produced in South Asia are not produced for the local (South Asian) market. Instead, these services are largely exported to developed countries where demand for them is much higher.

Table 3.2 shows that in India the production of software is one of the main components of Indian service exports: more than half of the services' share in total GDP in India comes from software production (compare the percentage of software production in GDP to total 'other services' percentage in GDP in Table 3.1). Further, the bulk of this production was aimed at the export market: software exports increased even faster, increasing more than twenty times to US$ 23 billion in 2006. As of today, 80 per cent of India's total software production is

TABLE 3.2   Software Production and Exports in India (1996–2006)

	Software Exports (million US$)	Software Production (million US$)	% of Software Production in GDP	% Software Production for Export
1996–7	1,099	1,775	0.46	61.9
1997–8	982	2,683	0.65	36.6
1998–9	2,600	3,777	0.91	68.8
1999–2000	3,958	5,619	1.24	70.4
2000–1	6,206	8,263	1.79	75.1
2001–2	7,653	9,933	2.08	77.0
2002–3	9,526	12,294	2.43	77.5
2003–4	12,674	16,210	2.7	78.2
2004–5	17,845	22,683	3.27	78.7
2005–6	23,310	29,286	3.67	79.6
D 1996–2006	20.2	15.5	3.21	17.7

Sources: Department of Information Technology, *Annual Report 2005–6* and previous editions. Exchange rate and GDP (current prices) used for conversions and calculations of column 3 from Reserve Bank of India.

aimed at the export market. This is a prime example of internationally traded services where from the South Asian perspective demand, and hence market access considerations are relatively unimportant (software demand in South Asia is low), and where from an NEG perspective all the relevant action is on the supply side. The question is what accounts for the increased importance of South Asia, and India in particular, as the location for tradable services production.

A first determinant is the fall in communication costs. This fall has been spectacular. The WDR (World Bank 2008) shows that the price of a telephone call from London to New York fell from a staggering US$ 293 to only a few cents in 2006. Figure 3.2 shows the fall in costs of a three minute telephone call to the US over the last decade. Over this period the fall in costs has particularly been markedly for non-Organisation for Economic Co-operation and Development (OECD) countries. In South Asia it went down from an average US$ 6 in 1997 to about US$ 2 in 2004.

The fall in communication costs has been even more pronounced when one takes the rise of the internet into account. Where it used to take several days or even weeks to send documents (let alone whole databases) from one country to the other, nowadays this takes no more than the click of a button. NEG theory's most straightforward prediction is

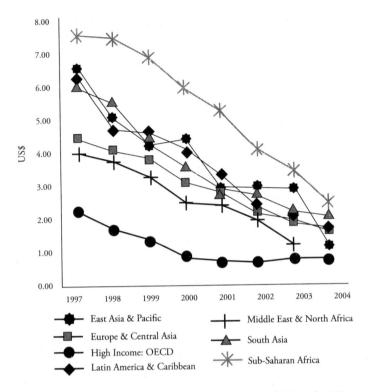

FIGURE 3.2   Average Cost of Telephone Call to the US
(*$ per 3 minutes*)

Source: World Bank (2008).

that this fall in communication costs will, all other things being equal, increase both the volume and range of tasks or services that are or can be traded.

Figure 3.3 shows that this is exactly what has happened. Business services exports of many countries have grown rapidly (outpacing overall export growth) over the last decade coinciding with the period of marked decreases in communication costs. Notice that India ranks second in Figure 3.3.

From the South Asian perspective, the international trade in services is still relatively limited in terms of overall size (see Chapter 2 of this volume); its growth rate, however, is (more than) impressive and in some countries (notably India and to a lesser extent Pakistan), and in some sectors (IT and software) the trade in services is thus also important in

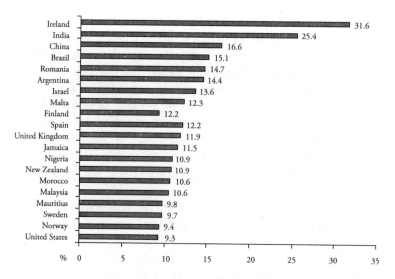

FIGURE 3.3   Average Growth Rate of Business Service Exports for
Selected Countries (1995–2005)

Source: IMF, Balance of Payments Statistics.
Note: The 'Business Services' category includes communication, construction, insurance, financial, computer and information, other business, personal, cultural and recreational services, as well as royalties and license fees.

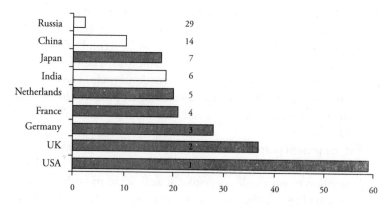

FIGURE 3.4   Largest Insourcing Countries (2002)
(US$ billion)

Source: Based on Amiti and Wei (2005).
Note: Number indicates rank.

quantitative terms. In this respect, also see Chapter 1, which shows that the growth experience of South Asia is indeed different from East Asia (China) since services and not, as is the case in East Asia, manufacturing are the drivers of export-led growth. To take just one (non-randomly chosen) example, India is nowadays responsible for 60 per cent of non-US software exports and also for 60 per cent of global software outsourcing (see Chapter 4 of this volume). Based on Amiti and Wei (2005), Figure 3.4 corroborates the importance of India. It illustrates the global importance of India in this respect by giving the value of in-sourcing for the largest in-sourcing countries (India was ranked sixth worldwide in 2002).

This tremendous increase in the amount and type of services that are nowadays traded has not remained unnoticed among popular media, sparking unrest among skilled workers in high-wage countries afraid of losing their jobs, policymakers, and academics alike. According to an influential paper by Baldwin (2006), the world depicted by Krugman (1991) and the subsequent NEG models is one of the first great unbundling, where largely thanks to the fall of transport and trade costs it became possible to spatially un-bundle manufacturing production and consumption. From the late twentieth century onwards, however, Baldwin (2006) states that we have started to witness the rise of a second great unbundling where the firm's production process itself gets spatially un-bundled. The spatial fragmentation of the value or production chain has increased trade but not so much of final goods as in that of intermediate goods or, even more generally, tasks or services. A large part (if not all) of the international trade in services belongs to the second unbundling. A recent influential analysis by Grossman and Rossi-Hansberg (2006) develops the first full-blown model of international trade in tasks where, for instance, (standardized) tasks like accounting are produced in low-cost countries like those in South Asia and then exported (back) to firms in the OECD countries.

For our present purposes, however, the drawback of the analysis in the vein of Grossman and Rossi-Hansberg (2006) is that it is not a model of agglomeration or economic geography. It analyses so to say for a single representative firm whether it makes sense to engage in the trade in tasks or not. What happens when one marries this idea of services outsourcing or trade in services with the key NEG notion of the spatial agglomeration or clustering of those activities? The only paper that we are aware of that offers such a view is the very recent contribution by Robert-Nicoud (2008). He specifically incorporates trade in services in a 'standard NEG model' that aims to explain the effect of decreased trade costs of services (that is, communication costs) on the spatial distribution of both goods and tradable tasks or services production. Even more specifically, the model seems to have been developed with the case of India and the outsourcing of (routine) tasks by 'western' firms to India in mind—or as put by Robert-Nicoud (2008: 534) 'my model applies to the unbundling of intangible tasks.... [it] fits the patterns of offshoring to "IT dragons like India"'. We explain his model in some detail in Box 3.2.

**BOX 3.2   NEG and Tradable Services: An Overview
of Robert-Nicoud (2008)**

To illustrate what NEG tells us about agglomeration once we allow for the 'second unbundling', Robert-Nicoud (2008) introduces a production process that consists of complex/strategic tasks as well as routine tasks. The North (OECD countries) has an advantage as a location for complex tasks, whereas routine tasks can be undertaken at lower (wage) costs in the South (South Asia). But the fragmentation of the production process, that is, outsourcing the routine tasks to the South, is subject to communication costs. To mimic what we have observed in South Asia in recent decades, he first assumes that communication costs are (still) very high but that transport costs are starting to fall. This results in the first great unbundling (see above). But, and here lies the paper's innovation, when communication costs start to drop as well because of ICT-driven innovations that make it less costly to transfer routine service tasks from the North to the South, Robert-Nicoud shows that once communication costs are low enough, the North will be home to the production of complex tasks and the South to the production of routine tasks (that is, it can explain the second unbundling). From the perspective of South Asia, introducing the offshoring option implies that in case of low transport and communication costs the South may indeed end up with a very specific part of global footloose economic activity, that is, the production of tradable tasks and/or services. Also, Robert-Nicoud shows that this shift of the production of tradable tasks to the South is an important channel for catch-up in welfare terms for the South (that is, the South benefits more substantially from this second unbundling than the North).

Robert-Nicoud (2008) is the first example of a NEG model that sheds light on the surge in services exports that we have observed over the last decade. Although showing the potential of NEG in offering theory-based insights into the trade in services, for our present purposes his model is too stylized. One important drawback of the analysis of a modern NEG services model like Robert-Nicoud (2008) is that it treats the 'South' (that is, South Asia and other developing regions) as homogeneous. But we know, for instance, that the engagement of the various South Asian countries or even sub-national regions in the international trade in tasks or services differs enormously (in the case of South Asia, see Chapter 2 of this volume and Table 3.3); firms that take part in this trade are predominantly located in India and within India itself the regional distribution is also rather uneven with a few large cities (Bangalore, Delhi, and Mumbai) dominating its production of tradable services.

When looking at (the type of) service exports, instead of at export services' share in total GDP as in Table 3.1, so far a surge in tradable business services really only seems to have occurred in India. In India about 78 per cent of exported services are 'other services' and of these other services 89.1 per cent are 'computer and business' services—exactly the type of exports that most casual observers refer to when discussing the drivers of India's recent economic success.

TABLE 3.3   Service Exports of South Asian Countries Decomposed

(in million of US$)

YEAR: 2006	Bangladesh	India	Maldives	Nepal	Pakistan	Sri Lanka	South Asia
Exports (total)	1,334	75,354	473	386	3,506	1,625	82,678
% Transportation services	6.7	10.1	5.5	9.1	32.0	46.2	12.0
% Travel services	6.0	11.9	91.8	33.2	7.0	25.2	12.0
% Other services	87.3	78.0	2.7	57.8	61.0	28.6	76.0
Other Services in More Detail							
% Communications	5.3	3.7	0.0	15.7	7.0	14.7	4.0
% Construction	1.9	0.7	0.0	0.0	1.0	6.3	1.0
% Royalties and license fees	0.0	0.2	76.9	0.0	2.0	0.0	0.0
% Finance and insurance	2.9	5.4	7.7	0.9	4.0	12.3	5.0
% Computer and business services	26.8	89.1	0.0	23.3	26	62.1	85.0
% Other services	63.0	0.9	23.1	60.1	59	4.5	4.0

Source: Adapted from Bosworth and Maertens (2008), Table 2.6, Chapter 2 of this volume.

In the other South Asian countries where service exports dominate the 'other services' sector (Nepal, Bangladesh, and Pakistan), the 'computer and business' services constitute less than a quarter of these exports. Again, it seems that India in particular has been able to respond to the global decrease in communication costs and has expanded its tradable service sector. It does not (or only marginally so) seem to be the case for the other South Asian countries. Note also the stark difference with the Maldives and Sri Lanka (see also Chapter 2): the Maldives specializes much more in the tourist industry, whereas in Sri Lanka—with its major transhipment port at Colombo—the transport service sector is dominant. It seems that the main predictions from the modern NEG literature, recall also the explicit claim by Robert-Nicoud (2008), first and foremost apply to India; the other South Asian countries have not witnessed a marked increase in the trade in previously non-tradable business services.

This raises the question why some South Asian countries and regions do better than others when it comes to the location of the service sector. To answer this, we tentatively go beyond Robert-Nicoud (2008) and approach the issue regarding the relevance of economic geography theory in explaining the recent (and possibly future) developments in the tradable service sector more broadly (at the cost of losing out on theoretical rigour). To do so, we ask the more general question whether NEG theory provides useful guidelines that can help us understand the spatial evolution of the tradable service sector and that of South Asia in particular. As in the case of non-tradable services, we turn to NEG's trinity of increasing returns, trade costs, and factor mobility for some possible clues.

The presence of localized increasing returns to scale combined with inter-regional factor mobility creates, what NEG models are renowned for, cumulative causation. This is important when it comes to explaining the current uneven spatial allocation of internationally tradable service production across South Asia. Once a region has established itself as an important and successful service exporter (for example, Bangalore), this is likely to start a process of cumulative-causation driven by the well-known Marshallian externalities that we know from the urban economics literature: skilled people from other regions will flock to this city in search of jobs, starting new companies, exchanging knowledge with other skilled people (and with foreign markets), making them more productive, attracting even more foreign investment, making the service sector grow further, and attracting even more people. In this sense sub-national hubs of the production of export services are likely to appear. The negative economies of scale (congestion costs, high land and housing rents, etc.) that go along with agglomeration are probably less relevant for services. Service firms literally take up less space, use less local resources, do not cause traffic jams when shipping their goods, and pollute less (at the location site itself at least). Based upon the scale economies argument, we thus expect the production of tradable services to show an even more concentrated spatial pattern than manufacturing production.

Figure 3.5 shows some tentative evidence of this hub effect to be relevant for the case of India. It shows that cities with an already large exporting service sector are able to maintain their lead over the smaller national service exporting centres. There is no evidence for significant catch-up between the service exporting cities—with Pune as a marked exception to this rule.[3]

Where such hubs appear and how they evolve depends on the relative strength of other factors, which from an NEG perspective would be spreading and agglomeration forces. This brings us naturally to NEG's

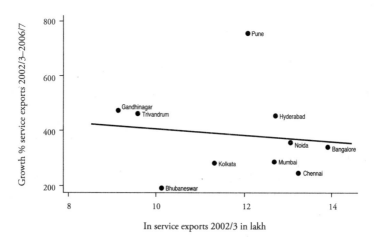

FIGURE 3.5   Catching Up among India's Largest Service Exporting Cities

Note: The slope of the line depicted is −11.94 and highly insignificant (p-value is 0.582).

[3]When considering the many places in India without any significant growth or even presence of a service exporting sector, one would very likely even find a divergence between the leading service exporting centres in India and its manufacturing or agriculture focused counterparts (see Bosker and Garretsen 2008) for evidence on divergence in terms of overall GDP per capita among Indian states.

most important spreading or agglomeration force, namely, part two of its trinity—trade costs.[4]

A marked difference with the (standard NEG) case of manufacturing goods is that in case of the trade in services, variable trade costs are today almost zero. The costs of a telephone call, or of sending data from one place to the other, have virtually disappeared due to the tremendous improvements in communication technology. However, this cannot be said of fixed costs, that is, the costs of setting up reliable broadband bandwidth services, electricity provision, etc. Even though communication costs between locations are virtually non-existent in a technical sense once an adequate communication infrastructure has been set up, countries and regions still differ widely in terms of their ability to participate in the global ICT revolution. In order to be attractive for foreign firms as an outsourcing destination, countries compete in terms of the quantity and quality in the provision of high-speed internet, reliable power, and telecom networks. Also less tangible trade costs such as language, cultural, or institutional differences are arguably much more prominent when it comes to the trade in services.

In fact these fixed costs are to some, or maybe even a large, extent determined by the presence of good quality non-tradable services (internet, electricity provision, language education, institutional quality, how easy is it to set up a business, contract enforcement, etc). The importance of these fixed costs in the overall cost of trading services have an important implication in terms of economic geography. Differences between locations in the availability of good-quality ICT infrastructure, institutions, or an educated workforce can make the difference between locations in determining which one will attract an (exporting) tradable service sector and which one does not. Both at the national as well as at the state level these fixed trade cost reducing measures do seem to exert a strong influence in determining which country (that is, India), state, or even city (Bangalore, Mumbai and, Noida [very close to Delhi]: recall Figure 3.5) attracts the tradable service sector and to what extent (see Figure 3.1 for some evidence for this at the state level in India).

Table 3.4 shows some evidence as to the possible reasons for the dominance of India in the overall tradable services market over its South Asian neighbours.

---

[4]As explained earlier, these trade costs are defined broadly to include all costs associated in moving a good or, in the case at hand, a tradable service from one place to the other. As such they include both tangible (cost of telephone call, tariffs, etc.) and non-tangible (language barriers, etc.) costs.

Table 3.4 shows that so far the internet infrastructure is most extensive in India: 17 per cent of the population regularly uses the internet followed at some distance by Pakistan and Maldives (both about 11 per cent). Of interest is the fact that India does not have the highest share of people subscribed to the internet (not shown here) but does have the highest share of people using the internet. Apparently, although many people cannot afford to subscribe to a regular internet scheme (or buy their own computer), they do use the internet regularly either at internet shops or maybe more likely at work. In terms of telecommunication infrastructure, India is not doing very well compared to, for example, Maldives, Pakistan, and Sri Lanka, the countries with the largest coverage of their telecom networks.[5] Turning to the quality of education services provided, Sri Lanka has the best educated population (tertiary enrollment rates are lacking, but we expect these to be the highest in South Asia as well). Notably, India comes in second, with 59 per cent secondary and 13 per cent tertiary enrollment rates, respectively. Pakistan comes in last with a 32 per cent secondary enrollment rate and 5 per cent tertiary enrollment rate (both around half that of India). When it comes to the share of the population speaking English, in all South Asian countries with the exception of Afghanistan about 10 per cent of the population speaks English. Overall, combining the level of education and the language ability of the population, it shows that (as in the case of infrastructure) India's educational performance is one of the best (only Sri Lanka has a similar, or better, educational record) in South Asia.

When it comes to labour mobility and its relevance for tradable services in South Asia, it is important to distinguish between international and inter-regional labour mobility. Given the still limited degree of international labour mobility, both between South Asia and the rest of the world, and between the South Asian countries, labour can largely be considered to be immobile from an international perspective. In fact, in the (few) NEG models that analyse tradable services, labour is indeed assumed to be immobile (see Krugman and Venables 1995; Robert-Nicoud 2008). The limited degree of labour mobility contributes to the higher wage costs in the developed (OECD) countries and thereby provides a main incentive for firms to re-locate their (routine) services to countries like India (in case of perfect labour

[5]Note that it is not impossible that much of the voice traffic in India takes place over the good quality internet network instead. Also note that Maldives' exceptional internet and telephone infrastructure may in fact only be in use by its many foreign tourists.

TABLE 3.4 South Asian Countries' Quality of Communication Infrastructure (2000–6)

Country/Year	Electrification Rate 2005	Internet Users (1000s) 2005	Internet Users per 100 People 2005	Broadband Subscribers per 100 People 2005	Telephone Subscribers per 100 People 2005	Secondary Enrollment Rate (%)—Male (Female) 2005	Tertiary Enrollment Rate (%)—Male (Female) 2005	No. of English Speakers (1000s) 2000–6	% English Speakers 2000–6
Afghanistan	0.07	580	2.14	0	18	–	–	–	–
Bangladesh	0.32	500	0.32	–	22	43 (45)	8 (4)	3,500	2.2
Bhutan	–	40	4.6	–	21	49 (43)	7 (4)	75	11.4
India	0.56	200,000	17.1	0.27	23	59 (49)	13 (9)	90,000	10.7
Maldives	–	33	10.8	1.57	115	–	–	–	–
Nepal	0.33	337	1.2	–	6	49 (42)	8 (3)	–	–
Pakistan	0.54	17,500	10.7	0.08	51	32 (25)	5 (4)	17,000	10.4
Sri Lanka	0.66	772	4	0.33	56	83 (89)	–	1,910	9.9

Source: Infrastructure—Cecot and Wallsten (Chapter 7 in this volume) and World Bank (2008). In the columns with year 2000–6, the latest observation possible in this period is taken. Education—Table adapted from Chapter 2 of this volume.

Note: Figures in parenthesis refer to female enrollment rate.

mobility, the wages would be the same everywhere as workers can take immediate advantage of the higher wages offered in other places).

Within South Asian countries, labour mobility is certainly relevant. Workers move to those regions where the production of tradable services is concentrated thereby strengthening the core–periphery like the pattern one observes notably in India with respect to the location of tradable services production. As opposed to the international setting where (the absence of) labour mobility stimulates the spreading of tradable services activity, in the case of intra-national labour mobility in South Asia, labour mobility strengthens agglomeration patterns. In fact, as seen from WDR 2009, when (policy induced) measures are taken to stimulate labour mobility within and between South Asian countries, this will tend to further increase regional differences in the sense of a more uneven spatial allocation of economic activity, in case of services.

NEG and Tradable Services—What Have We Learned?

Our discussion of the relevance of NEG's main ingredients for the tradable service sector shows that, and in contrast with the case of non-tradable services, NEG can provide useful insights into the question: why does the tradable service sector cluster in only a few locations in South Asia? The substantial drop in the variable costs of trading services has placed even more emphasis on the fixed cost of trading services. Providing a reliable, high-quality communication infrastructure is crucial for being able to attract tradable service firms. In addition, the fall in communication costs has accentuated the role of a location's amenities in attracting service exporting firms. Locations with good access to a well-educated population, able to work in the tradable service sector, and locations with interaction between firms and research institutes or universities will be the most attractive for tradable service producing firms.

Finally, NEG's focus on processes of cumulative causation is very relevant for the tradable service sector in our view. Once a location has been successful in attracting a fair share of tradable service firms, these provide further incentives to other firms, possibly also foreign, and workers to also locate there. These incentives arise from externalities such as knowledge spillovers between firms, workers, and/or universities. But besides offering these productivity enhancing externalities, the established larger locations also tend to provide more amenities to workers as well as better quality (communication) infrastructure, making it even more difficult for other (non-established) locations to attract firms or people. As a result, established regional centres of production in South Asia will most likely maintain their lead and it will be relatively hard for newcomers to compete with the overall level of 'amenities' offered by the established centres.

NEG, SERVICES, AND SOUTH ASIA: POLICY IMPLICATIONS

Is the observed clustering or agglomeration of tradable services unwanted? Or, in other words, is there a role for active government policy in enhancing the tradable service sector in locations that currently do not undertake such activity? Similarly, what can India do to maintain its tradable service-led growth experience? And, what can the other South Asian countries do to emulate (or even take advantage of) India's tradable services success? We now tentatively address these questions, but we have to be modest in the sense that to date little evidence is available on the effectiveness of active government policy in trying to attract or expand its tradable service sector.

In principle, the clustering of the tradable service sector is not unwanted, as clustering firms and workers can enhance productivity, taking advantage of the externalities outlined earlier. In essence, and similar to the conclusions of World Bank (2008), the clustering of economic activity is a natural stage in the development process, which will at some point be followed by a return to a more equal (spatial) distribution of economic activity. However, it is not unlikely that the clustering of tradable services production will turn out to be more persistent than the clustering of manufacturing. In order for growth to be inclusive, people who are not located in the centres of service production also have to be able to reap the benefits of the positive development in the tradable services hubs. To ensure this, the following two observations seem of particular relevance:

1. Given that the skill requirements in an average tradable services job are higher than those in agriculture or manufacturing, investing in education is of paramount importance. Without a good education, people (and this of course also holds for those already living in the hubs) will simply not be able to benefit from the developments in the tradable service sector as they will not be able to perform the tasks required.

2. People outside the tradable services hubs have to be able to take advantage of the jobs and opportunities available in these hubs. In order to ensure this, impediments to people's mobility have to be removed. Any impediments to factor mobility will hamper those who

happen not to live in the flourishing hubs in taking full advantage of the developments there. Another strategy would be to encourage ICT exports from new places (for example, the Indian government aims to stimulate ICT exports from second-tier cities). This could be successful if these locations are carefully selected. It will most likely be successful in urban places already offering a large and well-educated pool of workers, as well as having good quality infrastructure in place. Given the costs and uncertainty associated with such a strategy (and the fact that it has a necessary focus on urban areas only), we would argue that enabling people is a strategy that will more likely benefit a larger share of the total population.

In essence, these two observations can be combined into the following statement: the clustering of tradable services in a few locations will not be beneficial to all countries' inhabitants if those not already living in these hubs are hampered in their possibility (either in terms of education or mobility) to also take advantage of the opportunities offered by these hubs. If these minimum conditions are not met, the inequality between the successful tradable services hubs and other places will persist (and possibly even worsen).

What can India do to maintain its successful tradable services export-led growth, and what can the other South Asian countries do to try and emulate India's success story by also becoming attractive locations for the production of tradable services? Given its already well-established position in the world markets for tradable services, India's story is mainly one of trying to maintain its competitiveness. Its relatively low wages were one of the most important triggers for foreign firms to outsource their tradable task production to India. Keeping this competitive advantage is crucial and we see three important ways in which it can achieve this:

1. Maintain and upgrade both the quantity and quality of its communication infrastructure, electricity provisions, etc. These are crucial for ensuring the possibility of engaging in tradable services trade in the first place.
2. Innovate: Upgrade and expand the range of tradable tasks and services in which it can compete in world markets—India's leading position in software development is a case in point here.
3. Educate: Enable more people to perform the tradable tasks. A large supply of relatively skilled labour will have a dampening effect on wages. Compared to manufacturing, this is a crucial element, and more difficult to achieve than, for example, in China with its focus

on relatively low-skilled manufacturing for which it has a seemingly unlimited supply of workers.

The policy conclusions are, of course, somewhat different when considering the other South Asian countries that have not yet established themselves in the market for tradable services. We would argue that these countries do have a lot to gain from services export-led growth (as is already apparent in the emergence of some localized clusters in Pakistan, Sri Lanka, and Bangladesh). However, the example of Bangladesh shows that a service-led growth experience may not be the only viable option; there manufacturing industries have largely driven recent growth. As a comparison between the benefits of manufacturing versus services export-led growth is beyond the scope of this chapter, we abstract from the (maybe more important, and surely more difficult) question of whether or not these countries should strive to emulate India in the first place. Instead, we focus on the (somewhat easier) question of what they should do, were they to strive to emulate India and aim to also develop a modern tradable service sector that can compete in the international market for tradable services:

1. Start with services in which in it easier to compete on wages with, for example, India. Immediately competing on quality or focusing on innovation is very unlikely to be successful. Instead a focus on the relatively low-skilled tasks, in which it is easier to find suitable workers, and in which one can attain similar quality levels as in India much more quickly, will be much more likely to be successful. In essence, such a strategy would copy India's strategy of the last decade(s). India also started by offering relatively low-skilled services (call centres, etc.) and from there moved up the value chain and is nowadays also competing on much more skill-intensive services such as software programming or accounting.

2. Focus on creating a tradable services hub. Given the large fixed costs associated with setting up the necessary infrastructure to be able to trade in services, and given the positive externalities that can be reaped to a much greater extent in an agglomerated service hub, focusing on only one location (investing in research centres and communication infrastructure) will likely be most successful. Although enhancing spatial inequality in the short run, if successful, these benefits will eventually spread to the country as a whole (in the absence of the mobility and education constraints outlined earlier).

3. Where to locate such a hub? The quickest, and probably also most successful, strategy is to focus attention on one of the big cities that

generally already provides a much larger and better educated pool of workers and has a better stock of infrastructure in place, compared to more rural areas.

We have outlined in the previous sections that NEG offers a useful framework with respect to studying the service sector, and in particular the tradable service sector. How can the NEG analysis be reconciled with the (sparse) evidence on the service sector for South Asia as presented in the earlier sections?

As argued earlier, NEG has relatively little to say about the non-tradable service sector. The supply of non-tradable services will follow demand, so that the non-tradable service sector will flourish in places that are doing well in economic terms. People will start demanding more services in places that prosper. Given that income levels in most South Asian countries are quite similar and low, it is not surprising to see that the non-tradable service sector is not very well-developed yet (and contributes only about 2 per cent of GDP) in any of the South Asian countries. Moreover, within the South Asian countries, non-tradable service provision is concentrated in cities, exactly those places where people can afford to buy these services to a greater extent than in the rural areas and where the supply of these services is profitable.

However, as outlined earlier, the non-tradable service sector can play an indirect role in determining the location pattern of the tradable service sector where the latter is to a large extent influenced by the forces stressed by NEG. Given the crucial importance of high-quality reliable communication infrastructure for most tradable services production, and given the fact that tradable service production is in principle even more footloose than, for example, manufacturing production (it is easier to move a call-centre than a factory), places that are able to offer high quality non-tradable services (broadband internet, reliable power, and high quality education), and a high quality of life (restaurants, parks, clean air, and cinemas, etc.), are more likely to succeed in attracting the tradable service sector than others. To some extent this explains why India (with its large internet-literate and relatively well-educated population) outperforms the other South Asian countries is terms of being a successful service exporter. This is in particular true from the firms' perspective when one considers that many foreign services firms moved to India not only because of low wages and rents but also because of a reliable communication infrastructure and skilled people. It also explains why within India, we observe that tradable service production is heavily clustered in a few places (Bangalore, Noida, Pune, etc.) only; these are all large cities offering a good quality communication infrastructure, and access to a large pool of well-educated employees.

Another feature of NEG that seems to be relevant for the location of the internationally tradable services production in South Asia is that of cumulative causation. Not only is the production of tradable services highly concentrated only in a few Indian cities, it is also these cities that display the fastest growth in the tradable service sector, thereby further extending their lead over other cities. This is not surprising from an NEG point of view, as these places, by virtue of their already established tradable service sector, offer substantial benefits for new firms or firms from other places in the form of productivity enhancing externalities, and well-established and easily maintainable and improvable provision of important non-tradable services to firms and workers alike.

These positive externalities in the service sector that sustain and promote the clustering of tradable services firms are, however, different from those in the manufacturing sector, but we argue that they are at least as important in enhancing agglomeration. In the standard NEG model, the focus is on the manufacturing sector where trade-cost savings is one main driver of agglomeration: by locating in economic centres, firms are close to their intermediate supply and final demand and thus save on trade costs. Such a trade cost motive is much less important for the tradable service sector. Here we find that productivity enhancing externalities (of the type explained earlier) are arguably much more important drivers of the observed clustering of tradable services' firms.

In addition, we would like to argue that in the tradable service sector, the diseconomies of scale amenities of large agglomerations are much less apparent compared to the manufacturing sector. Combining agglomeration and spreading forces, we thus expect the production of tradable services to show an even more concentrated spatial pattern than manufacturing. This is not only true for developed countries, with notable tradable services hubs in New York, London, Silicon Valley, or Tokyo but also in the case of South Asia, and we expect this pattern to prevail, or even to strengthen in the near future.

REFERENCES

Amin, M. and A. Mattoo. 2008. 'Human Capital and the Changing Structure of the Indian Economy', Working Paper S4576, 2008/03, World Bank, Washington, D.C.

Amiti, M. and L. Cameron. 2007. 'Economic Geography and Wages', *Review of Economics and Statistics*, 89(1): 15–29.

Amiti, M. and S-J Wei. 2005. 'Fear of Service Outsourcing: Is It Justified?', *Economic Policy*, 20(42): 308–47.

Arnold, J., B. Javorcik, M. Lipscomb, and A. Mattoo. 2008. 'Services Reform and Manufacturing Performance: Evidence from India', Mimeo, University of Oxford, Oxford.

Au, C-C. and J.V. Henderson. 2006. 'Are Chinese Cities Too Small?', *Review of Economic Studies*, 73: 549–76.

Baldwin, R. 2006. Paper for the Finnish Prime Minister's Office, Economic Council of Finland as part of EU Presidency.

Baldwin, R., R. Forslid, P. Martin, G.I.P. Ottaviano, and F. Robert-Nicoud. 2003. *Economic Geography and Public Policy*. Princeton: Princeton University Press.

Blinder, A.S. 2006. 'Offshoring: Big Deal, or Business as Usual?', CEPS Working Paper 149, Princeton University, Princeton, NJ.

Bosker, E.M. and H. Garretsen. 2008. 'Economic Geography and Economic Development in Sub-Saharan Africa', CESifo Working Paper 2490, Centre for Economic Studies, Munich.

———. 2009. 'The New Economic Geography of South Asia and Its Lagging Regions', in *South Asia's Lagging Regions*. Washington, D.C.: World Bank.

Brakman, S., J.H. Garretsen, and M. Schramm. 2006. 'Putting New Economic Geography to the Test: Free-ness of Trade and Agglomeration in the EU Regions', *Regional Science and Urban Economics*, 36(5): 613–35.

Breinlich, H. 2006. 'The Spatial Income Structure in the European Union—What Role for Economic Geography?', *Journal of Economic Geography*, 6: 593–617.

Fujita, M. and J-F. Thisse. 2002. *Economics of Agglomeration*. Cambridge, UK: Cambridge University Press.

———. 2009. 'New Economic Geography: An Appraisal of Paul Krugman's 2008 Nobel Prize in Economics', *Regional Science and Urban Economics*, 39(2): 109–19.

Grossman, G.M. and E. Rossi-Hansberg. 2006. 'The Rise of Offshoring: It's Not Wine for Cloth Anymore', Mimeo, Princeton University, Princeton, NJ.

Hanson, G.H. 2005. 'Market Potential, Increasing Returns, and Geographic Concentration', *Journal of International Economics*, 67(1): 1–24.

Helpman, E. 1998. 'The Size of Regions', in D. Pines, E. Sadka, and I. Zilcha (eds), *Topics in Public Economics*, pp. 33–54. Cambridge, UK: Cambridge University Press.

Hering, L. and S. Poncet. 2008. 'Market Access Impact on Individual Wages: Evidence from China', *Review of Economics and Statistics*.

Information Technology. *Annual Report 2005–2006*. New Delhi: Government of India, Ministry of Communications and Information Technology, Department of Information Technology.

Krugman, P.R. 1991. 'Increasing Returns and Economic Geography', *Journal of Political Economy*, 99: 483–99.

Krugman, P.R. and A.J. Venables. 1995. 'Globalization and the Inequality of Nations', *Quarterly Journal of Economics*, 110: 857–80.

Mayer, T. 2008. 'Market Potential and Development', CEPR Working Paper DP6798, Centre for Economic Policy Research, London.

Ottaviano, G.I.P. and J-F. Thisse. 2004. 'Agglomeration and Economic Geography', in J.V. Henderson and J-F. Thisse (eds), *Handbook of Regional and Urban Economics*, Volume 4, pp. 2563–608. Amsterdam: Elsevier North-Holland.

Puja, D. 1999. 'The Rise and Fall of Regional Inequalities', *European Economic Review*, 43(2): 303–34.

Redding, S. and A.J. Venables. 2004. 'Economic Geography and International Inequality', *Journal of International Economics*, 62(1): 53–82.

Robert-Nicoud, F. 2008. 'Offshoring of Routine Tasks and Deindustrialisation: Threat or Opportunity—and for Whom?', *Journal of Urban Economics*, 63(2): 517–35.

World Bank. 2008. *World Development Report, 2009: Reshaping Economic Geography*. Washington, D.C.: World Bank.

————. 2007. *World Trade Indicators*. Washington, D.C: World Bank.

II
Service Exports

4

Software Production
Globalization and Its Implications

Rafiq Dossani

This chapter examines South Asia's software industry—its origins, growth, value addition, and potential, through a study of four countries in the region: Bangladesh, India, Pakistan, and Sri Lanka.

The logic for discussing the software industry is its rising economic importance, globally and in South Asia. Globally, in 2007, the information technology (IT) industry's revenue was US$ 2.5 trillion. Of this, hardware sales generated US$ 478 billion. The rest was comprised of software-related items: software services, business process outsourcing (BPO), packaged software, and Research, Development, and Engineering Services (RDES) (NASSCOM 2008: 31). Over the past two decades, software has overtaken hardware as the primary contributor of value in the IT industry.

Not only has software grown in importance within the IT industry, it is of growing importance to South Asia, particularly to India. For the financial year ended March 2008, the Indian IT industry, for instance, earned a revenue of US$ 64 billion and employed about 2 million persons. The other South Asian economies earned about US$ 2 billion and employed about 1,00,000 persons. Most of that revenue came from software services exports.

Our findings on the industry's growth trajectory are:

1. The industry's origins in the four countries (in the 1970s and 1980s)[1] were remarkably similar. In all cases, the software industry was export-oriented. All were established by US-educated returnee engineers. Foreign capital, foreign management, the diaspora, government policy, government capital, and state-owned enterprises played no role.

2. The industry's most rapid growth occurred in the 1990s, following key technological changes and government policy support. By the late 1990s, the industry's engineers in all the four countries did the same work—writing programmes at clients' sites overseas for projects managed from their home countries. Though this was relatively low value-added work, it was a dramatic change from the earlier decade when clients ran projects.

3. Over the decade till 2007, two trends occurred. First, by 2002, due to the capabilities of the internet, all the four countries had moved their programmers back home. Onsite personnel were used mainly for marketing and finalization of projects. After 2002, the work they did diverged. Indian firms established a range of high value-added software businesses that spanned the supply chain; in Pakistan, some high value-added businesses were established, though they were less integrated than in India. Bangladesh and Sri Lanka's software industries did not change significantly after 2002. The causes for the divergences lay in differentials in policies, their implementation, and external politics.

4. As of 2008, India accounts for 60 per cent of all non-US software exports and 60 per cent of all global software outsourcing. India is central to any large, global software outsourcing project. However, it is still an insignificant force in some components of software, notably packaged software.

Our investigation of the endowments that critically mattered and the critical factors in the institutional environment covered entrepreneurship, developed-country multinationals (DMNCs),[2] infrastructure and clusters; state policy; and rules for accessing capital, education, and foreign participation. Our summary finding on what is needed to develop a software industry suggests that entrepreneurship alone can spark a software industry, without policy support, foreign investment,

[1]The Indian software industry began in 1974, a decade before the others.

[2]Several developing countries, including India, have MNCs, including in the software industry. DMNC refers to an MNC headquartered in a developed country.

or infrastructure. However, to move up in value addition, openness to foreign participation and policy support for education are important. India and, to a lesser extent, Pakistan succeeded in moving up in value addition for these reasons; Bangladesh and Sri Lanka stagnated due to failures on these fronts. However, there is no evidence that special infrastructure or targeted fiscal policies are critical.

The South Asian experience reveals several facets of why DMNCs are important. DMNCs are traditionally both welcomed as carriers of knowledge and feared for their potential to crowd out domestic players. In the South Asian software offshoring industry, DMNCs played only the first role in the 1980s, when firms such as Texas Instruments (TI) pioneered remote software project management in Bangalore. This was of foundational value to domestic players, which learned from the DMNCs and rapidly adopted this new business model. However, the DMNCs' role was purely catalytic. In other respects, such as work type or share of industry revenue, they were minor participants.

A decade later, DMNCs were to play a new role: that of creating trust. In important segments such as systems integration and engineering services, South Asian firms had the capability to undertake such work remotely, but had to wait for a DMNC to do such work in South Asia before clients would trust them. More recently, the role of trust-creation has diminished because South Asian firms—primarily from India—have been able to bridge the 'trust barrier'.

Finally, we assess the potential for linkages within South Asia, which, as of 2008, were minimal. Some examples of existing linkages include: a few Bangladeshi banks use Indian software, the Sri Lankan BPO operations of some multinational firms are managed out of their Indian offices, and some venture capital managed by the Bangalore subsidiaries of US firms has been invested in Pakistan. In other words, the scale is tiny (while perhaps demonstrating India's central role in a future South Asian software cluster).

The low level of linkages is because the smaller countries' policymakers fear India's potential to overwhelm them otherwise. Intra-regional trade generally, and in software particularly, supports these fears of economic colonialism. In consequence, there are significant policy barriers to intra-regional work.

Will greater regional integration in software lead to a replication of the current supply chain, but on a larger scale, that is, of India managing the supply chain, keeping the highest-end work to itself and assigning low-end work to the other countries in South Asia? On the other hand, if regional integration is of value to the smaller countries, does greater regional integration need greater regional policy coordination? On the first matter, we show that many high value-added components of software production are scale neutral and easily fragmented. This, by itself, does not benefit the smaller countries of South Asia since their skills are lower than India's. However, they will benefit in other ways such as access to Indian MNCs and DMNCs and deploying their best talent more suitably, while losing little. Hence, greater regional integration will lead to large net benefits for all of South Asia and could spark the development of a regional software cluster in which India will play a pivotal role.

India's role in a potential South Asia software cluster has both similarities and differences with the role played by China in the East Asian manufacturing cluster, where China is both a large-scale manufacturer of low-end components and provides capacity for assembling components of higher value addition designed and manufactured in the rest of East Asia (Athukorala 2008).

Greater regional integration, we argue, does not imply a need for greater regional policy coordination. This is because, as of 2008, the policies that matter—in the areas of finance, infrastructure, and education—are similar (with the exception of Sri Lanka's higher education policy). However, greater understanding of the risks and benefits of regional integration will help clear the worries about economic colonialism that invariably surround intra-regional policy dialogues. For this to happen, India must step up and play the role of partially guaranteeing against the risks, rather than shrink from its regional responsibilities, as at present. This is a matter of political economy rather than policy.

Our method of analysis is to focus primarily on India and draw the rest of South Asia's features in relation to it. This is partly because the latter's evolution is similar to India's, though less advanced; hence, an explanation of the rest of South Asia benefits from such a comparative analysis. Second, India accounts for 97 per cent of the South Asian software industry's revenue; any analysis of the potential of a South Asian software cluster and the impact that it may have globally must necessarily assign India the central role.

The first section covers the software industry and its offshoring. The second section addresses offshoring to South Asia. The third focuses on regional comparisons. The fourth section covers workforce issues while the role of institutions is covered in the fifth section. The final section covers the potential and prospects for regional integration. The annexures explain the different types of software and the industry's organization.

THE SOFTWARE INDUSTRY AND ITS OFFSHORING

Software programmes are written for several purposes, usually classified
into the following three types: software for managing a computer's

TABLE 4.1   Global Software and R&D Services Spending
by Categories of Work (2007) and India's Market Share

	Global Software Services Spending ($ bn)	India's Global Market Share, 2003 (%)	India's Global Market Share, 2007 (%)	US Wage Rate ($/hour)
Software applications				
Consulting	59.6	< 0.1	1.4	80–120
Applications development	25.2	16.4	39.3	25
System integration: hardware and software deployment and support	119.3	< 0.1	1.3	18–25
System integration: applications, tools, and O/S	84.9	< 0.1	0.8	40
IT education and training	23.3	0	1.3	40
Managed services	182.7	1.6	5.1	60–120
RDES	802	< 0.1	0.8	40–120
Total	1,297			

Source: NASSCOM (2008: 30, 35, 163) for columns 2 and 4; NASSCOM (2004:
24) and author's interviews for columns 3 and 5.

Notes: *Consulting* refers to IT strategy, system conceptualization, architecture and
design. It is comprised of IS consulting and network consulting and integration. It
requires the highest level of skills, including system design and an understanding
of client requirements. *Applications development*, or, more commonly, applications
programming, refers to creating the applications programmes. The skills required
are primarily programming skills, and hence are less than those needed for the
consulting function. *Systems integration*: Hardware and software deployment and
support refers to making the software and hardware components compatible and
interoperable. The skills required vary, but are less than those needed for programming.
Systems integration: Applications, tools, and O/S refers to integration of the software
components (both products and custom software) in a software project. The skills
required include an understanding of client requirements and programming.
Managed services refer to services such as managing applications either onsite or
remotely over the web, managing networks, managing information systems, and
system infrastructure remotely. The skills required vary greatly. *RDES* (Research,
Development, and Engineering Services) refers to services such as chip design and
developing software embedded in special purpose computer chips. The largest users
of such special purpose chips are the IT, telecom, automotive, and pharmaceutical
sectors. The skills required vary, being highest for embedded software development.

internal operations (systems software), applications such as word processing (applications software), and hosts for applications such as data-base management software or web browsers (platform software). Annexure 4A.1 shows why systems and platform software are invariably sold as one-size-fits-all packages (such as the Windows Operating System), while enterprise level applications software is often custom-made.

Custom-made software creation is part of a larger category called software services. Table 4.1 explains the different types of software services. Table 4.1 also presents data on global software services spending by category and (for later use) India's market share. The software services business is five times as large as the packaged software industry (2007 revenue: US$ 250 billion).

The categories tend to change when new technologies are introduced. For instance, managed services are internet-age businesses. On the other hand, system software maintenance is no longer outsourced (since the introduction of Windows). In the computer industry's early days, software vendors (termed 'independent software vendors' or ISVs) tended to be large, integrated firms offering all the software services listed in Table 4.1. Over time, the service layers listed later in the chapter were modularized,[3] leading to industry fragmentation and firm-level specialization. Annexure 4A.2 details the growth of the ISV industry.

Table 4.1 describes three activities, software applications services (its components are in the first five rows of the table), managed services, and RDES. Software services start with the consulting function, at the end of which the functions of the software to be developed are specified. The software must then be produced by writing a software programme. This is the applications development function. Once written, the software must be integrated with the rest of the IT system and the users trained on the resulting system. The last two activities in Table 4.1, managed services and RDES, are self-contained services as of 2008, though this will likely change as new technologies create new modularizations.

THE OFFSHORING OF SOFTWARE TO SOUTH ASIA

Software production was first offshored by American IT firms in the 1970s to India, Ireland, and Israel (the '3 Is').[4] The widespread knowledge

---

[3]Modularization is the conversion of a component of the production process with one or more proprietary inputs, design, or fulfillment techniques into a component with standardized inputs, design, and fulfillment techniques.

[4]This was a decade after the offshoring of hardware manufacturing. Siwek and Furchgott-Roth (1993: 93–4) suggest that the delay was because, unlike manufacturing,

TABLE 4.2   US New Work-types in Software Services and South Asian Exports

Period	US New Work-type (A,B,C,D,E)	India	Bangladesh	Pakistan	Sri Lanka
1961–70	A: System software maintenance	Nil	Nil	Nil	Nil
1971–80	B: Applications development	Engineers exported—A	Nil	Nil	Nil
1981–90	C: System integration	Engineers exported—A, B	Engineers exported—A, B	Engineers exported—A, B	Engineers exported—A, B
1991–2000	D: Consultancy	Engineers exported—B	Engineers exported—B	Engineers exported—B	Engineers exported—B
2001–7	E: Managed services	Engineers in India—B, C, D, E + RDES	Engineers in Bangladesh—B, E	Engineers in Pakistan—B, C, E	Engineers in Sri Lanka—B

Source: Author's compilation, based on material in Annexure 4A.1; author's interviews for Columns 3–6.

Note: RDES—Research, Development, and Engineering Services.

of English and relatively low costs for technical labour were common attractions. Small domestic markets and weak domain knowledge (less so for Israel) were common disadvantages. From the 1980s, many other countries exported software to developed countries, including Bangladesh, Pakistan, Sri Lanka, and the Philippines. In the 1990s, the new entrants included Brazil, Bulgaria, China, the Czech Republic, Hungary, Mexico, Poland, Romania, Russia, and Vietnam.

Table 4.2 shows the South Asian software industry's evolution relative to the US. Column 2 lists the highest value-added work in the US software services industry for the period. Columns 3–6 list the work done in the South Asian software industry.

In the 1970s, the best US software engineers shifted from system maintenance to applications programming. Indian engineers were

---

software development was more closely linked to customer requirements and required close coordination within the firm.

then imported to support system maintenance. In the 1980s, systems integration became the highest value-added work in the US; the rest of South Asia entered the industry and, along with Indian engineers, took on applications development (programming) tasks. Thus, South Asian engineers moved ahead in value addition, but remained a decade behind the US. Thereafter, the time-gap increased. In the 1990s, high-end work focused on consultancy. During this time, the South Asian firms continued to write applications programmes overseas.

The next step up the value chain for South Asia was the shift of South Asian programmers to their home bases during the 1995–2001 period. This was technically enabled by the internet. From the business side, it was pioneered by DMNCs who had set up shop in India. Another business enabler was Y2K.[5] The sudden, overwhelming demand for software programmers due to Y2K led firms to outsource the work offshore as a matter of urgency, overcoming their managers' reluctance to send work overseas.

By 2002, all the South Asian companies had shifted most of their programmers back home. At that point, South Asia was still three decades behind the US (see Table 4.2). Thereafter, the shift to high-end work offshore accelerated. System integration shifted in 2004 (two decades later), managed services in 2004 (three years later), and contract RDES in 2003 (two years later). Once again, DMNCs operating in India were the pioneers, though the bursting of the internet bubble in 2002 played a role by forcing IT managers overseas to consider lower-cost locations urgently.

By 2007, the entire software services range was being provided by firms out of India. However, all four countries still primarily provide programming services. Bangladesh, due to multilateral agency support, also provides some managed services, despite poor bandwidth. Pakistan, due to a rapidly improving engineering workforce and bandwidth, provides system integration and managed services. Sri Lanka still only provides programming services. We turn now to the individual countries, and focus on the industry's domestic drivers.

India

Table 4.3 shows the growth of India's software industry. The rise in the number of firms between 1984 and 1990, the rise in revenue per employee

---

[5]Y2K work involved re-coding legacy software programmes to recognize dates after the year 2000. The Y2K problem had arisen from the days when computer memory was expensive, as a result of which programmers saved memory by allowing only the last two digits of a year to be recorded. Y2K rectification was considered low-end work.

TABLE 4.3   Growth of Indian Software Exports

Year	Total Exports ($ m)	No. of Firms	Average Revenue per Firm ($)	Average Revenue per Employee ($)	Exports/Total Revenue (%)
1980	4.0	21	190,476	16,000	50
1984	25.3	35	722,857	18,741	50
1990	105.4	700	150,571	16,215	N/A
2000	5,287	816	7,598,039	32,635	71.8
2004	12,200	3,170	7,003,154	35,362	73.9
2007	29,300	N/A	N/A	33,900	74.0

Source: Heeks (1996: 93) for 1980–90 data and NASSCOM (2004, 2005) for 2000 and 2004 data.
Notes: Data for 1980, 1984, and 1990 are from Heeks (1996: 72, 73, 87, 88). Data for 2000 (financial year ended March 2001) are from NASSCOM (2002) and NASSCOM (2004: 23, 26, 64). Data for 2004 (financial year ended March 2005) are from NASSCOM (2005: 75–6). The 2004 data for number of firms and average revenue is based on software, software services, and IT-enabled services (ITES) because disaggregated data is not available. Data for 2007 are from NASSCOM (2008: 163). Number of employees for 1980, 1984, 1990, 2000, and 2004 were 250, 1,350, 6,500, 162,000, 260,000, and 345,000, respectively.

and per firm between 1990 and 2000, and the continuing dependence on exports are its key features.

Unlike Ireland and Israel, where government policy provided incentives for private sector entry, the Indian software industry began during a time when policy was 'statist, protectionist and regulatory' (Rubin 1985). An industrial licensing regime and state-owned banks were used to strictly regulate private sector activity. In IT, the state created 'national champions' and granted them monopolies (Sridharan 1996). The Foreign Exchange Regulation Act of 1973 (FERA 1973) restricted foreign ownership to 40 per cent, leading many DMNCs to shut down. This included IBM (which served local markets), on concerns about intellectual property (IP) protection.

Offshored software development began simply enough with Indian programmers being sent to developed countries. In 1974 the mainframe manufacturer, Burroughs, asked its India sales and maintenance agent, Tata Consultancy Services (TCS), to send programmers to the US to install system software (Ramadorai 2002).[6] TCS's CEO, a returnee,

[6]Burroughs' request to TCS was a key trigger of the business. Since DMNCs were excluded from domestic operations, Burroughs had no option but to ask a domestic firm. While this bolsters those who make the 'infant industry' argument for initial protectionism

saw the business opportunity and sent programmers to other American clients. Other Indian firms followed TCS's lead, including foreign IT firms that formed FERA 1973 compatible joint ventures.[7] Initially, the exported programmers worked for global IT firms. Later in the decade, as IBM's global market share increased, end-users such as banks used Indian firms to convert existing applications software into IBM-compatible versions.

The state remained hostile to the software industry through the 1970s. Import tariffs were high (135 per cent on hardware and 100 per cent on software), and software was not considered an 'industry', that is, exporters were not eligible for bank finance. Even opening an overseas sales office was disallowed until 1979 (Ramadorai 2002).

Programmers returning from overseas assignments were the main source of learning about new opportunities, but their short duration overseas—typically less than a year—limited the depth of the learning (Ramadorai 2002). Also, many chose to remain overseas after completing their assignments. As a result, during its first decade, firms did little other than recruit engineers and send them to locations where they were assigned work by their clients.

A firm wishing to enter the business needed capital, primarily for advance recruitment and marketing overseas. Given India's strict capital regime, small firms were excluded; conglomerates became the industry's dominant players and Mumbai, the country's commercial capital, became the centre of the business. Of the top eight exporters in 1980, five had a large firm pedigree, including the top four. Seven of these eight were headquartered in Mumbai with a 90 per cent market share (Table 4.4). This was to change later, as Table 4.4 indicates. Note also the background of the founders—some were from pioneering firms such as TCS and Patni. Many had an American education, common to the pioneers of the software industry in the rest of South Asia.

The industry's activities gradually evolved in the mid-1980s with the global industry's adoption of the Unix-Workstation (U-W) standard (Annexure 4A.2) and the consequent modularization of programming.

The state at that time coincidentally began a long-debated, gradual abandonment of its protectionist and statist stance. The New Computer

---

(for example, Arora and Athreye 2002), in a technologically intensive industry like software, learning from DMNCs is far more important. This was first demonstrated by the impact of TI in India in the 1980s.

[7]These included Datamatics (a joint venture between the US minicomputer maker, Wang, and ex-employees of TCS), Digital, and Data General.

Policy (NCP) of 1984 was one outcome. NCP 1984 consisted of a package of reduced import tariffs on hardware and software (reduced to 60 per cent), recognition of software exports as a 'delicensed industry', that is, henceforth eligible for bank finance but not subject to the intrusive licensing regime (Heeks 1996: 44–5), permission for foreign firms to set up wholly-owned, export-dedicated units and a project to set up a chain of software parks that would offer infrastructure at below-market costs. In 1985, income from all exports (including software exports) was exempted from income tax.

The new policies successfully induced entry by DMNCs, who introduced new businesses and new business models. Some DMNCs

TABLE 4.4   Top Eight Indian Software Exporters

Rank	1980, India HQ	1990, India HQ	2008, India HQ	Founder, Education, Experience
1st	TCS—Mumbai	TCS—Mumbai	TCS—Mumbai	Kanodia (MIT)
2nd	Tata Infotech—Mumbai	Tata Infotech—Mumbai	Infosys—Bangalore	Murthy (ex-Patni, U. Mysore, IIT Kanpur)
3rd	Computronics—Mumbai	Citibank—Mumbai	Wipro—Bangalore	Premji (Stanford) and Soota (IISc)
4th	Shaw Wallace—Kolkata	Datamatics—Mumbai	Cognizant—Chennai	Lakshmi Narayanan (ex-TCS, Bangalore U)
5th	Hinditron—Mumbai	TI—Bangalore	Satyam—Hyderabad	Raju (Loyola College, Chennai; Ohio U)
6th	Indicos Systems—Mumbai	DEIL—Mumbai	HCL—Delhi	Nadar (PSG College, Coimbatore)
7th	ORG—Mumbai	PCS—Mumbai	PCS—Mumbai	Patni (MIT)
8th	Systime—Mumbai	Mahindra—BT—Mumbai	i-Flex—Mumbai	Hukku (BITS, Pilani) (ex-TCS, Citicorp)
Market share of top 8 firms (%)	90	65	69	

Source: Heeks (1996: 89) for columns 2 and 3; company websites and author's interviews for columns 4 and 5.

did research and development (R&D) and wrote packaged software using cross-country teams (such as TI and Hewlett Packard), others wrote custom software for in-house use, again using cross-country teams (such as ANZ [Australian and New Zealand] Bank and Citigroup). The DMNCs thus replicated successful approaches that they used in other environments, such as Ireland and Israel.

However, facing daunting communication costs and intrusive regulation (Parathasarathy 2000), the product-focused DMNCs remained small, although the initial entrants such as TI were important in persuading the government to improve infrastructure.[8] Domestic firms that sought to imitate the DMNC product-software model such as Wipro also failed due to the weakness of domestic markets as a source of domain expertise (Athreye 2005) and the absence of a flourishing venture capital industry.[9] In consequence, product development accounted for less than 5 per cent of exports by 1990 (Heeks 1996: 88–9), and had reached only 8 per cent by 1999 (NASSCOM 2002: 28).

However, the combination of the U-W standard and lower costs engendered a successful new business model, first proven by TI for internal use, and later pioneered by TCS for outsourcing. Under this model, domestic firms coded the software entirely in India, and relied on a foreign co-vendor for programme design, specification, and integration. This model reduced costs by keeping programmers at home—although the decline in the personnel dispatched overseas was initially slow.[10] Due to the reduced costs, many new firms were established. The number of software firms went up from 35 in 1984 to 700 in 1990.

It is worth noting that the shift to coding in India was only possible after the DMNCs had demonstrated that it could be done, though within the different setting of software product development. So, although the product-focused DMNCs had no significant direct impact on India's software exports during this period, they played two very important indirect roles: first, demonstrating to Indian IT firms that work could be performed in India, and second, demonstrating to clients that the

[8]According to Naidu (2002) TI's decision to enter India was conditional on the state providing adequate power and telecommunications bandwidth.

[9]Through the 1980s, domestic venture capital was concentrated in state-run firms. Two of today's leading IT firms, Wipro and Infosys, were both turned down for funding by state-run venture capital firms in the 1980s.

[10]By 1988, 10 per cent of the Indian software industry's labour force was located in India; this had risen to 41 per cent by 2000 and 71 per cent by 2004 (NASSCOM 1999, 2002: 28, 2005: 58).

work could be performed more cheaply in India rather than in clients' sites overseas.

This shift raised the required standards for physical infrastructure in India. This marked a new phase for IT in Bangalore because its real estate was cheaper than Mumbai. Infosys and Wipro were among the early movers, induced by cheap real estate (Premji 2003). The first software technology park under NCP 1984, with assured supply of electricity and telecommunications bandwidth, was located in Bangalore.

Bangalore's advantages included a small-firm culture, low labour costs, and relative freedom from trade union influences, unlike Mumbai and Delhi (Heitzman 1999: 6). Further, Bangalore is located at the centre of the four southern states of Karnataka (whose capital is Bangalore), Tamil Nadu, Andhra Pradesh, and Kerala, which together produced 52 per cent of India's engineering graduates at the time. Bangalore was the site of the elite Indian Institute of Science (IISc) and several of the state's 'national champions' in IT were located in Bangalore, and contained a trained labour force (Balasubramanyam et. al. 2000: 351). There is some dispute regarding their importance, though. According to some industry observers, the quality of the labour force was dubious and provided only a small percentage of the software industry's needs (Ramadorai 2002). The biggest success from IISc was Wipro Technologies, India's third largest software exporter. It was founded at IISc by a group of engineers working under Ashok Soota, an academic at IISc (Parthasarathy 2003).

Policy reforms in the 1990s and 2000s reduced import tariffs to near zero[11] and regularized foreign ownership, IP protection, venture capital, stock market listing, and telecommunications policies to global best practices. In addition, technological changes during this period, particularly the internet, led to a sharp decline in data storage and transmission costs. These changes induced a new round of entry of DMNCs, particularly foreign outsourcers, and US-based start-ups and opened new opportunities for existing firms in remote software services such as email management and remote software maintenance. The

---

[11]Import tariff reductions were a key feature of the 1990s reforms. These had risen to 110 per cent by 1991 but were reduced to 85 per cent in 1993, 20 per cent in 1994 for applications software, and 65 per cent for systems software and, in 1995, to 10 per cent for all software (Heeks 1996: 49). Duties on hardware ranged from 40 to 55 per cent in 1995, but by 2000 had come down to 15 per cent for finished goods such as computers, and 0 per cent for components (microprocessors, storage devices, ICs and sub-assemblies, display screens, tubes, etc.) (Government of India 2000).

management of software projects also started moving during this time from clients to their vendors located in India.

Interestingly, the DMNCs initially adopted the domestic firms' approach of focusing on programming only—for both in-house product development by firms such as TI, Agilent, HP, Oracle, and GE, as well as services by firms such as ANZ Bank, ABN Amro Bank, Accenture, IBM, and Dell. During this phase, DMNCs and foreign start-ups overwhelmingly chose Bangalore for their IT operations (Naidu 2002). Later activities included system integration (from 2004), managed services (from 2004), and RDES (from 2003). In these cases, DMNCs were important for removing the 'trust deficit': they already did such work overseas and simply shifted activities to India. Once the practice was established, Indian firms also got such business.

As Table 4.5 shows, the share of routine programming work and maintenance accounted for 68.9 per cent of the total export revenue in 2001. By 2007, this had fallen to 33.7 per cent. During this period, the share of foreign firms in total revenue rose from 14.5 per cent to 31 per cent. We believe that the correlation was partly causal, that is, the declining share of routine work was caused by the entry of foreign firms doing more sophisticated work.[12] Confirmatory evidence comes from Sridharan (2004), who notes the presence of 230 DMNCs in Bangalore employing about 25,000 engineers in R&D work by 2001 and that an estimated 30–40 chip designing start-up firms had been established all over India between 1999 and 2002 (see also case studies of foreign firms doing sophisticated work later in this chapter).

TABLE 4.5   Share of Custom Programming Work in Indian Software Exports

Financial Yr Ending March	2001	2008
CAD ($ bn)	$3.65 bn	$9.9 bn
Total software exports ($ bn)	$5.3 bn	$29.3 bn
Share of CAD (%)	68.9	33.7
Share of software products and RDES (%)	10	21

Source: NASSCOM (2008: 163; 2006: 47, 59, 60, 70; 2005: 50, 51; 2004: 36, 40; 2003: 39; 2002: 29, 30).
Note: CAD—Custom application development; RDES—Research, Development, and Engineering Services.

[12]Unfortunately, data on employment in foreign firms is not available, preventing proof of a direct causality. In 2001, the only year for which data is available, foreign firms employed 13 per cent of the workforce (NASSCOM 2002).

As the share of routine programming work declined, the share of engineering services, R&D, and product development rose from 9 per cent in 2001 to 21 per cent in 2007. Of course, several domestic firms also do high-end work. Wipro, the third largest domestic firm, had 14,000 employees providing contract RDES, and filed 68 US patents on behalf of overseas clients in 2005 (Premji 2003).

The large-scale contract RDES business was invented in India. Contract RDES had always been a small-firm activity of American and other developed-country software developers. These mostly provided services to small fabless chip designers—primarily start-ups in Silicon Valley. Indian firms, led by Wipro, entered this field by offering the same services from India. Later, they added new and more established industries as clients including the automotive, pharmaceutical, and telecommunications industries, while also providing RDES to large semiconductor firms.

Thus, this is the second case of indirect linkages between DMNCs and domestic firms, following the earlier (1980 to 2000) case of software services. Once again, DMNCs doing in-house work in India demonstrated to overseas clients that a certain new kind of work could be done in India, the move being followed by Indian outsourcers.

Eager to overcome the trust deficit early in the game, Indian firms, as of 2008, had begun onsite demonstration projects—they established 'centres of excellence' (COEs) in the US where new work-types could be undertaken at the same time as a western outsourcing company, and quickly moved to India. For instance, TCS launched its first major COE in Cincinatti in 2008. Wipro, in 2008, announced plans to open its first non-Indian global software development centre in Atlanta.

This review shows that the Indian software industry is well-diversified and spans the software services supply chain. It accounts for 60 per cent of all non-US software exports and 60 per cent of global software outsourcing. It has demonstrated that weak domestic markets—a concern of several studies (for example, D'Costa 2002; Rosenberg and Mowery 1978)—are not an insurmountable barrier. Its remaining weak spot appears to be packaged software development.

Bangladesh

Software development in Bangladesh started in the early 1980s. The industry started, as it did in the rest of South Asia, by sending programmers to the US. In the late 1990s, the business grew substantially due to Y2K work. Upgrading of the telecommunications facilities led to a gradual shift to remote programming. By 2002, most of the work was done in Bangladesh. By 2005, managed services had been introduced including information systems outsourcing, which is a high value-added business. By 2007, there were about 100 companies in the software export business. Most were small firms with fewer than ten employees. While a few large, domestically-owned firms exist, the few large firms with over 100 employees were mostly joint ventures with foreign companies or 100 per cent subsidiaries of foreign companies.

The industry, as of 2009, is constrained by a number of factors. An independent regulator, the Bangladesh Telecommunication Regulatory Commission, was established only in 2001, and focused primarily on mobile voice services. As a result, bandwidth is expensive and of poor quality. Bangladesh also faces a shortage of software engineers, with 5,500 computer science graduates annually (compared with 20,000 in Pakistan and 3,50,000 in India). The government permits private higher education providers to operate, a strategy that has paid dividends in India and Pakistan, where over 80 per cent of the engineers are graduates of private colleges. However, weak regulation and the shortage of workers have led to a slippage of quality standards. This had been India's experience as well in its early days, so this might be a temporary issue. Table 4.6 summarizes the value of software exports in Bangladesh.

Pakistan

The Pakistani software industry started in the 1980s, again by sending programmers to the US to undertake projects directed by overseas clients. The establishment of the U-W standard (Annexure 4A.2) led to the gradual shift of work to Pakistan. The process accelerated with the establishment of the internet and the imperatives of Y2K.

By 2007, the export industry had crossed the one billion dollar mark. Pakistan's initiatives in the late 1990s to enable private provision of higher education have paid off. The country graduated 20,000 engineers in

TABLE 4.6   Value of Export of Software and ITES from Bangladesh

(in million US$)

Fiscal Year	2003	2004	2005	2006	2007
Value of export	4.20	7.19	12.68	27.01	26.08
Growth rate		71.2	76.4	113.0	–3.4

Source: Bangladesh Bank (2008).
Note: The year above refers to the fiscal year ending in March.

TABLE 4.7   Value of Export of Software from Pakistan

(*in million US$*)

Year	2004	2005	2006	2007
Value of export	600	720	960	1200
Growth rate %		20	33	25

Source: Pakistan Software Houses Association (2008).

2008 and the rate of growth of the engineering workforce is the highest in South Asia at 30 per cent.

The industry's telecommunications sector lagged behind India's for several years due to limited reforms. However, in 2004, the regulator, the Pakistan Telecom Authority, was given greater independence, and later proposed new, improved rules—though still short of best practice standards. The private sector has responded to improved regulation with greater provision of bandwidth, although it remains relatively expensive and of poorer quality compared to India and other global-standard providers.

The combination of improved bandwidth and better human capital has enabled Pakistan's software industry to provide higher value-added services such as systems integration and managed services.

Since 2002, the country's software exporters have faced the challenge of countering negative perceptions of the country due to 9/11. It is impossible to quantify the loss of business, but as the case study of Align Technologies indicates (discussed later in this chapter), they are substantial. Table 4.7 outlines the value of software exports for Pakistan.

Sri Lanka

After a similar start and progression as in Pakistan, the Sri Lankan software industry has stagnated since 2004. This is despite the presence of state support for the industry, entrepreneurship, and good bandwidth. The problem is that the number of skilled graduates is relatively low. The higher education system is state-owned and managed, and due to a shortage of resources has not expanded adequately. The result is that Sri Lanka, despite having the highest literacy rate in South Asia, has a tertiary enrollment rate of 6 per cent, less than that in India and Pakistan. The island's severe internal political problems have raised perceptions of risk. As in India's early days, the industry is dominated by firms that grew out of conglomerates. An example is John Keells Computer Services (JKCS), a subsidiary of John Keells Holdings, one of the country's large conglomerates. JKCS has over 1,000 employees and has achieved a

TABLE 4.8   Value of Export of Software and ITES from Sri Lanka

(in million US$)

Year	2004	2005	2006	2007
Value of export	80	90	100	150
Growth rate %		12.5	11.1	50

Source: http://www.slicta.lk/advantage/industry/, 2004 data, accessed on 8 September 2008; www.adb.org/Documents/Books/ADO/2006/documents/sri.pdf, 2005 data, accessed on 8 September 2008; http://www.dailynews.lk/2007/08/30/bus005.asp, 2006 data, accessed on 8 September 2008; http://srilanka.usembassy.gov/22march07.html, 2007 data, accessed on 8 September 2008.
Note: Exports include ITES; figures for financial year ending in March.

CMM Level 3 rating. Table 4.8 shows the value of software exports for Sri Lanka.

COMPARISON OF THE SOFTWARE INDUSTRIES OF SOUTH ASIA

Software firms in South Asia have several similarities: reliance on services rather than software products, origins based on domestic capital and enterprise, dependence on US markets, and focus on programming services. Underlying these is a reliance on a well-trained cohort of engineers, now being refreshed by the entry of private colleges (except in Sri Lanka), and government policy that is supportive through tax incentives, cheap bandwidth, and industrial parks. India, as the oldest software services exporting industry in the region and the world, has started developing clusters, has a growing presence of multinational subsidiaries, has entered product development, has a growing venture capital industry, and has advanced most in the level of sophistication of work performed. It also has the advantage of scale and scope: the large Indian firms have reached a scale of workforce rivalled only by the very largest of their global competitors. They also undertake a range of work that is second only to the US in scope and sophistication. These advantages have yielded higher revenue per employee than their South Asian counterparts, and higher starting wages for employees.

The software industries in Bangladesh, Pakistan, and Sri Lanka were established about a decade after India. As in India, the initial drivers were local entrepreneurs, many with overseas education, looking to the US market as a source of business. The governments in these countries supported their industries by providing tax exemptions and subsidized infrastructure in the 1980s and 1990s. Up to 2001, their industries followed similar trajectories and had caught up with India in the kind of work done—primarily sending engineers overseas to work on programming projects for their clients. Over the past decade, however, there have been divergences.

1. Offshored work versus body-shopping: From 2001, the work type for all four countries shifted to an offshoring model, in which there was minimal onsite requirements. As discussed earlier, this raised value addition.

2. The programming function: In India, programming for applications (applications development) has risen from a 16 per cent global market share to 39 per cent. This suggests that India is probably central to any large IT outsourcing project anywhere in the world. At the same time, the share of applications development in Indian software exports has fallen to a third from two-third in 2001. This shows that while expanding its presence in the programming function, India has started to span the supply chain. Meanwhile, Pakistan has started moving away from its near complete dependence on programming applications a decade ago, although the dependence is still at two-third. The new fields are managed services and system integration, both of which are significantly more lucrative fields (Table 4.1). Meanwhile, Bangladesh and Sri Lanka's software industries almost entirely undertake applications programming, which is lower value-added.

3. Managed services: The difference in the experiences of the three countries offering managed services appears to be, at least in large part, related to bandwidth availability. Due to successful telecom reforms in India in 1998–2001, new private providers entered the field. Since then, India has experienced a large increase in bandwidth availability and declining costs. This has enabled it to enter the lucrative field of managed services. Pakistan went through similar reforms in the period 2004–6. Though competition is still limited, bandwidth costs have moved downwards since 2006 and this, in turn, is leading to a rising share of work done in Pakistan, including the move to managed services. Bangladesh and Sri Lanka have been unsuccessful with telecom reforms, so bandwidth costs remain high. For instance, in Bangladesh, a leased E1 line costs US$ 3,000 per month which is three times the price in India.

4. Systems integration: While the growth of managed services is driven by bandwidth costs, the rise in systems integration work in India and Pakistan has different reasons. The initial driver of this, oddly,

appears to have been the low-end work created by Y2K. Though this was relatively unsophisticated work even by the standards of regular applications development, it was 'project' work rather than piece work. US firms offshored the business of making their software Y2K compliant to South Asian firms due to the shortage of labour in the US at that time. Their success in doing such work convinced American firms that overseas firms could deliver on projects, leading to higher levels of trust. System integration, which is similar to turnkey project management, was thus deemed to be within the capability of South Asian engineers. The first practical step by clients was to entrust such work to DMNCs in South Asia, following which local firms gained such business as well.

5. Engineering services: The growth of engineering services in India has different reasons. The work started with the downturn in the US economy in 2001. At that time, 'fabless' design firms in Silicon Valley were urgently looking for ways to save on costs due to a drop in venture funding. India offered a way to do this. Some of these firms were start-ups, while others were established firms. Subsequently, firms like Wipro undertook such work on a contract basis, and thus developed competence in it. The work initially done was simple, such as verification of designs. Over time, a greater component of more sophisticated work, such as architecting the chip's layout, writing embedded software, and taking responsibility for whole projects based on specified outcomes resulted. As of 2008, two of the largest firms, TCS and Wipro, each expect to generate annual revenue of US$ 0.5 billion from engineering services.

   Pakistan will undoubtedly also be able to supply engineering services, but it will be a slower process led by the diaspora rather than by multinational firms. Workforce constraints in Bangladesh and Sri Lanka are likely to limit such work in these countries.

6. The impact of multinationals, the diaspora, and returnees: In India, the impact of multinationals is, as discussed earlier, significant. Whether as bearers of good management practices, bridges of trust, or institutional approaches to innovation, the DMNCs have started playing a significant role. In the other three South Asian countries, the diaspora plays an important role, but the multinational firms do not. There are several reasons for this. Primarily, India currently offers a multinational firm both scale and sophistication, and is thus their natural locus for South Asian work. However, transacting with

the rest of South Asia is difficult due to regulatory restrictions and high transaction costs. DMNCs tend to be further constrained by perceptions of high risk arising from volatile internal politics in all the three countries, and in the case of Pakistan, geopolitical concerns. Interestingly, the large Indian multinational firms such as TCS, Infosys, and Wipro have not looked at other countries in South Asia to locate their work. Even if less deterred by internal politics and geopolitical issues, the transaction costs of doing business across the borders is high. Although labour costs are lower in the rest of South Asia relative to India, the size of the workforces in these countries is low relative to India. Pakistan is the only country in which work of scale (which is the Indian firms' specialty) is possible. This ought to improve Pakistan's attractiveness in the event of regional integration. Unlike in India, where Indian firms are unable to recruit the best engineering talent due to competition from multinationals, Pakistan offers them its best. They, as in Sri Lanka and Bangladesh, are as good as those produced by the best Indian colleges.

The diaspora has been more important for Bangladesh, Pakistan, and Sri Lanka due to the relative absence of multinationals in these countries. Unlike India, where the software business was pioneered, and continues to be led by domestic residents (albeit many with an American education), the software industries in the other three countries are much more dependent on the diaspora.

The Challenges in Developing Packaged Software in South Asia

Packaged software is the lifeblood of Silicon Valley, and globally it generates annual revenues of US$ 250 billion. The US dominates this business with an 80 per cent global market share in tradable packaged software. It is the highest value-added component of its software industry. All the South Asian countries have invested, but largely failed to progress, in developing packaged software either for domestic or global markets.

One reason is that packaged software development requires higher levels of coordination than custom-made software. In the latter, there is a single client, while for the former the intended client-base is always a large number. When market conditions change, for instance, due to new technologies, these trigger new requirements to be fulfilled by the software. Given the larger potential client base, packaged software needs to undergo more complex changes in response to new market information than custom-made software. This may explain why packaged software development is so difficult to offshore. The new requirements need to be communicated offshore, which is a costly task requiring high levels of coordination.

The case studies discussed now are intended to illustrate these causes by studying firms that have offshored packaged software development.

Case Studies of Packaged Software Offshoring

For purposes of this discussion, we consider packaged software development by two types of firms: (a) start-ups and (b) established firms. The former tend to be staffed very tightly. For start-ups, offshoring leads to high coordination costs as a share of total costs. Hence, they tend to use offshoring as an integral part of product development. The latter have established sources of revenue. They may choose to use offshoring as a non-integral part of product development for purposes such as product upgrades or second generation product maintenance.

Case Study: Align Technology

Align Technology Inc. of Sunnyvale, California was the first company to manufacture and market an aesthetic alternative to traditional metal braces for adults, the Invisalign System. The Invisalign System consists of a series of removable, plastic, nearly invisible orthodontic 'aligners' that let adults straighten their teeth without braces. The company was founded in 1997. The technology consists of applying advanced 3-D computer imaging graphics in the field of orthodontics. The standard polysulfide or equivalent dental impression is converted to 3-D images, and the movement of each tooth to its final occlusion is also sequenced on the computer. The individual aligners are prepared accordingly.

Align Technology initially used Pakistan as its offshore (and only) manufacturing base, employing 700 persons. This was a successful business model and showed the importance of offshoring right at the beginning, thus minimizing the trust deficit and building in the coordination issues from the beginning. Following the upheaval in the global political environment occasioned by 9/11, the board of Align transferred the work to Mexico.

The Align Technology case shows:
1. how changes in the global political environment can change the assumptions behind a proven business offshoring model, and
2. that the coordination problem can be minimized by building it into management structures from the initial stages.

Case Study: Agilent Technologies[13]

Agilent, a maker of test and measurement equipment, chose India as a base for software development in 2001. Its choice of India was based on the potential talent pool; the judicial system, which it deemed mature relative to East Asia; favourable intellectual protection rules compared with other developing countries in Asia; and mature management talent. Concerns about IP protection and managerial control drove its choice to do most of the work in-house rather than outsource (some software maintenance and programming work was outsourced). To manage these concerns, and also concerns about reversibility of work in the event of failure, all offshored operations had a six-month overlap in staffing between the US and India.

The work started with simple activities and moved to more complex activities over time (Figure 4.1). The engineering services group was the first user of the Indian operations. The initial work done was to provide parts' lists to customers worldwide and data entry for the design group in the US. Over time, most support services were moved to the Indian operations.

In early 2002, the second user within Agilent, the communications solutions group, established a ten-person team to automate test suites

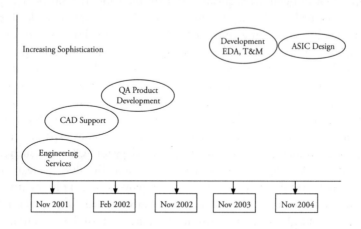

FIGURE 4.1   Activity Transfer to Agilent's Indian Operation by Date

Source: Dossani and Manwani (2005).
Note: CAD—Computer Aided Design, EDA—Electronic Design Automation, QA—Quality Assurance, and ASIC—Application Specific Integrated Chip.

[13]Based on Dossani and Manwani (2005).

for one of Agilent's projects, Netexpert. However, lack of coordination between the Indian and US teams led to the initial failure of this experiment. Increasing the time allocated for coordination and introducing a quality enhancement programme in the Indian operations led to an improvement. By 2005, the development and maintenance of Agilent's EDA software products was being done jointly by multi-country teams located in both the US and India. The success of the India operations has been measured in various ways. Overall, there is a 37 per cent reduction in headcount attributed to consolidating the work in India.

The Agilent case study demonstrates that packaged software development can be successfully done in India. However, it shows how difficult it was to overcome the problem of trust. The focus on second generation test and maintenance work shows that in offshoring packaged software development, the firm preferred to develop software for which the coordination costs that arose from new market conditions were minimal.

Case Study: Broadcom

Broadcom, a Silicon Valley based fabless chip firm, acquired an India operation through the acquisition of Armedia Labs. The Silicon Valley based Armedia Labs was founded in 1997 to develop a single-chip (popularly, system-on-a-chip, or SOC) solution for HDTV. From its inception, work in Silicon Valley was tightly integrated with its Bangalore subsidiary, except for market development, for which the Silicon Valley team took responsibility (Khare 2006). This meant that all other work such as design and developing the embedded software and libraries was shared. When Broadcom acquired Armedia in 1999, its 25-person Indian subsidiary became Broadcom India. Broadcom expanded the team and brought in complementary technology for SOC work such as in graphics and digital conversion and processing. By 2006, the team in Bangalore had grown to 190 persons. Employees were, as in the firm's San Jose offices, divided into functional teams and each functional team was part of a global team consisting of engineers in San Jose and Irvine, USA, Israel, Andover MA, and Singapore.

As of 2008, the process of software development is driven by the engineering director of the project based in San Jose, working with the marketing team based in Irvine. The team members might consist at any one time of over 100 people located in various places, who travel across the various locations as needed. The final chip integration design (tapeout), which may take up to two months, is always performed at one location because of the need for close coordination. This initially used to be either San Jose or Irvine, but is increasingly being done in Bangalore. Early in the chip development process, one of these three locations takes the lead.

The logic for allowing Bangalore to share the lead position in product development (a status not granted to other locations including Broadcom's offices in Andover, Israel, and Singapore) is that of scale and capability. The Indian team had, between 2003 and 2005, filed for 140 US patents and been granted ten.

Interestingly, despite the progress with the Bangalore team, proximity still matters in some cases. Once a chip has been fully designed, that is, after tapeout, software libraries and firmware are needed to accommodate the specific requirements of different types of customers. These may also change considerably during and after the product's first release. Understanding customer needs was found difficult to undertake from Bangalore (Khare 2006). Hence, in the event that the project is led by Bangalore, one member of the Bangalore team is located in the US on an 8-week rotation after the first release and until maturity.

Broadcom attempts to reduce coordination costs by recruiting key engineers from the US, mostly of Indian origin, as a result of which about 5 per cent of its Indian workforce are Indian expatriates. The firm claims that India has become established as a centre of expertise in embedded software and very large chip development.

The Broadcom case study shows first, that building in offshoring from the beginning into the management structure of a chip project improves the chances of success. The case also shows that coordination costs can be significant; however, strategies such as relocating engineers from their US operations to India appear to make coordination costs lower. However, over time, the expatriate engineers tend to lose the market knowledge that made them valuable, requiring regular rotations between India and the US. Several other firms recognize this constraint and organize such rotations.[14]

Implications of the Case Studies

Extrapolating from this admittedly small base of information, we found two basic models: in the first model, offshoring is a supplement to onshore operations, that is, the offshore facility is intended to lower costs and/or to speed product or product line extensions. In the second

[14]Including Google and Yahoo! (author's interviews).

model, offshore operations are an integral part of the business model. In the first model, the ultimate goal is the same as for the second model, to make them an integral part.

Interestingly, both start-ups and established firms often choose to begin by using an outsourced provider rather than establish their own facilities. The advantage of outsourcing is that it can facilitate a rapid ramp-up. Also, through the operation of the outsourcer it may be possible to learn more about the local environment, thereby facilitating the later establishment of a subsidiary. There are risks to this approach as one cedes control over the labour force to an outside vendor and there are risks of losing IP. The ultimate goal, as noted earlier, for both new and established firms, appears to be to make the offshored operations an integral part of the firm's business. This requires, at some point, the establishment of a subsidiary. While this may sound like an irrevocable end point, we have observed cases of firms in which the more routine in-house work is later contracted out. Established firms have less critical cost concerns and are more likely to create a subsidiary and begin with in-house work right away.

In all cases, coordination costs have been surprisingly high. The fault for this does not lie in inadequate communications facilities but appears to lie in the complex nature of the work, as discussed earlier. The other primary constraint to doing higher value-added work is the difficulty in finding and retaining qualified persons. This most likely arises from the small size of domestic markets and inadequate educational systems. A third finding is that overcoming the problem of the 'trust deficit' is significant even within a firm. It often requires an unusual situation, such as a severe downturn, to convince the management to offshore work.

Table 4.9 summarizes the stages of offshoring described in these cases. Undoubtedly, there will be further stages of evolution.

WORKFORCE ISSUES

Most university education in India is provided by individual states, and these are largely poorly resourced relative to the few well-funded central universities. This creates a quality gap. The generously-funded central universities occupy the upper quality tier and the state universities are, in general, significantly behind. This feature also restricts the natural flow of the best students to successively higher tiers within state-level institutions.

Although private higher education has been a feature of the system from the beginning, it has become important only over the past decade. The change has been policy-driven based on the failure of the pure

TABLE 4.9   Stages of Software Offshoring by US Firms to India

Firm	Work Offshored	Initial Stage Onshore	Offshore Stage 1	Reason for Stage 1*	Offshore Stage 2	Reason for Stage 2
Agilent	Embedded software	In-house	In-house; Non-integral	Control	In-house; Integral	Stabilized coordination in Stage 1
Broadcom	Chip design	In-house	In-house; Integral	Scale		
Align	Production	In-house	In-house; Integral	Scale	Revert to onshore	Geopolitical situation

Note: *in addition to labour cost arbitrage.

public provision approach. Until recently, faculties at even the best engineering institutions, almost all of which are public universities, were not required to do research. Those that chose to do so faced, according to the government's own reckoning, severe problems.

[O]bsolescence of facilities and infrastructure are experienced in many institutions...the IT infrastructure and the use of IT in technical institutions is woefully inadequate...the barest minimum laboratory facilities are available in many of the institutions and very little research activity is undertaken... engineering institutes have not succeeded in developing strong linkages with industry...the curriculum offered is outdated and does not meet the needs of the labor market. (Ministry of Human Resource Development [MHRD] 2001)

Until very recently, nearly all of the best students migrated (Siwek and Furchgott-Roth 1993: 140), although, with increasing opportunities at home, this is likely to lessen.

Prior to 1991, the state took the view that higher education should only be provided by the state. However, the country has seen low rates of enrollment that have increasingly been attributed to exclusive state provision. India's gross enrollment ratio, that is, the number of age-unadjusted enrollees as a share of the eligible population that goes to university is, as of 2008, only 11 per cent, compared with 35 per cent who complete secondary school. While the absence of private provision has not always led to rises in enrollment in other countries—for instance, the state might reduce its commitment to higher education as a result, in

India it has prompted a policy initiative since 1991 to increase the share of private provision. The other driver of private participation has been the policy decision to reverse the historical bias of the state's education spending in favour of tertiary education. Historically, the government has spent about 3–4 per cent of GDP on education and this accounts for 13 per cent of public spending (Kapur and Mehta 2007). These numbers are comparable to many other developing countries such as China. About 15 per cent of the total budget (equal to Rs 120 billion or US$ 3 billion in 2004) is spent on higher education (NUEPA 2007: 23). Of this, about a fourth is spent on technical education. (NUEPA 2007: 5) On a per capita enrollment basis, however, the amount spent on tertiary education is three times that spent on primary and secondary education combined. By contrast, in China, about two-thirds on a per capita enrollment basis is spent on primary and secondary education.

About 15,00,000 students were enrolled in undergraduate degree courses in engineering (all fields) as of 2008. The impact of private provision can be seen in the following data: from a negligible presence up to 1990, as of 2005, they accounted for half of the total undergraduate enrollment of about 10 million students and over 60 per cent of the number of degree-awarding institutions. In more commercially lucrative fields such as engineering, they accounted for over three-fourths of the number of institutions. In engineering, 95 per cent of the increase in enrollment since 1997 has been in private colleges. The storied state-owned Indian Institutes of Technology (IITs), which made up 10 per cent of national engineering enrolment in 1990, now account for less than 2 per cent and graduate 5,000 students a year (NUEPA 2008).

One of the desirable outcomes is increased access. Ten years ago, a child of an agricultural worker was, if educated through secondary school, likely to have studied only in the vernacular, and would thus have been excluded from the higher education engineering degree, which is taught only in English. Even if there was money in the family to pay for tuition, the nearest college was probably too far to allow the student to stay at home; even if she had the money for staying away from home, competition for the limited number of available seats would likely exclude her from even the least meritorious college.

Today, even though private colleges charge, on average, Rs 50,000 a year for tuition, which is three times the tuition fee at a comparable state college, affordability has increased. This is for two reasons. First is the proliferation of colleges. There is a college, most likely two or three, in most small towns. Big cities have many more. Bangalore alone has 110 engineering colleges—almost all private. Small-town students no longer need to live away from home, thus saving on living costs. This can be a significant saving as, for instance, rent for a single room in Bangalore, more than makes up the difference in private and state tuition fees. Second, many of the private colleges have tied up with banks for loans which usually cover half the tuition costs.

The private providers are rapidly catching up with the IITs in quality. The top quartile of the graduates of the top local private colleges in Bangalore is now considered equal in quality to those at the fiftieth percentile in the IITs. The top quartile at national colleges such as the National Institutes of Technology, are deemed equal to the seventy-fifth percentile of the IITs. A thousand colleges (of the nearly 2,000 that offer engineering degrees in India) are deemed to meet the standards of the top three IT firms and their graduates are thus eligible for recruitment. A decade ago, there were only fifty colleges that met their standards.[15]

There are caveats to the seemingly successful story of higher education. One of the concerns of regulators is that as control has shifted from New Delhi to the states, the weak states have not been able to keep up with the strong states, thus increasing the intellectual gap between them. A second concern is the continued absence of a research agenda in these colleges.

Table 4.10 summarizes the situation with regard to workforce supply as of 2008 in the other countries of South Asia in relation to India.

TABLE 4.10   Workforce Supply in South Asia (2008)

Country	Annual No. of Graduates in IT/ Related Fields*	Annual Growth Rate (%)	Share of Private Provision	Starting Wage in IT Services per Annum
Bangladesh	5,500	20	25	$3,500
India	350,000	25	80	$7,500
Pakistan	20,000	30	30	$7,500
Sri Lanka	3,500	16	0	$2,000

Source: Bangladesh—'Software and IT Industry in Bangladesh', Basis Report (2008); India—NUEPA (2007, 2008); Pakistan—http://www.hec.gov.pk/QualityAssurance/Statistics/; Sri Lanka—SLICTA (2007).

Note: *refers to computer science, computer engineering, electrical engineering, electronics engineering, communications, and IT.

[15]Author's interviews and Dossani and Patibandla (2008).

In summary, the workforce differences between the four countries appear to pivot on a single issue: one of output rather than the quality of output, and the driving force for change is the enabling of private sector provision in higher education. On the first aspect, all four countries' engineers appear to be able to do the full range of software work. For various reasons, such as scale, only India and Pakistan appear to get the more sophisticated work. Only India, of the four South Asian countries, delegates significant responsibility for higher education to individual states. Yet, Pakistan's more centralized approach appears to be succeeding because of enabling private access. Bangladesh also enables private provision and so might appear to be a counter-example to the proposition. However, its reforms are still in the early days, which may explain why the quality of private provision is weak. India went through the same situation in its first five years after reforms. Sri Lanka does not allow private provision largely due to lack of political consensus and appears to have suffered severely in workforce output as a result.

THE ROLE OF INSTITUTIONS

The Indian software industry is unique among the IT industries of developing nations in a significant respect: the limited, almost non-existent, role of government policy in the inception of the industry. Countries as diverse as Ireland, Israel, and Taiwan would not have IT industries today without government initiatives from their origins in the 1970s onwards. Yet, in India, the state did not just neglect the industry, it was actively hostile—it wanted the public sector to succeed and so would not allow private firms to do any domestic business, either in hardware or software.

The fundamentals that instead drove the software industry were two: (a) a cadre of engineers, educated over the previous decades in the best engineering colleges of the country, who had limited opportunities in India. Many left India to study or work in developed countries, including a majority of graduates from IITs, but there were enough working in India's stagnant engineering industries who were available to join the initiatives of the US-educated returnees when they started the industry; and (b) entrepreneurs who were returnees of US engineering colleges, and who received the support of local conglomerates to set up their businesses.

In the 1980s, the Indian state turned positive towards private software, as did the other states in South Asia. Since India, for the previous decade, had merely been exporting engineers, the others were not disadvantaged by being latecomers. That is why they started at the same level of value addition.

During the 1980s, the policy reforms detailed for India in the earlier sections were also implemented in the rest of South Asia—industrial parks, openness to foreign firms, tax breaks, and reduced tariffs. Although education policy remained backward and unchanged, there was a sufficient stock of engineers to keep the industry growing.

A question often raised in IT is the role played by IP protection. In fact, it played no role for several decades. The reason is that the Indian markets were too small for the packaged software business to be developed. This is the reason why the Indian software industry was devoted entirely to services, which is not an IP-protected business.

As of 2008, the countries of South Asia have signed WTO/TRIPS protocols on IP protection, although the quality of implementation varies. If the countries of South Asia become proficient in packaged software production, this will improve their policymakers' incentives to strengthen implementation.

By the 1990s, the IT industry in India and Pakistan had grown large enough to become the largest employer of engineers in the two countries. As labour shortages loomed, government policy in education started to respond. The system was gradually 'privatized' by allowing private provision and through state subsidy for private provision.

The state of telecommunications also started becoming a constraint in the 1990s, primarily because of the advent of the internet. As more and more business was done over the internet, the IT sector started facing bandwidth constraints in accessing and implementing business. Once again, government policy was responsive. Indian policy turned favourable in 1999 and Pakistan policy in 2004.

Unfortunately for Bangladesh and Sri Lanka, the state has been slower to respond in both education and telecommunications. Although Bangladesh's policy, as of 2008, is similar to India's and Pakistan's, its quality of policy regulation is significantly weaker. In Sri Lanka, on the other hand, while the quality of telecommunications regulation is high, the state has not yet started reforming education.

This section has shown that the 'endowments' that really matter are entrepreneurship and education, while the policy fundamentals that matter are in education and telecommunications. Other privileges and targeted incentives, such as tax breaks, do not matter critically.

PROSPECTS FOR REGIONAL LINKAGES

We have shown in this chapter that India has become an important participant in the global IT industry. India's software exports of US$ 29 billion for the fiscal year ended March 2008 accounted for 60 per cent of non-US exports of software and 60 per cent of global outsourcing of IT services. In certain fields of software development, notably customs applications development, India is rapidly becoming the global centre of the industry.

The rest of South Asia is another 2.5 per cent, accounted for mainly by Pakistan's IT exports of US$ 1 billion in 2007 (Table 4.11). Software exports are also an important source of employment, as seen in Table 4.11.

The achievements of South Asia are remarkable given that they were built on the capital and enterprise of domestic firms. This is still the case for Bangladesh, Pakistan, and Sri Lanka. By contrast, Vietnam's software industry, which is FDI-driven, exported US$ 300 million in 2007 and employs 15,000 engineers (see http://www.business-in-asia. com/software_industry_in_vietnam.htm).

As of 2008, there are almost no linkages among the region's software industries. India's software industry—perhaps because of its relatively early start in South Asia and also due to the high quality of its workforce—spans the supply chain. This raises the important question of how the supply chain may be restructured if there was greater openness to intra-regional trade and investment in South Asia.

TABLE 4.11   Software Exports and Employment

Country	Exports ($ m)	Workforce	Revenue/Employee
Bangladesh	26	1,200	21,600
India	29,300	865,000	33,900
Pakistan	1,000	40,000	25,000
Sri Lanka	150	9,000	16,000

Source: Bangladesh—Bangladesh Bank (2008). India—NASSCOM (2008: 50–1); Pakistan—http://www.pseb.org.pk/item/industry_overview, accessed on 6 June 2008; http://pashanews.org/wp-content/uploads/2008/05/psha_study_executive_summary. pdf; and http://www.pasha.org.pk/show_page.htm?input=page_131220070524, accessed on 6 June 2008. Sri Lanka—http://srilanka.usembassy.gov/22march07. html, accessed on 8 September 2008.

Notes: All data are for financial year 2007/8, except Bangladesh, which is for financial year 2006/7; Bangladesh and Sri Lanka data include ITES such as BPO; India and Pakistan data exclude ITES. Pakistan's exports consist primarily of software services. India's exports are comprised of software services (78 per cent). The rest are engineering and R&D services.

The first aspect is technical. The components of the supply chain are largely scale-neutral. Evidence for this comes from the US where, except for the programming function (applications development), the software services business is fragmented by service layers, and small firms dominate the business.

The scalability of the programming function is partly because a large firm can deploy its best programmers for the most difficult parts of the programming function such as system specification, while using the weaker programmers for more routine work such as running quality checks. It, therefore, helps to have a large number of programmers of different qualities (and corresponding costs).

However, scalability is also an outcome of how the business has changed. The average size of the time taken to create enterprise software in the financial services industry is typical: it rose from less than five programming man-years in the 1980s to over twenty man-years by 2000 (Ramadorai 2002). The reason is the increasing complexity of the underlying business.

As a result, both in the US and India, large firms that undertake the programming function have risen in market share. In India, for instance, as Table 4.4 shows, the share of large firms rose between 1990 and 2008. As a share of value, however, programming's share is small, accounting for about 25 per cent of the value of the typical finished software, even though it accounts for a majority of the engineer man-hours. This is because the other software components are higher value added, as shown in Table 4.1.

In the event of greater regional integration of the software industry, fragmentation in the style of East Asian manufacturing would be a favourable outcome. In East Asia's relations with China in manufacturing, there is considerable evidence of fragmentation of the manufacturing supply chain (Athukorala 2008). China plays the role of assembler and the rest of East and Southeast Asian countries either build components (Malaysia, Indonesia, the Philippines, and Thailand) or undertake design (Singapore, Korea, Taiwan, and Japan). This is a consequence of many reasons: China's later starting point for liberalization in some cases (vis-à-vis ASEAN), and its less well-educated workforce relative to the NIEs.

At present, the smaller South Asian countries focus on programming, and only Pakistan has a presence of any significance in system integration. Will the smaller countries of South Asia, in the event of regional integration, undertake the high value-added components while India will put it all together (system integration) as well as do the programming work? This is an unlikely outcome.

This is because of the skills in each country. Unlike China's position in East Asian manufacturing, India has the highest levels of skills in software among the South Asian countries. Hence, in the event of regional integration, it is likely *ceteris paribus* that India will capture the scalable work (programming) as well as the skill-intensive work such as system integration.

In reality, this has already happened. The software industry relies primarily on exports, and overseas clients have already chosen to pass on the programming work to India. The only reason why any programming work goes to the smaller South Asian countries is that the wage rates are low enough to compensate for reduced productivity (Table 4.10).

This implies that opening up to regional integration will not adversely affect the industry in the smaller countries. But can it help? The answer is an unqualified yes. This is for the following reasons: First, as of 2008, the best engineers in the smaller countries, who are capable of more sophisticated work such as system integration and RDES, are excluded from such work. DMNCs have largely avoided programming operations in such countries due to the small pool of talent available. Their systems integration projects are then fulfilled in countries that have demonstrated capabilities to do such work and, therefore, excludes the smaller countries of South Asia. Second, in the event that India gets such work, it fulfils it internally due to the lack of regional integration. In the event of integration, at the right wage rate, a system integrator from the smaller countries would be able to compete with an Indian firm, while still earning more than at present as a programmer.

Presumably, Indian firms are more likely to be willing to set up shop in the smaller countries in the event of permitted integration than DMNCs, due to their greater familiarity with the operating environment. This will help overcome the trust deficit, a key factor, as discussed earlier.

In summary, in the event of greater integration, India's role will show some similarities to China's role in East Asia because India will be the producer of scalable activities (in this case, programming), and due to DMNC presence, will provide the capacity to assemble sophisticated projects together (system integration). But, India will also compete in scale-neutral activities such as design due to its advanced skills. Hence, unlike China, India will span the supply chain.

Of course, political and social contexts matter as well. The political context has two aspects of relevance, the first being the difficult internal political situations in Bangladesh, Pakistan, and Sri Lanka, as well as the geopolitical challenges raised by the US war on terror, in which

Pakistan plays a role that is seen to have negative implications by US firms. The social context is the role played by the diaspora, particularly in the US, and the cultural resistance to offshoring in many developed country firms.

In both these respects, despite the economic advantages to integration, there are tough challenges ahead to achieving it. This is where India ought to play a far more responsible role than it has played to date. At present, India tends to avoid describing itself to the world as a South Asian country for fear of being tainted by the political difficulties of its neighbours. While this may be an appropriate face for the West, India should realize that it, too, will benefit economically from greater integration of the software industry.

The following are some steps for Indian policymakers to consider that ought to be acceptable to South Asian policymakers. First, Indian IT firms should be incentivized by the Indian government to open production operations in neighbouring countries, thus offering employment and helping to bridge the trust deficit. Second, Indian venture capital firms should be allowed to operate in the rest of South Asia. This will lead to a transfer of process knowhow to the rest of South Asia. Third, software engineers from the smaller countries of South Asia should be allowed to work in the Indian IT industry.

CONCLUSION

The objective of this chapter was to describe the evolution of the software industry in India and the potential for a regional cluster. We showed that in India's case, the industry started due to the initiative of returnee engineers working for big firms, while surrounded by hostile government policies. A stagnant industrial environment led to adequate (and low-cost) supplies of trained manpower. By the 1980s, the policy environment became positive; the demonstration effect of India, similar manpower policies, and now-positive government policies sparked off software industries in the rest of South Asia. Foreign participation, which had played no role in the industry's origins in India, started to play an important role in India by demonstrating new business models and resolving the trust deficit. As education, fiscal, and infrastructure policies turned positive in South Asia (though at different rates in the different countries), all four countries' software industries took off. As of 2008, India is the most sophisticated and spans the supply chain; Pakistan follows in size and sophistication, while Bangladesh, hampered by weak regulation, and Sri Lanka, suffering from an ineffective tertiary education policy, remain behind.

As of 2008, India accounts for 60 per cent of all non-US software exports and 60 per cent of all global software outsourcing. India is central to any large, global software outsourcing project. However, it is still an insignificant force in some components of software, notably packaged software. The latter is true of the rest of South Asia. We showed that this was primarily due to weak domestic markets and the problems of coordination.

Finally, we considered whether regional integration would produce a South Asian software cluster and the consequent policy requirements. Investment liberalization in South Asia will likely lead to higher trade. The Sri Lanka–India bilateral agreement shows this. In software, India can be the hub for organizing the work, while fulfilment can happen in the other countries of South Asia. Cross-recognition of certifications and degrees, followed by allowing professionals to work anywhere in South Asia will also help. The best software professionals from Bangladesh, Pakistan, and Sri Lanka will then probably spend some years in India, enhance their competence, and some will return to their home countries. However, no other significant policy coordination is needed. Instead, what is primarily needed is to overcome the political barriers to integration, for which India could play an enabling role—a role that it has hitherto shrunk from playing.

ANNEXURE 4A.1 PACKAGED AND CUSTOM-MADE SOFTWARE

Software is usually classified by type of use and customization.
Types of software by usage:

1. System-level software: Programmes that manage the internal operations of the computer such as operating system software, driver software, virus scan software, and utilities.
2. Tools/platform software: Programmes that help applications to work better such as database management software.
3. Applications: Programmes that deliver solutions to the end-user such as word processing software and financial accounting software.

We define two categories of software, differentiated by their degree of customization. We use the North American Industry Classification System (NAICS) definitions for the difference between packaged software and customized software.

Software publishers such as Microsoft come under NAICS 5112 Publishers of Packaged Software, that is:

establishments primarily engaged in computer software publishing or publishing and reproduction. Establishments in this industry carry out operations necessary for producing and distributing computer software, such as designing, providing documentation, assisting in installation, and providing support services to software purchasers. These establishments may design, develop, and publish, or publish only. (http://www.census.gov/epcd/naics02)

Enterprises that fall in the NAICS 5112 category create software products or packages. Similar in some respects to mass manufacturing, software products target the general consumer market and capitalize on economies of scale. Software products may be shrink-wrapped and transported physically or made available for download over the internet.

This is distinct from NAICS 54151 Computer Systems Design and Related Services, which comprises:

establishments primarily engaged in providing expertise in the field of information technologies through one or more of the following activities: (a) writing, modifying, testing, and supporting software to meet the needs of a particular customer; (b) planning and designing computer systems that integrate computer hardware, software, and communication technologies; (c) on-site management and operation of clients' computer systems and/or data processing facilities; and (d) other professional and technical computer-related advice and services. (see http://www.census.gov/epcd/naics02)

In contrast to one-size-fits-all software products enterprises in NAICS 54151 create custom software. Custom software is often employed where there are no software products available, as in highly specialized processes, or to integrate disparate software products into a cohesive system. The latter process is quite common where large software products such as ERP or CRM suites must be integrated into already existing enterprise systems. Custom software may be constructed by using traditional programming languages and tools or, as is the case with many large software products, proprietary scripting or configuration languages.

Being made-to-order, custom software is more geographically constrained than products. Proximity to the stakeholder is often crucial, especially if tacit (uncodified) knowledge is to be exchanged. In consequence, software products are more readily exportable than custom software.

Nearly every computer needs systems software and the mass market provides an almost ideal condition for creating systems software as a packaged product. Thus, today systems software has evolved to where it is marketed almost exclusively as a packaged product. Over time, the need to maintain compatibility across operating systems has been a critical requirement of both enterprise and retail users, and this has grown with the internet.

As a result a few operating systems dominate the computing landscape and, in turn, have considerable pricing power. Demand for systems software, when compared to demand for applications software, is relatively inelastic with respect to pricing. Consumers of systems software such as high-availability server operating systems and real time embedded operating systems are willing to pay higher prices for quality and interoperability. Consequently, the producers of such software are less sensitive to production costs when compared to product quality and the need for highly specialized skills.

Although packaged software is designed to serve a range of customer requirements, there is a limit to the variation it can incorporate. Beyond this limit, software will need to be written to a customer's specifications. In an industry such as banking, for example, customer requirements vary significantly so that there is often a need for custom software. In general, the more varied an end-user's needs from another end-user, the more likely is the software to be customized. Since variations in needs appear most at the stage of applications, most customized software is applications software. These attributes are summarized in Table 4A.1.1.

The US is the market leader in software product development, accounting for 41 per cent of the industry, which had revenue of US$ 250 billion in 2007. Its share of exported software products is undoubtedly higher because many countries like Japan and Brazil that produce software products do so for protected local markets.

Custom software is part of a larger category called software services. We also display India's market share as a proxy for offshoreability. As discussed earlier, and as may be seen in Table 4.2, software services comprise a significantly larger market than software products. The programming function, which has been modularized and, as discussed, is technically the easiest to offshore (even with poor bandwidth) is relatively small in market share. Yet it remains the most significant work-type for

TABLE 4A.1.1   Software Types and Programmes Used

	Packaged Software Used by	Custom Software Used by
Operating system	All users	None
Tools	Most users	Some users
Applications	Small and large users	Large users

Source: Author's compilation.

South Asia. Managed services are the next easiest to offshore, assuming that the host country has adequate bandwidth and is not perceived to be a politically risky destination. Software system integration and contract RDES offer opportunities for offshoring, and are relatively high value-added activities. However, they usually need the most technical and managerial skills. The remaining activities in the table below, that is, hardware and software system integration, and IT education and training remain activities with a high need for face-to-face interaction. Hence, their offshoring is occurring relatively slowly.

ANNEXURE 4A.2 THE ISV INDUSTRY

The ISV industry was created by two events, both related to market leader IBM: First, in 1956, in order to settle a long-standing antitrust suit by the federal government, IBM agreed to cease offering computer consulting advice, as part of a consent decree (McKenna 2006: 20).[16] Leading accounting firms such as Arthur Andersen then began offering computer consulting services. Second, in 1969, IBM decided to un-bundle its mainframe operating system, applications software and hardware by creating open standards. Subsequently, some end-user firms set up in-house software development and maintenance operations (Table 4A.2.1, column B) while others outsourced the work (columns C–E). The resulting ISV businesses are shown in Table 4A.2.1.

TABLE 4A.2.1   Client–Vendor Grid during 1970–9

Clients' actions =>	External data processing and managed services	Client owns hardware			
		Develop and maintain own software	Buy bundled software and outsource maintenance services	Buy software products from ISVs	Buy custom software services
	(A)	(B)	(C)	(D)	(E)
ISVs' respon-ses =>	Managed services, electronic data processing	No role for ISVs	Integration of hardware and software; software maintenance	System level and applications products	Custom applications software

Source: Author's compilation based on Steinmuller (1996).

[16]When the consent decree was lifted in 1991, IBM immediately created an IT consulting group. Within five years, it had an annual revenue of $11 billion (McKenna 2006: 23).

Columns A to E are not intended to describe mutually exclusive choices. For example, a firm might purchase system level software products while developing its own applications.

The columns are arranged by sequentially dominant work-types over the decade, starting with the shift from external data processing and managed services (Column A) to in-house hardware at the start of the decade. Initially, firms developed their own software (B). As the 1970s progressed, hardware and software became more complex making in-house software development and management more difficult. This led to the outsourcing of system integration (C) and then to the sourcing of system level and applications products (D). The move to outsourcing customized applications (E) was due to the failure of industry-specific products to meet the needs of the more sophisticated users, particularly large banks (Steinmuller 1996: 30).

In the 1980s, the IBM PC was introduced. Over the subsequent decade, IBM lost control of the operating system to Microsoft Windows, which combined with the Intel microprocessor (Wintel) to become a market-created standard by the late 1980s. The result was a decline in hardware prices and rising demand for applications. Unlike mainframes, the PC was for individual users, and they were reliant on packaged software.

The PC of the 1980s lacked both the programming capacity and performance needed by mid-size and large enterprises. Hence, it had no impact on the custom software business. However, it spawned the creation of a mass market for retail packaged software.

The workstation, introduced in the early 1980s, had many end-uses for enterprises, but could also be used for stand-alone programming for mainframes. The widespread adoption of Unix as the operating system for all computers, jointly with the workstation (in short, the U-W standard), revolutionized the ISV industry. An ISV could now own a workstation made by any manufacturer, yet write programmes for a client whose installed hardware might be of a different brand (including a mainframe). In other words, software creation became platform independent or modularized from the hardware component. With the simultaneous widespread adoption of C as the programming language, the other functions of software creation such as system architecture, design, and integration could be done separately from programming, thus modularizing the programming component and enabling its remote production. Programming could now be done anywhere in the world by programmers whose only raw material, apart from a workstation, was a specified software system, that is, the programmers did not need to know which firm's hardware the programme would work on and even the type of application the programme was intended to support. In the 1990s, the success of database software packages further simplified the creation of applications software. The platform independence that arose from the U-W standard, combined with the rise in demand for custom software by small firms, resulted in the growth of a large custom software industry.

The workstation also had sophisticated graphics and the computational capacity needed by small enterprises. Such firms shifted from outsourcing data processing services to running their own workstations. In the 1980s, the first workstation-based local area networks were established and increased the demand for more sophisticated software for running such networks and for applications compatible with networked users.

In the 1990s, the rising computing power of the PC improved its capacity to process programmes written in Unix/C, thus increasing its acceptability in the enterprise. Given its relatively low and declining costs due to its mass market, the PC would supercede the workstation as the hardware platform for programming. Later in the decade, the success of PC-based networks increased the accessibility of applications to many more users within the enterprise.

The spread of the internet from the late 1990s was accelerated by declining bandwidth and storage costs. The internet provided a platform for networked development of software, and for software installation, hosting, and maintenance. This influenced the location of data, which moved away from servers located at the premises of the enterprise to remote data centres. The internet also significantly reduced the cost of collaboration among remote teams. These factors further reduced the need for proximity between user groups and between developers and users.

Since the internet has become established, several new models of preparing and delivering software have appeared. These include service-oriented architecture that provides a standards-based environment for sharing services, independent of development technologies and platforms; network-based access to and maintenance of software (software-as-a-service); and open source software, that is, software based on a non-proprietary code, whose development relies on the voluntary contributions of networked developers. With the exception of the Linux open-source operating system software, whose market share of webserver operating systems is believed to be about a third, (although less than 2 per cent of all operating systems) these have not impacted the spatial distribution of software development (see www.idc.com/getdoc.jsp?containerID=202388).

The new twist in the provision of software services is that the required interaction between the seller and the consumer has been substantially limited. The advances in IT made possible the parsing of the provision of certain services into components requiring different levels of skill and interactivity. Apart from the standardization of hardware and software platforms and reduced cost of computing power discussed earlier, new language structuring mechanisms such as object-orientation were important. Further, the internet allowed for the standardization of data-transmission platforms. As a result, certain portions of the serviced activity—that might or might not be skill-intensive, but required low levels of face-to-face interactivity—could be relocated offshore.

REFERENCES

Arora, A. and S. Athreye. 2002. 'The Software Industry and India's Economics Development', *Information Economics and Policy*, 14(2): 253–73.

Athreye, S. 2005. 'The Indian Software Industry and Its Evolving Service Capability', *Industrial and Corporate Change*, 14: 393–418.

Athukorala, Prem-Chandra. 2008. 'China's Integration into Global Production Networks and Its Implications for Export-led Growth Strategies in Other Countries in the Region', RSPAS Departmental Working Papers 2008–04, Australian National University, Canberra.

Balasubramanyam, V. and A. Balasubramanyam. 2000. 'The Software Cluster in Bangalore', in John Dunning (ed.), *Regions, Globalization and the Knowledge-based Economy*, pp. 349–63. Oxford: Oxford University Press.

Bangladesh Bank. 2008. *Software and IT Services Industry in Bangladesh*. Dhaka: Bangladesh Bank.

D'Costa, A. 2002. 'Software Outsourcing and Development Policy Implications: An Indian Perspective', *International Journal of Technology Management*, 24(7/8): 51–87.

Dossani, R. and M. Patibandla. 2010. (forthcoming). 'Preparing India for a Services Economy: An Evaluation of Higher Education in IT', in H. Bidgoli (ed.), *Handbook of Technology Management*. Hoboken: John Wiley & Sons.

Dossani, R. and A. Manwani. 2005. 'Agilent's Supply Chain: A Locational Analysis of its Indian Operations', paper presented at Stanford University Conference on Globalization of Services, Stanford, C.A., June.

Government of India. 2000. *Finance Minister's Budget Speech*, Ministry of Finance, Government of India, New Delhi.

Heeks, R. 1996. *India's Software Industry*. New Delhi: Sage Publications.

Heitzman, J. 1999. 'Corporate Strategy and Planning in the Science City: Bangalore as Silicon Valley', *Economic and Political Weekly*, 34(5): 2–11.

Kapur, D. and P.B. Mehta. 2007. 'Indian Higher Education Reform: From Half-Baked Socialism to Half-Baked Capitalism', Working Paper, Brookings Institution, Washington, D.C.

Khare, R. 2006. CEO of Broadcom, India. Personal Interview with Rafiq Dossani, 2/1/06.

McKenna, C. 2006. *The World's Newest Profession*. Cambridge: Cambridge University Press.

Ministry of Human Resource Development (HRD). 2001. 'Technical Education Quality Improvement Project of the Government of India', Ministry of HRD, New Delhi.

Naidu, B. 2002. Personal Interview with Rafiq Dossani, 15 February 2002.

NASSCOM. 2002–8. *The IT Industry in India: a Strategic Review*. New Delhi: NASSCOM.

NUEPA (National University of Educational Planning and Administration). 2007. *Annual Report*. New Delhi: NUEPA.

———. 2008. *Annual Report*. New Delhi: NUEPA.

Parathasarathy, B. 2000. 'Globalization and Agglomeration in Newly Industrializing Countries: The State and the Information Technology Industry in Bangalore, India', PhD thesis, University of California, Berkeley.

Parthasarathy, S. 2003. CEO Aztec, Personal Interview with Rafiq Dossani, March 2003.

Pakistan Software Houses Association. 2008. Available at http://www.pasha.org.pk/, accessed in October 2009.

Premji, A. 2003. Chairperson of Wipro, Personal Communication with Rafiq Dossani, 12 Februray 2003.

Ramadorai, S. 2002. CEO of TCS, Personal Communication with Rafiq Dossani, 29 November 2002.

Rosenberg, N. and D. Mowery. 1978. 'The Influence of Market Demand upon Innovation: A Critical Review of Recent Empirical Studies', *Research Policy*, 8: 102–53.

Rubin, B. 1985. 'Economic Liberalization and the Indian State', *Third World Quarterly*, 7(4): 942–57.

Siwek, S. and H. Furchgott-Roth. 1993. *International Trade in Computer Software*. Westport, C.T.: Quorum Books.

SLICTA. 2007. *Rising Demand*. Colombo: Sri Lanka Information and Communication Technology Association.

Sridharan, E. 1996. *The Political Economy of Industrial Promotion: Indian, Brazilian and Korean Electronics in Comparative Perspective*. Westport, C.T.: Praeger Publishers.

———. 2004. 'Evolving Towards Innovation? The Recent Evolution and Future Trajectory of the Indian Software Industry', in A. D'Costa and E. Sridharan (eds), *India in the Global Software Industry: Innovation, Firm Strategies and Development*, pp. 27–50. New York: Palgrave Macmillan.

Steinmuller, W. 1996. 'The U.S. Software Industry: An Analysis and Interpretive History', in D. Mowery (ed.), *The International Computer Software Industry: A Comparative Study of Industry Evolution and Structure*, pp. 15–52. Oxford: Oxford University Press.

5

Migration and Remittances

Sanket Mohapatra and Çağlar Özden

Services and economic growth go hand in hand. The service sector contributes a larger portion of the gross domestic product (GDP) in Organisation for Economic Co-operation and Development (OECD) and developing countries and its share tends to increase with economic growth. Yet, the role of services in economic growth and development is generally overlooked in literature and policy debates. One of the main reasons for this bias is the implicit assumption among development economists and policymakers that growth and development accompany the rise of the manufacturing sector in general, and manufactured exports in particular. East Asia, especially China, is the prime example of this phenomenon where massive investment in manufacturing fuelled rapid economic growth, and integration with the global economy occurred through manufactured goods trade. However, a close observation of the more advanced OECD economies clearly indicates that this assumption may be wrong. Services are important both as direct contributors to economic growth and as efficiency increasing inputs into other sectors of the economy.

The assumption that global integration has to occur through trade in manufactured goods has also proven to be wrong in the case of South Asia. For example, the most exciting feature of the Indian miracle is the story of the information technology (IT) and other service sectors which catapulted parts of the Indian economy to the forefront of the technology frontier. The exports of these services can be impersonal where the provider does not cross national boundaries and services are exported digitally from an office in Bangalore. Or the software engineer from South Asia might physically move to a company in Silicon Valley joining thousands of other highly educated immigrants.

In addition to IT services, there is another range of mostly low-skilled services sold in international labour markets by millions of South Asian workers. These are the migrants who work as maids, cooks, and construction workers in relatively difficult social and physical environments, mostly in the Middle East. They work, save, and send billions of dollars every year to lift millions of other people back home out of poverty. Their remittances have so far been a very stable and important source of foreign exchange earnings for countries in South Asia, especially during the recent global financial crisis. This chapter analyses the main patterns of these migration flows and remittances to the region.

As the rest of the chapter argues, migration and remittances are a very important part of the economic growth and poverty reduction story in South Asia. While millions of highly skilled engineers, scientists, and managers work in the western OECD markets or for companies located in South Asia but supply these markets, a significantly larger number of unskilled or semi-skilled workers have migrated to the Persian Gulf countries as well as many other parts of the world. The highly skilled workers form the link between Western and South Asian companies and become the main conduits of technology transfer that create the IT sector in South Asia. On the other hand, the remittances sent by unskilled temporary migrants sustain higher living standards, enable children to attend school, and families to afford medicines for millions of people at the lower end of the social and economic spectrum. The migrants' savings become the capital for small enterprises which would otherwise suffer from lack of access to financing. In short, both the South Asian engineers building the next generation internet applications or the construction workers at the site of another dream hotel in Dubai contribute significantly to the South Asian economic development.

MIGRATION PATTERNS

International migration is a response to differences in living standards, wages, and other supply and demand conditions in labour markets in different countries. This is most clearly exemplified in South Asia, which has been a net exporter of millions of migrants to other parts of the world

TABLE 5.1   **Migrants from South Asia in 2000**

(in thousand)

	EU	USA and Canada	Middle East	Other South Asian	Rest of the World	Total
Afghanistan	94	70	2,338	44	106	2,652
Bangladesh	285	122	666	5,534	266	6,873
India	793	1,400	4,049	2,045	755	9,042
Nepal	19	14	188	911	63	1,195
Pakistan	513	313	28	1,422	178	2,454
Sri Lanka	197	118	967	278	147	1,707

Source: Parsons et al. (2007).

(starting with the British colonial rule) due to its high population density and excess labour supply. Descendants of those migrants constitute large portions of the current populations in many countries in the Caribbean, Africa, and East Asia. Despite the end of British colonial rule, South Asian migration continues to this day with western OECD countries and the oil-rich countries in the Persian Gulf becoming the main destinations over the last decades (see Table 5.1).

Currently, almost 24 million people born in South Asia are living outside their countries of birth. This is around 1.5 per cent of the total population of the region. Indians constitute a majority of the migrants due to the sheer size of the country, but the rate of emigration is higher for smaller countries such as Nepal, Sri Lanka, and Afghanistan. In terms of destinations, 35 per cent of the migrants are in the Middle Eastern countries, close to 20 per cent are in the wealthy OECD countries, and 43 per cent are in other countries in the region. Among the most important examples of the latter are the Nepalis, Pakistanis, and Bangladeshis who are currently living in India.

The characteristics of migrants and nature of migration are quite different for migrants heading for western OECD countries versus the oil-rich Middle Eastern countries. Migrants to OECD tend to be relatively high-skilled, are able to migrate with their families, and are likely to migrate permanently if they choose to do so. They enjoy greater employment rights and assimilate more easily. On the other hand, migrants in the Middle East are mostly single people who migrate for limited time periods to save and send remittances to their families back home. The main reasons for this stark divergence are the types of labour demands and migration policies in the destination regions.

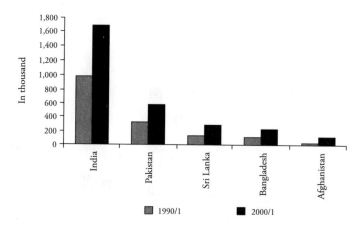

FIGURE 5.1   Total Migration from Main South Asian Countries
to OECD

Source: Docquier and Marfouk (2006).

Figure 5.1 shows the current distribution of migrants from the five major South Asian countries in the labour forces in the OECD countries. India has the largest number of migrants to OECD countries and the difference between India and the other four countries is significant. Data show that in 2000 there were close to 1.7 million Indians in OECD labour markets followed by Pakistanis (581,000) and Sri Lankans (292,000).

The preferred destinations for South Asian migrants are the UK and US which jointly account for 43 per cent of the total migrants to the OECD countries as of 2001. The main reasons for this pattern are colonial linkages, linguistic familiarity, and the relatively liberal migration policies of these countries. Data indicate that the US and Canada have also experienced the largest increase in South Asian migration between 1990 and 2000. The number of South Asian migrants in the US labour market jumped by 160 per cent (from 427,000 to over 1.1 million) while in Canada the number rose by 118 per cent from (193,000 to 422,000). This rapid growth implies that the US saw its share of South Asian migrants in the OECD more than double from 10 per cent in 1990 to 25 per cent in 2001, making it the largest single destination. This rapid flow of migration to the US is clear in Figure 5.2.

Number of South Asian Migrants in Major OECD Destinations

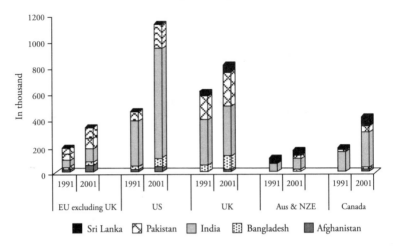

FIGURE 5.2   Main Destinations of South Asian Migrants

Source: Docquier and Marfouk (2006).

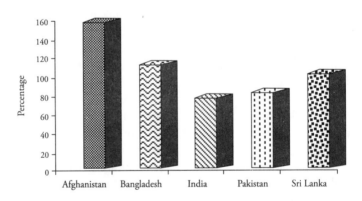

FIGURE 5.3   Change in the Number of Migrants from South Asia
to OECD Countries

Source: Docquier and Marfouk (2006) and authors' calculations.

South Asian countries exhibit variations in terms of recent migration
trends. Afghanistan had the largest increase in the number of migrants
to OECD countries between 1991 and 2000, followed by Bangladesh
and Sri Lanka (Figure 5.3). While it is still the largest source of migrants

in absolute terms, India had the smallest percentage increase in the number of migrants during that period. There are various reasons and implications for these rapid changes. Political and economic conditions have spurred the increase in migration from Afghanistan and Sri Lanka, while economic stability and growth decreased the incentives to migrate from India. These patterns imply that the pace of migration from India is likely to slow further if economic conditions in the country continue to improve.

Another important feature of South Asian migration to the OECD countries is the relatively high level of the education of the migrants which might have both negative and positive effects on source countries. Among South Asian countries, Sri Lanka and Afghanistan have the largest share of the tertiary educated labour force emigrating. Figure 5.4 shows that in 2000, migrants with tertiary education or higher accounted for 25 per cent of the total tertiary educated labour force in Afghanistan and over 20 per cent in Sri Lanka. Another striking feature about migration trends among skilled workers is the surge in the ratio of educated migrants from Afghanistan since 1980 and from Pakistan since 1990.

Migration of highly-educated workers is generally driven by the same forces that motivate overall migration. These are the differences in economic and political conditions as well as future prospects at home and in the destination countries. Educated workers have the linguistic and professional skills that are highly demanded in the destination countries, and hence they are more adaptive to new

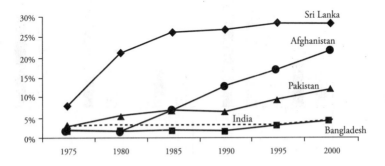

FIGURE 5.4   Immigration Rates of Tertiary Educated Workers to OECD Countries between 1975 and 2000

Source: Docquier and Marfouk (2006).

environments and capable of dealing with migration procedures. As a result, they are likely to respond more readily than unskilled workers to worsening economic or political conditions at home. Therefore, the ratio of skilled migrants to the overall labour force might increase as conditions deteriorate in the home country. However, this leads to further economic decline and hampers reconstruction efforts in the long run.

Even though OECD countries are similar at the outset, there are large differences in terms of the distribution of highly skilled South Asian migrants among them. Several factors are important: migration policies of the destination countries, the social and cultural familiarity of the migrants with the destination country (such as colonial or linguistic links), and perceptions among migrants about labour markets and social conditions in destination countries (that is, in countries where they could perform better and would be socially accepted).

The US and Canada are the most attractive destinations for the highly educated migrants from South Asia. As seen in Figure 5.5, in 2000, 75 per cent of the South Asian migrants in the US labour force and 57 per cent of those in Canada had tertiary education. An important observation is that the share of educated workers among South Asian migrants in the US remained constant and increased only slightly in Canada between 1990 and 2000. By comparison, the share of educated

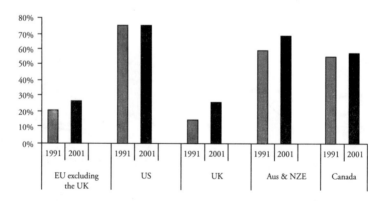

FIGURE 5.5   Percentage of South Asian Migrants with Tertiary Education

Source: Docquier and Marfouk (2006).

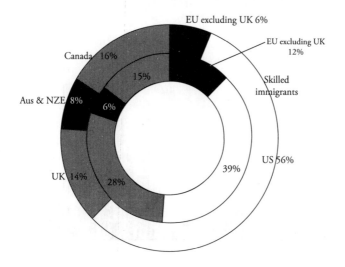

FIGURE 5.6   Share of Major OECD Regions among Immigrants
and Highly Educated Immigrants (2001)

Source: Docquier and Marfouk (2006) and authors' calculations.

migrants increased noticeably in the UK, from 14 per cent to 26 per
cent, and in the European Union (EU) from about 19 per cent to 25
per cent. But these are still rather low compared to migrants in the US,
Canada, and Australia.

Overall, the US attracts a larger share of educated migrants. Figure
5.6 shows that 56 per cent of educated migrants choose the US while
only 39 per cent of all migrants are in the US. On the other hand, 40
per cent of all South Asian migrants are in Europe but only 20 per cent
of tertiary educated migrants choose to migrate there.

Another critical issue, in addition to the education levels of the
migrants, is their occupational choices. Detailed data exist for the US
and is presented in Figure 5.7. As indicated earlier, over 75 per cent of
South Asian migrants in the US labour market have college and graduate
degrees. The four largest sectors of the economy that employ South Asian
migrants are: (a) education, health, and social services, (b) professional,
scientific, and management services, (c) manufacturing, and (d) retail
trade. These four sectors account for 70 per cent of the South Asian
labour force in the US.

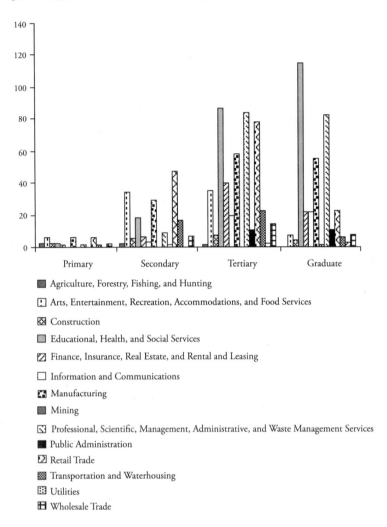

FIGURE 5.7   Occupational Choices of South Asian Migrants
in the US (2000)
(in thousand)

Source: US Census (2000).

SOUTH ASIAN IMMIGRANTS IN THE PERSIAN GULF

The Persian Gulf started emerging as a major destination for South Asian immigrants in the mid-1970s, with the onset of the oil boom. Subsequent large-scale development activities in the six Gulf Cooperation Council

(GCC) countries of Saudi Arabia, Bahrain, Kuwait, Oman, Qatar, and the United Arab Emirates (UAE) drew a growing flow of labourers initially from India and Pakistan, and later from other South Asian countries. Over the past three decades, millions of South Asian workers have migrated to the Gulf countries in search of work opportunities and the ebbs and flows of migrants have been closely correlated with movements in oil prices during this period.

Despite the decades-long and economically significant immigration flows, data on numbers and attributes of South Asian migrants in the Gulf are still very limited. Available figures are mainly estimates that are based on reports by a variety of sources in host and source countries. The main reason for the scarcity of data is not the lack of data collection but the reluctance by destination countries to release detailed information on migration characteristics.

A recent report by the United Nations (UN) on international migration in the Arab region estimated the total number of South Asian immigrants in the Gulf in 2004 at 6 million, with over half the number accounted for by Indian migrants. Some reports put the number of South Asian migrants at much higher levels. For example, Sri Lanka's Bureau of Foreign Employment estimates the number of Sri Lankan workers alone in the major six Gulf destinations at around 1 million.

Table 5.2 shows the number of migrants from major South Asian countries in the six major destinations in the Persian Gulf. Saudi Arabia is by far the single largest destination, hosting almost half of all South Asian in the region.

As mentioned earlier, a large majority of South Asian migrants in the Persian Gulf is comprised of semi-skilled and unskilled workers, with white-collar workers and professionals accounting for only a small share. This composition has remained largely unchanged even as demand for professionals and highly-skilled workers grew rapidly in the Gulf. In

TABLE 5.2   **South Asian Communities in the Persian Gulf**

					(estimates in thousand)	
	Bahrain 2004	Kuwait 2003	Oman 2004	Qatar 2002	Saudi Arabia 2004	UAE 2002
India	120	320	330	100	1,300	1,200
Pakistan	50	100	70	100	900	450
Bangladesh					400	100
Sri Lanka		170	30	35	350	160

Source: Kapiszewski (2006).

TABLE 5.3   Distribution of Indian Immigrants by Profession in
Saudi Arabia in 2001

	(per cent)
	Share
Professionals	5
Technicians	20
Non-specialist	10
Administrative staff /semi-skilled labour	50
Domestic/agricultural workers	15

Source: Kapiszewski (2006).

the absence of reliable data on numbers and attributes of workers from host countries, information reported by various government agencies in sending countries becomes the main source. While such data is also limited, it still provides a useful insight into the overall patterns and trends of South Asian immigration to the Persian Gulf.

Table 5.3 shows the distribution of Indian immigrants according to their professions in Saudi Arabia in 2001. Only 5 per cent of the immigrants were professionals with the remaining 95 per cent comprising semi-skilled and unskilled workers.

A similar composition is apparent among Sri Lankan immigrants where unskilled migrants make up the majority of all immigrants to the Gulf region. The distinguishing feature of Sri Lankan immigrants to the Gulf is the large number of women who mostly work as housemaids and domestic employees. Figure 5.8 and Table 5.4 show that in 2005 over 100,000 Sri Lankan women went to work as housemaids to the six major Gulf countries. This is 50 per cent higher than the number of skilled and unskilled male workers that migrated to the Gulf in the same year.

The selection bias in favour of unskilled workers in the Gulf may be an outcome of regulations in Gulf countries which make it difficult for families to accompany migrants to these countries and, equally important, limit foreigners' ability to own businesses and property. The educated and highly-skilled workers are less likely to accept such conditions than unskilled workers, and therefore are less inclined to seek work opportunities in the Gulf. Further, highly skilled migrants can enter OECD countries more easily where they can enjoy better labour market and social opportunities.

The data in this section highlight the main patterns of South Asian migration—highly skilled migration to mainly English-speaking OECD countries and low-skilled migration to the oil-rich Persian Gulf countries.

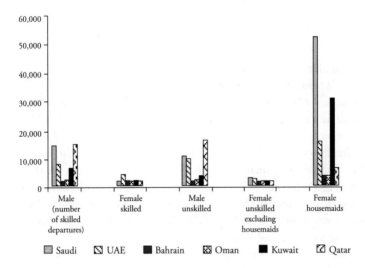

FIGURE 5.8 Number of Sri Lankan Workers in the Persian Gulf by Skill Level

Source: *Annual Statistical Report of Foreign Employment*, Sri Lanka Bureau of Foreign Employment (2005).

TABLE 5.4   Number of Departures of Sri Lankan Workers to the Persian Gulf by Gender and Skill Level

	Male Skilled		Female Skilled		Male Unskilled		Female Unskilled excl. Housemaids		Female Housemaids	
	2001	2005	2001	2005	2001	2005	2001	2005	2001	2005
Saudi	11,932	12,280	110	131	11,309	8,740	2,147	1,323	37,483	50,091
UAE	3,153	6,001	5,423	2,178	3,879	7,700	1,852	1,090	11,211	13,646
Bahrain	324	318	580	572	373	262	89	60	2,051	2,142
Oman	517	570	471	134	268	379	46	2	1,805	1,551
Kuwait	3,300	4,321	1,587	74	2,348	1,996	596	207	26,327	28,562
Qatar	4,648	12,903	226	125	5,430	14,359	409	211	2,201	4,858

Source: *Annual Statistical Report of Foreign Employment*, Sri Lanka Bureau of Foreign Employment (2005).

They are both critical to the services exports of the South Asian countries and their integration into the global economy. What is clearer is the need for more detailed data on the migrants and their characteristics. The next section explores the main channel through which migration impacts the source countries—remittances.

REMITTANCES IN SOUTH ASIA

Remittances as a Source of External Finance

Remittances play an extremely important role among external financial flows for South Asian countries according to estimates compiled by Ratha and Mohapatra (2009). Officially, recorded remittance flows to South Asia are expected to have reached US$ 73 billion in 2008. Migrant remittances were more than half the size of private medium and long-term capital flows received by South Asia in 2007, and more than four times the official development assistance (ODA) to the region in the previous year (Figures 5.9 and 5.10, Table 5.5). Remittances are the largest source of external financing after private capital flows to the region. The true size of remittances is likely to be higher, due to significant unrecorded flows through formal and informal channels.

India accounts for a bulk of the external financial flows to the region.[1] More specifically, total external flows to India increased from US$ 21 billion annually during 1999–2001 to US$ 34 billion during

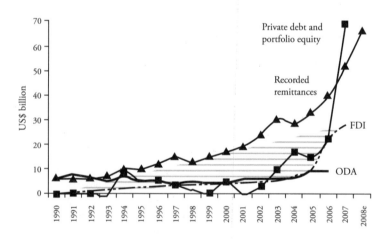

FIGURE 5.9   **Remittances and Other Resource Flows to South Asia**
(1999–2007)

Source: Ratha and Mohapatra (2009); Migration and Remittances team, World Bank.

[1]External resource flows include foreign direct investment (FDI), private debt and portfolio equity flows, ODA, and migrant remittances. 2007 is the latest year for which data was available for all categories of resource flows other than remittances from the Global Development Finance database at the time of writing this paper (Table 5.5). Data and estimates of migrant remittances were available until 2008 from Ratha et al. (2008).

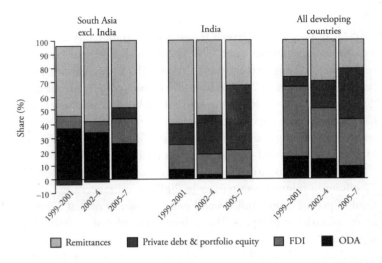

FIGURE 5.10   Sources of External Financing for South Asia (1999–2007)

Sources: Ratha and Mohapatra (2009); Global Development Finance 2008 database.

TABLE 5.5   Financial Flows to South Asia, India, and South Asia Excluding India

(US$ billion)	1990	1995	2000	2005	2006	2007	2008e
South Asia							
ODA	6.0	5.2	4.2	9.2	9.2		
Private medium and long-term flows	2.1	5.6	12.6	22.4	50.8	90.0	
Migrant remittances	5.6	10.0	17.2	33.9	42.5	54.0	73.3
India							
ODA	1.4	1.7	1.5	1.7	1.4		
Private medium and long-term flows	1.8	4.4	11.9	18.0	43.7	79.7	
Migrant remittances	2.4	6.2	12.9	22.1	28.3	37.2	51.6
South Asia excl. India							
ODA	4.6	3.4	2.7	7.5	7.8		
Private medium and long-term flows	0.3	1.2	0.7	4.3	7.1	10.3	
Migrant remittances	3.2	3.8	4.3	11.8	14.2	16.8	21.7

Source: Ratha and Mohapatra (2009); Migration and Remittances team, World Bank; Global Development Finance 2008 database.

2002–4, and then more than doubled to US$ 76 billion annually during 2005–7. India is also the largest recipient of migrant remittances in the region, receiving an estimated US$ 52 billion in 2008 which is 70 per cent of the total migrant remittances received by South Asia during that year. In comparison, in 2007 India received nine-tenths of private capital flows to the region and less than a fifth of ODA. As private flows to India have become more important, the share of remittances among external resource flows progressively decreased from 60 per cent in 1999–2001 to 54 per cent in 2002–4, and to 32 per cent in 2005–7.

South Asian countries outside India received an estimated US$ 22 billion in migrant remittances in 2008. Remittances were about a third of private capital inflows and twice the size of official aid in this set of countries in that year. The recipients in order of declining levels were Bangladesh (estimated US$ 9.0 billion in 2008), Pakistan (US$ 7.0 billion), Sri Lanka (US$ 2.9 billion), and Nepal (US$ 2.7 billion) (Figure 5.11).

Compared to all developing countries as a group, migrant remittances have accounted for a larger share of external flows to South Asia. While the share of remittances in external flows to all developing countries ranges from 21 per cent to 29 per cent during 1999–2007, the share for remittances in South Asia has been much higher, accounting for 55 per cent and 58 per cent of total flows in 1999–2001 and 2002–4, respectively, and 37 per cent in 2005–7 (The decrease in the share in 2005–7 was primarily due to the sharp increase in portfolio flows to India).

As a share of GDP, remittances were 3.7 per cent of GDP for South Asia in 2007, compared to 2 per cent of GDP for all developing countries. Remittances as a share of GDP were the highest in Nepal (15.5 per cent),

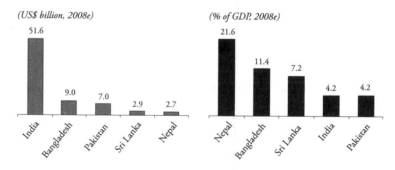

FIGURE 5.11   Remittance Inflows to South Asian Countries

Source: Ratha and Mohapatra (2009).

followed by Bangladesh (9.5 per cent), Sri Lanka (8.1 per cent), Pakistan (4.2 per cent), and India (3.1 per cent) (Figure 5.11 and Table 5.5).

Stability of Remittances Compared to FDI and Other Resource Flows

Other key characteristics of remittances are their stability or reliability. At the macroeconomic level, unlike private capital flows, remittances tend to be resilient when the recipient economy suffers an economic downturn following a financial crisis, natural disaster, or political conflict (Clarke and Wallsten 2004; World Bank 2005; Yang 2006; Yang and Choi 2007). In the Caribbean, a 1 per cent decrease in real GDP is associated with a 3 per cent increase in remittances after a two-year lag (Mishra 2005). In Sub-Saharan Africa, where official aid flows have fluctuated considerably from year to year, remittances were more stable than both FDI and official aid (Gupta et al. 2007). Remittances can thus contribute to macroeconomic stability in recipient economies by offsetting foreign exchange losses that arise due to negative macroeconomic shocks.[2] The main reason behind the stability and predictability of remittances is that they are flows between private individuals—mostly members of the same household—and they are targeted for consumption, rather than, for example, speculative portfolio investments. As such, they tend to be more isolated from economic cycles.

In order to examine the resilience of remittances to South Asia, the coefficient of variation of remittance flows is constructed relative to three other categories of external financial flows—FDI, private debt and portfolio equity, and ODA for 1998–2007. These findings are presented in Figure 5.12. Private debt and portfolio equity flows to South Asia were the most volatile, with a coefficient of variation of 134 per cent, followed by FDI with the coefficient of variation of 89 per cent. Migrant remittances were significantly less volatile than both categories of private flows, with a variation coefficient of 40 per cent during 1998–2007. The volatility of migrant remittances was slightly higher than that of official aid during this period. Migrant remittances received by South Asia were, therefore, more stable than FDI and other private capital flows and behaved similarly to official aid between 1998 and 2007.

---

[2]Even at the household level, remittances can smooth macroeconomic shocks. For example, in rural Mali, households use remittances to insure themselves against adverse shocks: a 500 kilogram drop in grain output leads to a 48 per cent increase in remittances (Gubert 2007).

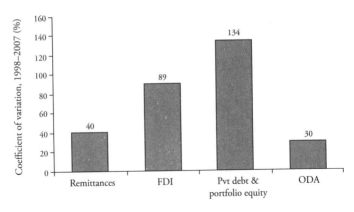

FIGURE 5.12   Stability of Remittances in South Asia Relative to
Other Financial Flows

Source: Migration and Remittances team, World Bank; Global Development Finance
2008 database.

Recent Trends in Remittances and Outlook for 2009[3]

The current crisis leads to many questions and concerns about the
future of financial flows, especially remittances, as they are central to
development and growth in the region. The data for the last two years
indicate robust growth for remittances during 2007 and 2008, especially
for countries outside India. Remittances to the South Asia region rose
by 27 per cent in 2006–7 with an increase of 15 to 20 per cent for
Bangladesh, Pakistan, Nepal, and Sri Lanka in 2007. Flows to India
rose by 31 per cent in that year. This pattern appears to have continued
into the first half of 2008. Pakistan and India have also reported robust
growth in remittance flows in 2007–8, with growth of 17 per cent in
Pakistan and 39 per cent in India. Flows to Bangladesh, Nepal, and Sri
Lanka grew by 37, 57, and 17 per cent, respectively. Officially recorded
remittance flows to the South Asia region are estimated to grow by 36
per cent in 2007–8 (some 9 per cent higher than the previous year), from
US$ 54 billion in 2007 to an estimated US$ 73 billion in 2008.

The growth of remittances to South Asia is expected to moderate
significantly in 2009 as a result of the global financial crisis. This pattern
is similar to that for all developing countries. After several years of

[3]This section draws on Migration and Development Brief 'Revised Outlook for
Remittance Flows 2009–11', by Dilip Ratha and Sanket Mohapatra. Available at www.
worldbank.org/prospects/migrationandremittances.

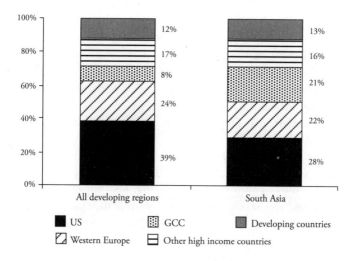

FIGURE 5.13   Sources of Remittances for South Asia

Source: Ratha and Mohapatra (2009).

strong growth, remittance flows to all developing countries began to slow down in the third quarter of 2008—with growth slowing from 23 per cent in nominal dollar terms in 2006–7 to an estimated 17 per cent in 2008.

This slowdown is expected to deepen further in 2009 in response to the global financial crisis, although the exact magnitude of the growth moderation (or outright decline in some cases) is hard to predict given the extreme level of uncertainty about global growth, commodity prices, and exchange rates. As discussed earlier, there is some evidence that migrant remittances to developing countries have been relatively stable or resilient compared to other types of resource flows and to downturns in the country of origin. However, unlike past emerging market crises, the current financial crisis is affecting both the host and origin countries.[4] The projections of Ratha and Mohapatra (2009) explicitly take this into account by modelling remittances as a function of bilateral migrant stocks and the World Bank's projections of growth of GDP in the major receiving

[4]Remittances do not appear to have been affected by economic cycles in the host countries in the past. For example, Roache and Gradzka (2007) find that remittance flows to Latin America were relatively insensitive to business cycle fluctuations in the US during 1990–2007. However, given the magnitude of the current financial crisis, there is a strong possibility that it could affect the incomes of migrants and their ability to send money home.

regions, including the US, western Europe, the Gulf, and other receiving regions. The remittance projections thus take into account a 'recession channel', whereby the economic situation in the host country influences the employment prospects and incomes of migrants, and thereby their ability to send money home (see Annexure 5A for the methodology for constructing these estimates).

Under the base case projections, the growth of remittances to South Asia would fall drastically, from about 36 per cent growth in 2008 to –2 per cent growth in 2009 under their base case scenario. Remittances to South Asia will decline by even more under a 'low case' scenario which takes into account the possibility that new migration flows stop altogether, and recent migrants have to return as they lose employment in the destination countries.

The economic prospects for sources of remittances will be among the main determinants of remittance flows. The top sources of remittances for the South Asia region were the US (an estimated 28 per cent of inflows), the 15 EU countries (22 per cent of inflows), and the GCC countries (21 per cent of inflows) (Figure 5.13).[5] The share of remittances inflows from the US and Europe is lower for South Asia compared to the average for all developing regions.

For India, studies by India's central bank indicate that North America accounted for 44 per cent of inward remittance flows, followed by the Gulf countries (24 per cent), Europe (13 per cent), East Asia (8 per

TABLE 5.6   Remittance Flows to South Asian Countries (2006–8)

	US$ (million)			Growth Rate (per cent)	
	2006	2007	2008e	2006–7	2007–8
South Asia Region	42,523	54,041	73,293	27	36
Afghanistan	–	–	–	–	–
Bangladesh	5,428	6,562	8,995	21	37
Bhutan	–	–	–	–	–
India	28,334	37,217	51,581	31	39
Maldives	2.8	2.982	3.13	7	5
Nepal	1,453	1,734	2,727	19	57
Pakistan	5,121	5,998	7,039	17	17
Sri Lanka	2,185	2,527	2,947	16	17
All developing countries	235,403	289,376	337,761	23	17

Source: Ratha and Mohapatra (2009).

[5]See Ratha and Mohapatra (2009) for the methodology used to compile these bilateral remittance estimates.

cent), and South America (6 per cent) (see Reserve Bank of India 2006a, 2006b; Chisti 2007).

The prospects for recovery of economic growth in the source countries (the US, EU, and the GCC countries) can influence remittance flows to receiving countries in the region. Data available from the central banks of Bangladesh and Pakistan show that remittance flows from oil-rich GCC countries accounted for 63 per cent and 52 per cent, respectively, of the remittance flows to Bangladesh and Pakistan in the 2008 fiscal year (Figure 5.14).[6]

There are an estimated 2.2 million Indian migrants in the UAE (the fourth largest migration corridor in the world excluding the former Soviet Union), and 1.3 million in Saudi Arabia (Ratha and Xu 2008). Remittances received by Bangladesh and Pakistan from the GCC

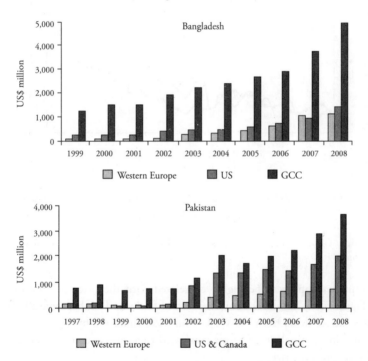

FIGURE 5.14   Sources of Remittances for Bangladesh and Pakistan

Sources: Central Banks of Bangladesh and Pakistan.

[6]See Bangladesh Bank (www.bangladesh-bank.org) and State Bank of Pakistan (www.sbp.org.pk).

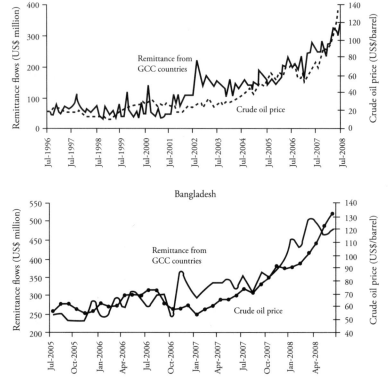

FIGURE 5.15   Relationship between Crude Oil Prices and Remittances
from the GCC Countries

Sources: Central Banks of Bangladesh and Pakistan; World Bank Commodities
Team.

countries appear to be highly correlated with the price of crude oil
(Figure 5.15). Under the base scenario of Ratha and Mohapatra (2009),
remittance flows from the GCC countries would fall by 3 per cent in
2009 in nominal dollar terms compared to an increase of 38 per cent
in the previous year.

Ratha and Mohapatra (2009) suggest that this decline in remittance
flows is expected to be smaller than the fall in private or official capital
flows in the South Asia region, implying that remittances are expected
to remain resilient relative to many other categories of resource flows to
the region.

Remittance Costs

The costs and other barriers on remittances are among the main determinants of the size and nature of flows (such as via formal or informal channels). The remittance receiving countries in South Asia represent some of the most competitive remittance corridors in the developing world, although costs are still high compared to other mature corridors such as that between the US and Mexico. It is also relatively difficult to send remittances within the South Asia region, for example from Bangladesh to India or from India to Nepal due to restrictions on outward flows in these countries.

The average cost of sending US$ 200 from Saudi Arabia to Bangladesh, India, and Pakistan is between US$ 10 to US$ 11, or about 5 to 5.5 per cent of the total amount—with the exchange rate commission accounting

TABLE 5.7   Cost of Sending US$ 200 to Selected South Asian Countries

Receiving Country	Sending Country	Fee	Exchange Rate Margin (%)	Average Total Cost US$	(%)
Bangladesh	Saudi Arabia	5.2	2.5	10.2	5.1
	Singapore	9.7	2.7	15.1	7.5
	United Kingdom	10.4	2.8	16.0	8.0
India	Canada	19.6	3.2	25.9	13.0
	France	18.6	0.0	18.6	9.3
	Germany	17.7	1.9	21.4	10.7
	Italy	10.3	2.0	14.3	7.1
	Saudi Arabia	5.4	2.2	9.8	4.9
	Singapore	10.3	1.5	13.3	6.6
	United Kingdom	13.3	1.7	16.8	8.4
	United States	8.3	1.5	11.2	5.6
Pakistan	Saudi Arabia	5.8	2.8	11.4	5.7
	Singapore	19.8	3.6	27.0	13.5
	United Kingdom	8.2	3.2	14.6	7.3
	United States	9.1	2.6	14.3	7.2
Sri Lanka	Italy	15.0	4.8	24.6	12.3
	United Kingdom	13.5	2.1	17.7	8.8
Other regions					
Mexico	United States	8.4	1.6	11.6	5.8
Philippines	Saudi Arabia	6.9	1.3	9.6	4.8
Kenya	United Kingdom	15.9	5.5	26.8	13.4

Source: Remittance Prices Worldwide database, World Bank.

for half of the total. The cost for sending US$ 200 from the US to India is also less than 6 per cent of the transfer amount, although the fee is higher and the exchange rate commission lower. The cost of transferring money from Saudi Arabia to South Asia is similar to that in the mature corridors such as from the US to Mexico, where the cost for sending US$ 200 is about US$ 12, or 6 per cent for the transfer amount.

The cost for sending a similar amount from the UK to Bangladesh, India, Pakistan, or Sri Lanka is between US$ 16 and US$ 18 (or 8 to 9 per cent of the transfer amount), most of it accounted for by higher fee. Remittance fee is somewhat higher in some South Asia corridors, for example, between 12 and 14 per cent of the transfer amount in Canada–India, Singapore–Pakistan, and Italy–Sri Lanka, comparable to costs in other corridors such as UK to Kenya.

Although there is significant intra-regional migration in South Asia—with an estimated 3.5 million migrants from Bangladesh in India, for example—it is relatively difficult to send remittances within the South Asia region due to restrictions on outward flows in the countries in the region. Bangladesh and India require migrants to obtain authorization before the central bank processes international remittances (Ratha and Shaw 2007).

Remittances and Financial Sector Development

Policies to increase the level of competition and lower the transactions costs in the remittance industry will have significant welfare effects. In addition to increasing the net amount received by the families back home, lower fees, and increased availability to remittance services can improve overall financial access of migrants and remittance recipients. Remittances sent through the formal financial sector influence financial sector development in several ways: banks' loanable funds increase with deposits linked to remittance flows; remittance recipients can gain greater access to credit and other financial services due to the relative stability of remittance flows; and providing remittance transfer services allows banks to 'get to know' and reach out to unbanked recipients or recipients with limited financial intermediation (Aggarwal et al. 2006). Increasing access to bank accounts for migrants and their families back home would not only provide them a lower cost and a more secure remittance channel, it would also enable them to save more. Banks, private firms, and microfinance institutions in Bangladesh and India offer transnational consumer loans, mortgage loans, and microfinance products.[7] Indian migrants in many OECD countries are relatively wealthier than the average, which can increase the propensity to invest in real estate.

The remittance industry has also seen the introduction of cell phone-based remittances and several pilots involving remittance-linked financial products.[8] In India, Visa has tied up with some of the major commercial banks to extend its domestic card-to-card transfer service to mobile phones. Western Union and the GSM Association have also announced a pilot project for mobile phone remittances. Mastercard Worldwide, one of the largest credit card issuers, is offering a service known as MasterCard MoneySend, which allows customers of major banks in India to send funds from a MasterCard credit, debit, or prepaid account to any other MasterCard account through the MoneySend system (http://www.mastercard.com/in/personal/en/moneysend/faq. html). California based Obopay Inc. announced a partnership with Bangladesh-based Grameen Solutions Ltd. to develop a system for payments and fund transfers through mobile phones called the 'Bank a Billion' initiative. This initiative will be initially piloted in Mumbai, India, and in Bangladesh (http://www.grameensolutions.com/News-Events/grameen-solutions-ltd-enters-partnership-with-obopay-inc-to-bring-low-cost-mobile-banking-to-poor.html).

New card-based remittance technologies are now starting to be used for a variety of payments, including the delivery of public assistance to those in remote rural areas in South Asia. The use of prepaid/reloadable smart cards and cash cards can revolutionize the delivery of both private and public payments at the micro-level.[9] For example, smart cards that use biometric technology for identification have been distributed by card-provider FINO to nearly half-a-million people in rural areas in India receiving payments under the Indian government's National Rural Employment Guarantee (NREG) scheme (Hindu Business Line 2008).

---

[7]Similar products are available in other remittance recipient countries such as Mexico, El Salvador, Peru, and the Philippines.

[8]In the Philippines, G-Cash and SMART provide deposit, credit, and money transfers through mobile phones. In Kenya, Vodafone through its subsidiary Safaricom, has launched a mobile banking service M-PESA which has more than 2 million clients.

[9]The use of remittance channels for public aid delivery is not new in South Asia. In Afghanistan, an informal money transfer system has been used in recent years by aid agencies to distribute cash to poor households in remote rural areas, according to an Overseas Development Institute report (Savage and Harvey 2007).

Role of Post Offices in Remittances

Post offices typically have very strong networks in both urban and rural areas, with significant potential to reach poor populations. While commercial banks are inaccessible to the poorest in many countries, post offices are typically more familiar and more accessible. This provides postal networks a unique opportunity to become key players in both international and domestic remittances, and to bring in the unbanked into the formal financial system.

For international remittances, post offices in South Asia (such as India Post) have either de jure or de facto exclusivity agreements, that is, an agreement to work with one international money transfer company. Studies show that such exclusive partnerships keep costs high for the migrants, reduce the amounts that are sent, and can therefore limit the development impact of remittances for recipient households (World Bank 2005).

These exclusive partnerships raise the issue of policy incoherence, since the lack of competition encourages the partner money transfer operator to keep the remittance fee high, which acts as a form of tax on remittance senders and recipients. This usually goes directly against national policies and international recommendations not to tax remittances or direct them to specific uses. A clear policy recommendation is to eliminate exclusive partnerships, and encourage post offices to partner with more money transfer companies (and even banks). This will put downward pressure on costs. The revenue losses in the short-term will most likely be offset by larger volumes, benefitting the postal networks, migrants, and remittance recipients.

The Impact of Migration and Remittances on Poverty and Development Outcomes

Experience from other developing regions shows that migration and remittances have a significant effect on reducing poverty and improving many development outcomes. Adams and Page (2005), using cross-country regression analysis, show that a 10 per cent increase in per capita international remittances in a developing country can lead to a 3.5 per cent decline in the share of people living in poverty. International remittances have reduced poverty in Latin America by 0.4 per cent for each percentage point increase in the remittances to GDP ratio (Acosta et al. 2007). Remittance receiving households typically have better asset ownership and have been more entrepreneurial when compared to others.

Similar poverty reduction and development benefits of remittances have been observed in South Asia. In Nepal, between a fifth and half of the decline in poverty between 1995 and 2004 has been attributed to increased internal and international migration (Lokshin et al. 2007; World Bank 2006). Migration and remittances have also contributed to significant improvements in human capital accumulation and health outcomes, particularly for women. According to Mansuri (2007), in rural Pakistan school enrollment rates increased by 54 per cent for girls in migrant households as opposed to only 7 per cent for boys in migrant households. Ratha and De (2005) find that children of Sri Lankan migrant-sending households had higher birth weight and spent more on private tuition, a possible contributor to better education outcomes.[10]

Using Remittances to Improve Capital Market Access of Countries

Ketkar and Ratha (2005, 2008) have examined how remittance securitization and diaspora bonds can be an attractive instrument for developing countries to access the wealth of the diaspora, especially during times of crisis when external sources of finance dry up. It can attract that part of migrant remittances that are directed towards investment motives.

Diaspora Bonds

India has raised some US$ 11 billion in the last decade by issuing 'diaspora bonds' targeted at Indian migrants in the US, Europe, and the Gulf, often in times of crisis (Ketkar and Ratha 2008).[11] Although the diaspora bonds tap into the savings of migrants, studies show that a significant share of the proceeds of diaspora bonds have been converted to local currency and have remained as remittances (Chisti 2007; Ratha and Shaw 2007).

The Indian authorities, through the state-owned State Bank of India, first issued the India Development Bonds worth US$ 1.6 billion following the balance of payments crisis in 1991 (at 9.5 per cent coupon in US$ terms). In the period following sanctions after the nuclear tests in 1998, India issued the Resurgent India Bonds for US$ 4.2 billion (at 7.75 per cent in US$). It raised India Millennium Deposits worth US$ 5.5 billion in 2000 (at 8.5 per cent in US$). Sri Lanka has also raised resources from

---

[10]This finding is similar to the finding of higher birth weight and lower mortality for children born in rural Mexican migrant-sending households (Hildebrandt and McKenzie 2005).

[11]A diaspora bond is a debt instrument issued by a country—or potentially, a sub-sovereign entity or a private corporation—to raise financing from its overseas diaspora.

the diaspora using Sri Lanka Development Bonds (SLDBs) targeted at both resident and non-resident Sri Lankans.

Securitization of Future Remittance Flows

Remittances can improve access to international finance of countries of origin. Large banks in some countries (for example, Turkey and Brazil) have used their access to foreign currency-denominated remittances as collateral for raising international bond financing at lower costs and longer maturities. These mechanisms can be used to raise funds for development projects such as low-income housing, or power and water supply.

Despite the current economic climate, a recent Standard & Poor's research report found that remittance securitization and securitization of other future flow receivables in emerging markets are performing well, bucking the trend in global credit markets. Ketkar and Ratha (2005) found the securitization of future remittances and trade, tourism, credit card, and other future receivables (together called 'Diversified Payment Rights' or DPRs) a useful tool that can help South Asian countries maintain access to international capital markets especially in times of crisis.

A typical remittance securitization transaction is in the investment grade (BBB, or higher) category since future flows are heavily overcollateralized. It would take a huge slowdown in future remittances (of more than 95 per cent) for a typical remittance securitization to default.[12] This makes them a safe bet for 'buy and hold' investors such as pension funds and institutional investors.

South Asian countries such as Bangladesh, India, and Pakistan can potentially issue bonds backed by future remittances, with amounts ranging from a tenth to a fifth of their annual remittance flows. The remittance securitization potential is US$ 1 billion–US$ 2 billion for Bangladesh; US$ 1 billion–US$ 1.5 billion for Pakistan; and US$ 3 billion–US$ 6 billion for India, depending on the level of overcollateralization required for implementing these transactions.

POLICY CHALLENGES

The remittance industry in South Asia has experienced a shift in remittances from informal to formal channels and remittance costs

---

[12]Future flow securitization structures are typically resilient to adverse events. For example, a $250 million bond backed by telephone receivables issued by Pakistan Telecommunications Company Limited (PTCL) continued to perform even in the face of deteriorating credit ratings and selective default on Pakistan's sovereign debt following nuclear tests in 1998 (Ketkar and Ratha 2001).

appear to have fallen in recent years, but they remain high relative to other main remittance receiving countries such as Mexico and the Philippines.[13] Sending money between countries within the South Asian region (South–South remittances), however, continues to remain difficult, if not impossible.

Policy measures can improve competition and transparency in the market for remittance services, and improve accessibility of the poor to less costly and more reliable remittance transfer mechanisms. Some of the reasons for continued use of informal channels include regulatory barriers to outward remittances from South Asian countries (despite high volumes of intra-regional migration); lack of access to formal financial institutions by families in rural areas; and in many cases, relatively high cost and poor reliability of formal remittance service providers. Regulations have also contributed to reducing competition and increasing costs and entry barriers.

Regulations relating to anti-money laundering and countering the financing of terrorism appear to have become a constraint in reducing remittance costs, especially for smaller remittance service providers and mobile operators dependent on correspondent banks in South Asia. For example, some South Asian countries such as India are now considering simpler prudential regulations for money transfer companies and ways to harmonize telecom and financial services regulations.

Governments in South Asia can help expand the formal market for remittance services by improving access of rural unbanked recipients to formal remittance services, easing the constraints on outward remittances, and facilitating bilateral and regional agreements with the major destination countries to harmonize regulations governing the provision of remittance services.

LESSONS FROM THE PHILIPPINES

As discussed earlier, Nepal, Sri Lanka, and Bangladesh, and to an extent India and Pakistan, are relying heavily on export of mainly unskilled labour and the receipt of remittances to ease domestic labour market pressures and to generate hard currency for financing the current account. The governments of the sending countries can play a role in facilitating these traditional service exports. South Asian countries can

[13]Costs have fallen in other corridors as well. Average remittance costs in the US–Mexico corridor, one of the largest remittance corridors, fell dramatically by nearly 55 per cent between 1999 and 2004, but appear to have levelled off lately.

learn useful lessons from the experience of the Philippines, which has perhaps had the longest history of a managed labour export programme. It has created mechanisms for pre-departure training for overseas workers, a migrants' welfare fund that provides essential services to overseas workers and helps in re-integration of returnees, and bilateral labour migration agreements with the major destination countries.

Pre-departure Training

The Philippines requires workers departing abroad for employment to attend pre-departure orientation seminars (PDOS). The topics covered in the PDOS include travel regulations, immigration procedures, settlement concerns, employment and social security concerns, and rights and obligations of Filipino immigrants. It also provides language training and cultural familiarization programmes tailored to the country of destination to departing Filipino workers, in particular household service workers (HSWs), who may face language barriers in interactions with employers. These pre-departure seminars, offered sometimes in partnership with the private sector, provide skills related to work at destination, financial literacy, tools to respond to mistreatment, exploitation and abuse, and educate workers on remittance channels.[14] The Skills for Employment Scholarship Programme (SESP) and the Seafarer's Upgrading Programme (SUP) provide technical and vocational courses for overseas jobs.

Migrants' Welfare Fund

The Philippines has introduced a welfare fund for migrants, the Overseas Workers' Welfare Administration (OWWA), which is funded by a US$ 25 membership fee from migrants going abroad as temporary workers. The fund provides for repatriation, emergency evacuation of workers, life, health and disability insurance, and burial benefits while abroad, legal assistance of migrants, and education and training programmes. The fund also provides loans for pre-departure expenses such as medical examinations and other costs. Bangladesh, Pakistan, the Philippines, Sri Lanka, Thailand, and, most recently, India have introduced migrant welfare funds that provide a similar but more limited range of services (Agunias and Ruiz 2008).

[14]This is run by the Commission for Filipino Overseas (CFO) for permanent migrants and by the OWWA for temporary migrants (see http://www.cfo.gov.ph/ and http://www.owwa.gov.ph).

Return and Re-integration of Returnees

The Philippines OWWA fund also provides loans and other assistance for the re-integration of returning migrants through the National Livelihood Support Fund (NLSF) Livelihood Development Programmes for OFWs which provide credit facilities for small and medium enterprises in trading, services (repair shops, restaurants, parlours), manufacturing (meat/fruit processing, shoes), and agri-business (tilapia piggery, poultry) (http://www.owwa.gov.ph/page/programs/). The fund also finances the OFW Groceria Project which provides OFWs and their families interest-free loans for setting up retail stores.

Bilateral Agreements with Destination Countries

One of the major costs that migrants face is the lack of transparency in employment contracts (with salaries often lower than what is promised), withholding of passports, non-payment or late payment of salaries by employers in the receiving countries, and abuse and exploitation by employers, in particular of domestic workers. Bilateral agreements between sending and destination countries can help in regulating the recruitment process and protect the rights of migrant workers. A bilateral agreement between the Philippines and the UAE, a major destination of OFWs, provides a 'model' employment contract drafted jointly by the Department of Labour and Employment (DOLE) of the Philippines and the Ministry of Labour of the UAE. The agreement requires labour contracts to be drafted in both Arabic and English and applications for workers by UAE employers to state the required specifications and qualifications for the job and conditions of employment including salary, accommodation, and transportation (www.poea.gov.ph/docs/ uae_moa.pdf). For workers bound for Canada, the Philippines Overseas Employment Administration (POEA) has signed a bilateral agreement that requires an employment contract, a manpower request that specifies the position and salary of the worker to be hired, and verification of business license or commercial registration of the employer.

Similarly, other migrant-sending countries have concluded bilateral agreements with receiving countries. A bilateral agreement between Indonesia and Malaysia requires employers to sign contracts that specify rights and obligations of both employers and workers, specify minimum salary, prohibit withholding of salary by employers, and require a bank account to be opened in the name of the domestic worker and full salary deposited directly into the bank account. Korea has signed fourteen

Memorandum of Understanding (MoUs) with sending countries (Hugo 2009). Indonesia has signed MoUs with Malaysia, Korea, Taiwan, Japan, Australia, UAE, Jordan, Qatar, and Syria. India has signed bilateral agreements with some of the major receiving countries in the Gulf and in Europe.

Some of the other measures that the Philippines government has put in place to protect migrants include having labour attaches in embassies, auditing employers, and verifying offer/employment letters and documents, regulating recruitment agencies, and limiting fees that would-be migrants pay recruiters.

CONCLUSION

South Asia, especially India, has shown the importance of the service sector in development and poverty reduction. In addition to providing important intermediate inputs into other sectors of the economy and forming a large portion of the domestic final consumption, services have become an important export sector. In this regard, the focus has been on the IT and related services provided by the relatively high-skilled portion of the labour force. The goal of this chapter was to argue that there is another highly relevant, yet ignored, range of services exported by South Asian countries. These are the services of the millions of migrants' working in OECD countries and in the Persian Gulf.

The migrants in the OECD countries tend to be highly educated, migrate permanently with their families, and enjoy numerous privileges. On the other hand, migrants in the oil-rich Persian Gulf countries are generally low-skilled, temporary, and have the main goal of saving and sending remittances back home. This chapter argued and showed the importance of both types of migrants and the remittances they send for poverty reduction, financial market development, and investment.

It is especially important to focus on remittances during a time of great financial chaos in the global markets where most financial flows have already dried up. There is emerging evidence that remittances tend to be more stable and resilient in the face of financial uncertainty and they may become more important in pulling South Asia out of the current chaos in the global markets.

The key policy messages in this chapter are clear. Policies restricting migration flows—whether these are the highly skilled engineers heading to Silicon Valley or semi-skilled workers in European or Persian Gulf countries—are likely to be welfare reducing for all parties involved. Especially given the rapidly aging populations in Europe, increased migration from regions with excess labour supply such as South Asia are needed for the provision of many services that need to be locally supplied.

The second set of policies involves remittances and the financial markets. It is especially important to lower all market barriers and transaction costs that especially discourage the use of formal financial channels. Not only does the lowering of such costs benefit the consumers of the services, it also enables more appropriate policy responses and development of stronger financial markets which further encourage stronger and more sustainable economic development.

ANNEXURE 5A   FORECASTING REMITTANCES WORLDWIDE

This annexure describes the methodology for forecasting remittances used by Ratha et al. (2008) and Ratha and Mohapatra (2009). Remittance flows are broadly affected by three factors: the migrant stocks, incomes of migrants, and the income differential with the source country. We assume that migrant stocks will remain unchanged during 2008 to 2010. This is not an unreasonable assumption as argued in the main text. We prepare the forecasts for remittance flows for 2009 and 2010 by examining the effects of income changes in destination countries worldwide. For this purpose, a bilateral remittance matrix estimated by Ratha and Shaw (2007) is used to estimate remittance intensities—the share of remittance outflows in GDP—for the remittance source countries.

$$r_{ij} = \frac{R_{ij}}{Y_j}$$

where 'i' is the remittance receiving country and 'j' is the remittance source country.

Then, remittance flows for 2008 until 2010 are estimated using these remittance intensities and the latest available projections of GDP for all remittance source countries from the World Bank's global macroeconomic forecasts.

$$R_{ij} = \sum_j r_{ij} Y_j$$

In order to avoid attributing flows in dollar terms that are simply due to movements in the Euro-dollar exchange rate, a constant exchange rate at the current level is assumed.

Other factors such as remittance costs and migrants' vintage also play a role (see World Bank 2005; Lueth and Ruiz-Arranz 2008). The data on remittance costs are not easy to model, although we know that remittance costs are falling and causing remittance flows to increase. The migrants' vintage, or the number of years lived in the destination country, is also a plausible determinant of remittance flows to the origin countries. New migrants may send more remittances as a percentage of their income, since they have better ties back home. However, there is anecdotal evidence that new migrants often have financial obligations (such as repaying loans incurred while migrating) and therefore are unlikely to send remittances immediately after arrival in the host country. Ratha and Mohapatra (2009) try to capture the vintage effect examining a low case scenario where recent migrant inflows of the last one or two years are forced to go back as the economic crisis deepens in the major destination countries, an unlikely but high-impact scenario (see discussion in the main text).

Source: Ratha et al. (2008); Ratha and Mohapatra (2009).

REFERENCES

Acosta, Pablo, Pablo Fajnzylber, and Humberto Lopez. 2007. 'The Impact of Remittances on Poverty and Human Capital: Evidence from Latina American Household Surveys', in Çağlar Özden and Maurice Schiff (eds), *International Migration, Economic Development, and Policy*, pp. 59–99. Basingstoke: Palgrave Macmillan.

Adams, Richard H. and John Page. 2005. 'Do International Migration and Remittances Reduce Poverty in Developing Countries?', *World Development*, 33(10): 1645–69.

Agunias, Dovelyn Rannveig and Neil G. Ruiz. 2008. 'Protecting Migrant Workers: Migrant Welfare Funds from Developing Countries', *Migration and Development Brief*, 7, World Bank, Washington, D.C.

Aggarwal, Reena, Asli Demirguc-Kunt, and Maria Soledad Martinez Peria. 2006. 'Do Workers' Remittances Promote Financial Development?', Policy Research Working Paper 3957, World Bank, Washington, D.C.

Chisti, Muzaffar. 2007. 'The Rise in Remittances to India: A Closer Look', Migration Policy Institute. Available at www.migrationpolicy.org, accessed on 23 February 2009.

Clarke, George and Scott Wallsten. 2004. 'Do Remittances Protect Household in Developing Countries against Shocks? Evidence from a Natural Disaster in Jamaica', unpublished manuscript, World Bank, Washington, D.C.

Docquier, Frederic and Abdeslam Marfouk. 2006. 'International Migration by Education Attainment', in Çağlar Özden and Maurice Schiff (eds), *International Migration, Remittances and the Brain Drain*, pp. 151–201. Basingstoke: Palgrave Macmillan.

Global Development Finance. 2008. Available at www.worldbank.org/data, accessed on 23 February 2009.

Gubert, Flore. 2007. 'Insurance Against Poverty', *Journal of African Economies*, 16(1): 172–5.

Gupta, Sanjeev, Catherine A. Pattillo, and Smita Wagh. 2007. 'Impact of Remittances on Poverty and Financial Development in Sub-Saharan Africa', Working Paper 07/38, International Monetary Fund, Washington, D.C.

Hildebrandt, Nicole and David McKenzie. 2005. 'The Effects of Migration on Child Health in Mexico', Policy Research Working Paper 3573, World Bank, Washington, D.C.

Hindu Business Line. 2008. 'FINO Plans Smartcards for Money Transfers', 12 August.

Hugo, Graeme. 2009. 'Labour Migration for Development: Best Practices in Asia and the Pacific', Working Paper 17, International Labour Organization Regional Office for Asia and the Pacific, Bangkok, Thailand.

Kapiszewski, Andrzej. 2006. 'Arab Verus Asian Migrants Workers in the GCC Countries', United Nations Expert Group Meeting on International Migration and Development in the Arab Region, UN Population Division, Beirut, Lebanon.

Ketkar, Suhas Laxman and Dilip Ratha. 2001. 'Development Financing during a Crisis: Securitization of Future Receivables', Policy Research Working Paper 2582, World Bank, Washington, D.C.

————. 2005. 'Recent Advances in Future Flow Securitization', The Financier, 11/12. Available at: www.the-financier.com, accessed on 23 February 2009.

————. (eds). 2008. *Innovative Financing for Development*. Washington, D.C.: World Bank.

Lokshin, Michael, Mikhail Bontch-Osmolovski, and Elena Glinskaya. 2007. 'Work-Related Migration and Poverty Reduction in Nepal', Policy Research Working Paper 4231, World Bank, Washington, D.C.

Lueth, Erik and Marta Ruiz-Arranz. 2008. 'Determinants of Bilateral Remittance Flows', *The B.E. Journal of Macroeconomics*, 8(1): 1–23.

Mansuri, Ghazala 2007. 'Temporary Migration and Rural Development', in Çağlar Özden and Maurice Schiff (eds), *International Migration, Economic Development, and Policy*. Basingstoke: Palgrave Macmillan.

Mishra, Prachi. 2005. 'Macroeconomic Impact of Remittances in the Caribbean', unpublished paper, International Monetary Fund, Washington, D.C.

Parsons, Christopher, Ronald Skeldon, Terrie Walmsley, and L. Alan Winters. 2007. 'Quantifying International Migration: A Database of Bilateral Migrant Stocks', in Çağlar Özden and Maurice Schiff (eds), *International Migration, Economic Development, and Policy*, pp. 17–59. Basingstoke: Palgrave Macmillan.

Ratha, Dilip and Prabal De. 2005. 'Migration and Remittances in Sri

Lanka', unpublished paper, Development Prospects Group, World Bank, Washington, D.C.

Ratha, Dilip and Sanket Mohapatra. 2009. 'Remittances Expected to Fall by 5 to 8 per cent in 2009', *Migration and Development Brief 9*, World Bank, Washington, D.C.

Ratha, Dilip and William Shaw. 2007. 'South-South Migration and Remittances', Working Paper 102, World Bank, Washington, D.C.

Ratha, Dilip and Zhimei Xu. 2008. *Migration and Remittances Factbook*. Washington, D.C.: World Bank, Development Prospects Group.

Ratha, Dilip, Sanket Mohapatra, and Zhimei Xu (2008). 'Outlook for Remittances: 2008–2010', *Migration and Development Brief 8*. Washington, D.C.: World Bank.

Remittance Prices Worldwide database, World Bank. Available at remittanceprices. worldbank.org/, accessed on 23 February 2009.

Reserve Bank of India. 2006a. *Report of the Working Group on Cost of NRI Remittances*.

———. 2006b. 'Invisibles in India's Balance of Payments' *RBI Bulletin*. November.

Roache, Shaun K. and Ewa Gradzka. 2007. 'Do Remittances to Latin America Depend on the U.S. Business Cycle?' Working Paper 07/273, International Monetary Fund, Washington, D.C.

Savage, Kevin and Paul Harvey. 2007. *Remittances during Crises: Implications for Humanitarian Response*. London: Overseas Development Institute.

Sri Lanka Bureau of Foreign Employment. 2005. *Annual Statistical Report of Foreign Employment—2005*. Battaramulla, Sri Lanka.

World Bank. 2005. *Global Economic Prospects 2006: Economic Implications of Remittances and Migration*. Washington, D.C.: World Bank

———. 2006. *Nepal: Resilience Amidst Conflict: An Assessment of Poverty in Nepal, 1995–96 and 2003–04*. Washington, D.C.: World Bank.

Yang, Dean. 2006. 'International Migration, Remittances, and Household Investment: Evidence from Philippine Migrants' Exchange Rate Shocks', Working Paper W12325, National Bureau of Economic Research, Cambridge, M.A.

Yang, Dean and Hwa Jung Choi. 2007. 'Are Remittances Insurance? Evidence from Rainfall Shocks in the Philippines', *World Bank Economic Review*, 21(2): 219–48.

III
Infrastructure

6

Education and Growth of Services

Carl J. Dahlman

The volume of literature linking education (especially higher education) and growth is large. Workers with better education are generally more productive and may also raise the productivity of co-workers (see Hanushek and Woesmann 2007). Higher stocks of human capital facilitate investments in physical capital, enhance the development and diffusion of new technologies, and raise output per worker (Organisation for Economic Co-operation and Development [OECD] 2005b). Higher education and skills are also very complementary to technological advance.[1]

However, in South Asia, there appears to be an additional special relationship between higher education and growth. It is the growth of services which require higher levels of education. Services have been the main source of growth in South Asia over the last 25 years.[2] This has been particularly marked in the case of India, which has had the highest rate of growth in South Asia, and spectacular growth of exports of information-enabled services based on a critical mass of highly educated workers. The average level of education of workers in the service sector in South

[1]See De Feranti et al. (2003).
[2]See Chapter 1 of this volume.

Asian countries is higher than in industry or agriculture.[3] In addition, the fastest growing services have been the most education intensive,[4] which has led to a popular belief in the existence of a new development model based on high skill service growth.

In the global economy, services now account for nearly 70 per cent of gross domestic product (GDP)[5] and that share generally rises with the level of GDP. Commercial service exports have also been growing faster than GDP. They have increased to nearly 19 per cent of total merchandise and commercial service exports, and are growing faster than goods exports.[6] The rapid rise in service exports is due to increasing liberalization of trade and advancements in information technology (IT). Improvements in information and telecommunications technologies (ICTs) are making it increasingly possible to trade any service that can be digitized and that does not require face to face contact.

South Asia's share in global goods exports in 2006, at 1.30 per cent, is only slightly more than half its share of global GDP at 2.37 per cent. On the other hand, the region has developed a comparative advantage in the export of commercial services. South Asia's share of world commercial service exports is 2.91 per cent and 62.3 per cent consists of information-enabled services.[7] However, this is not yet a widespread phenomenon in South Asia, as 93 per cent of South Asia's commercial service exports are from India, and 73.7 per cent of India's exports are information-enabled services (World Bank 2008a).[8] The virtuous circle of higher education leading to the growth of high value information-enabled service exports feeding back to faster growth and more investment in higher education shows the potential that the populous South Asian region has in higher education based growth (Box 6.1).

[3]The average years of education in services, compared to industry, ranged from 10 per cent higher in Sri Lanka to 52–3 per cent higher in India and Pakistan (Bosworth and Maertens (2009, Table 7).

[4]See Bosworth and Maertens (2009), Chapter 2 in this volume, Tables 2A.2.1–2A.2.5 in Annexure 2A.2 which has details on the average level of educational attainment of workers in different service categories.

[5]Although it is 75 per cent and 76 per cent for the UK and the US, respectively, and 91 per cent for Hong Kong,

[6]WDR 2008 with trade data for 2006.

[7]The category in World Bank (2008a) is actually computer, information, communications, and other commercial services.

[8]See Blinder (2007) for the argument that information and communications enabled services constitute a 'third industrial revolution'.

BOX 6. 1   ICT-enabled Service Exports from India

The rise of ICT-enabled services from India has been covered in detail in many other studies (see Pack and Saggi 2006; Gordon and Gupta 2006; Dossani this volume. The focus here is on the link to tertiary education. Many elements played a role in the rise of India in this sector. To a large extent India was able to get into this business thanks to earlier investments it had made in high quality engineering education, particularly through the Indian Institutes of Technology (IITs) and to their English language ability. Indian engineers were already doing some off-shoring work when the Y2K crisis hit at the end of 1999. That boost in demand to help fix the Y2K problem in computer and program software was a great boost to Indian ICT exports. Another key factor was the diaspora of Indian engineers and managers in companies in Silicon Valley and other places that got their companies to source, first software services, and latter more general business from India. A large part of these services are being done by Indian engineers working for subsidiaries of US and other foreign companies in India. These companies have set up affiliates in India to take advantage of the lower cost of high-skilled labour. Thus the success of this sector is mostly due to the high quality engineering and management graduates in India. However the rapid rise in demand for skilled engineers and other higher education graduates led to rapidly rising wage rages because of supply and regulatory constraints. Many thought this would be a major problem for the continued growth of the IT-enabled industry and for high value service-based growth. However the private IT sector was able to address these constraints. This has created a virtuous circle through which the rise in demand for high level human resources has led to an increased supply. This excellent example of how the private sector can solve some of the supply problems will be developed later in the chapter.

This chapter focuses on the role of education in South Asia's service growth. There is a paradox in that South Asia (primarily India) has a comparative advantage in the export of high-skilled services, although its average educational level is low. On the other hand, China has a comparative advantage in the export of manufactured products although it has a higher educational level than South Asia.

The chapter starts with an overview of education in South Asia relative to the rest of the world and focuses in particular on the demand and supply of higher education. The next section examines in more detail the situation of higher education in the five largest South Asian countries—Bangladesh, India, Pakistan, Nepal, and Sri Lanka. This includes a discussion on the role of the ICT industry in overcoming the supply and quality constraints in engineering education that threatened to choke its growth in India. The next three sections explore distance education in South Asia, trade in education services, and the challenges for higher education in South Asia as well as the opportunities for regional collaboration.

The chapter also deals with the broader issue of the role of education in South Asia's service growth. It compares education in India with China, then examines the role of education in the different economic and export structures in the two countries, and draws some implications. The final section looks broadly at the challenge of education for South Asia. It notes the importance of seeing higher education in the context of the population and education pyramid in the countries. It focuses on the need to improve education in order to leverage the advantage of South Asia's rapidly growing population, and identifies issues that warrant further attention.

HIGHER EDUCATION IN SOUTH ASIAN COUNTRIES

South Asian economies are very diverse, ranging in size from Bhutan and the Maldives with populations of less than one million, to the small economies of Nepal and Sri Lanka with populations between 20 and 30 million, to the large economies of Bangladesh and Pakistan with populations of about 160 million, to the giant of India, with a population of 1.1 billion. This chapter provides some detail on all but the two smallest. Even within the remaining five there are wide differences on many aspects. In per capita income, they range from a low of US$ 320 in Nepal, to high of US$ 1,310 in Sri Lanka. This variance is paralleled in the average number of years in education which ranges from 2.43 years in Nepal to 6.87 years in Sri Lanka. They also differ in other education indicators including literacy, primary enrollment rates and completion; and secondary and tertiary enrollment rates (Table 6.1).

Besides having a generally low position on all average educational indicators, South Asia has a poor relative position in tertiary enrollment rates. South Asian countries doubled their enrollment rates between 1990 and 2000, but have not been able to increase them ever since (Table 6.2). They have a weighted average tertiary enrollment rate of 9 per cent and a large dispersion from just 5 per cent (Pakistan) to a high of 11 per cent (India) versus 20 per cent for East Asia (where China is currently 22 per

TABLE 6.1   Basic Population and Education Statistics

(2006 except as noted)

	Bangladesh	India	Nepal	Pakistan	Sri Lanka
Gross national income/capita	450	820	320	800	1,310
Population (million)	156	1110	28	159	20
Av. pop. growth rate 1900–2006	2.0	1.7	2.3	2.4	1.0
Av. pop. growth rate 2006–15	1.6	1.2	1.7	2.1	0.3
Literacy male/female	54/41	73/48	63/35	64/35	92/89
Primary net enrollment rate	89	90	79	66	97
Primary cohort survival rate (percentage of children in 1st grade that reach 5th) male/female 2005	63/67	73/73	75/83	68/72	–/–
Percentage of previous year's primary enrollment entering secondary enrollment male/female 2005	86/92	87/83	79/74	69/75	–/–
Secondary gross enrollment rate	44	54	43	30	87
Tertiary gross enrollment rate	6	11	6	5	–
Average yrs educational attainment of adults (2000)	2.58	5.06	2.43	3.88	6.87

Source: World Bank (2008a and 2008b).

cent). Given its much larger population and higher enrollment rates, total enrollments in India are 12.9 million. These are 12 times those of the second largest—Bangladesh, with 1.1 million, which is followed by Pakistan, with 0.9 million (Table 6.3). Globally, India has the third largest highest tertiary education enrollments in the world, after China with 23.4 million and the US with 17.5 million. The South Asia region, with 14 million higher education students, has the critical mass to have a world class higher education system as is developed in the following section.

TABLE 6.2   Rising Tertiary Enrollment Rates, World Regions and Selected Countries (1986 to 2006)

	1980	1990	2000	2006
EAP	4	5	14	20
China	2	3	13	22
ECA	31	34	48	51
LAC	14	17	23	30
MNA	11	12	–	24
SA	5	5	10	9
Bangladesh	3	4	6	6
India	5	6	11	11
Nepal	3	5	5	6
Pakistan	–	3	–	5
Sri Lanka	3	5	–	–
SSA	1	3	–	5
High Income	36	47	61	67
World	13	16	24	24

Source: World Bank (2008a, 2004, 2002).

Note: EAP stands for East Asia and the Pacific, ECA for Eastern and Central Europe, LAC for Latin America and the Pacific, MNA for Middle East and North Africa, SA for South Asia, and SSA for Sub-Saharan Africa. For the specific groupings under each regional heading see the source above.

The Demand for Higher Education in South Asia

Since higher education is widely seen as means to better jobs, in South Asia, as in the rest of the world, there has been an explosion of demand. Excess demand for education can be seen from three factors. The first is the rapid proliferation of private higher education institutions in all the countries, but is most evident in India. In Bangladesh 47 per cent of the students are in private higher education institution, in Pakistan just 8 per cent (Table 6.3).[9]

A second indicator is that many students who do not get into higher education in their native countries opt to study abroad. They represent anywhere from 1 per cent to 6 per cent of the tertiary students in the home country (discussed later on in the chapter and in Table 6.7).

A third indicator of the strong demand for education in the region can be seen from the rates of return to education. Psacharopoulos and Patrinos (2004) have estimated that the average social rate of return to education is 10.8 per cent, while the average return to primary education is 18.9

[9]Percentages from private institutions are from UNESCO (2007). More detailed country information is provided in the following discussion.

per cent. However the returns to higher education range from 9.7 per cent to 17 per cent depending on the specific conditions of the country in question and the degree of high skill shortages. In the last 15 years the returns to higher education have increased by almost 2 percentage points, while those to secondary education have decreased by 2.0 percentage points (Psacharopoulous 2006). Also, the returns to higher education are generally higher than the returns to physical investment.

Time series data (available for three South Asian Countries) reveals that the returns to education, particularly for higher secondary and tertiary education, increased during 1992–2004.[10] The rates of return are especially high for females at the middle, secondary, and higher secondary levels. The returns also tend to be higher for India and Pakistan (which are countries with faster and more continuous economic growth), than for Sri Lanka where growth has been more variable. The returns to education for males are the highest in India with rates of 15 per cent. These higher returns clearly indicate that the demand for educated and skilled workers has been increasing faster than the supply. This is consistent with evidence from other countries.

In addition, there are differences in the return to education by sector. Riboud et al. (2007) find that in India the rates of return to secondary education first increased but then fell for all but utilities and construction, which was the highest throughout. For tertiary education, the rates of return increased for all sectors over the 20-year period. Business services had the highest returns among all the sectors. By 2004, the last year covered, they increased from 12 per cent in 1989 to 18 per cent, consistent with the well publicized growth in demand for ICT-enabled services.

In Pakistan, rates of return to secondary education were highest for business services and manufacturing, rising throughout the period. The returns to public administration fell throughout the period, and were the lowest among all the sectors by 2004. The returns to utilities and construction and wholesale and retail trade rose, but only slightly. However, for higher education, the returns to utilities and construction and public administration rose to become the two highest categories. Those for business services and manufacturing fell. This may have been related to the greater variability in Pakistan's growth rate.

In Sri Lanka, for secondary education there was a dramatic fall in the returns to business services and public administration since the

---

[10]Riboud et al. (2007) calculate the rates of return to education based on wage equations derived from household surveys in the respective countries.

TABLE 6.3   **Total Tertiary Students Enrolled and Female and Private Percentages (2006)**

(in thousand)

	Total Enrollment	Per cent Female	Per cent Private
World	143,889	50	–
Arab States	7,038	49	–
Central and Eastern Europe	20,125	55	–
Russian Fed.	9,167	57	12
Central Asia	1,974	52	–
Ukraine	2,819	54	–
East Asia and Pacific	43,777	47	–
China	23,361	47	–
Indonesia	3,657	–	–
Japan	4,085	46	80
Republic of Korea	3,204	37	80
Thailand	2,504	54	17
Latin America and Caribbean	16,247	54	–
Brazil	4,572	56	72
North America and Western Europe	33,752	56	–
USA	17,487	57	26
South and West Asia*	17,253	41	–
Afghanistan	28	20	–
Bangladesh	1,054	35	49
Bhutan	4	33	–
India	12,853	40	–
Iran	2,829	52	52
Nepal	147	28	–
Pakistan	955	45	33
Sri Lanka	–	–	–
Sub-Saharan Africa	3,723	40	–

Source: UNESCO (2008, Table 8); De Ferranti et al. (2003).
Note: * UNESCO groups Iran in this regional aggregate.

mid-period. The other three did not change much, although returns to manufacturing did dip in the mid period. For higher education there was not that much variability in the returns, except for public administration which was much lower.

Noticeably only India shows rising returns to business services in tertiary education and these are higher than that of the other sectors, suggesting a rapid demand for IT-enabled services (ITES). This is

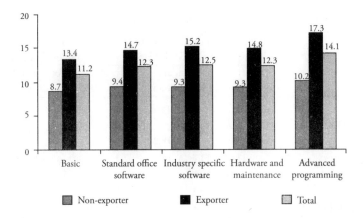

FIGURE 6.1   Average Annual Percentage Change in Average
Wages by Type of Skills (2003–6)

Source: World Bank (2008c)

consistent with a micro data indicator of excess demand for ICT skills
in India from the World Bank Investment Climate surveys (Figure
6.1). It shows that average wages have been rising faster for higher
levels skills, and that the increase is larger for firms that export (and
presumably have to perform to higher quality standards) than for firms
that do not export.

It is also noteworthy that the level of education tends to be higher for
the services sector. Bosworth and Maertens (Chapter 2 in this volume)
found that the average educational attainment increases in South Asian
countries from agriculture to industry to services. Higher rates for
industry than agriculture are expected, but the higher levels for services
are somewhat surprising, as traditional service employment is low skilled.
However, the high-skilled part of services, such as business services and
finance, showed the fastest growth. In India and Pakistan, the average
years of education in services was more than 50 per cent higher than that
in industry. In Nepal and Sri Lanka the average years in services were
just 10 per cent higher than in industry.

The Supply of Higher Education

The expansion in the supply of public tertiary education in South Asia has
not kept its pace with the demand. Supply has been constrained by the

TABLE 6.4   Expenditure on Education, Selected Regions and Countries

	Public Expenditures per Student as per cent of GDP/Capita						Public Expenditure on Education
	Primary		Secondary		Tertiary		Per cent GDP
	1991	2006	1999	2006	1999	2006	2006
EAP	–	–	7.0	–	32.2	–	3.5
China	–	–	11.5	–	90.1	–	
ECA	–	13.6	–	18.2	–	21.8	4.2
LAC	–	11.4	14.8	14.1	37.1	–	4.0
MNA	–	–	–	–	–	–	–
SA	–	–	13.1	–	90.8	–	2.2
Bangladesh	–	7.6	12.4	14.6	46.3	49.4	2.5
India	–	9.2	24.9	27.0	90.8	61.0	3.8
Nepal	–	–	13.1	–	141.7	–	–
Pakistan	–	–	–	–	–	–	2.6
Sri Lanka	–	–	–	–	–	–	–
SSA	–	11.8	–	–	–	–	4.2
High Income	15.8	19.2	24.3	24.8	32.8	29.0	5.4
World	–	14.5	–	21.1	–	–	4.6

Source: World Bank (2008a).
Note: Regional data are means, not weighed averages.

generally weak fiscal position of these countries as well as by regulatory barriers and biases against private sector supply. The share of public expenditure on public education in South Asia is the lowest compared to the global average (less than half) and just 40 per cent of the share spent by high income countries (Table 6.4). India has the highest share of public expenditure on public education among the South Asia region, but it is still almost one percentage point below the global average.

Another constraint on the growth of public higher education, particularly in South Asia, is the fact that tertiary education costs more per student than secondary and primary education (Table 6.4). In 1999, for example, the average per pupil cost of higher education in Nepal was ten times that of secondary education, and in Bangladesh and India it was four times the cost of secondary education. Furthermore, there are many pressing needs on limited government budgets, not only to extend access to basic and secondary education to a larger proportion of the population, but also for many other government services such as preventive health, infrastructure, and other public goods.

THE SITUATION OF HIGHER EDUCATION IN THE FIVE LARGEST SOUTH ASIAN COUNTRIES

The higher education systems have been under pressure in all the countries as they strive to cope with increasing demand. A synopsis of the situation is presented below for each of the five countries.[11]

Bangladesh

There are two categories of higher education institutions—degree awarding universities and colleges affiliated to the National University (NU). The higher education sector in Bangladesh has recently undergone an expansion. At independence in 1971 there were only 4 public universities, and now there are 29. However, excess demand in the 1990s saw the rapid growth of private universities. Currently there are 54 private universities, mostly around Dhaka and other large cities. There are also 1,400 colleges affiliated to the NU which serves about 80 per cent of the student body.

The University Grants Commission (UGC) is responsible for funding public universities and approving private universities. The colleges are controlled by the NU but there is no effective quality assurance mechanism. Each university establishes its own mechanism, but does not provide results for external review. The UGC is supposed to monitor the private universities, since it approves their operation. However, most private universities have failed to meet the minimum requirements regarding infrastructure, full time faculty, libraries, and other facilities. The government recently developed a National Strategic Plan for Higher Education for the next 20 years which is supported by a World Bank loan.

India

India has the largest and most developed system of higher education in South Asia. There are four types of institutions—universities (established by an Act of Parliament or of a state legislature), deemed universities (institutions which have been accorded the status of a university with authority to grant their own degree through central government notification), institutes of national importance (such as the IITs which are awarded that status by an

---

[11]This section draws heavily on a series of summary tables on the higher education sector of the three countries prepared by the World Bank Education Sector. See World Bank (2008d) for details on enrollment from each country.

Act of Parliament), and colleges affiliated to universities (which may or may not be aided by the government or the state and which have to follow the curriculum dictated by the affiliated university). The system has been growing rapidly in the last ten years, particularly private institutions. In 2005/6, enrollment in private and unaided institutions was estimated to be 31 per cent of total enrollments.

The UGC allocates public resources to the universities and colleges (including the so-called 'aided' private colleges) and recognizes colleges (a prerequisite to receive public funds). Quality assurance is done primarily by the National Assessment and Accreditation Council (NAAC) established by the UGC, although there are other institutions for technical colleges and professional schools. However, this is relatively new and only a small proportion of institutions have been accredited. A burning issue in India is that of equity. As part of an affirmative action programme, the number of places reserved for the lower castes and scheduled tribes was raised to 50 per cent, sparking a widespread public debate. As part of the 11th Development Plan, the federal government announced that it proposes to raise enrollment rates from 10 to 15 per cent. This includes creating 30 new central universities, 8 new IITs, 20 Indian Institutes of Information Technology (IIITs), 7 new Indian Institutes of Management (IIMs), several high grade medical institutes, and one degree college in each district in the country.

Nepal

The first university in Nepal (Tribhuvan University-TU) was established in 1958. In 1971 all community colleges were nationalized and became part of TU. Currently there are 6 universities and 567 colleges. TU has 91 per cent of the students. It appears that 9 per cent of total enrollments are in private institutions.

The Ministry of Education and Sports is responsible for the education sector, but the UGC (which funds and monitors higher education) is under the Ministry of Health. A Quality Assurance and Accreditation Council has been established in the UGC. The government has been preparing a 20-year strategic vision for the higher education sector.

Pakistan

There are two types of higher education institutions—the university/ degree awarding institutes (DAIs) and the affiliated colleges sector. The UGC has recently been replaced by a Higher Education Commission (HEC) and is responsible for public funding and accrediting degree programmes. Although almost half the 120 universities and one-third of the 1,135 colleges are private, the education sector is mainly public; 75 per cent of university students and 91 per cent of college students are in the public system. (This does not take into account the large number in the distance education programme.)

Although Pakistan's higher education system was neglected for two decades, in the early 2000s the government increased funding and created the HEC to implement major reform outlined in the 2005–10 Medium-Term Development Framework. This sought to improve, access, quality, and governance. Enrollment grew significantly and there were improvements to procedures and greater focus on quality and merit. However, much still remains to be done.

Sri Lanka

There is no reliable information on enrollments in Sri Lanka's higher education sector, other than for the public sector. There are 17 public universities with about 70,000 students. This gives an enrollment ratio of just 3 per cent. However, there is also an open university, 13 post graduate and specialized institutes, and an estimated 1,50,000 'external students' who take exams without attending classes. There are more than 50 private higher education institutions, and their numbers continue to grow. Adding all students in this broader system gives an enrollment rate of about 18 per cent and rising. Greatest growth has been in the private system, accounting for nearly 7 per cent of total tertiary students (counting distance education and 'external students'). Until 2006, higher education was under the Ministry of Education, but in January 2007 a Ministry of Higher Education was created as greater importance was given to the sector

Higher education in Sri Lanka used to be highly regarded, but it has not maintained this reputation as the system expanded. Student assessment reflected low quality and employers' assessments were negative. The UGC has initiated stronger steps to improve quality assurance, but this excludes private HEIs. A move towards an independent accreditation board is being considered. The government launched a 10-year Horizon Development Framework (2006–16) to create a knowledge economy with higher education as one of the main pillars.

Besides the weak performances of South Asian countries on formal higher education, the countries in the region do not do compare well in post-school or in-service training by employers. An analysis based on labour force surveys found that the incidence of post-school training was low in

South Asia. It was lowest in Pakistan with just 2.4 per cent, and highest in Sri Lanka with 12 per cent. The returns to post-school training were positive and statistically significant, even when controlled for educational attainment and other worker attributes (Riboud et al. 2007, chapter 5). In addition, based on cross country investment climate surveys, it was found that the incidence of in-service training in South Asia is among the lowest in the world, less than half the average for East Asia, Europe and Central Asia, and Latin America and the Caribbean. Since such training is required for technological change and productivity growth, the low incidence of training has negative implications for the competitiveness of the region's countries (Riboud et al. 2007, chapter 6).

Common Challenges, Differing Approaches

Essentially the same generic issues arise, to different degrees, across all five countries. They are access, quality, relevance, finance, and governance. Moreover, they are all related to the increasing demand for higher education across all the countries, which is part of the global trend in education and competitiveness outlined above. In addition, there are strong interrelationships among most of these issues.

Access

As has been seen, all the countries are struggling to deal with the problem of increasing access. The public system has not been able to respond to increasing demand, let alone extend access on an equitable basis. As a result, the private sector has jumped in to respond to unmet demand. While that has helped address part of the problem, it has created other problems, including those of equity and quality. In addition, as was seen in Table 6.1, even with the entry of the private sector, the South Asia region is not increasing tertiary enrollment as fast of other developing areas, particularly East Asia, and especially China.

Quality

Concerns about the quality of higher education stem from three causes. One is that there is great variation in the graduates of both the public and private systems. Most countries have some very good first tier public universities. However, they also have a much larger tier of universities and colleges that produce very poorly prepared students. Similarly, there are some excellent private universities, and at the same time a very large number of diploma mills that have emerged to take advantage of the excess demand. The second cause is that none of the countries have effective systems of quality assurance, either for the public or the private sector. The third is that it is hard to maintain quality when systems go through significant expansions, as is the case in some of the countries. Compounding this problem is a shortage of qualified faculty in all the countries. That arises, in part, because faculties are generally not well compensated. This is a particularly severe problem for good faculty in high-demand programmes, such as IT and other hot fields. The public universities simply cannot compete with career opportunities in the business world to retain their faculty or to expand their staff. In addition, salaries for faculty even in the private higher education sector are often controlled by the government (as in the case of India) generalizing the problem to the private higher education sector.

Relevance

There are various indications of lack of relevance in the output of higher education. In many countries too many tertiary graduates are produced in fields for which there is limited demand, while not enough are produced in areas in higher demand. This is caused by rigidities in the number of places allocated to different disciplines in the public system. Another part of the problem is due to outdated curriculum and pedagogical methods that still rely too much on rote learning rather than creative thinking, problem solving, and team work that is needed by the market. A study by the McKinsey Global Institute based on interviews with multinational companies, for example, found that only one quarter of Indian engineering graduates were considered to be qualified to be hired by the companies.[12]

Finance

Much of the problem of access and some of the problems of quality and relevance stem in large part because of limited finance. However, much can, and should still, be done to improve efficiency of public higher education, including the use of distance education and computer based learning. Another strategy is to charge tuitions to help offset public cost of expanding access, as has been done in China. It can be argued that since graduates are likely to get better paying jobs, they should be able

---

[12]Farrell et al. (2005: 96), based on interviews carried out by McKinsey, estimated that on average only 25 per cent of the engineering graduates in India were suitable for employment by multinational companies. Problems were language skills, too much emphasis on theory rather than practice, and lack of cultural fit (interpersonal skills as well as attitudes towards teamwork and flexible work).

to finance it through their higher earning potential. Another solution is to let the private sector grow further to service a larger part of the growing market. However, shifting the financial costs to the students by increasing tuitions in the public system or pushing them off into a private system increases the problem of equity. Increasing the private costs of higher education makes it more difficult for poor and disadvantaged students to access the better job and income opportunities associated with increased education. Therefore, governments will have to focus more on addressing the equity problem through grants and other support schemes for qualified students who cannot afford the increasing cost of higher education. In addition, they will have to do more to develop a student loan market as is being done in India.

Governance

As noted, the formal higher education system in all five countries now has both public and private higher education providers. There are also many more providers of post-secondary education and training services including specialized certificates in everything ranging from certain software certification to professional qualification certificates in accounting, legal, financial, or other services. As the system becomes more complex with multiple players and multiple pathways, new and better systems of governance have to be established. The public sector has to improve governance arrangements for the public institutions under its direct control by developing better incentives, monitoring, performance assessment, and accountability both for the internal processes of the education as well as for students. However, it also has to help set up systems and processes to improve the performance of the broader post-secondary system, including better quality assurance mechanisms as well as better information on career prospects and on the quality of different education providers. Thus its role needs to change from the earlier paradigm where it was the sole provider of higher education, to one where it is just one of the providers in a more complex system with multiple providers and many more pathways to higher education skills and degrees.

As can be inferred from the quick overview of the situation in different countries, they have tried different degrees of privatization as well as of liberalization or regulation of their higher education sector and they have had mixed results. The mixed results are not only due to the different approaches, but also how vigorously and effectively they have implemented them. While there are different ideologies on the role of government and of the market, it is interesting and quite instructive to briefly review the spectacular rise of the ITES exports from India. We outline what was done by the private sector to overcome many of the challenges enumerated above, and what challenges were compounded by a fairly unresponsive public education sector.

Tackling the Challenges: The Example of the ICT Sector in India

The rise of the IT/ITES sector in India is a remarkable example of development. It also illustrates the power of market demand and of a strong private sector in bringing about fundamental reform in the higher educational system. The growth and contribution of the sector to the Indian economy can be traced through various figures. These include its direct contribution to GDP, its export earnings, direct and indirect employment generation, its multiplier effects, and other indirect effects on the rest of the Indian economy.[13]

The share of the IT/ITES industry to GDP has risen rapidly from just 1.2 per cent in FY 1998 to 5.2 per cent in FY 2007. Exports have increased from US $1.8 billion to US $40 billion over the same period. Direct employment has risen from 1,90,000 to 20,00,000. Although this was just 0.5 per cent of India's labour force, it made the sector the largest employer in the organized private sector in the country.[14] According to NASSCOM, studies show that for every job created by the IT/ITES industry, three to four additional jobs are created in the rest of the economy. These include direct service providers such as catering, transport, housekeeping, security; and spending on housing, infrastructure, food, clothing, entertainment, travel, etc. Thus the sector is estimated to provide indirect employment for another 6.5 million workers (most of which do not require higher education). NASSCOM also estimates that spending US$ 15.83.billion in FY 2006 by the IT/ITES sector has an output multiplier of two on domestically sourced goods driven by firm outlays on domestic capital and operating expenditure, and

---

[13]This section draws heavily on a recently completed study by NASSCOM with the assistance of the consultancy and accounting firm of Deloitte. It was based on the data base and studies done by NASSCOM and others, a survey of 123 member firms, and direct interviews with firms and government officials (see NASSCOM Deloitte 2008).

[14]The Indian labour force is about 400 million, but only 11 per cent work in the organized sector (roughly equivalent to the formal sector consisting of firms employing ten workers or more and paying regular wages). However, roughly two-thirds of workers in the formal sector work for federal, state, or local government, so formal private sector employment is roughly just 3.5 per cent of total employment.

consumption expenditure by its professionals generating an additional output of US $15.5 billion through direct and indirect backward linkages with other sectors and induced effects of wages and salaries.[15]

Another indirect effect of the rise of the IT/ITES industry includes fuelling the growth of the venture capital and private equity funding industries in India (the IT and ITES sectors accounted for more two-thirds of the deals by 2000) and spurring the growth of first generation entrepreneurs.[16] But perhaps the most important indirect contribution of the success of the Indian IT/ITES industry has been to boost the confidence of Indian entrepreneurs and to raise the image of India in global markets. The industry has definitely put India on the global map and led to increased foreign investment by MNCs seeking to benefit both from the skilled higher education graduates who have been the driving factor behind the growth of this sector, plus the now rapidly growing domestic market.

The main motivation for firms to offshore services internationally is the lower cost of foreign knowledge workers. However, low wages for professionals in the information industry and other business services is not the only element taken into consideration. Firms also give weight to other costs including information infrastructure, the supply of skills, and the general business environment. In the 2007 global ranking of the top 50 countries as evaluated by A.T. Kearney, which includes these four factors, India is rated the most attractive overall. Particularly noteworthy is the high score it receives on people and skills availability (Annexure 6A)

India's reputation for world quality human capital has attracted much foreign investment into India to capitalize on this valuable resource. Apart from setting up subsidiaries in India to do business process outsourcing (BPO) and information and computer related services, firms have also hired Indian graduates to do research, consulting, and investment analysis, and provide other knowledge-intensive services for both their domestic and global operations. In addition, there have been spillover effects and impressive gains in other knowledge-intensive production and service sectors such as pharmaceuticals, biotechnology, auto parts,

[15]See NASSCOM Deloitte (2008).

[16]These include Narayana Murthi who started Infosys with initial capital of USD 250 in1981 but by FY 2007 had 60,000 employees and a turnover of USD 3.2 billion and Shiv Nadar and five other engineers, who launched Hindustan Computers Limited (HCL) in 1976 which launched its first computer in 1982, and is now India's second largest computer and office equipment manufacturer (Nassom Deloitte 2008).

etc. Thus there has been a more general boom in knowledge-intensive activities in the Indian economy.

All this demand for knowledge workers has put tremendous pressure on supply. In addition, the poor quality of the bulk of the graduates of the higher education system soon became obvious. Companies that hire offshore talent, tend to follow each other so there is often clustering in particular locations. This can create excess demand and local wage inflation. Farrell et al. (2005: 99) estimates that salaries of engineers in hot cities in India could have doubled between 2005 and 2008.

Overall, the supply of high quality education has become a major preoccupation for the ITES industry. The 2005 NASSCOM McKenzie Study identified a shortage of qualified talent for the IT/ITES industry of 5,00,000 by 2010. Since the educational sector was not able to respond to the massive need, individual firms developed their own training programmes. The top software companies, Infosys, Wipro, TCS, HCL Technologies, and Satyam were said to be spending US $430 million in 2007–8 to train 100,000 engineers hired during this period. For most companies 80 per cent of the hires are entry level and 80 per cent of the budget is spent on these new entrants.[17]

The industry association NASSCOM also set up various initiatives targeting three levels of talent requirements.[18] For the *entry level* it launched NASSCOM's Assessment of Competence in 2006 as an industry standard assessment and certification programme to test the skills and capabilities of entry level manpower. It is working with universities and colleges to help align their curriculum with the needs of the ITES-BPO sector. It aims to reduce hiring costs, improve efficiency, enlarge the candidate pool, and reduce escalating costs.

For the *middle level* it launched NAC-Tech, a similar testing and accreditation programme for evaluating students seeking jobs in the technology engineering industries. It aims to help both students and higher education institutions understand the skills required by the industry. With the Ministry of Human Resources Development (MHRD),

[17]Some firms have also developed specific programs with institutes of higher education. These include: 'Fellowship Program' from Infosys at top institutes for PhD work in computer sciences, management, law, and accounting; 'Campus Connect' programme, also from Infosys, focused on aligning the needs of engineering colleges, faculty, and students with the needs of the industry; and the 'Sarvodaya Program' of TCS with departments of Education and Science and Technology in various universities to help students upgrade technology and programming skills, enhance communication and presentation skills, and many others (NASSCOM 2007).

[18] This section is based on NASSCOM (2007).

it also launched in 2007 a 'Finishing Schools for Engineering Students Programme' to raise the skills of graduates to the needs of the industry. The curriculum reinforces some basic engineering skills and provides industry specific knowledge and skills, soft skills, and management and employment skills. The programme provides feedback on the ability of students in rational analytical thinking capabilities in a problem solving environment and includes the NAC-Tech test. It has also launched an IT Workforce Development programne aimed at improving the interaction between the industry and academia. It includes workshops on the needs of the industry, faculty training workshops and sabbaticals, and a 12–24 month mentorship programme with specific colleges and institutions to close the gaps in teaching methods and improve educational quality. It also works with formal academic bodies such as the MHRD, the All India Commission on Technical Education (AICTE), and the UGC to improve and standardize curriculum and pedagogy. Finally it promotes research and white papers in key areas such as curriculum requirements and skill sets needed by the industry.

For the *top level* it is working with the MHRD to develop highly specialized professionals in 'on the horizon' technologies that are not yet mainstream. This includes sectors ranging from banking, remote sensing, water, agriculture, energy, transportation, environment, geosphere, natural sciences, nanotechnology, healthcare, networks and mobile computing, image processing, cyber security, etc. The objectives include not only research, but the creation of competent professionals, and the incubation of new companies and clusters. This involves collaboration on the establishment of five new IIITs based on the public-private partnership model by the end of 2008, with in MHz's plan to have 20 IIITs during the current plan period.

This shows the tremendous impact this strong and growing sector is having on the higher education system. Although there are limits to what can be done by the market, and there is surely an important role for government, it shows how the private sector has been able to improve the quality of engineering education by the following:

1. Developing a *de facto* certification exam to test the competence of graduates
2. Working directly with universities to reform and update the curriculum
3. Training faculty in new technologies and pedagogies
4. Putting new entrants through a rigorous boot camp to improve standards

While other industries have not been subjected to such strong shortages of quality students, and while the technology base in those industries may not be changing as fast, the case of the Indian ICT industry does illustrate the need to reform and update antiquated and dysfunctional systems. It also illustrates how these standards, pushed by industry are becoming *de facto* standards. Since students want to get jobs in this industry they are paying attention to how well the graduates of different programmes do on these accreditations tests and using that to select where to study. At the same time universities and training institutions are taking note of the search for quality by students and are aiming to improve the quality of their programmes. Furthermore, the government has responded to the demands of the market and the value that can be contributed by quality education by expanding the number of IITs, IIMs, IIITs, and other high quality higher education institutions.

THE POTENTIAL OF DISTANCE EDUCATION IN SOUTH ASIA[19]

The Potential

Given the large demand for tertiary education as well as the constraints on public budgets there is enormous potential for open and distance learning (ODL) education programmes.[20] These programmes have been given a strong boost from the rapid advances and falling costs of information and communication technologies. The advantage of using ODL centres is that they have the potential to provide a cost effective delivery of tertiary education, as well as short-term courses to persons who have already left the formal educational system and are in the labour force.

The Situation in South Asian Countries

There already are large, well established ODL programmes in South Asian countries. India has the largest system. It includes nine tertiary institutions, dominated by the Indira Gandhi National Open University

[19] This section is based on Raza (2008), for some of the specifics for South Asia, Perraton (2000), and UNESCO (2007) for the more general discussion of the benefits and lessons of ODL and OECD (2008) for some of the future directions.

[20] Distance education is defined as 'an educational process in which a significant proportion of the teaching is conducted by someone removed in space or time from the learner'. Open learning is defined as 'an organized educational activity based on the use of teaching material, in which constraints on study are minimized either in terms of access, or of time and space, pace, method of study, or any combination of these' (Perraton 2000: 12).

(IGNOU). Moreover India's Tenth Five Year Plan (2002–7) aimed to expand ODL to reach 40 per cent of all tertiary level students by 2007.[21] Pakistan has the Allama Iqbal Open University (AIOU) which is Asia's oldest single mode ODL tertiary institution. Sri Lanka has the Open University of Sri Lanka (OUSL). Bangladesh Open University (BOU) emerged from the National Institute for Education Media and Technology (NIEMT) which in turn has resulted from the fusion of a correspondence school and a school of broadcasting.

There is incomplete information on the actual enrollments and graduates in these systems. In Bangladesh, the BOU had more than 2,00,000 students in 2001 in programmes ranging from high school to certificate and tertiary degree programmes. In India, by 1995, there were more than 2,00,000 in tertiary ODL programmes (UNESCO 2007). In Pakistan, AIOU accounted for 7.8 per cent of the bachelor degrees, 1.7 per cent of the masters, 13.8 per cent of the M.Phils, and 0.4 per cent of the PhD of the public sector graduates between 1996 and 2001. In Sri Lanka, data for 1999 indicated that while OUSL's share of graduates at the undergraduate level was very low, they accounted for 31 per cent of the postgraduate degrees in arts and 32 per cent of those in management (Raza 2008).

There is also little analysis of their cost effectiveness. In part this is because there is little information on completion rates since students enrolled in these programmes typically have a longer period of time to complete than in conventional institutions. In addition, in many systems that have fixed completion dates, students are allowed to re-enroll.

Lessons and Implications from the South Asian Experience

Raza (2008) analyses ODL in various South Asian countries and provides some interesting findings with important policy implications. The pass rates (percentage of students who sit for an examination and actually pass) are roughly equal to those of students at conventional tertiary institutions. However, the completion rates (percentage of students who complete a programme compared to the intake over a period of time) are lower. This is primarily because a large number of students who register do not attend any course, and many drop out after attending some classes. However, completion rates vary greatly across ODL institutions, types of programmes, and specific subject matter. The data for South

[21]This includes converting conventional institutions to dual mode institutions. By 2001 at least 64 traditional face-to-face institutions had converted to dual mode institutions.

Asia is consistent with that, in other parts of the world (Perraton 2000). Completion rates are better for short term certificate programmes and for postgraduate programmes, and they are lower for bachelor and diploma levels. Moreover, they are lower for technical subjects (such as engineering or accounting) than for non-technical subjects (such as liberal arts). The study also found that per students' costs for those who completed programmes at IGNOU and AIOU were not lower than those at conventional tertiary institutions in India and Pakistan, respectively, if they were based on comparisons of completion rates per student.

The lack of cost savings was attributed to wastage resulting from high dropout rates (around 70 per cent) from the ODL programmes. These comparisons did not explicitly take into account the possible saving in opportunity costs for ODL students who may be working while taking the ODL courses versus students at conventional tertiary institutions who may tend to be full time. However, the study does suggest that ODL programmes may not be as cost effective as many had expected.

Despite these lapses, there have been subsequent improvements in ICT delivery, pedagogy, organization, and management of ODL systems. While the study used data from 1996 to 2002, it does bring about certain relevant implications. One is that more complete data has to be collected on the relative performance of ODL programmes versus conventional tertiary education programmes. This should include more attention to direct and indirect costs and outcomes—for example, what is the benefit for students who participate in some ODL programmes, but do not complete the programme; how does the market evaluate the graduates of ODL versus those of conventional programmes; and is there any difference in their relative performance over time? A second is that it is important to tailor and focus on the programmes and subject areas where experience has shown that it tends to be more successful. A third is that more has to be done to reduce the high wastage rates of ODL programmes, and to concentrate on successful completion rather than simply on expanding enrollments.[22]

TRADE IN EDUCATIONAL SERVICES IN SOUTH ASIA

Students from South Asian Countries Studying Abroad

International student enrollments are increasing, particularly in higher education. In 1975 there were 0.6 million tertiary level students studying

---

[22]For lessons of the experience in distance education from OECD countries see OECD (2005a).

TABLE 6.5   International Flow of Mobile Students at
Tertiary Level (2006)

	Total Students Studying Abroad	As Percentage of Tertiary Students in Country	Students from Abroad in Country	Net Flow of Students (inbound– outbound)	Net Flow as Percentage of Tertiary Students in Country
Afghanistan	2,993	10.8	–	–	–
Bangladesh	16,687	2.8	939	–	–
Bhutan	626	–	–	–	–
India	1,39,459	1.1	7,589	–1,19,340	–0.9
Iran	19,720	0.9	2,092	–	–
Maldives	1,216	–	–	–	–
Nepal	10,572	5.3	–	–	–
Pakistan	23,795	3.3	–	–	–
Sri Lanka	11,266	–	–		

Source: UNESCO (2008, Table 10).

outside their home countries. By 2006, the figure stood at 2.8 million students (UNESCO 2008). China accounts for 15.2 per cent of the tertiary students studying outside their home country, followed by India (5.1 per cent), the Republic of Korea (3.7 per cent), Germany (2.5 per cent), and Japan (2.2 per cent).[23]

Table 6.5 shows the number of South Asian students studying outside their home country at the tertiary level. The highest ratio of tertiary students studying abroad to those in their own country are in Afghanistan (10.8 per cent) and Nepal (5.3 per cent), followed by Pakistan (3.3 per cent). The large percentage outside Afghanistan is due to domestic instability. The high percentage in Nepal and Pakistan may reflect limited options in those two countries, and domestic constraints on the quality as well as supply.

The GATS as It Applies to Trade in Educational Services

The General Agreement on Trade in Services (GATS) classifies trade in services into four types.[24] Bulk of the trade takes place through direct

[23]The largest host countries are the US (5,84,814), the UK (3,30,078), Germany (2,59,797), France (2,47,510), and Australia (2,07,264). Australia and the UK are making education a major export business, with net tertiary (domestic students studying abroad minus foreign studies studying in country) accounting for 19.0 per cent and 13.0 per cent of their total tertiary enrollments, respectively.

[24]Mode 1 is cross-border supply of educational services using distance technologies.

consumption abroad (mode 2). Restrictions include immigration requirements in the host country, foreign currency controls, and difficulties having degrees recognized in the home country. Therefore, agreements regarding standards for degree conversion/recognition would be helpful. On a more ambitious note, agreements on licensing and accreditation would also help. However, there has been an increase in cross-border education services (mode 1) facilitated by developments in IT and internet infrastructure. The main barriers here include the quality of the service, and the lack of recognition of the degree by the host country.

There are three common forms of commercial presence (mode 3): franchises, joint programmes (where students may spend time in the foreign country for part of the studies), and full local presence. Franchises and joint programmes tend to be more common than full local presence. Barriers to commercial presence include: inability to be recognized as a degree/certificate granting institution in the host country, limits on foreign direct investment (FDI), including specific caps on foreign ownership percentage, nationality requirements, restrictions on recruiting foreign teachers, and unequal competition from government subsidies to local institutions.

Barriers to presence of natural persons (mode 4) include immigration requirements, nationality restrictions, and recognition of credentials.

The Situation of the Five Largest South Asian Countries

Bangladesh

Bangladesh has not undertaken any commitments under the World Trade Organization (WTO), but has opened its education system to trade in services. Major destinations for education abroad are the US, Canada, the UK, and India. Bangladesh attracts students from Nepal, Bhutan, India, and some African countries.

Bangladesh already has relationships regarding education with Bhutan, India, and Nepal. It would appear that Bangladesh would benefit from opening trade in educational services. Bangladeshi students studying abroad at the tertiary level are 1.7 per cent of total tertiary students in Bangladesh. It is likely that by opening up more to trade in educational services, more students would study in Bangladesh and save

---

Mode 2 is students going abroad for study. Mode 3 is commercial presence of the foreign education provider in the country through the establishment of a foreign affiliate. Mode 4 is movement of teachers temporarily to the country of the consumer to provide the service.

the country some foreign exchange and strengthen Bangladesh's higher education sector.

India

India did not undertake commitments under the Uruguay Round or during its initial offer. However, it has a revised offer which includes commitments in higher education. Because of the strong excess demand for education services in India and constraints on public supply, there has been significant interest from foreign providers.

Students have also been recruited from India by foreign institutions to study abroad. The number of foreign providers offering programmes in India increased from 27 to 144 from 2000–4, although one-third were not universities, and an equal number of their Indian collaborators were not part of the higher education system either (Asian Development bank [ADB] 2008: 166).

Although 100 per cent entry by foreign higher education providers is permitted, in practice it is very difficult for foreign providers to enter because of India's vast and complex regulatory system for higher education. For example, the AICTE which oversees engineering and management education requires that besides being accredited in their home country, their degrees must be the same; and there are no provisions for conversion to the nomenclature approved by the UGC. In addition, the UGC, the AICTE, and other statutory councils prescribe minimum standards on infrastructure, faculty, duration of programme, eligibility criteria, and fees. Furthermore, the institutions are also subject to additional regulations at the level of the state they operate in.

Pakistan

Pakistan did not make commitments under the Uruguay Round, but its initial offer includes education services and is relatively open as compared to other South Asian countries. Pakistan has offered full commitments in modes 1–3. Mode 4 is unbound, but refers to horizontal commitments where it is quite open to entry of professionals. The main restrictions are: foreign equity cap of 60 per cent for commercial presences, no sectoral mode 4 commitments, and no national treatment with regards to subsidies.

Because of excess demand and limited supply of higher education there has been an expansion of private higher education institutions in Pakistan. However higher education in Pakistan lags behind that of some other countries in the region. As a result, it has a higher proportion of students studying outside the country (Table 6.5). Therefore, it would probably do well to open up to more FDI in education, as it may provide better quality higher education at a lower cost than having students to go abroad for very expensive education.

Nepal

Nepal undertook commitments with no limitations on modes 1 and 2 in market access. However, mode 3 has a maximum foreign ownership of 51 per cent (to be raised to 80 per cent by April 2008 when it completes five years of joining the WTO).

Nepal has the lowest enrollment rates at the tertiary level among the five major South Asian countries. It also has a problem of brain drain in tertiary education. There is a mismatch between the skills provided by the existing system and the needs of the market. This is particularly so for the IT market which suffers shortages even though there are various specialized foreign training institutes such as NIIT, STG, SSi, Pentasoft, and APTECH in the IT sector, in addition to training provided by the formal higher education system. Various Indian higher education institutions already operate in Nepal. A leading example is a medical college run by the Manipal College of Medical Sciences which is ranked as the best college in Nepal. Currently students from Nepal studying abroad are 5.3 per cent of the total number of students studying in Nepal. Nepal would benefit from opening up more on its trade in education services, particularly with respect to greater foreign ownership limits, and immigration of teachers as it will benefit from having more capacity in the sector to improve economies of scale and probably also save foreign exchange.

Sri Lanka

Sri Lanka has not undertaken any sectoral commitments in education services, but it did allow up to 100 per cent foreign ownership under the Uruguay Round. Private tertiary education has been very contentious in Sri Lanka and the government is the only provider of accredited tertiary education. Although there are ambiguous rules regarding private tertiary education, several private degree granting institutions have been established, especially in tertiary programmes in accounting, management, and IT. Many of these are in collaboration with foreign institutions. By some estimates, less than 15 per cent of the eligible students are admitted to public universities.

As a result, students who can afford it study abroad, especially in the US, the UK, and Australia. India is also appealing to Sri Lankan

TABLE 6.6   **Summary of Commitments for Each Mode, by Country**

	Trade in Educational Services Mode 1	Students Studying Abroad Mode 2	Foreign Institutions in Country Mode 3	Foreign Teachers in Country Mode 4
Bangladesh	No formal commitments.	No formal commitments.	No formal commitments	No formal commitments.
India	India requires service providers to follow same regulations as domestic providers.	No formal restrictions.	No maximum foreign equity cap, but lots of regulations constrain commercial presence. Fees subject to approval by domestic authority. Institutions that have prior investments need permission from the FIPB to open additional universities. Regulation of higher education institutions at Federal and State levels and by more than one body	Unbound, however with respect to national treatment which is quite liberal across other service areas, educational services are not included. This may negatively impact teachers from other Asian countries.
Nepal	No national commitment to provide foreign exchange to pay foreigners for cross-border services.	No formal limitations.	Maximum foreign equity at 51 per cent, but being raised to 80 per cent in 2009. Foreign	Unbound and refers to horizontal section where there is no special provision for education.

(contd...)

(Table 6.6. contd...)

	Trade in Educational Services Mode 1	Students Studying Abroad Mode 2	Foreign Institutions in Country Mode 3	Foreign Teachers in Country Mode 4
		investment and reinvestment of earnings require permission.		Therefore movement of teachers and related professionals seems to be closed.
Pakistan			Incentives and subsidies available only to wholly Nepal owned enterprises. Maximum foreign equity limited to 60 per cent. High minimum land and endowment requirements imposed on private institutions to set up a campus.	Liberal entry of professionals, and others having skills to supply education, but is limited to imparting training.
Sri Lanka	No sectoral commitments	No sectoral commitments	No sectoral commitments. However 100 per cent foreign equity allowed on a case by case basis in consultation with relevant state agencies was agreed to earlier during Uruguay Round.	No sectoral commitments.

Source: Based on Asian Development Bank (2008).

students because of lower costs and proximity. However, many Sri Lankan students who earn degrees in India face problems getting them recognized by the Sri Lankan authorities, and often have to pass Sri Lankan certification exams. It would make sense for India and Sri Lanka to develop mutual recognition agreements, given the already existing level of interaction. In addition, Sri Lanka would benefit from greater trade in higher education services, given limited domestic supply.

CHALLENGES FOR HIGHER EDUCATION AND OPPORTUNITIES FOF REGIONAL COLLABORATION

Challenges

As global competition is becoming more demanding, obtaining tertiary education has become more critical for job seekers to compete successfully. Demand for higher education in South Asia is increasing rapidly with the growing population. Other countries are moving ahead dramatically, particularly China (discussed later in the chapter). There is ample evidence that higher education is important for economic growth. In the case of India, in particular, it is clear that the critical mass of skilled English speaking engineers was a crucial factor in the development and growth of the ITES. These have been leading sectors in the rapid growth of the modern service sector in India as well as other South Asian countries. Higher education also has been very important in the rapid growth of other modern high skilled service sectors in India and other South Asian countries. These include financial services, real estate, and education services.

However, in spite of the success in the growth of modern high skilled services in South Asian countries, they lag behind the rest of the world in the expansion of higher education. In addition, it is clear that there has been a constraint in the supply of quality higher education. This can be seen from the rapid expansion of the private higher education sector, the sizable number of South Asian students who pay large sums to study abroad, the still high and even rising returns to higher education in most South Asian countries, and the rapidly rising salaries of graduates from the best engineering schools.

There are many problems in the higher education sector in South Asian countries.[25] The challenges of the higher education system across the five countries are very similar—access, quality, relevance, financing,

[25]See Kapur and Crowley (2008) for a general discussion of some of the problems of higher education in developing countries.

and governance. The countries have taken somewhat different approaches to deal with these challenges. This has included different degrees of regulation and privatization. They have had mixed results across the five countries not only because they have come from different perspectives, but also due to differences in degree and capacity for implementation. Some of the key issues requiring special attention include:[26]

1. Higher education has a long gestation process. It is the apex of a pyramid that has typically been 18 years in the making. While it is possible to implement some reforms that will improve higher education in the short run, it is also important to begin to reform the whole education pyramid (later in the chapter).

2. Countries need to invest both in expanding higher education as well as in expanding access to, and quality of, basic education. This requires careful thinking through of the rationale for public investments in education. The critical role of government is to invest in education as a public good. This includes most of basic education, maybe some of secondary education, and just a portion of tertiary education. Many areas of higher education—namely the professional schools—can be delivered by private providers.

3. South Asian governments should consider charging higher tuitions for elite public higher education institutions such as at the IITs and IIMs. The graduates of these institutes receive very large wage premia and would be able to afford tuitions that cover most of their costs. China was able to rapidly expand its public higher education system by charging tuition that covers 40 per cent of costs. The government should instead focus on financing research universities and areas of higher education that have a public good content, and typically will not be financed by the private sector or pay high wage premia. The government can support them directly or indirectly through competitive grants that private universities can also compete for.

4. More has to be done to improve the effectiveness in the allocation and use of public education budgets as well as to find more cost effective ways of delivering education, including more efficient distance education, blended learning, IT-based instruction, short duration professional courses, etc.

5. Governments also have to develop alternative funding mechanisms, including developing more effective student loan systems. In addition,

[26]For some excellent analysis the key issues in reforming Indian higher education, see Kapur and Metha (2007).

as more of higher education is provided privately for a fee and as tuitions are raised in public institutions, the government will have to do more to address the equity problem in access to higher education. This involves grants to needy but qualified students. It may also involve affirmative action. The higher education system is typically the means through which inequality is perpetuated. While affirmative action efforts can offer excluded groups an opportunity to get education that can improve their earning potential, overly ambitious affirmative action goals may undermine quality of higher education if the target groups are not up to standard. Therefore it is important to open access to quality education for disadvantaged groups from the earlier stages in the education pyramid—going all the way to down to primary education. This is a complex area especially given excess demand for education and limited supply. Governments can mitigate some immediate trade-offs by enlarging the number of places in higher education, as is being done in India, but they also have to create enrichment programmes to improve the qualifications of the affirmative action candidates so they may succeed in higher education.

Growth of the Indian ICT industry has driven demand for quality higher education. Many education providers have entered the market to fill the growing needs of this skill-intensive sector. The industry has been able to overcome some of the challenges that stifle the supply of high quality higher education, including governance and regulatory constraints on the system. While this may not be easily generalizable to other sectors, it does show that the constraints can be broken when the private sector takes a strong initiative and works directly with higher education institutions as well as the government.

South Asia pioneered distance education and virtually all countries have some element of distance education. This technology has the potential to significantly reduce the costs of delivering tertiary education services to many students. However, the review of distance education initiatives indicated that there are still many problems with the effective implementation of the technology. More work needs to be done to harness the potential of this mode of education delivery.[27]

South Asian countries are participating in different degrees of trade in educational services. The most developed is the GATS mode 2 whereby South Asian students go abroad for study. Some of this foreign study is

[27]See OECD (2005a) for more on the experience of developed countries.

to other countries in the region, particularly India. However, most of this is movement of students is to the UK, Australia, the US, and other European countries, which implies high foreign exchange costs. There is scope for greater liberalization in mode 3 (foreign presence), mode 4 (foreign teachers), and mode 1 (international distance education). This could mean more cost effective ways of meeting the shortage of domestic supply of quality higher education. Also greater use of modes 3 and 4 could increase economies of scale and specialization to strengthen higher education in South Asian countries as competitive sectors in their own right. This could also strengthen the prospects for South Asian countries themselves to be larger exporters of educational services, not only for trade among themselves, but also to countries outside the region.

The Opportunities for Regional Collaboration in Higher Education

The rationale for a regional approach is based on two elements. The first element is that the issues South Asia confronts on education are very similar. There are large economies of scale in developing common frameworks and in applying them over the larger population of the South Asian region. South Asian countries are faced with a more complex international environment and the increased importance of, and demand for, quality higher education. Thus there is scope for intra-regional cooperation in many areas. There is scope to share general experiences on how they are dealing with the challenges, what is working, and how things can be improved. At a more specific level there is scope for cooperation on issues such as: standards, accreditation, and certification; curriculum development; distance education delivery platforms; and the political economy of the reform process. There is also scope for developing joint programmes where the region can build economies of scale by working across national boundaries.

Regional cooperation is already happening in the ITES service area. Some of the large foreign and regional companies and international universities are already working across national borders. Joint programmes exist to train new students as well as to upgrade the skills of persons already employed in this sector. However, there should be scope for more formal collaboration across national boundaries by the public higher education sector.

Opening up more to mode 3 (trade in services) would help relieve the domestic supply constraint and may provide a lower cost and way of addressing the demand. Since a lack of qualified teachers is another important constraint, allowing greater movement of teachers (mode 4) would help relieve that supply constraint. Upgrading teacher training would also help. India is the already a major provider of educational services to the South Asia region through all four modes. Currently India gets thousands of students from Bangladesh, Nepal, and Sri Lanka. They get some concessions at Indian public institutions. There is also great potential for more trade in education services through mode 1, facilitated by the internet which will require regional cooperation on accreditations and recognition of degrees.

The second element of the rationale for regional cooperation rests on the shared history and culture of many South Asian countries. There is a common legacy of the British heritage—the English language and in the structure and key institutions in South Asian higher education systems. This gives them a common ground which facilitates interaction. There is much greater commonality across the South Asian countries than with the world as a whole. It makes sense for regulatory bodies, such as the UGC and various accrediting agencies, to work with their counterparts in the countries in the region to develop some common standards in curricula, licensing, accreditation, recognition of qualifications, and monitoring both profit and non-profit institutions.

However, in spite of the common British heritage in higher education, there is one important caveat. South Asian countries must decide whether that heritage is helping or hindering them compared to what is happening in the rest of the world. They also have to take into account how they should relate to standards being set up by the rest of the world. One place to start is to see how the British system itself has been going through important transformations to improve the efficiency, relevance, and competitiveness of British higher education with respect to the rest of the world.[28] The second is to decide which system or what combination of higher education systems and standards they want to align themselves with. In the important area of engineering education there are two systems. One is the US system. The other is the evolving European Community system. There are also economies of scale and scope in studying the advantages and disadvantages of these systems for their own specific situations, and how they should be factored into their own accreditation and certification standards.

[28]Note for example, that there has been significant reform of the British higher educational system including making state financed colleges and universities more responsive to the needs of the productive sector, as well as significantly increasing tuition fees in order to improve their quality and competitiveness.

On a more ambitious note and looking more towards a period when there is greater regional integration in trade, South Asia may also want to look at the model of what the European Community has been doing in to integrate higher education. This is the Bologna Process which aims to establish a European Higher Education Area by 2010. The Bologna Process uses four objectives to create a convergent system of education. This includes: a common framework of recognizable degrees; a two cycle—undergraduate and graduate—system in all participating countries; a European credit transfer system to recognize course credits and learning experiences in other member countries; and a system of common quality assurance, including an overarching framework of qualifications. While this is not to suggest that South Asia needs to do the same, it would be worthwhile to explore avenues for collaboration, including perhaps some collaboration with the EU system itself. In the short run, there is also scope for more international cooperation on phasing in international standards in professional areas such as engineering, medicine, nursing, and accounting.

EDUCATION AND THE DEVELOPMENT STRATEGIES OF INDIA AND CHINA

There is an education paradox in the comparison of the export structure of India and China. India has developed a comparative advantage in the high-skilled service sector exports, while China has developed a comparative advantage in the export of manufactured products, even though India has a lower general education attainment than China. There is the notion that India's rapid growth based on services shows there is an alternative development model based on skipping from agriculture to services rather than the traditional development model from agriculture to industry, and eventually to services. There is also the concern of whether services can be the engine of growth for South Asia.

Although this is a topic that requires more extensive analysis, this section attempts to provide some insights into this discussion by first comparing education in India and China. It will then summarize some of the critical elements of the broader development strategy of these two countries which may help to explain the different structures. It also has some implications for future development strategies in South Asia.

Education in India and China

This section first compares literacy, primary, and secondary education. It then compares secondary and higher education enrollment rates and stocks, and makes concluding comments on lifelong learning.

Literacy and Primary Education

As a very poor developing country just 25 years ago, China had very low average levels of education, although it already had a literacy rate that was more than 60 per cent higher than India's (see Table 6.7 for all the comparative education figures). Over the last 25 years it has made massive investments in basic education and now has a literacy rate nearly as high as developed economies. India still has a very low literacy rate. Illiteracy is 52 per cent among women and 27 per cent among men. Its basic education system is still very poor with tens of millions of primary school children out of school.

Secondary Education

China also invested earlier in secondary education. By 1980, secondary enrollment rates were already 50 per cent higher than in India. Although India has increased secondary enrollment rates over the last 25 years, China has also increased its enrollment rates and has maintained its 50 per cent lead over India. China's edge in secondary education has been very important in preparing its large labour force for a massive expansion of the industrial sector. It has also been one of the attractions for labour-intensive, export-oriented foreign investment.

Tertiary Education

China has undertaken a massive expansion of its tertiary education system starting in the late 1990s to make up for the havoc reeked on the educational system after the Cultural Revolution (1965 to 1975). In 1980 China had less than half the tertiary enrollment rates of India. By 2005, its enrollment rate reached 22 per cent. Starting in the 1950s, India set up seven IITs and later several IIMs, which produced a critical mass of well-educated, English-speaking professionals who have been instrumental in India's emergence in software and ICT-enabled services. India has expanded tertiary enrollment rates, but it has not done so as fast as China. Although India enrollment rates were more than twice those of China's in 1980, in 2006 they were just half of China's. Also, the quality of higher education is poor with the exception of IITs, IIMs, IIITs, (which produce less than 7,000 graduates a year), the Indian Institutes of Science (IIScs), and some of the regional engineering colleges. The low quality of tertiary education and the regulatory constraints on expanding high quality institutions appeared to be a road block to India's continued rapid growth in knowledge-intensive services. However, as noted earlier, the ICT industry in India took the initiative in addressing this concern and

TABLE 6.7   Education Comparison: China and India

	China	India
Literacy rate, population 15 and above		
1980	67.1	41.0
1990	78.3	49.3
1995	80.8	53.3
2006	90.9	61.0
Av. ed. attainment of adult pop. (2000)	6.35	5.06
gross primary enrollment rate		
1980	113	83
2006	111	115
Secondary education enrollment rate		
1980	46	30
2006	76	54
Higher education enrollment rate		
1980	2	5
2006	22	11
Total stock of persons with higher education (2005 in millions)	70.3	52.6
Scientists and engineers in R&D		
1995	5,31,997	1,45,115
2006	9,26,252	1,17,528
Skilled labour	*Well developed* Training market inside and outside firms	*Very under developed* Very poorly developed training market

Source: Stock of persons with higher education, OECD (2008); Scientists and Engineers in research and development (R&D), World Bank (2008b); World Bank (1997 and 2008).

it appears that the higher education system is responding at least with respect to quality IT education. The challenge remains as to what extent these reforms can be expanded to the existing higher education system.

Because of China's rapid expansion of higher education (expanding new enrollments by 50 per cent per year starting in 1998), the stock of persons with higher education in 2005 is 70 million, compared to 53 million in India (OECD 2007). In addition, China has nearly one million scientists and engineers involved in R&D, which is almost eight times the number in India. In 2006, China spent 1.4 per cent of GDP on R&D versus 0.85 per cent spent by India. In purchasing power parity terms, this amounts to US $82 billion dollars in China versus US $23 billion in India. In addition, Indian universities only perform 4.4 per cent of this R&D versus 10.0 per cent in China and 14.4 per cent in the US (Dahlman forthcoming 2009). Thus, India is falling behind China because of its weaker education system in general and its tertiary education system in particular.

Education and the Development Strategies of India and China

There are four factors that help to explain the different economic and trade structures of India and China—trade, FDI, infrastructure, education, and language.

Trade Policy

Arguably the most important has been trade policy. China started trade liberalization in the late 1980s, about a decade earlier than India. Learning from the success of its Asian neighbours such as Hong Kong, Korea, Singapore, and Taiwan it opted for labour-intensive manufactured exports (see Naughton 2007). This started with four export processing zones across from Hong Kong and Taiwan. These were successful in generating foreign exchange and employment growth so they were expanded to another 19 zones. In addition, China eventually committed to joining the WTO and as part of that process it committed to significant liberalization in goods and services. Furthermore, because of a more open trade policy, China has been rapidly increasing the technology intensity of its exports. In 1996, the share of high technology products in its manufactured exports was 21 per cent compared to 10 per cent in India. In 2006, the share of high technology products was 30 per cent in China, compared to only 5 per cent in India (World Bank 1999, 2008a). This difference is partly because China imports a lot of high technology components for the electronic products it exports. Another reason is that a lot of these exports are made by foreign multinationals exporting from China. However, a third part of the explanation is that China has a highly skilled workforce that is able to produce more sophisticated products and also China has been investing very rapidly in higher education and in science and technology, as noted above.

India was largely a closed economy until it was forced to undertake trade liberalization after the 1991 financial crisis, as part of the IMF conditionality for structural adjustment. India has liberalized further since then (see Panagariya 2008). However, even by 2006, the average weighted tariffs on manufactured products in India, at 14.5 per cent, was more than three times that in China, at 4.3 per cent (World Bank 1999, 2008a).

In China, the rapid development of a very large labour intensive manufacturing export sector led to massive migration of workers from the interior of China to the coastal provinces. This is one of the largest internal migrations in history. Exports of manufactured products were 50.5 per cent of manufactured value added in 1995 and increased to 102.1 per cent by 2006 in China. In India, they went from 32.5 per cent in 1990 to 69.2 per cent in 2006. However, the total volume of manufactured exports from India in 2006 was less just 60 per cent of the increase in manufactured exports from China between 2005 and 2006.[29]

Foreign Direct Investment

A key element of China's trade strategy was to use FDI to get into exports. China used FDI to get access to technology and to markets. FDI was allowed into the first export processing zones, and they were important in the subsequent zones (see Naughton 2007: chapters 16, 17). India was very suspicious of FDI inflows, and only liberalized slowly in the 1990s. Even since 2000, the inflows of FDI into India have only been a fraction of those into China. Average gross FDI into India as a percentage of GDP for 2000–5 has only been 0.9 per cent versus 3.1 per cent for China. Estimates are that as much as 60 per cent of Chinese manufactured imports into the US are products made by US multinational companies.

Infrastructure

Another important element as to why China has a comparative advantage in manufactured exports is that it has relatively efficient port and transport infrastructure and less bureaucracy in imports and exports. India's much higher cost of infrastructure and more bureaucratic procedures to get goods in and out make it less competitive in manufacture product trade. The International Finance Corporation (IFC) (2009) *Cost of Doing Business Report* ranks China 48th and India 90th among 181 economies in the ease of doing business across borders.[30] One reason why India has a comparative advantage in exports of ICT-enabled services is that they do not have these high transactions costs.

[29]Based on calculation with data in World Bank (2008a).
[30]The measure includes the number of documents and number of days and the cost required to import and to export a container of freight—see IFC (2009).

Education and Language

Finally, China had a more literate labour force and was able to rapidly expand secondary education which greatly contributed to the capabilities of the very large number of workers required for its labour-intensive manufactured products export industry. The low cost and good skill levels of its labour force were the key attractions of putting labour-intensive operations in China. On the other hand, the core stock of English speaking engineering and technical graduates in India, as well as the strong connection of the Indian diaspora to the ICT industry in the US and Europe were the main attractions in off-shoring ITES to India. In addition, once India developed a reputation for good quality higher education services many foreign firms chose to set up subsidiaries in India to tap that talent pool and they developed a virtuous circle for the rapid growth of high skilled services.

Sustainability of Service-led Growth in South Asia

How sustainable is India's continued rapid growth in information-enabled services exports and its service-based growth more generally? It is clear that India has developed a strong comparative advantage in IT-enabled exports and that these can increase, particularly now that the IT sector has adopted standards and is working with higher education institutions and the government to address the issue of graduate quality. There is also some evidence of ITES export growth from other countries in South Asia.

The ITES sector growth has been decoupled from the domestic economy since so much of it has been driven by exports, in particular to the US.[31] In the short run, the demand for these services is likely to be negatively affected by the sharp global economic downturn which will reduce demand. There is also the risk of a protectionist backlash in some developed market economies such as the US given the severity of the downturn and the very rapidly rising unemployment rates. In the medium run there is some concern that some of the more routine work that was being off-shored can also be done by automated machine-based processes. In addition, other countries, including China, as well as in Central and Eastern Europe, the Middle East, Latin America, and Africa and are moving into this export sector.

However, India developed strong capabilities in this sector. Its IT firms are also moving up the value chain to more knowledge-intensive activities

[31]The US market represents 60 per cent of Indian ITES (NASSCOM 2009).

including software development and IT integration services, and are beginning to offshore some of the more routine work to other countries in the region with lower wages. There is likely to be increasing globalization of services work. But attracting this work to South Asian countries is not just a matter of improving tertiary education. As noted in rankings such as those used by A.T. Kearney (Annexure 6A), other important considerations are total compensation costs, work force availability and flexibility, tax and regulatory costs, the country and business environment, infrastructure costs (not just IT services, but also electricity, travel, and rental costs), intellectual property, and security. Thus it also requires making progress on the broader investment climate and improving infrastructure—which has been a challenge for South Asian countries.

The sustainability of rapid service-based growth beyond the ITES sector depends on the broader growth prospects in India, South Asia and the world more generally. This is difficult to predict now given the magnitude of the crisis and the probability that it will lead to significant restructuring of the financial as well as the real sector in the US and other developed economies. Looking beyond the crisis, though, there certainly is strong potential for continued high productivity increases in the service sector in South Asia because these countries are still far behind the technological frontier in many areas, and particularly in distribution and retail trade. This continued productivity increase will be spurred by increasing deregulation and competition.

The concern however is that the high growth, high productivity sector is not generating much employment relative to the size of the rapidly growing labour forces in South Asian countries.[32] The challenge will be how to absorb that labour productively into the modern economy. That will require strengthening the general education base of the workers and greater employment in manufacturing as was done in China. Based on its track record the modern service sector itself cannot absorb the rapidly growing labour force. Moving to more labour-intensive and inclusive growth will require addressing broader constraints such as excessively rigid regulation of labour and land markets; further reduction in red tape and in the cost of doing business; and significant improvements in power, transportation infrastructure, and social services.

South Asian countries need to improve the competitiveness and labour absorption capacity of their manufacturing sectors. Manufacturing wages

[32]Even by 2009, the ITES industry in India does not employ much more than 0.5 per cent of the labour force.

in China have been rising faster than in India. To the extent that they continue to rise faster after the crisis, space will be opened up for greater labour-intensive manufactured exports from India and South Asia more generally, provided that the labour force is better educated and that some of the broader regulatory and infrastructure constraints are addressed.

However, it should be emphasized that India and other South Asian countries need to continue to improve the quality and supply of higher education. Quality higher education has become critical for countries to compete in the increasingly knowledge-intensive global knowledge economy. As noted, China is also moving up the value chain very rapidly and investing heavily in R&D and its own innovation sector. India and other South Asian countries need to increase their capacity to absorb knowledge from the rest of the world as well as to generate more of their own knowledge. This requires a strong higher education sector and greater research capability.

Thus, South Asian countries need to make significant improvements in the quality and supply of basic and secondary education, as well a higher education. The education sector itself can be a relatively important source of employment at the same time that it is a critical input into improving the performance of an economy.[33]

THE BROADER CHALLENGE OF POPULATION, EDUCATION, AND GROWTH IN SOUTH ASIA
Population Education and Growth

South Asia has a large population. It is also a rapidly growing population. Some suggest that this young and growing population can give South Asia a 'youth dividend' as the growing number of young workers join the labour force. However, for that dividend to materialize, this new labour force has to be educated, trained, and productively employed. A key issue therefore is how to turn this large and growing population into an asset than can contribute to growth rather than to have it become a liability, as new entrants to the labour force fail to find other than low productivity, subsistence-type employment.

South Asia's school population is almost as large as East Asia's (and will soon be larger given their higher population growth rates). On the other hand, public spending on education is smaller even than their

---

[33]The education sector accounts for 10 per cent of service employment in Sri Lanka and 12 per cent in India (the two countries for which there is a disaggregated breakdown of total service employment). The health sector is another important part of the service sector that can be expanded and provide more employment opportunities.

share of global GDP. The challenge therefore is how to educate this enormous population.

Literacy and educational attainment of the population in South Asian countries is very low. It is the lowest for any region, including Sub-Saharan Africa. Literacy ranges from a low of 28 per cent in Afghanistan to a high of 96 per cent in the Maldives. Bangladesh is just 44 per cent, Pakistan 50 per cent, and India 61 per cent.

Recent research has been showing the importance of agglomeration economies that occur in large urban centres (see Gill and Kharas 2007). The South Asia region has the highest population density of any region in the world (Table 6.8). It should be able to benefit from these economies of agglomeration if it has a more educated population. It must be noted, nevertheless, that South Asia has the highest percentage of rural population among all the regions, and the lowest percentage of population in cities of over 1 million. However, it does have many thriving cities with potential for strong knowledge agglomeration.

Given the large population and extensive higher education system, South Asia should be able to become a major education platform. As demonstrated by India, South Asia has some world class educational institutions. In economics jargon, they have the production function for quality higher education. South Asia has the critical mass of high quality tertiary institution, a rapidly growing number of young cohorts clamouring for higher education, economies of scale, and economies of agglomeration. Therefore it should be able to turn its abundant population advantage into a strategic asset. China has in fact explicitly followed a strategy of turning abundant natural resources to competitive assets (see Chinese Ministry of Higher Education 2003).

Population Education Pyramids

It is important to understand the population and education pyramid of South Asian countries because this has implications for the expected future size of the educational system. Figure 6.2 presents the population and education pyramids for the five South Asian countries covered in this chapter, as well at that of China for comparative purposes.

Pakistan, Nepal, Bangladesh, and India still have the highest population growth rates (Table 6.8) and therefore have population pyramids that are still very broad at the bottom and narrow down rapidly. Sri Lanka has already gone through a demographic transition with average population growth rate of just 1 per cent for 1990 to 2006 and an expected rate of just 0.3 per cent for 2006 to 2015. Therefore,

TABLE 6.8 Basic Population Indicators, World Regions and Selected Countries (2006–15)

Region or Country	Population in Million		Average Annual Growth Rates	Share of Population (in 2006) between		Population Density (2006)	Percentage of Population (2006)	
	2006	2015	1990–2006/ 2006–15	0–14 yrs	15–64 yrs	Per sq. km	Urban	In cities > 1 million*
EAP	1,899	2,033	1.1/0.8	23.5	69.4	120	42	–
China	1,311	1,382	0.9/0.6	21.1	71.1	141	41	18
ECA	460	461	0.1/0.0	19.4	68.9	20	64	17
LAC	556	616	1.5/1.1	29.6	64.1	28	78	34
MNA	311	362	2.0/1.7	32.7	63.0	35	57	20
South Asia	1,499	1,695	1.8/1.4	33.4	61.9	314	29	12
Bangladesh	156	180	2.0/1.6	34.7	61.7	1,198	26	12
India	1,110	1,233	1.7/1.2	32.5	62.4	373	29	12
Nepal	28	32	2.3/1.7	38.5	57.8	193	16	–
Pakistan	159	192	2.4/2.1	36.4	59.7	206	35	18
Sri Lanka	20	21	1.0/0.3	23.7	69.7	308	15	–
SSA	782	963	2.6/2.3	43.3	53.6	33	36	–
HIGH Y	1,031	1,071	0.7/0.4	17.9	67.1	31	78	–
EURO ZN	317	320	0.4/0.1	15.5	66.7	128	73	18
WORLD	6,538	72,001	1.4/1.1	28.0	64.6	50	49	20

Source: World Bank (2008a, 2008b).
Note: * Percentage of population in cities of more than one million is for 2005.

it already has a shrinking of the population cohorts at the younger ages and the shape of its population pyramid is closer to that of China which instituted strong population control in the 1980s. All the countries except Pakistan nominally have full enrollment rates at the primary level, although they all also suffer from the problem of repeaters which is why their enrollment rates are above 100 per cent (see enrollment rates in the pyramid). Pakistan is an outlier having primary enrollment rates that are just 74 per cent for females and 94 per cent for males, thus also showing a strong gender bias. However, these numbers for all the countries hide that fact that many children drop out of school before completing primary education.

At the secondary level Sri Lanka has much higher enrollment rates than the four other South Asian countries (even higher than China) because of its early strong focus on education. India does better than Bangladesh and Nepal, and Pakistan again comes in last. The same pattern is true at the tertiary level. As already noted, enrollment rates in China are twice those of India. What is also striking is just how fast the education pyramid narrows (with the exception of Sri Lanka), as well as the very significant problem of gender inequality in the South Asian countries. It is also very likely that ethnic and other social groups (caste, low-income) that have been discriminated against are those that are most excluded from advancing up the educational pyramid. In addition, those that advance are likely to be segregated in the lower quality schools, and therefore are at disadvantage even in the education they receive. Designing affirmative action policies at the higher education level for women, disadvantaged castes, or other special target groups needs to take this into account. Measures need to be put into place to give them more equality of opportunity at the lower levels of the educational pyramid so that they are well prepared for entry to higher education.

The pyramids in Figure 6.2 give a sense of the flow of education. The small box insert in each pyramid shows a stock measure—the average years of educational attainment of the population 15 years and above in 2000. This ranges from a low of just 2.4 years in Nepal to a high of 6.87 in Sri Lanka. In China it was 6.35 years. However, as China has had a massive drive to increase enrollment rates in upper secondary and higher education since 1998, the average educational attainment of its population over 15 reached more than 8 years in 2006 (see Dahlman et al. 2007). Thus the South Asian countries still have a long way to go to turn their abundant human resources to a source of competitive advantage the way China has been doing.

Moving Forward

The key challenges in education and training for South Asian countries are many. All countries need to improve the quality of primary education. All still need to expand access to secondary education and particularly to higher education which is now becoming critical for participation in the knowledge economy. They have to improve the quality of the whole educational system from pre-school to university. They also have to improve the content and relevance of what is taught in the formal educational system.

In addition, they have to move from an exclusive focus on the formal educational system to the development of lifelong learning systems. The half life of knowledge is getting shorter because of the speed-up in the generation and diffusion of knowledge. This can be provided at the work site, or in specialized schools and training facilities, or at home or elsewhere.

The education and training systems of most countries, developed as well as developing, are seriously fragmented. The biggest part of the system is the formal education typically provided by the Ministry of Education. But many other ministries are still involved in the provision of education, including many sectoral ministries. Similarly, while training is provided primarily by the Ministry of Labour and Social Security, many other ministries and organizations as well as trade unions and private enterprises are also involved in training. In addition, there are multiple non-government domestic and foreign providers of education and training with their own standards and qualification systems.

The government alone cannot build a lifelong learning system by itself and it is not just because of limited public finance.[34] In virtually all the South Asian countries, there has been significant growth in private higher education, given the importance that parents and students put on obtaining degrees to improve their livelihoods. However, beyond allowing excess demand to be met by the private providers, an effective education and training system must involve the multiple players and develop multiple pathways. This requires a broad partnership and a streamlined and effective governance structure. That also requires appropriate regulatory, finance and information systems, and making effective use of ICT to deliver education and training services. To this end, the role of government needs to change from being the controller and main provider to architect, coordinator, facilitator, integrator, monitor, innovator, and quality assuror. It can help set the regulations, the rules of

[34]For a detailed application of this to China, see Dahlman et al. (2007).

the game, the standards of quality, and the accreditation and monitoring system, making sure that the system works efficiently. Meanwhile, the private sector, intermediaries, and NGOs need to be fully mobilized to provide multiple pathways to lifelong learning. The example of what was done by the Indian ICT industry in attacking the problems of quality of the educational system is very instructive in this regard. This needs to be replicated for other areas.

In conclusion the South Asia region faces many challenges in sustaining its growth and even more in improving growth with equity, particularly given its rapidly growing population. The service sector has contributed more strongly to growth than to employment. The rapidly growing, high skilled service sector can only provide employment to a very small percentage of the growing labour force. The ICT sector in India appears to be on its way to releasing the supply constraint of quality higher education. While higher education is very important for competing in today's ever more demanding knowledge economy, it is not enough.

The comparison in the development strategy of India and China suggests that sustaining high growth also requires making significant improvements across the board in education. Better education more generally can help South Asia leverage its large and growing population into a source of wealth and competitiveness. It can enable it to participate not just in information-enabled service, but also to take advantage of globalization and the two unbundlings to participate more effectively in trade in goods as well. Furthermore, improving education in general and higher education in particular can help to make more effective use of the rapidly expanding stock of global knowledge and to improve productivity and raise welfare. The challenges are great but so are the opportunities and the potential rewards.

The South Asian countries therefore face a large challenge in improving education and training at all levels. This is challenging but not impossible. China has shown what can be done. South Asia can do as well if not better. South Asia is well positioned given it has some high quality higher education institutions, critical mass in skilled people, and agglomeration and scale economies. Furthermore, the different countries know what needs to be done. It requires commitment, undertaking some politically difficult decisions, and developing better governance and information systems. It also requires reforming other policies and institutions. All this is within their grasp. The only thing holding them back is their own policies and institutions. Hopefully this chapter can stimulate more awareness and lead to concrete actions to improve the situation.

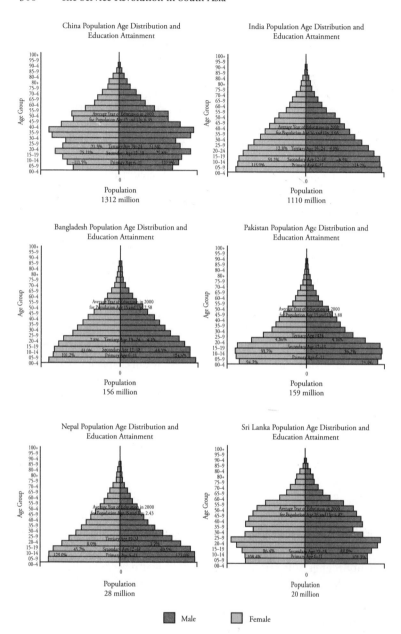

FIGURE 6.2   Population Structure and Enrollment Rates,
Selected Countries (2005)

Source: United Nations Statistics Division (2008).

ANNEXURE 6A   A.T. KEARNEY LOCATION INDEX

Category	Sub-categories	Metrics
Financial attractiveness (40%)	Compensation costs	• Average wages • Median compensation costs for relevant positions (call-centre representatives, BPO analysts, IT programmers, and local operations managers)
	Infrastructure costs	• Rental costs • Commercial electricity rates • International telecom costs • Travel to major customer destinations
	Tax and regulatory costs	• Relative tax burden • Corruption perception • Currency appreciation or depreciation
People and skills availability (30%)	Remote services sector experience and quality ratings	• Size and existing IT and BOP sectors • Contact centre and IT centre quality certifications • Quality ratings of management schools and IT training
	Labour force availability	• Total workforce • University-educated workforce • Workforce flexibility
	Education and language	• Scores on standardized education and language tests
	Attrition risk	• Relative IT and BPO sector growth and unemployment rates
Business environment (30%)	Country environment	• Investor analyst ratings of overall business and political environment • A.T. Kearney Foreign Direct Investment Confidence IndexTM

(contd...)

(*Annexure 6A contd...*)

Category	Sub-categories	Metrics
		• Security risk
		• Regulatory burden and employment rigidity
		• Government support for the ICT sector
	Infrastructure	• Overall infrastructure quality
		• Quality telecom, internet, and electricity infrastructure
	Cultural exposure	• Personal interaction score from A.T. Kearney Globalization IndexTM
	Security of intellectual property (IP)	• Investor ratings of IP protection and ICT laws
		• Software piracy rates
		• Information security certifications

Source: A.T. Kearney (2007).

REFERENCES

Asian Development Bank. 2008. *UNCTAD Report*. Manilla: ADB.

Blinder, Alan S. 2007. 'Offshoring: Big Deal or Business as Usual?', Center for Economic Policy Studies Working Paper 149, Princeton University, Princeton, NJ, June.

Chinese Ministry of Higher Education. 2003. *China's Education and Human Resource Report—Stride from a Country of Tremendous Population to a Country of Profound Human Resources*. Beijing: Higher Education Press.

Dahlman, Carl. 2009 (forthcoming). 'Innovation Strategies in Brazil, China and India: From Imitation to Deepening Technological Capability in the South', in Xiaolan Fu and Luc Soete (eds), *The Rise of Technological Power in the South*. London: Palgrave Macmillan.

Dahlman, Carl, Douglas Zhihua Zeng, and Shuilin Wang. 2007. *Enhancing China's Competitiveness through Life Long Learning*. Washington, D.C.: World Bank.

De Ferranti, David, Guillemo E. Perry, Indermitt Gill, J. Luis Guasch, William F. Maloney, Carolina Sanchez-Paramo, and Norger Schady. 2003. *Closing the Gap in Education and Technology*. Washington, D.C.: World Bank.

Farrell, Diana, Martha A. Laiboissiere, and Jaeson Rosenfeld. 2005. 'Seizing the Emerging Global Labor Market', *The McKinsey Quarterly*, 3: 93–103.

Gill, Indermit, and Homi Kharas. 2007. *An East Asian Renaissance: Ideas for Economic Growth.* Washington, D.C.: World Bank.

Gordon, James and Poonam Gupta. 2006. 'Understanding India's Services Revolution', in Wanda S. Tseng and David G. Cowen (eds), *India's and China's Recent Experience with Reform and Growth.* New York: Palgrave Macmillan.

Hanushek, Eric A. and Ludger Woessman. 2007. 'The Role of Education Quality in Economic Growth', Policy Research Working Paper 4122, World Bank, Washington, D.C.

International Finance Corporation. 2009. *Cost of Doing Business 2009.* Available at http:www.doingbusiness.org, accessed on 9 June 2009.

Kapur, Devesh, and Megan Crowley. 2008. 'Beyond the ABCs: Higher Education and Developing Countries', Mimeo, Global Development Center, Washington, D.C., January.

Kapur, Devesh and Pratap Bhanu Mehta. 2007. 'Mortgaging the Future? Indian Higher Education', Brookings-NCARD, *India Policy Forum*, 26 December.

Kearney, A.T. 2007. *Offshoring for Long Term Advantage: The 2007 A.T. Kearney Global Services Locations Index.* Available at http://www.atkearney.com/res/shared/pdf/GSLI_2007.pdf, accessed on 24 March 2009.

NASSCOM. 2007. 'NASSCOM'S Education Initiatives: Sustaining India's Talent Edge to Fuel the Next Wave of IT-BPO Industry Growth'. Available at http://www.yogyata.com/resources.html, accessed on 19 February 2009.

—————. 2009. *Strategic Review Executive Summary.* Available at http://www.nasscom.org/upload/60452/Executive_summary.pdf, accessed on 30 May 2009.

NASSCOM Deloitte. 2008. *Indian IT/ITES Industry: Impacting Economy and Society 2007–08.* Available at http://www.slideshare.net/nasscom/indian-itites-industry-impacting-economy-and-society-200708, accessed on 20 February 2009.

Naughton, Barry. 2007. *The Chinese Economy: Transitions and Growth.* Cambridge: MIT Press.

Organisation for Economic Co-operation and Development. 2005a. *E-learning in Tertiary Education: Where Do We Stand?* Paris: OECD.

Organisation for Economic Co-operation and Development. 2005b and various other years. *Education at a Glance.* Paris: OECD.

—————. 2007. *Science Technology and Industry Scoreboard 2007.* Paris: OECD.

—————. 2008. *Tertiary Education for the Knowledge Society.* Paris: OECD.

Pack, Howard, and Kamal Saggi. 2006. 'The Case for Industrial Policy: A Critical Survey', Policy Research Paper 3839, World Bank, Washington, D.C.

Panagariya, Arvind. 2008. *India: The Emerging Giant.* London: Oxford University Press.

Perraton, H. 2000. *Open and Distance Learning in the Developing World.* London: Routledge.

Psacharopoulos, George. 2006. 'The Value of Investments in Education: Theory, Evidence, and Policy', *Journal of Education Finance*, 32(2): 113–36.

Psacharopoulos, George and Harry Patrinos. 2004. 'Returns to Investments in Education: A Further Update', *Education Economics*, 12(2): 111–34.

Raza, Reehana R. 2008. 'New Evidence on Outcomes from South Asian Distance Tertiary Institutions: Some Implications for Future Policy', *Compare: A Journal of Comparative Education*, 38(4): 483–500.

Riboud, Michelle, Yevgeniya Savchenko, and Hong Tan. 2007. *The Knowledge Economy and Education and Training in South Asia*. Washington, D.C.: World Bank.

United Nations Educational, Scientific and Cultural Organization. 2007 and 2008. *World Education Digest*. Paris: UNESCO.

United Nations Statistics Division. 2008. Demographic and Social Statistics. Available at http://unstats.un.org/unsd/demographic/default.htm, accessed on 23 July 2008.

World Bank. 2008a, 2004, 2002, 2000, 1999, 1997. *World Development Indicators*. Washington, D.C.: World Bank.

World Bank. 2008b. *Knowledge Assessment Methodology*. Available at www.worldbank.org/kam, accessed on 21 September 2009.

World Bank. 2008c. 'India: Employment Generation, Regional Conversion and Enhancing Productivity Growth', India ICA report draft, World Bank, Washington, D.C.

World Bank. 2008d. 'Country Summaries of Higher Education', Mimeo, South Asia, Washington, D.C.

7

Telecommunication Development and the Role of Regional Cooperation

Caroline Cecot and Scott Wallsten[#]

Telecommunications is universally recognized as a crucial component of a country's infrastructure. Competition, resulting from both technology and institutional reforms that reduced entry barriers, has yielded tremendous investment in telecommunication networks around the world. This investment, in turn, has led to marked improvement in the well-being of hundreds of millions, if not billions, of people who even a decade ago had little or no access to even a pay phone. This chapter focuses on telecommunications in South Asian countries and the potential and reality of regional cooperation in the sector.

Scholars and policymakers alike intuitively believe that an improved telecommunication infrastructure is a crucial component of economic development. Because income and telecommunication development are endogenous, however, a positive correlation between gross domestic product (GDP) and any measure of telecommunications does not demonstrate how—or even whether—telecommunications contributed to development. Research is beginning to confirm that while GDP is, indeed, probably the most crucial determinant of investment in telecommunication, investments in telecommunications also contribute to GDP growth. Roller and Waverman (2001), for example, find

[#]The authors thank Stephanie Hausladen and Piotr Pilarski for valuable research assistance. Any opinions and mistakes are solely those of the authors.

a significant causal link from telecommunications to GDP among Organisation for Economic Co-operation and Development (OECD) countries. They note, however, that this positive effect seems to be most pronounced once penetration is nearly universal. They warn that 'non-OECD countries might only realize the growth effects through telecommunication investments like their OECD counterparts if a significant improvement in telecommunications infrastructure is achieved' (Roller and Waverman 2001: 921).

Most countries in South Asia are not even remotely close to universal access, so we are unlikely to observe an effect of telecommunications on an indicator as broad and as poorly measured as GDP. Nevertheless, other research shows benefits of connectivity on a more microeconomic scale. Clarke and Wallsten (2006), for example, find that higher internet penetration in a developing country increases trade with developed countries, even controlling for the endogenous nature of telecommunications development. That is, higher internet penetration appears to facilitate trade with countries that already have high internet penetration, but not with other developing countries. Similarly, Clarke (2008) revisits the issue using a panel of firm-level data in Eastern Europe and Central Asia and finds that firms connected to the internet were more likely to export than firms that were not connected, even after controlling for the firm's choice to connect to the internet. It seems reasonable to assume, therefore, that better access to telecommunications would, at a minimum, aid the ability of firms in South Asia to export, thereby promoting economic growth.

Policies that promote competition within a country are the most well-established ways of promoting telecommunication development. The regulatory environment, in particular, is crucial. Wallsten (2005) finds that entry and price regulations can hamper internet development in poor countries. Certain types of regulations are better able to attract investment and growth in the telecommunication industry. Kessides (2004) discusses the importance of best-practice regulations, which include expressing the regulator's mandate in statutory law in order to reduce the chances of subjecting the regulator to volatile short-term political pressures, and a commitment to promoting competition.

There is no lack of advice on the best institutional structure for a new regulator. Many argue that a regulatory body should be independent, transparent, accountable, and adequately staffed.[1] Some of this advice

---

[1] See Noll and Wallsten (2005) for a more detailed discussion of these elements.

is indisputable. Clearly, any government agency should be transparent, accountable, and competent. However, it is much more difficult to know precisely what transparency means in practice and how best to hold the regulator accountable. For example, should an aggrieved party be able to appeal directly to a court or should it go through a round of appeals with the regulatory body? And if the courts are involved, how effective and transparent are they? In addition, while the independence of the regulator has become nearly an article of faith, little research to date has demonstrated that independence, per se, matters. In the first place, 'independence' can be defined in many ways. For example, does the regulator rely on the government for its budget or does it raise its own revenues? Raising its own revenues may contribute to its independence, but relying on industry fees can encourage the regulator to require license fees simply to fund itself, potentially imposing costs or entry barriers. Similarly, should the country's chief executive or legislative body be able to remove the regulator, and if so, under what circumstances? On the one hand, such an ability may make the regulator subject to short-term political pressures. On the other hand, in a democracy it is not obvious that a governmental agency should be completely separate from elected officials who, presumably, represent the peoples' will in some form.

Of course, in addition to institutional details, regulatory rules can matter a great deal. Rules can encourage competition by liberalizing international gateways, for example, making it easy to obtain licenses, and allocate spectrum in ways that allow it to be used for high-value services.[2]

Other factors, such as the degree to which foreign ownership is allowed, are also likely to be important, especially in very small countries that may not be large enough to support many indigenous firms. It is in part for this reason that regional cooperation is so appealing, in principle. Small countries can pool resources—investment and regulatory—to overcome disadvantages of a small market. In reality, however, successful regional telecommunication efforts are rare, in part because the political economy does not typically support sustainable real initiatives, and in part because the potential economies may not be as large as advertised.

In the next section, we present an overview of telecommunications in South Asia, and then discuss each market separately. We then proceed

---

[2]People often interpret the phrase 'high-value services' to mean services like wireless broadband. In some cases that may be true, but in some cases it may mean lower-tech devices such as additional cellular voice and SMS services.

to discuss the evidence of regional initiatives, and finally provide a conclusion.

OVERVIEW OF THE SOUTH ASIAN TELECOMMUNICATIONS MARKET

Although South Asian countries differ significantly in many respects, the region includes some of the world's poorest, densely populated, and under-developed countries. The telecommunication sector reflects this makeup.[3] Table 7.1 summarizes some basic economic and telecommunication indicators and demonstrates the range of telecommunication development. Maldives, the smallest country, has the highest GDP per capita as well as the highest number of telephone subscribers per capita, with about 90 per cent of the subscribers using mobile cellulars. At the other end of the spectrum, Nepal, the poorest country as measured by GDP per capita, has only six telephone subscribers per 100 people. The largest country, India, has about 20 telephone subscribers per 100 people, approximately the regional

TABLE 7.1   Basic Economic and Telephone Indicators
by Country (2007)

Country	Population (in million)	Population Density (in km²)	GDP per Capita (year 2006 in US$)	Total Telephone Subscribers (in thousand)	Telephone Subscribers per 100 People	Per cent using Mobile Cellular
Afghanistan	31.06	43	800	4,749	18	98
Bangladesh	158.66	1,102	404	35,557	22	97
Bhutan	0.87	23	1,121	179	21	83
India	1,169.02	369	813	272,870	23	86
Maldives	0.31	1,025	3,107	351	115	91
Nepal	28.20	199	271	1,769	6	65
Pakistan	163.90	204	815	83,793	51	94
Sri Lanka	19.30	294	1,289	10,726	56	74

Source: Data from the International Telecommunication Union (ITU) World Telecommunication Regulatory Database, except in the case of GDP per capita for Afghanistan, which was unavailable. We use the GDP per capita for Afghanistan from the *CIA World Fact Book* (2007).

[3]There is some controversy about exactly which countries to include in the region known as South Asia. We use the World Bank's categorization which includes Afghanistan, Bangladesh, Bhutan, India, Maldives, Nepal, Pakistan, and Sri Lanka. We focus on telephone and internet use; radio and television are also components of telecommunication but are not the focus of this chapter.

median. In all countries, more subscribers use mobile cellular telephony than fixed line telephony.[4]

This snapshot, however, masks differing levels of telecommunication development within countries. In all countries, rural telephone subscribership is lower than in urban areas and is sometimes almost non-existent. Table 7.2 summarizes the percentage of households in Bangladesh, India, Nepal, and Pakistan that own a telephone according to the Demographic and Health Surveys (DHS) for 2006. In Pakistan, rural ownership is about half of urban ownership, while the difference is much larger in the other three countries for which we have data.[5] Telecommunication in rural areas is problematic because a majority of the population in South Asian countries resides in rural areas. In addition, these data provide no information on issues such as quality of service, which may be low.

TABLE 7.2   Urbanization and Telephone/Computer Ownership (2006)

Country	Per cent Urbanization	Telephone Ownership, by Household			Computer Ownership by 100 People
		Urban	Rural	Total	
Afghanistan	21	–	–	–	0.32
Bangladesh	26	15.6	1.8	4.8	2.42
Bhutan	31	–	–	–	1.95
India	29	36.3	7.4	16.8	2.76
Maldives	35	–	–	–	20.08
Nepal	16	22.5	2.1	5.5	0.49
Pakistan	35	65.9	35.2	45.7	0.52
Sri Lanka	15	–	–	–	3.54

Source: Per cent urbanization and computer ownership from Asian Development Bank (ADB) (2008). Data for Pakistan, Nepal, and Sri Lanka is from 2005, and data for Bhutan is from 2007. Telephone ownership data from the DHS. Data for Bangladesh is from the 2004 survey. Data is for 'telephone' ownership in Bangladesh and Pakistan and 'mobile telephone' ownership in India and Nepal. The telephone ownership data for India, Nepal, and Pakistan is compiled from the 2006 DHS final report for each of these countries.

[4]Building mobile cellular networks requires lower initial investments than does building fixed line networks. Andonova (2006) also finds that mobile technology is less dependent on institutional characteristics, making it more likely to develop even in poor institutional settings.

[5]Computer ownership is even more unevenly distributed. The 2006 DHS survey for Nepal and India records that 8 per cent of urban households own a computer, compared to only about 0.6 of rural households (computer ownership per 100 people is summarized in Table 7.2).

Internet, and particularly broadband, deployment is low. Table 7.3 summarizes basic statistics for 2007. Maldives and Pakistan, leaders in the region for internet deployment, have little more than two subscribers per 100 people. The rates for broadband subscribership are lower, with all the countries, except Maldives, averaging less than one subscriber per 100 people. As with telephones, rural internet penetration rates are even lower.

Several factors account for these low penetration rates. Most importantly, these countries are generally quite poor, reducing demand for communications services and especially for advanced services. Table 7.4 summarizes the electrification and literacy rates in the region, demonstrating the low level of general development and likely demand. In addition, as Bosworth and Maertens discuss in Chapter 2 of this volume, rapidly growing service industries, which make up the demand for advanced telecommunications, rely on relatively highly educated workers, which are in limited supply in much of South Asia. In fact, they find that the average literacy rate is the lowest of any major geographic area, which can slow the growth of telecommunications.[6]

Although not apparent from the low rates of telecommunication deployment, much progress has been made in the region over the last decade in at least some countries. Maldives, Sri Lanka, and Pakistan have

TABLE 7.3   Basic Internet and Broadband Indicators
by Country (2007)

Country	Internet Subscribers (in 1000s)	Internet Subscribers per 100 People	Internet Users (in 1000s)	Internet Users per 100 People	Broadband Subscribers (in 1000s)	Broadband Subscribers per 100 People
Afghanistan	50	0.18	580	2.14	0.50	0.00
Bangladesh	150	0.10	500	0.32	–	–
Bhutan	10	1.15	40	4.60	–	–
India	13,490	1.15	200,000	17.11	3,130.00	0.27
Maldives	6	2.03	33	10.80	4.70	1.57
Nepal	67	0.24	337	1.20	–	–
Pakistan	3,500	2.14	17,500	10.68	128.70	0.08
Sri Lanka	202	1.05	772	4.00	63.30	0.33

Source: ITU World Telecommunication Regulatory Database.

[6]For a more detailed discussion on the link between education and the rise of IT-enabled service exports from South Asia, see Chapter 6 of this volume.

TABLE 7.4   Infrastructure Barriers in South Asia (2005)

Country	Electricity Consumption (billion kWh)	Electricity Consumption per Capita	Electrification Rate %	Literacy Rate %
Afghanistan	0.80	25.12	7.0	28.1
Bangladesh	19.49	129.55	32.0	43.1
Bhutan	0.38	163.24	–	47.0
India	488.50	432.35	55.5	61.0
Maldives	0.16	506.45	–	96.3
Nepal	1.96	67.82	33.0	48.6
Pakistan	67.06	407.06	54.0	49.9
Sri Lanka	7.07	337.95	66.0	90.7

Source: Electricity consumption is from the *CIA World Fact Book* (2007). Electrification rate is from the International Energy Agency. The electricity consumption total for Nepal is from 2006.

made great progress over the last decade, especially in the last few years. While wealth plays a role, despite relatively constant GDP per capita, a few countries have managed fast growth in telecommunication.

Eliminating barriers to entry is also important. Afghanistan imposes no limitations on any telecommunication providers or operators; in contrast, Nepal and India only allow up to 80 per cent and 74 per cent foreign ownership of operators and providers in most services. We discuss these limitations in more detail in the country-level analysis for these countries.

Promoting competition is especially crucial to spurring investment in telecommunication. Competition brings lower prices and more services. Table 7.5 shows our index of competition in each country, created using information from the International Telecommunications Union (ITU). Although crude, the index provides an overview of the degree of liberalization in each country. According to this index, India and Pakistan have, on paper, the most competitive overall telecommunication framework in the region. Pakistan, especially, has over 100 different service providers, with services ranging from fixed long distance to wireless broadband. In contrast, the telecommunication market in Maldives is the least liberalized with monopoly control of local services and national and international fixed long distance services and partial competition in all other available services. Sri Lanka is a close second with monopoly control of local services and international fixed long distance services and partial competition in all other available services.

TABLE 7.5   Level of Telecommunication Competition in South Asia

Country	Number of Operators/Service Providers	Level of Competition (0–2)	Above/Below Regional Average (1.33)
Afghanistan	2	1.08	Below
Bangladesh	8	1.25	Below
Bhutan	1	1.33	Average
India	51	2	Above
Maldives	1	0.7	Below
Nepal	37	1.47	Above
Pakistan	134	2	Above
Sri Lanka	20	0.89	Below

Source: Authors' calculations, using the ITU World Telecommunication Regulatory Database.

Note: ITU has classified various telecommunication services as being fully competitive, partially competitive, or monopolistic for each country. We assigned 'full competition' a value of 2, 'partial competition' a value of 1, and 'monopoly' a value of 0, in order to calculate a competition index between 0 and 1, where 0 represents monopoly in all available services and 2 represents full competition in all available services. We do not count unavailable services. Data is from 2007, except for Afghanistan, Bangladesh, and India where the data is pre-2007. Services include local services, domestic fixed long distance, international fixed long distance, wireless local loop, data, DSL, cable modem, VSAT, leased lines, fixed wireless broadband, mobile, paging, cable TV, fixed sat, mobile sat, GMP CS, IMT 2000, internet services, and international gateways. This table summarizes the ITU's classification of each country's level of competition in telecommunications after taking all these services into account. Of course, the level of competition may vary from service to service within a country. For the levels of competition in each country in these services individually, see the country-level analysis.

Tables 7.3, 7.4, and 7.5 in particular suggest that the official regulatory framework is not the sole driver of the deployment of telecommunications services. Maldives and Sri Lanka have some of the highest rates of telecommunication penetration in the region despite the lack of competition. Although an open regulatory environment and increased competition generally stimulate telecommunication deployment, it is important to remember that other factors seemingly unrelated directly to telecommunication such as wealth, human capital, and even geography can affect investment. In the following section we discuss each country in more detail.

COUNTRY-LEVEL MARKET ANALYSIS

The diverse nature of South Asian countries makes it difficult to draw general conclusions. This section briefly discusses the regulatory environment in each country individually.

Afghanistan

In addition to being quite poor, with a GDP per capita of about US$ 800 in 2006, Afghanistan has been politically volatile in the last few decades. Its infrastructure in particular is very poor. As demonstrated in Table 7.3, only about 7 per cent of the population has access to electricity and only about 28 per cent are literate. It has only 18 telephone subscribers per 100 people and a negligible number of internet subscribers.[7] About 98 per cent of those with access to telephone services rely on mobile services.

The Afghanistan Telecom Regulatory Authority (ATRA) was established in 2005.[8] ATRA's mission is to 'facilitate the rapid development of affordable, high quality telecom services to the entire population of Afghanistan' through a transparent regulatory environment that encourages private participation. Since its inception, ATRA has worked to privatize the incumbent service providers and to license new entrants in order to increase competition. Afghan Telecom, the main telecommunication company is now partially privatized, with the government retaining 20 per cent ownership. Accordingly, ITU now considers Afghanistan to be at least partially competitive in all available services, which include domestic and international fixed long distance, wireless local loop, VSAT, leased lines, mobile, cable TV, fixed satellite, GMPCS, internet services, and international gateways. Afghanistan is fully competitive in local fixed telephone services.

Certain aspects of regulation are relatively transparent. For example, interconnection agreements and prices, defined as the technical and commercial arrangements under which service providers gain access to customers, are publicly available, as are licensing agreements and spectrum information.[9] According to ITU, ATRA plans to issue additional licenses

[7]In general, telecommunications statistics are from the ITU, available at http://www.itu.int, unless otherwise noted.

[8]See the ATRA website at http://www.atra.gov.af. See also the ICT Regulatory Decisions Clearinghouse, an online resource that provides decisions by telecommunications regulators, among others at http://www.ictdec.org/.

[9]For a discussion of interconnection agreements in India versus other countries, see Jasuja and Agrawal (2002).

in the future. The government also encourages foreign investment in the sector by allowing 100 per cent foreign ownership for facilities-based and spectrum-based operators, local, long distance, and international service operators, and value-added service operators and issuing laws protecting private investment. Although Afghanistan's telecommunication sector is still underdeveloped, there has been a marked increase in telephone subscribers in the country since 2005. Internet and broadband subscribership is low, however, and individual users are not allowed to make voice over IP phone calls.

Bangladesh

Bangladesh is one of the poorest countries in the region with about US$ 400 GDP per capita and is the most densely populated country in the region, with over 1,000 people per square kilometre. About a third of the population has access to electricity, and less than half of the population is literate. Not surprisingly, Bangladesh has low telephone subscribership and almost non-existent Internet subscribership. About 97 per cent of those with access to telephone services rely on mobile services.

The Bangladesh Telecommunication Regulatory Commission (BTRC) was established in 2001.[10] Its mission is to 'facilitate affordable telecommunication services...for all...' BTRC has liberalized many telecommunication service areas including local services, domestic fixed long distance, data, DSL, VSAT, mobile, and internet services. International fixed long distance, paging, fixed satellite, and international gateways remain under monopoly control. Bangladesh is also making licensing agreements and spectrum information publicly available on the BTRC website and strengthening its overall regulatory capacity under the supervision of the World Bank.[11] Many advanced services such as broadband and voice over IP telephony are not yet generally available, and neither the regulator nor the companies make interconnection agreements and charges publicly available.

Since 2005, Bangladesh has seen some improvement in telecommunication penetration, but penetration has grown more slowly than some other countries in the region such as in Pakistan.

[10]See the BTRC website at http://www.btrc.gov.bd.
[11]See the project website, available at http://www.btrc.gov.bd/projects/world_bank_funded_projects/overview.php.

Bhutan

In contrast to Bangladesh, Bhutan has higher per capita income and is more sparsely populated, with about 20 people per square kilometre, though the literacy rate in the two countries is similar. Despite Bhutan's higher relative wealth, telecommunication penetration in Bhutan and Bangladesh is similar. Bhutan has about 20 telephone subscribers and one internet subscriber per 100 people.

Bhutan's telecommunications regulatory body, called the Bhutan InfoComm and Media Authority (BICMA), was established in 2000.[12] Though its fixed line services and wireless local loop are still under monopoly control, its data, VSAT, leased lines, fixed wireless broadband, mobile, cable TV, internet services, and international gateways are, in principle, fully competitive due to deregulation in 2004.[13] Mobile services were deregulated more recently in 2007. About 80 per cent of all telephone subscribers use mobile cellulars. Licensing agreements are publicly available, and individual users are allowed to make voice over IP phone calls. Spectrum information and interconnection agreements and charges are not publicly available and broadband internet service is not yet generally available.

India

India is the largest country in South Asia in terms of geography and population. India's telecommunication penetration remains low, with only about 20 telephone subscribers per 100 people. While the penetration rate is similar to several other countries in the region, India's large population means that its total subscribership is still impressive—more than 270 million people are telephone subscribers, and more than 13 million people are internet subscribers.

Despite its low overall telecommunication penetration, India has also gained a reputation for a strong information technology market in its urban centres.[14] Many foreign firms outsource components of their business to India, taking advantage of its highly-skilled and cheap labour force making Indian call centres increasingly popular. In 2007 information technology services exports totalled US$ 18 billion, while

[12]See the BICMA website at http://www.bicma.gov.bt.

[13]In 2008, the incumbent BTL launched DSL and Third generation (3G) services.

[14]The overall rate is so low because of the low penetration of telecommunications service into rural markets.

the entire information technology industry contributed US$ 48 billion to GDP.[15]

Two government agencies in India oversee portions of the telecommunication sector. The Telecom Regulatory Authority of India (TRAI) was established in 1997 and re-organized in 2000 to 'create and nurture conditions for growth of telecommunications' so that India can emerge as a leader in the global information society.[16] TRAI has opened all available telecommunication services to full competition, and over fifty service providers operate in the country.[17] The foreign ownership cap has also been raised to 74 per cent for most services.[18] Two of the four main fixed line operators are fully private.[19] Interconnection charges, licensing agreements, and spectrum information are publicly available. Individual users are allowed to make voice over IP phone calls. Each year, TRAI releases a report on telecommunication developments and it recently published a report on its achievements since 1997. In addition to TRAI, the Ministry of Communications and Information Technology—especially the Department of Telecommunications (DoT) within the Ministry—develops various government initiatives to further increase India's leading position in information technology.[20] For example, a 2004 Broadband Policy Initiative set ambitious goals for broadband penetration in India by 2010, although it does not appear that India will meet these goals.[21]

India is attempting to increase telecommunication deployment into its rural areas where a majority of the population lives.[22] India's Universal Service Fund (USF) is intended to reimburse the net cost (cost minus revenues) of providing rural telecom services. Because costs may

[15]See India's National Association of Software and Services Companies (NASSCOM) factsheet at http://www.nasscom.in.

[16]See the Telecom Regulatory Authority of India's website at http://www.trai.gov. in.

[17]DSL, leased lines, fixed wireless broadband, fixed and mobile satellite, GMPCS, and IMT 2000 are not yet available.

[18]The cap for internet service provider ownership is 100 per cent, according to the ITU.

[19]Reliance and Bharti (AirTel) are private, and BSNL (the incumbent) and MTNL are partially privatized, according to ITU.

[20]See the Ministry of Communications and Information Technology's website at http://www.mit.gov.in.

[21]See Noll and Wallsten (2006) and Wallsten (2008) for more on telecommunication in India.

[22]The information on reverse auctions and universal service in India comes largely from Wallsten (2008).

differ across different types of services and different service segments, separate auctions determine the actual reimbursement to be awarded for each.[23] When awarding licenses for cellular telephone services, DoT divided the country into 20 telecom 'circles' (which loosely follow state boundaries). These circles were used as the basis for geographic reference in the rural subsidy auctions.

Telecommunication firms submitted bids to provide services. The firm that bid for the lowest subsidy, as long as the bid was no higher than a set benchmark, was eligible to be reimbursed that amount from the fund. Benchmarks were set using information primarily from the incumbent, BSNL. Any firm with a license to provide basic or cellular service in the relevant service area was eligible to bid (see DoT 2002). The winner received a subsidy for seven years, subject to review after three years.

India held several auctions, each for different types of telecommunication services. The first, in March 2003, was to install VPTs in 520,000 villages. The second, in September 2003, was to replace about 180,000 Multi-access Radio Relay-based VPTs. The third, held in September 2004, was to provide additional rural community phones in about 46,000 villages. The fourth, in November 2004, was to install VPTs in the 66,000 villages that had no public telephone facilities. The fifth, in March 2005, was to provide direct rural exchange lines in 227 regions. The most recent auction took place in April 2007 to provide mobile services.

The auctions yielded dramatically different results. The first two subsidy auctions, relating to Primary VPTs and replacing Multi-access Radio Relay-based VPTs, were disappointing. In 19 of the 20 circles, only the incumbent, BSNL, bid for the subsidies (Shayamal Ghosh, personal communication 2004).

Not surprisingly, given the thin market, BSNL bid exactly the benchmark amount, which was the maximum subsidy DoT was prepared to provide. By the final auction, however, some firms even

[23]According to commentators at the Indian National Council for Applied Economic Research (NCAER), six auctions have taken place, covering the following six services and service segments: operation and maintenance of village public telephones (VPTs) in certain villages (finalized January 2003); replacement of Multi-access Radio Relay-based VPTs installed before 4 January 2002 and technology upgrading of existing VPTs (finalized September 2003); provision of additional rural community phones in larger villages with at least one VPT (finalized September 2004); provision of VPTs in villages that remained uncovered (finalized October 2004); installation of high speed public telecom information centres (HPTICs) (not finalized as of the time of this writing); and provision of household telephones in rural and remote areas identified for subsidy support (finalized March 2005).

bid negative amounts, demonstrating that they were willing to pay to provide services.

In September 2004 the government held an auction to provide a second VPT in 300 areas (called secondary switching areas, or SSAs) that already had one. The incumbent BSNL and Reliance Infocomm were the largest winners, and two carriers bid against each other in 115 out of the 300 SSAs. The total subsidy awarded was 17 per cent below the benchmark amount.

A fourth auction in November 2004 was for the obligation to provide VPTs in the remaining 67,000 villages without one. The incumbent BSNL won in all 12 service areas. It faced bidding competition in three service areas, and that competition reduced the total subsidy by 15 to 20 per cent.

A fifth auction for subsidies to install rural household phones was concluded in 2005 as a first step towards distributing funds for connecting individual households. This step is potentially more important than the first. Many more telephone lines were at stake in devising a plan for implementing extensive residential access than for providing more public telephones. While even in the best of circumstances firms might not have found subsidies for a relatively small number of public telephones an attractive basis for entering rural areas, subsidies for a much larger number of residential lines clearly are more attractive. Indeed, the 2005 auction generated more interest among private operators, and the bidding reduced subsidies by 60 to 75 per cent of the benchmark. BSNL won subsidies for 1,267 Short Distance Charging Areas (SDCAs, the basic service unit identified for subsidies) while two private operators won subsidies for 418 SDCAs.[24]

In 2007, the government conducted two auctions for mobile services in 81 'clusters' that include 2,50,000 villages. The first auction was for the right to build infrastructure that could be used by other firms to provide services. BSNL won 80 per cent of the US$ 570 million to build this wholesale infrastructure. Although BSNL dominated the winning bids, bidding competition reduced the subsidy to 30 per cent below the benchmark (see *The Hindu* 2007 and *The Hindu Business Line* 2007).

The second mobile auction in 2007 was to provide service over this 'passive' network. Bidding was so intense that in many cases the winning bid was either zero or negative, meaning that the operator was willing to pay the government for the right to provide services.

---

[24]According to comments received from NCAER, December 2005.

These auction results demonstrate strongly that competition for subsidies can bring down the subsidy. Because these appeared to be bids to operate on a network being built by someone else, however, it is unclear why subsidies would be offered in the first place. The Government of India apparently decided to separate ownership and operation of the network from service provision. This wisdom of such structural separation is heavily debated and centres on whether consumers are ultimately better off when firms compete by investing in facilities or by offering service over the same facilities. Mandatory sharing of network facilities is likely to lead to more intensive use of those facilities, but can reduce the incentive to invest in the network itself. In this case, we do not know what the bidding might have revealed if firms had bid simply to provide service at the lowest cost.

Maldives

Maldives is the smallest of the South Asian countries, consisting of a series of islands off the coast of India. It has a much higher GDP per capita than the other countries (about US$ 3,100), almost three times the GDP per capita of Sri Lanka, the second wealthiest South Asian country. In addition, its literacy rate is almost 100 per cent, in contrast to the other South Asian countries, where the literacy rate averages 53 per cent. Perhaps not surprisingly, in the past decade these advantages have translated into high telecommunication penetration rates. Telephone subscribership in Maldives has increased from about 10 per 100 people in 1999 to 100 in 2007.

This surge in telecommunication penetration was not sparked by liberalization and deregulation. Local and long distance services are still under monopoly control, and all other available services are at best partially competitive. Dhiraagu, whose right of exclusivity expires in 2009, currently provides all telecommunication services.[25] However, Maldives' Ministry of Communication, Science, and Technology (MCST) recently promised some form of deregulation in the future, and Dhiraagu is currently partially privatized. In its *Science and Technology Master Plan*, MCST articulated the following policy decision: 'to liberalize (in the immediate future) the market for Internet services and possibly, at a later date, selected other devices not covered by current exclusivity arrangements'.[26]

[25]See the Maldives MCST website at http://www.mcst.gov.mv.
[26]See chapter 4, of the MCST's *Science and Technology Master Plan*, available at http://www.mcst.gov.mv/Downloads/Documents/S&T/Part2-04Telecommunication.pdf.

Already some deregulation has occurred in internet and broadband services, making those partially competitive. It is unclear whether Maldives will move to full competition in these services and whether competition will spread to telephone services. In 2003, a separate entity was formed in Maldives to regulate the telecommunication sector and foster competition in telecommunication services. The Telecommunications Authority of Maldives (TAM) has recently released a policy statement for telecommunications from 2006 to 2010.[27] Despite Maldives' high telephone coverage relative to other countries, there is still room for improvement in internet and, especially, broadband services. The policy statement sets goals such as implementing one universal tariff for service on all islands, lowering prices, enhancing existing networks, and supplying high-speed internet services to all by 2010. In addition, Maldives is expected to make licensing agreements and spectrum information publicly available in the near future.

Nepal

Nepal is the poorest country in South Asia as measured by GDP per capita. In addition, only a third of the population has access to electricity, and more than half of the population is illiterate. These formidable barriers have made telecommunication deployment in the country very difficult. Perhaps not surprisingly, Nepal has the lowest number of telephone subscribers per 100 people (six), less than one internet subscriber per 100 people, and broadband is not generally available.

In 1998, the Nepal Telecommunications Authority (NTA) was established to help foster competition to develop and expand telecommunication services in Nepal.[28] NTA has deregulated most of the available telecommunication services, making all at least partially competitive.[29] The main fixed line operator, United Telecom Limited, is almost fully privatized. Recently, NTA has allowed IP-based voice services to the two international telephone operators. The maximum foreign ownership restriction is 80 per cent for all operators, including facilities and spectrum-based operators, local, long distance, and international service operators, value-added service operators, and internet service providers.

[27]See the TAM website at: http://www.tam.gov.mv.
[28]See the NTA website at http://www.nta.gov.np.
[29]Data, cable modem, VSAT, cable TV, mobile satellite, GMPCS, and internet services are fully competitive, while local services, domestic and international fixed long distance, wireless local loop, leased lines, mobile, IMT 2000, and international gateways are partially competitive.

In 2000 the Nepalese government decided to use a reverse auction process to provide telecommunication services to the 534 village development committees (VDCs—the second-smallest administrative units in Nepal) that had no such access. Firms were to bid for a one-time subsidy and a ten-year renewable license with a five-year exclusivity guarantee. In exchange they were to provide two public access lines in each VDC. Unlike most reverse auctions, in Nepal the maximum available subsidy was not made public.[30]

Two firms bid in September 2000, but 'the security situation' caused the winning firm to back out of its agreement. The regulator, the NTA, attempted the auction again in 2003 with more success.

Two firms bid in the 2003 auction, and the winning bidder asked for US$ 11.9 million to do the project. The winner appeared to be on track to meet its first three rollout agreements by the end of 2004. The company notes that after rolling out service to more than 500 villages in 2004 it now serves 'over 1,800 sites' and plans to expand service into western Nepal.[31]

Pakistan

Although Pakistan has 164 million residents, India 1.2 billion, and Afghanistan only 31 million, they share a similar GDP per capita of about US$ 800. India and Pakistan also share similar access to electricity and literacy rates, and both are fully competitive in all available telecommunication services. Despite these similarities, the two countries have diverged in their telecommunication penetration rates, especially in the last few years. India's telecom sector has continued to grow steadily, but Pakistan's has surged. In 2007, Pakistan had over 50 telephone subscribers per 100 people, compared to only about two subscribers per 100 people in 1999.

In 1997, the Pakistan Telecommunications Authority (PTA) was established 'to regulate the establishment, operation and maintenance of telecommunication systems, and the provision of telecom services'.[32] Pakistan's telecommunication sector is fully deregulated, and all available telecommunication services are open to full competition.[33]

---

[30]Spectrum information is not publicly available.

[31]See http://www.stmi.com/index.php?option=com_content&task=view&id=125 ·&Itemid=277.

[32]See the Pakistan Telecommunication Authority's website at http://www.pta.gov.pk.

[33]Cable modem, paging, fixed and mobile satellite, and IMT 2000 are not available.

Pakistan's main fixed line operator, Pakistan Telecom Comp Limited, is partially privatized. Interconnection agreements and charges, as well as spectrum information, are publicly available. Its licensing process is technology neutral, though licensing agreements are not public. Telecommunication investment totalled more than US$ 4 billion in 2007.[34] Telecommunication companies themselves have invested more than US$ 8 billion during the last four years, mostly in the mobile sector. This large flow of investment into the sector is a large contributor to its rapid growth, despite Pakistan's low GDP per capita. Cooperation between Pakistan and China has also been helpful in that regard; China Mobile invested US$ 700 million in 2007 to expand their joint networks.[35] In its most recent annual list of achievements, PTA noted that more than 6,000 cities, towns, and villages are covered by mobile operators. In addition, PTA has already seen some success in its Rural Telephony Project, which aims to increase rural telephone deployment.

It appears that a large foreign investment, the deregulated environment, and PTA's proactive approach to increasing telecommunication penetration is promoting the rapid growth evident since 2005 despite Pakistan's relatively low GDP per capita and other barriers.

Sri Lanka

Sri Lanka has the second-highest GDP per capita and the second-highest telephone subscribership with 56 per 100 people in the region. In addition, its industry is advanced relative to other countries in that it has introduced 3G mobile services and a fibre optic cable link with Europe and India.[36] Sri Lanka is also planning to launch its first national satellite (see *Daily Mirror*, Sri Lanka 2008).

The Telecommunications Regulatory Commission of Sri Lanka (TRCSL) was established in 1996 to promote development in the telecommunication industry by ensuring that 'competition in the market is open, fair and effective'.[37] ITU defines the Sri Lankan market, however, as only partial competitive in all available services and with monopoly control in local services and international fixed long distance services.[38]

[34]See PTA's achievements 2006–7, available at http://www.pta.gov.pk/index.php?option=com_content&task=view&id=1077&Itemid=671.

[35]Ibid.

[36]See the *CIA World Factbook* at https://www.cia.gov/library/publications/the-world-factbook/geos/ce.html#Comm.

[37]See the TRCSL website at http://202.124.172.4/trc3/index.php#.

[38]Sri Lanka is partially competitive in domestic fixed long distance, wireless local loop, data, DSL, cable modem, VSAT, leased lines, fixed wireless broadband, mobile,

Sri Lanka does, however, make more telecommunication services available in South Asia than any other country (specifically, all services tracked by the ITU except paging). The main fixed line operator, Sri Lanka Telecom, is partially privatized and licensing agreements and spectrum information is publicly available. Interconnection agreements and charges, however, are not publicly available.

General measures of telecommunication development, such as total telephone subscribership, are low in most countries in South Asia. The generally poor state of telecommunication in the region has sparked interest in finding cooperative measures that may help promote investment and adoption. The next section describes the role of cooperation in recent years.

THE ROLE OF COOPERATION

Partly because of globalization and economic integration, South Asian countries have become increasingly interested in regional cooperation on many issues. The ADB (2006) notes that as economies become more integrated, governments are more likely to introduce cooperative measures, making integration and cooperation mutually interactive. In the aftermath of the financial crisis of 1997–8, for example, Asian governments expressed interest in cooperating to help prevent macroeconomic and financial instability. A large number of free trade agreements have been signed in recent years, including the South Asian Free Trade Agreement (SAFTA), which is expected to be operational by 2016. Increasing trade and investment between neighbouring countries can promote interest in cooperation in other areas.

REGIONAL TELECOMMUNICATION COOPERATION: POTENTIAL BENEFITS AND BARRIERS

The ADB (2006) considers the overall goal of regional cooperation to be poverty reduction. Through that perspective, regional cooperation allows developing countries 'greater access to key inputs, resources, technologies and knowledge, and enlarges the market for their products'. Through regional cooperation, less developed economies in a region can take advantage of the resources of the more developed countries. According to ADB, the more developed countries benefit from cooperation because they can relocate industries requiring less

---

cable TV, fixed and mobile satellite, GMPCS, IMT 2000, internet services, and international gateways.

skills to their less developed neighbours by comparative advantage principles and, in the long run, benefit from a more efficient allocation of resources, generating efficient investments.

Interest in regional cooperation and integration extends to telecommunication. In principle, cooperation can be beneficial. For example, large economies of scale in certain network industries could make it sensible for countries—especially small ones—to work together to achieve those economies. Similarly, very small countries may lack the resources necessary to implement a successful regulatory structure. A regional regulator, as opposed to several national regulators, could allow countries to pool the resources that an effective regulator would require.

The economics of telecommunication are unrelated to political boundaries and are thus also favourable to regional agreements. The marginal cost of voice or data transmissions does not have to increase just because they cross a political border. Just as free trade agreements can lower arbitrary costs of trading, regional cooperation can in principle reduce the costs of telecommunication to consumers if it reduces costs associated with crossing political boundaries.

Despite these arguments in favour of cooperation, other factors cast a doubt on some of the theoretical justifications and on whether real integration is feasible. First, simply because telecommunication networks exhibit economies of scale does not necessarily mean that the optimal scale is larger than what a small country can support. Historically, many successful telecommunication companies have been small, challenging the legitimacy of the economies of scale explanation. It remains true, however, that network effects mean that a small country's telecommunication network will be inherently less valuable on a per capita (or per line) basis if it lacks good interconnection agreements with other countries.

Second, a central, regional regulator may have advantages and disadvantages. A working document from a Connect Africa Summit contends that regional cooperation will lead to harmonized regulations and policies and sharing of best practices (ITU 2007). It is not clear, however, whether anything in particular about regional agreements creates incentives to create good regulations rather than bad regulations.

Finally, regional regulatory initiatives can have political–economic benefits, but face real political resistance. A regional authority could, for example, provide national policymakers a cover to make unpopular, yet economically wise, decisions. Nevertheless, small countries are often reluctant to cede any authority to a regional body for fear of being dominated by their much larger neighbours. At the same time, the very large countries see little to gain by cooperating with countries whose populations are a tiny fraction of their own. It is possibly for this reason that there are few examples of successful regional telecommunication initiatives.

EVIDENCE FROM OTHER COOPERATIVE VENTURES

A few examples of successful regional partnerships worldwide have moved beyond the earliest stage of economic integration and eliminated internal tariffs between member nations. Waheeduzzaman (2007) evaluates a range of regional integration groups and finds that only one, the European Union (EU), has accomplished complete economic integration, with no internal tariff, a common external tariff and free factor mobility, and a common monetary and fiscal policy.[39]

The only other partnership that has moved beyond the earliest stage of economic integration and created a free trade area is the North American Free Trade Agreement (NAFTA), since it has no internal tariff.[40] Waheeduzzaman's analysis puts the incidence of regional cooperation in perspective: true cooperative regional efforts are rare.

Economic Community of West African States (ECOWAS), a regional cooperative group founded in 1975, however, has made some progress in regional telecommunication cooperation. The external impetus for cooperation was the 2004 ITU and EU project to establish an integrated information and communication technology (ICT) market in West Africa.[41] After a series of workshops, ITU and EU finalized guidelines in 2005 based on best practices (ITU/EU 2005). The West Africa Telecommunication Regulators Assembly adopted these guidelines in 2005. The telecommunication committee from ECOWAS used the guidelines to formulate a set of ICT regulatory decisions in 2006. At the 31st session of ECOWAS in 2007, the decisions were adopted as supplementary acts (ECOWAS 2007). The supplementary acts define harmonized regulatory schemes by which member states could 'standardize their national telecommunications market...to promote

[39]See Waheeduzzaman (2007) for a full discussion of the criteria for various stages of economic integration as well as a classification of a majority of the regional partnerships in the world.

[40]For more information on cooperative agreements in Asia, see Song (2005).

[41]See the ITU's project page at http://www.itu.int/ITU-D/treg/projects/itu-ec/index.html.

reliable interconnection among [each other]' (ECOWAS 2007). Only two similar binding harmonized regulatory ICT frameworks exist worldwide: the West African Economic and Monetary Union directives and the EU New Regulatory Framework (ITU 2006). ECOWAS anticipates the acts will be used as a model for future cooperative regional groups of developing countries interested in creating a harmonized regulatory ICT framework (ITU 2006).

The ECOWAS supplementary acts are in the process of being translated into national legal frameworks (ITU 2007). Many ECOWAS member states are already experiencing fast growth in telephone subscribership, attracting more investment to the region (Vanguard 2008). In early 2008, Nigeria became Africa's largest mobile market with more than 45 million subscribers. Cote d'Ivoire's mobile subscribership increased almost 80 per cent to more than 8 million, while Guinea and Guinea-Bissau increased their small subscribership more than 140 per cent.

EXISTING AVENUES OF COOPERATION: BILATERAL AGREEMENTS, SAARC, AND SASEC

Cross-border cooperation occurs in two ways. One is through bilateral or multilateral agreements on very specific projects. The other includes official regional cooperation agreements and programmes sponsored by multilateral organizations. Official, high-level regional agreements receive the most attention, but have yielded the fewest results. By comparison, bilateral and multilateral project-based agreements have a better track record of success. For example, Bhutan received an optical fibre cable connection to the London Internet Exchange through Mumbai, India (see Kuensel Online, Bhutan 2008). Most recently, Pakistan was considering linking with China, India, Afghanistan, and Iran through a fibre optic connection.[42] Unfortunately, these agreements are limited and, because they typically lack a high-profile sponsor, difficult to identify.

Larger cooperative regional agreements receive far more attention, but have few concrete results. In December 1985, Bangladesh, Bhutan, India, Maldives, Nepal, Pakistan, and Sri Lanka established the South

---

[42]See the Pakistan Daily (2008). Other examples of regional cooperation, not related to telecommunications, include Sri Lanka and Pakistan signing a free trade agreement (Associated Press of Pakistan, 2008), and India and Pakistan agreeing to try to increase their trade with each other to $10 billion by 2010 (PTI News Agency India, 2007).

Asian Association for Regional Cooperation (SAARC) with the aim of facilitating the process of economic and social development in its member states.[43] With the addition of Afghanistan at the Association's 14th summit in April 2007, SAARC became an eight-member economic and political organization representing approximately 1.5 billion people, larger than any other regional trading block in the world.

To accelerate sustainable economic development, four of the SAARC member states—Bangladesh, Bhutan, India, and Nepal—formed their own regional cooperative block, the South Asian Growth Quadrangle (SAGQ) in 1996.[44] SAARC approved sub-regional cooperation among its member states at its ninth summit in May 1997, recognizing that competing interests among member states in the region and political tensions between some member states were hampering cooperation efforts. Monetary and human resource support for SAGQ came in 2001 from the South Asia Sub-regional Economic Cooperation (SASEC) programme, which was launched with assistance from the ADB.[45]

SOUTH ASIAN ASSOCIATION FOR REGIONAL COOPERATION: LOTS OF TALK, LITTLE PROGRESS

From its inception, SAARC designated telecommunication as one area of cooperation, although consensus on how to achieve cooperation did not come until May 1997 at the Association's ninth summit.[46] There, representatives of member states noted that poor telecommunication systems were preventing close cooperation.[47] Communications ministers were appointed and charged with the responsibility of drafting a telecommunication development plan that stressed cooperation in the

[43]See the SAARC website at http://www.saarc-sec.org/main.php. SAARC is one of the more than 13 regional 'cooperation' groups that Waheeduzzaman (2007) classified as being at the lowest level of economic integration because the groups did not even have serious tariff reductions among members.

[44]See ADB (2006) for more background on regional cooperation efforts in South Asia, including the formation of the SAGQ and SAARC's approval of the SAGQ as a sub-regional cooperative block.

[45]The SASEC programme was undertaken by the SAGQ with assistance from ADB; to avoid confusion, from this point forward we use 'SASEC region' to refer to the SAGQ and its member countries: Bangladesh, Bhutan, India, and Nepal.

[46]See the telecommunication section of SAARC's website at http://www.saarc-sec.org/main.php?t=2.3. The website was the source for all details summarized in this section, unless otherwise noted.

[47]See the telecommunication section of the SAARC website at http://www.saarc-sec.org/main.php?t=2.3.

development of infrastructure and communication networks among member states.

At their first conference in May 1998, SAARC's communication ministers adopted a plan of action on telecommunication. The plan was revised at the second conference in June 2004 in light of further developments in the telecommunication sector. The goals of the SAARC revised plan of action on telecommunication included promoting cooperation, minimizing disparities within and among member states in telecommunication, using telecommunication for economic development, and developing a coordinated approach on international telecommunication issues.

The revised plan of action reflected a push by member states towards general liberalization of telecommunication services, prioritizing universal access, affordable rural services, and real incentives to providers to achieve the plan of action's goals.[48] The most notable point in the plan of action is a joint member state promise to reduce telecommunication tariffs within the SAARC region to the lowest extent feasible within the framework of cost orientation. The revised plan of action also called on countries to increase efforts to use regional telecommunication hubbing and transit facilities for long-distance telephone communication, develop infrastructure and services that could assist travellers and entrepreneurs using cellular services, promote telecommunication research and development, share telecommunication expertise, and enhance and better use and share existing training facilities in order to develop human resources in the telecommunication sector.

Additionally, the revised plan of action notes the need for cooperation among regulatory authorities and administrations in an effort to increase the telephone density in the region and access to ICT at affordable tariffs, naming e-commerce, healthcare, and education as services that require particular ICT investment.

Further reflecting the growing importance of telecommunication in the SAARC's cooperative agenda, a working group on telecommunication and ICT was created after the Association's 12th summit in January 2004. The task of developing performance indicators for the successful development and dissemination of ICT in the region was assigned to the working group. The working group has convened once since its inception in September 2004.

---

[48]See the 'SAARC Revised Plan of Action', available on SAARC's website at http://www.saarc-sec.org/main.php?t=2.3.10.

A third conference of the SAARC communications ministers was to feature an exhibition of ICT products developed and manufactured in the region. The conference was planned for early 2005, but has yet to take place.

A repeated declaration for the need for closer regional cooperation in the ICT sector was made by member states at the Association's 14th summit in April 2007.[49] Nonetheless, examples of cooperation have been largely limited to meetings and declarations. For example, despite six consecutive meetings of the CEOs of ICT service providers and regulators from the SAARC region at the annual Voice and Data CEO Conclaves, cellular service roaming charges in the region remain among the highest in the world (Parbat and Philip 2007).

Notably, the Sixth Voice and Data CEO Conclave, held in December 2007, hosted the first summit of the SAARC Telecom Advisory Council (STAC), which drew up a roadmap for telecommunication in the region for 2008 and beyond (Swain 2007).[50] The STAC summit identified challenges that operators in the SAARC region face with respect to taking telecommunication growth to semi-urban and rural markets, the main agenda of this most recent CEO Conclave (Swain 2007). In addition, the STAC summit brainstormed country-specific strategies for operators to address challenges in telecommunication; assessed the preparedness of operators to implement these strategies in terms of technologies, regulations, infrastructure, and revenue models; and discussed the support that operators require from each other in the SAARC region (Swain 2007).

Despite SAARC's and the CEO Conclave's shared goals of increasing telecom penetration, quality of service, adoption of new technology, and affordability in the region, however, little reportable progress has been actually made on these fronts.

SOUTH ASIA SUB-REGIONAL ECONOMIC COOPERATION

As with SAARC, ICTs were designated one of six priority sectors of cooperation under the SASEC programme, but no work began on the issue until the second phase of the programme in October 2002.[51]

[49]See the 'New Delhi Declaration of the 14th SAARC Summit', available on SAARC's website at http://www.saarc-sec.org/data/summit14/ss14declaration.htm.

[50]See the Voice and Data CEO Conclave website for more information on the fifth and sixth CEO Conclaves at http://voicendata.ciol.com/content/CEOConclave/default.asp.

[51]See ADB (2006) and the SASEC programme website at http://www.adb.org/SASEC/default.asp for more information on the SASEC programme and its priority sectors

The first meeting of the SASEC ICT working group was held in March 2004 to develop a cooperation agenda, discuss major issues and activities for ICT development in the region, and identify priority areas from the developmental master plan.[52] Lack of connections between SASEC member countries was identified as a major contributing factor to the high cost and low penetration of telecommunication services in the sub-region. Likewise, the lack of strong infrastructure and low human capital development in the telecommunication sector were identified as major barriers to regional cooperation. To diminish these barriers, the SASEC ICT working group identified five areas of focus for the sub-region's ICT sector: enhancement of regional connectivity, establishment of community information centres, promotion of information sharing and human resources development in the ICT sector, strengthening and harmonization of regulations and standards in the ICT sector, and development of common software tools to enhance content available on the Internet.

ADB demonstrated its ongoing support for the SASEC ICT working group's activities by approving a US$ 450,000 project preparatory technical assistance instrument designated towards creating a SASEC ICT developmental master plan (ADB 2005).

Within a year, the ICT working group's pilot project, which called for the development of approximately 20 'community e-centers' in rural areas of the SASEC region, was approved and launched with US$ 1 million in financing from the Japan Fund for Information and Communication Technology (JFICT) and US$ 200,000 in financing from the United Nations Economic and Social Commission for Asia and the Pacific (UNESCAP) (ADB 2005). The goal of the community e-centers project is to increase community level productivity and profitability, improve the capacity of the local government and rural community to use ICT, and evaluate the impact of the e-centres on rural development. The project was implemented in September 2005 and was to be completed in February 2008, and an evaluation study of the impact of the e-centres is due. Upon evaluation, best practices from the initiative will be replicated to the ICT working group's national e-centre initiative in cooperation with other development partners.

---

of cooperation. Information from ADB (2006) and the SASEC programme website are the main sources for this section, unless otherwise noted.

[52]See ADB (2004) for full proceedings of the first meeting of the SASEC ICT working group.

A milestone in the region's telecommunication cooperation was achieved in August 2007 when the four member countries of the SASEC sub-region jointly agreed on the 'SASEC Information Highway Project' (ADB 2007a). The overall goals of the SASEC Information Highway Project are to create economic opportunity, facilitate trade and investments, encourage regional cooperation and integration, and extend the reach of public and private services to rural communities deprived of access to goods, services, markets, and information (ADB 2007b). Existing internet traffic in South Asia goes through third parties and often depends on satellite transmission; once developed, the SASEC Information Highway Project is intended to render third party connections unnecessary, optimize the costs of interconnection in the region, drive down prices for ICT services, and boost ICT use across borders (ADB 2007b). Moreover, the project also hopes to bridge the ever-widening rural–urban divide in ICT that has exacerbated the disparities between rural and urban areas, accomplishing goals set out by both the SASEC programme and SAARC (ADB 2007b).

The project calls for the development of a SASEC regional network with fibre-optic and data interchange capacity to directly connect the four member countries and decrease internet costs; building of a SASEC village network that will expand broadband wireless connectivity to 110 rural communities, enabling them to access services such as telemedicine, distance learning, and e-government services; and creation of the SASEC regional research and training network that will link communities, businesses, and research institutes in member countries and facilitate the movement of information, knowledge, and services among them (ADB 2007a).

ADB approved a US$ 500,000 project preparatory technical assistance instrument designated towards creating a development plan for the project in November 2006 (ADB 2007a). In December 2007, ADB made the landmark decision to provide US$ 21.2 million in funding for the development of the SASEC Information Highway Project upon review of the proposal (ADB 2007b). The US$ 24 million project will be financed by a US$ 4.7 million grant to Bhutan, a US$ 9 million grant to Nepal, and a US$ 3.1 million loan to Bangladesh, each provided by ADB (ADB 2007b). The remaining US$ 7.2 million of costs will be borne by the governments of the four member countries of the SASEC programme (ADB 2007b). An additional US$ 4.4 million grant will be provided by ADB to increase the technical and business skills of human resources in ICT research institutes responsible for developing local ICT and internet applications for the poor (ADB 2007b).

Why have SAARC Telecom Initiatives Largely Failed?

SAARC's progress towards economic cooperation has been criticized as being too slow.[53] The slow pace has most often been attributed to the consequences of political tensions between member states, especially between India and Pakistan over the disputed Kashmir region.[54] A key pre-requisite for regional cooperation in any sector is friendly political relationships and a strong political will to cooperate (Waheeduzzaman 2007). Many believe that the most recent three summits of SAARC, however, were more successful, reflecting an improvement in relations among member states and a strong desire to achieve the goals of the SAARC charter (see Table 7.6 for a summary of these key agreements).

Another pre-requisite for regional cooperation may be economic interdependency (Waheeduzzaman 2007). Intra-regional trade is small in comparison to trade between member countries of other regional trading blocks, representing only about 4 per cent of the region's total trade (De and Bhattacharyay 2007).[55] Table 7.7, reproduced from De and Bhattacharyay (2007), summarizes the intra-regional trade among Bangladesh, India, Maldives, Nepal, Pakistan, Sri Lanka, and South Asia in general.[56] De and Bhattacharyay (2007) report that the SAFTA, which will be fully operational by 2016, is expected to increase intra-regional trade from US$ 6 billion to US$ 14 billion within two years of its existence.

Nonetheless, the Association's summits are drawing the attention of increasing numbers of nations. China, EU, Iran, Japan, South Korea,

---

[53]See Waheeduzzaman (2007) and Hajni (2007) for a commentary on and criticism of SAARC's progress towards economic cooperation.

[54]See ADB (2006) for more background on barriers to economic cooperation in South Asia.

[55]See Hassan (2000) for an economic analysis of SAARC's viability as a cooperative group. See ADB (2006) for more background on barriers to economic cooperation in South Asia and Waheeduzzaman (2007) for a commentary on SAARC's progress towards economic cooperation.

[56]They cite the various issues of the IMF's *Trade Statistics Yearbook* and UNCTAD's *Handbook of Statistics* as sources for their table. As a reference, the ECOWAS *Handbook of International Trade* cites intra-regional trade in 2001 as higher than the SAARC intra-regional trade, with intra-ECOWAS exports making up nine per cent of all exports, and intra-ECOWAS imports making up 14 per cent of all imports (see http://www.ecostat.org/en/National-Accounts/EXTERNAL%20TRADE.pdf).

TABLE 7.6   Key Agreements from the Most Recent
SAARC Summits

Summit	Date	Location	Key Agreements
12th	January 2004	Islamabad, Pakistan	Drafting of the agreement on a South Asian Free Trade Area (SAFTA) with zero customs on nearly all goods by 2016; pledge to eradicate poverty; focus on the prevention and treatment of HIV/AIDS and tuberculosis; condemnation of and pledge to suppress terrorism in South Asia; renewed focus on ICTs; affirmation of improved relations among member states.
13th	November 2005	Dhaka, Bangladesh	Reaffirmation of commitment to make SAARC an effective instrument of cooperation; establishment of the SAARC Poverty Alleviation Fund (SPAF); pledge to further advance economic cooperation via SAFTA, strengthened transportation and communication links, and energy trade; pledge to address South Asia's pressing social and environmental challenges; reaffirmation of pledge to combat terrorism.
14th	April 2007	New Delhi, India	Welcoming of Afghanistan into SAARC; focus on connectivity (physical, economic, and people-to-people); recognition of need to move SAARC from a declaratory to an implementation phase, especially with regard to the operationalization of the SAARC Development Fund (SDF); pledge to collaborate on addressing environmental challenges; establishment of the South Asian University in India; welcoming of China, EU, Japan, Iran, South Korea, and the United States as observers.

Source: The Islamabad, Dhaka, and New Delhi Declarations of the 12th, 13th, and 14th SAARC summits, respectively. Available on the SAARC website at http://www.saarc-sec.org/main.php?t=7.1.

TABLE 7.7   Intra-South Asia Trade

Country	Trade with World (US$ million)			Trade with South Asia (US$ million)			Intra-South Asia Trade (per cent)		
	1991	1995	2003	1991	1995	2003	1991	1995	2003
Bangladesh	5,100	9,600	16,000	340	1,200	1,800	6.6	13	11
India	37,000	65,000	130,000	720	1,700	3,400	1.9	2.7	2.7
Maldives	220	400	580	33	58	190	15	14	32
Nepal	760	1,100	2,400	120	160	470	16	15	20
Pakistan	15,000	19,000	25,000	340	420	500	2.3	2.2	2.0
Sri Lanka	5,000	8,300	12,000	370	650	1,300	7.3	7.8	11
South Asia (total)	63,000	100,000	180,000	1,900	4,300	7,600	3.0	4.1	4.2

Source: Reproduced from De and Bhattacharyay (2007), rounded to two significant digits.

and the US were observers at the Association's 14th summit in April 2007.[57] Mauritius was granted observer status for the 15th summit to take place in August 2008 (*The Daily Star* 2007). Australia and Russia have also expressed interest in being granted observer status, while Iran and Myanmar have expressed interest in becoming member nations.[58] Increased international interest in SAARC's affairs implies that there is a growing perception that SAARC is doing something right, though perhaps not in the telecommunication sector.

CONCLUSION

South Asia is made up of largely poor countries with low telecommunication penetration. The few countries with higher than average deployment, namely Maldives and Sri Lanka, are also the region's wealthier nations. Pakistan, however, has managed a high rate of telecommunication growth despite a low GDP per capita by encouraging foreign investment and introducing regulatory reforms conducive to

[57]See *China Daily* (2007) for a commentary on China's and other nations' interests in the most recent SAARC summit.
[58]See *The Statesman* (India) (2007) for a commentary on Iran's interests in SAARC; as reported by *The Daily Star* (2007) and Rediff India Abroad (2006).

telecommunication growth. Despite the low overall telecommunication penetration rates in the region, a few countries have experienced high levels of growth in the last few years. Most of the growth is attributable to intra-country regulatory changes and outside investments. Little growth can be directly attributed to regional cooperation.

Nevertheless, the fundamental network economics inherent to telecommunications mean that tremendous gains are possible if countries can, at a minimum, reduce the costs of interconnecting communication networks across borders. That is, the value of the network to each person connected increases as more people connect. Thus, South Asia could reap real benefits by making it easier not just for people in the region to connect to industrialized countries, but also by making it easier for networks to connect within the region.

REFERENCES

Asian Development Bank. 2004. 'South Asia Subregional Economic Cooperation (SASEC): First Meeting of the Information and Communications Technology (ICT) Working Group'. Available at http://www.adb.org/Documents/Events/2004/SASEC/First_Mtg_ICT/SASEC-1st-Proceedings.pdf, accessed on 15 August 2008.

————. 2005. 'SASEC Information and Communications Technology Working Group (ICTWG): Progress and Next Steps'. Available at http://www.adb.org/Documents/Events/2005/SASEC/SASEC-II/SASECII-session-5.pdf, accessed on 15 August 2008.

————. 2006. 'Regional Cooperation Strategy and Program: South Asia (2006–2008)'. Available at http://www.adb.org/ Documents/CSPs/South-Asia/2006/CSP-SA-2006.pdf, accessed on 15 August 2008.

————. 2007a. 'Information Highway Project in South Asia targets ADB approval in 2007'. Available at http://www.adb.org/media/Articles/2007/12086-asians-highways-projects, accessed on 15 August 2008.

————. 2007b. 'ADB Provides $21M to Develop ICT in South Asia'. Available at http://www.adb.org/media/Articles/2007/12339-south-asian-ict-development.

————. 2008. 'Key Indicators for Asia and the Pacific 2008', 39th Edition. Available at http://www.adb.org/Documents/Books/Key_Indicators/2008/pdf/Key-Indicators-2008.pdf, accessed on 15 August 2008.

Andonova, Veneta. 2006. 'Mobile Phones, the Internet and the Institutional Environment', *Telecommunications Policy*, 30(1): 29–45.

Associated Press of Pakistan. 2008. 'Pakistan PM, Sri Lanka Minister Stress Close Ties', Lexis-Nexis.

Chinadaily.com.cn. 2007. 'China Makes First Visit to SAARC', Lexis-Nexis.

CIA (Central Intelligence Agency). 2007. *CIA World Factbook.* Washington, D.C.: CIA.

Clarke, George R.G. 2008. 'Has the Internet Increased Exports for Firms from Low and Middle-Income Countries?', *Information Economics and Policy*, 20: 16–37.

Clarke, George R.G. and Scott J. Wallsten. 2006. 'Has the Internet Increased Trade? Developed and Developing Country Evidence', *Economic Inquiry*, 44(3): 465–84.

Daily Mirror (Sri Lanka). 2008. 'Sri Lanka Working on Launch of First National Satellite', Lexis-Nexis.

The Daily Star. 2007. 'Mauritius Gets SAARC Observer Status'. Available at http://www.thedailystar.net/story.php?nid=14922, accessed on 15 August 2008.

De, Prabir and Biswa Bhattacharyay. 2007. 'Prospects of India–Bangladesh Economic Cooperation: Implications for South Asian Regional Cooperation', Discussion Paper No. 78, Asian Development Bank Institute, Tokyo.

Demographic and Health Survey (DHS). 2006. 'Final Reports from Bangladesh (2004), India, Nepal, and Pakistan'. Available at http://www.measuredhs.com/countries/browse_country.cfm?selected=2, accessed on June 2008.

Department of Telecommunications (DoT). 2002. *Guidelines for Implementation of Universal Service Support.* New Delhi: Government of India, Ministry of Communications and Information Technology.

ECOWAS. 2007. 'Supplemental Act A/SA. 1/01/07 on the Harmonization of Policies and of the Regulatory Framework for the Information and Communication (ICT) Sector', 31st Session of the Authority of Heads of State and Government.

Hajni, Mehraj. 2007. 'Why SAARC Has Failed', *Greater Kashmir*. Available at http://www.greaterkashmir.com/full_story.asp?Date=11_5_2007&ItemID=3&cat=11, accessed on 15 August 2008.

Hassan, M. Kabir. 2000. 'Is SAARC a Viable Economic Block? Evidence from Gravity Model', *Journal of Asian Economics*, 12: 263–90.

The Hindu. 2007. 'BSNL Bags 80% of Rs 2,500-crore Rural Mobile Telephony Project', Delhi, 28 March 2007.

The Hindu Business Line. 2007. 'India: Rural Mobile Auction Results'. Delhi, 13 April 2007.

ITU. 2006. 'ECOWAS/UEMOA Moves Forward Towards ICT Market Harmonization'. Press Release, May 2006.

————. 2007. 'Creating an Enabling Environment for Investment Background Paper—Session Five', Connect Africa Summit. Available at http://www.itu.int/ITU-D/connect/africa/2007/summit/pdf/Enable-environ-longv.pdf>, accessed on 15 August 2008.

ITU/EU. 2005. 'West African Common Market Project: Harmonization of Policies Governing the ICT Market in the UEMOA-ECOWAS Space—

Final Guidelines'. Available at http://www.itu.int/ITU-D/treg/projects/ itu-ec/Ghana/modules/Compil-Guidelines_final.pdf, accessed on 15 August 2008.

Jasuja, Nikhilesh G. and Bhuwan Agrawal. 2002. 'Interconnection Agreements in the Telecom Business'. Available at SSRN. http://ssrn.com/abstract=329580, accessed on 15 August 2008.

Kessides, Ioannis. 2004. *Reforming Infrastructure: Privatization, Regulation, and Competition.* Washington, D.C.: Oxford University Press and World Bank.

Kuensel Online (Bhutan). 2008. 'Bhutan Telecom on Global Fibre Network'. Available at http://www.kuenselonline.com/modules.php?name=News&fil e=article&sid=9735, accessed on 15 August 2008.

Noll, Roger G. and Scott Wallsten. 2005. 'Telecommunications Policy in India', SIEPR Working Paper, Stanford Institute for Economic Policy Research, Stanford.

————. 2006. 'Universal Telecommunications Service in India', in Suman Bery, Barry Bosworth, and Arvind Panagariya (eds), *NCAER/Brookings India Policy Forum*, pp. 255–88. New Delhi: Sage Publications.

Pakistan Daily. 2008. 'Pakistan Information Technology Mulling Fibre Link with Neighbours'. Available at http://www.daily.pk/technology/business-tech/78-business-tech/4037-pakistan-information-technology-mulling-fibre-link-with-neighbours.html, accessed on 15 August 2008.

Parbat, Kalyan and Joji T. Philip. 2007. 'Call for Lower Roaming Cost in SAARC', *The Economic Times*. Available at http://economictimes.indiatimes. com/News/News_By_Industry/Telecom/Call_for_lower_roaming_cost_ in_Saarc/articleshow/msid-2245622,curpg-1.cms, accessed on 15 August 2008.

Rediff India Abroad. 2006. 'Russia Keen to Join SAARC as Observer'. Available at http://www.rediff.com/news/2006/nov/22russia.htm, accessed on 15 August 2008.

PTI (India) News Agency. 2007. 'India, Pakistan Set 10bn-dollar Trade Target, Agree Two Cross-Border Banks', Lexis-Nexis, 1 August 2007.

Roller, Lars-Hendrik and Leonard Waverman. 2001. 'Telecommunications Infrastructure and Economic Development: A Simultaneous Approach', *American Economic Review*, 91(4): 909–23.

The Statesman (India). 2007. 'SAARC Iran Okayed as Observer', Lexis-Nexis, 1 April 2007.

Song, Hong. 2005. 'Increased Connectivity in Asia: Empirical Evidence and Issues', *Asian Economic Cooperation and Integration: Progress, Prospects, and Challenges*, pp. 353–64. Manila: Asian Development Bank.

Swain, Gyana. R. 2007. 'Telecom Kings in Himalayan Kingdom', Voice & Data. Available at http://voicendata.ciol.com/content/CEOConclave/107120306. asp, accessed on 15 August 2008.

Vanguard. 2008. 'West Africa: ECOWAS Telecom Market Upbeat As Abuja Hosts Business Leaders'. Available at http://allafrica.com/stories/200806021053. html, accessed on 15 August 2008.

Wallsten, Scott. 2005. 'Regulation and Internet Use in Developing Countries', *Economic Development and Cultural Change*, 53(2): 501–23.

———. 2008. 'Reverse Auctions and Universal Telecommunications Service: Lessons from Global Experience', Technology Policy Institute Working Paper, Stanford, C.A.

Waheeduzzaman, A.N.M. 2007. 'Why Is SAARC Progressing So Slowly?', *The Daily Star*, 28 April 2007. Reprinted in BBC Monitoring South Asia— Political as 'Bangladesh: Pundit Blames India for South Asian Cooperation Body Slow Progress', Lexis-Nexis.

8

Air Transport Liberalization

Yahua Zhang and Christopher Findlay

Surface transportation modes in many developing countries are more important than air transport. The view that relatively expensive air travel belonged only to an elite group was true in South Asia for some time. However, in the last two decades, with the implementation of deregulation and the resultant competition in airline markets, the emergence of low-cost carriers, and rising disposable income, air travel has become more affordable. Air transport has gained increasing importance and now plays a vital role in many South Asian countries. The effects of air transport on tourism and the movement of goods and people are particularly prominent.

Deregulation in the airline industry initiated by the US has been followed throughout the world, including the countries in South Asia, to various extents and at different speeds. South Asia is a huge area with a population of over 1.2 billion people. However, the countries within this area differ greatly in population and geographic size. This chapter reviews the development of air transport policy in South Asia in the past two decades, with a concentration on the last ten years. It appears that all South Asian countries—India, Pakistan, Bangladesh, Sri Lanka, the Maldives, and the landlocked Himalaya countries, Nepal and Bhutan—have started to embrace and formulate a liberal air transport policy in which some elements of the open skies concept have been incorporated.

Air transport is an important facilitator of other trades in goods and services. Modern supply chains are intensive users of air transport.

Services sectors like tourism, the most obvious example, purchase or have air transport as a complementary input. Other services sectors such as professional services in which the movement of people is important are also significant users of air transport. As we note below, mode 4 transactions are so important in South Asia, Bangladesh for instance, that they are a driver of the growth of air transport systems, which in turn supports their development.

This chapter explores air transport policy changes and their impacts, summarizing the key features of the policies and using them to construct indicators of the aviation environment. We then examine the performance of the national and private carriers in these countries to establish any link between their performance and national aviation policy. The relationships between the aviation environment index and the logistics performance, international traffic flows, and international tourist arrivals are also explored. We begin with a review of air transport activity in South Asia.

AIR TRANSPORT ACTIVITY

The scale of the air transport activity in South Asia is summarized in Table 8.1, which shows the air cargo and passenger movements in India, Pakistan, and Sri Lanka in recent years. International cargo movements in India are around 1 million tonnes, about three times the level in Pakistan, whose cargo movements are about twice the volume of that in Sri Lanka.

TABLE 8.1   Passenger and Cargo Movements for India, Pakistan, and Sri Lanka

	Domestic		International	
	Passengers	Cargo (tonnes)	Passengers	Cargo (tonnes)
India				
2005–6	50,970,000	477,150	22,370,000	920,150
2006–7	70,620,000	529,640	25,780,000	1,021,260
Pakistan				
2005–6	7,495,725	115,000	14,615,694	347,674
2006–7	6,985,869	98,172	14,199,431	312,604
Sri Lanka				
2005	63,954		4,239,161	142,354
2006	29,054		4,585,780	154,132
2007			4,840,998	154,413

Source: Directorate General of Civil Aviation of India; Pakistan Civil Aviation Authority; Civil Aviation Authority of Sri Lanka.

The World Bank (2008) reports an air cargo share in the region of about 0.5–1.5 per cent of international tonnage (the world average share is about 1 per cent) and a much higher share of the value of international trade (35–40 per cent). Domestic and international freight across the region grew at over 8 per cent a year from 1998 to 2005 (World Bank 2008: Table 24). India accounts for about 60 per cent of the traffic.

India's international passenger movements are about 26 million, compared to 14 million in Pakistan and 5 million in Sri Lanka. Domestic passenger movements in India are more than twice of those internationally, but domestic air freight is only about half that of the international volume. Domestic traffic in Pakistan is much smaller than its international movements.

Table 8.2 reports the international tourist arrivals for the six South Asian countries. India experienced the largest growth from 2000 to 2006, followed by Pakistan. Sri Lanka and the Maldives saw moderate growth while Bangladesh and Nepal have been stagnant or have deteriorated in terms of attracting international tourists. We later discuss some of the determinants of the variation in traffic growth.

Table 8.3 shows the pattern of flights from airports in South Asia. The main destinations after the region itself are the Middle East, followed by Southeast Asia and Europe. These patterns are shown to be significant later when we discuss options for new policy strategies.

TABLE 8.2   International Tourist Arrivals

Year	India	Pakistan	Bangladesh	Sri Lanka	Maldives	Nepal
1998	2,358,629	428,800	171,961	n/a	n/a	n/a
1999	2,481,928	432,200	172,781	n/a	474,473	421,188
2000	2,649,378	556,700	199,211	400,414	465,750	376,503
2001	2,537,282	499,700	207,199	336,794	465,750	298,456
2002	2,384,364	498,100	207,246	393,171	487,189	215,922
2003	2,726,214	500,900	244,509	500,642	567,539	265,600
2004	3,457,477	648,000	271,270	566,202	620,704	288,356
2005	3,918,610	798,300	207,662	549,308	398,146	277,129
2006	4,447,167	898,400	n/a	559,603	604,749	283,516
2007	4,977,193	839,500	n/a	n/a	n/a	n/a
Growth pa 2000–6	9.0%	8.3%	0.8% (to 2005)	5.7%	4.4%	–4.6%

Source: India Ministry of Tourism; Pakistan Ministry of Tourism; Bangladesh National Tourism Organisation; Sri Lanka Tourist Board; the Maldives Ministry of Tourism; Nepal Tourism Board.

TABLE 8.3   Distribution of Non-stop Flights from Major Airports
in South Asia

	Delhi (%)	Mumbai (%)	Dhaka (%)	Chittagong (%)	Colombo (%)	Karachi (%)	Islamabad (%)	Kathmandu (%)	Male (%)
S. Asia	68.8	64.1	41.5	69.0	41.6	57.3	44.5	65.6	67.3
M. East	8.0	14.6	34.9	20.7	31.2	29.6	30.5	17.7	9.1
SE Asia	3.6	5.2	11.9	10.3	16.2	4.2	2.3	7.3	2.7
W. Europe	11.3	6.5	6.7		7.5	3.3	16.4		17.3
NE Asia	4.3	5.0	4.4		3.5	2.8	4.7	8.3	1.8
N. America	2.2	2.0				2.4	1.6		
E/C Europe	1.0	0.3				0.5			0.9
Africa	0.3	1.7							0.9
C. Asia	1.0		0.7					1.0	

Source: Air Transport Intelligence (based on 14–20 April 2008).

Airline performance also varies considerably across the region and most national airlines experienced losses in recent years. As will be reviewed later, these national carriers have served social goals in addition to commercial performance. Martin and Parker (1997) contend that when state-owned firms pursue other objectives, the ability to achieve efficiencies is weakened. Backx et al. (2002) have examined the influence of an airline's ownership structure on aspects of its performance and find that pure private airlines outperform pure public airlines, with airlines with mixed ownership lying in between. Our review of airline performance data finds that privately owned airlines are more productive and more profitable.[1]

Privately owned Jet Airways' reported net profit margin, for example, is much higher than that of Air India and Indian Airlines. Sri Lankan, a national carrier with hybrid ownership, reported a positive net profit margin consistently from 2002 to 2006. This result is better than the government-owned Biman and the two Indian national carriers.

Employee productivity, defined as the ratio of total revenue to the number of employees, shows that privately owned airlines Jet Airways and Deccan have the highest employee productivity, followed by Air India and Sri Lankan. Indian Airlines, Biman, and PIA are at the bottom of the ranking. Employees per aircraft provide another measure of a carrier's efficiency: a smaller ratio of the number of employees over the number

[1]Details of the data on which the following three paragraphs are based are available on request.

of aircraft indicates greater efficiency. All the private carriers—Airblue, Jet Airways, and Deccan—report an employee–aircraft ratio of less than half that of the national carriers, indicating higher productive efficiency of the privately owned carriers.

Backx et al. (2002) find no strong evidence supporting the hypothesis that privately owned airlines exhibit higher passenger load factors than state-owned airlines. However, there is some evidence to that effect in South Asia, and airlines indicate that the private carriers had higher load factors than most of the national carriers.

Increments to capacity by some carriers in South Asia have lagged behind the growth of air travel demand. We hypothesize that national airlines do not have a strong incentive to expand compared to their private counterparts. We are unable to test this hypothesis using statistical methods, but the relatively small fleet sizes of the nationally owned South Asian carriers are relevant. These carriers also show slow passenger growth (compare Indian and Air India with Deccan and Jet, for example). The scale of the national airlines could be larger, we expect, given the huge populations of Indian, Pakistan, and Bangladesh and the booming economic activity over the past few years. In comparison, it is interesting to note that after the airline consolidations in China in 2002, the China Southern group alone had a fleet of 186 aircrafts even without considering other Chinese national carriers. Indian and Air India have a fleet of 93 aircrafts between them. Another obvious reason for the stagnancy of the aviation sector is that most governments in South Asia are unable to finance the investment required. These observations lead to a focus on the reform of ownership arrangements in this industry, to which we return below.

Online airfares (lowest economy class) of the routes from several South Asian capital cities to London, Singapore, Bahrain, New York, and Shanghai can be found in Annexure 8A.1. For many destinations, routes departing from Delhi exhibit lower fares than from most of other cities. Does India have a relatively liberal aviation environment and does this contribute to the result of relatively low fares? We examine the question of Indian policy compared to that of other South Asian economies in the next section and in the section following discuss the impact of policy on the performance of markets for air transport.

CIVIL AVIATION POLICY REVIEW

Variation in ownership structures exist across the region. Table 8.4 provides a summary of those structures in the context of other recent developments.

TABLE 8.4   Country Aviation Policy Summaries

India	India is one of the leaders in South Asia that initiated deregulation as early as the 1980s, partly driven by the growing demand from the tourism industry. The two state-owned airlines were corporatized and the private airlines were allowed to provide scheduled services in 1994. Since then, the private airlines have expanded at a very fast pace. Jet Airways became the largest domestic airline in August 2001. More private airlines, including low-cost airlines, mushroomed in the new century, but they are only permitted to fly international routes after five years of domestic operation, which has been a constraint for them to grow through international competition. Even though the eligible private airlines can service the international markets, the allocation of routes is made by the government. The two inefficient state-owned airlines merged in 2007, leading to a wave of consolidations between private carriers. The government has decided to privatize the national airline with a limit of 49 per cent for foreign equity, but this goal has not been achieved mainly because of political reasons and opposition from trade unions. Foreign investment into domestic air transport services is not allowed. An open skies agreement has been signed with the US.
Bangladesh	Private airlines emerged in 1996 in Bangladesh with the institution of a programme of deregulation. However, because of the low disposable income, the domestic market alone cannot generate enough revenue to enable Bangladeshi carriers to grow. The large movements of migrant workers between Bangladesh and the Middle East as well as South Asia in recent years have pushed up demand for air travel. Unfortunately, the national carrier Biman did not seize this opportunity for growth and instead has cut back on destinations in the last few years. The airline was restructured in 2007 and became a limited company, but failed to find a strategic partner. In contrast, the private carrier GMG has been relatively successful and could win more private investment. But its growth is still constrained by limited access to international markets. More liberal bilateral arrangements are being sought by the government, but an open skies negotiation does not seem to have been a priority.
Pakistan	Pakistan's deregulation in the aviation sector began in the early 1990s, but the government-owned national carrier, PIA, still dominates both the domestic market. The private airline Air Blue has gained popularity in recent years, but it is rather small in scale. Lacking funds to update its aircraft fleet, in 2007 PIA

(contd...)

Table 8.4 (contd...)

flights were banned from flying to Europe because of safety concerns. Although this ban has been lifted, PIA's reputation has been seriously damaged and its network has shrunk. The government's plan to privatize PIA to raise funds has been resisted by the trade unions. Pakistan intends to become a transportation hub linking East and West. To achieve this, it adopted a relatively liberal aviation policy in the 1990s and has signed several open skies agreements with a number of countries. The National Aviation Policy of 2007 committed Pakistan to seeking open skies arrangement in the freight sector and more liberal arrangement in passenger transportation. The government also committed to granting more rights to the private airlines to enter international markets.

Sri Lanka   Sri Lanka was the first South Asian country to privatize its national carrier when it handed the management right to a foreign company—Emirates. Ten years after the privatization, the national carrier, Sri Lankan, has become more competitive and has an improved financial status. However, because of the threat of terrorism, Sri Lanka's domestic air services have stagnated since the mid-1990s. Therefore, there is little opportunity for private airlines in the domestic market. Meanwhile, most of the international traffic rights have been retained for Sri Lankan. As a result, there is no competent private airline in this country. Sri Lanka has now concluded open skies agreements with the US, Thailand, Singapore, Malaysia, and Switzerland.

Nepal   Triggered by the high demand from the tourism industry and India's deregulation experience, Nepal started its liberalization in the aviation sector in 1992, hoping to bring in private investment. Private airlines were soon established but most have not survived for long, mainly because of fatal air disasters. Therefore, Nepal introduced a more liberal aviation policy in 2006 to replace that of 1993. The new policy clearly states the need to upgrade and expand domestic airports and to privatize the national carrier, Nepal Airlines. Private airlines can operate international flights after five years of domestic experience. Foreigners are allowed to have an 80 per cent stake of the Nepali airlines operating international services and a 49 per cent stake of those engaging in domestic services only.

Bhutan   Bhutan has only one airline and one airport, with no domestic services. Fifth freedom rights have been granted to its national

(contd...)

Table 8.4 (contd...)

	airline, Druk Air, for picking up traffic from a number of Indian cities to Singapore and Dhaka. Alternative airport construction is being considered. Communication and navigation facilities as well as staff training are main issues that need to be addressed in expanding this country's aviation sector.
Maldives	The Maldives has adopted a liberal aviation policy on international routes and has signed a full open skies agreement with the US. However, the domestic market is not open to foreign carriers and it is mainly serviced by the national airline and a number of private airlines. The national airline is now acquiring capital aiming to service the international market. Private investment has been invited to participate in the construction and development of the Maldives' airports.

Overall, there has been a trend towards further liberalization in civil aviation in all the countries since 2000. However, the actual achievement of liberalization varies from country to country. For example, although many countries have realized the value of loosening ownership control over the national carriers, few have achieved it, largely because of political responses by local communities and union objections. Some national carriers have failed to provide sufficient capacity to meet the increasing air travel demand, which is a significant impediment to the growth of the tourism industry and the overall economy. Limits on private airlines (for example, the restrictions on flying international routes) may have stunted their growth, which might otherwise have been possible through international operations.

We now compare more carefully the evolution of policy across countries and over time. The methodology is based on the application of a frequency measure that Hoekman (1995) developed to use as an index to quantify barriers to trade in service. This approach has been applied in telecommunications (Warren 2001), banking (McGuire and Schuele 2001), maritime transport (McGuire et al. 2001), and professional services (Nguyen-Hong 2000). To analyse the relationship between air transport liberalization, private ownership and competition, and airfares at national and route levels, Gonenc and Nicoletti (2000) constructed summary indices measuring country-level and route-level regulation, market structure, and infrastructure access. Following this approach, Doove et al. (2001) first constructed a bilateral index to quantify restrictions across various bilateral agreements and then examined the impact of such a policy index on airfares. They found significant fare reductions were associated with more liberal arrangements. We use a similar approach to the regulatory and market environment in the aviation sector in the seven South Asian countries.

Domestic Market Index

We consider the following eight issues, which are elements of the domestic index and that influence airline competition on domestic routes.

A Comprehensive Air Liberalization Programme

The enactment of the 1978 Deregulation Act in the US codified the developments in the policies of fare flexibility and more liberal entry and exit that had developed over the previous year, and allowed deregulation measures to be phased in. As a result, airlines had full freedom to enter any market in 1981, and the full freedom to set fares in 1982 (Pickrell 1991). The Act played an important role in guiding the development of the US civil aviation industry, leading to a climate change in this sector in the following three decades. The existence of this comprehensive air liberalization programme shows the resolution of the US government in pursuing openness and represents consensus among different interest groups towards this direction.

The 2003 Naresh Chandra Committee's report in India has served as a road map for the continuing reforms in the civil aviation sector, as has Pakistan's 2007 NAP (draft). Nepal and Bhutan have also formulated a clear policy in the civil aviation sector. Therefore, these countries are assigned a value of 0 when we consider the aviation policy in the period from 2005 to 2008. In contrast, Bangladesh has not promulgated a comprehensive policy to reform its airline industry although there are signs that it is seeking a liberal policy. In Sri Lanka, even though it was the first to privatize a national carrier, as early as 1998, the clarity of its aviation policy in 2007 and 2008 has lessened with the termination of the contract with Emirates. The Maldives lacks a comprehensive policy over its domestic market but it has opened its domestic market to private carriers in the 1990s.

In the period around 1999 to 2001, Sri Lanka receives a value of 0 because of its series of reforms in the aviation sector, including the privatization of the national airline and preparations for the establishment of the Civil Aviation Authority of Sri Lanka as a Public Enterprise (established in 2002). No other country in this period was prepared to adopt more liberal reforms.

The Privatization of National Airlines

Kemal (2000: 145) identified the major objectives of privatization in Pakistan as: 'improving the level of efficiency in the production processes; reducing the government's debt burden and fiscal deficit; broad-basing of equity capital; and releasing resources for physical and social infrastructures'.

Although there have been calls in almost all the South Asian countries for privatizing the national carrier, only Sri Lanka has achieved this goal. Too many government interventions and strong union opposition in countries such as India and Pakistan may have scared off the potential buyers.

Sri Lanka was one of the countries that adopted privatization as state policy in the 1980s. According to Kelegama (1995), the employees were appeased by being offered shares in the privatized entity and a voice in decision making. When Air Lankan was privatized in 1998, the privatization policy had been in place for more than ten years and the government had gained experience in dealing with the issues accompanying privatization. Knight-John and Athukorala (2005) note that the ownership change in the late 1990s in Sri Lanka largely retained the existing employees, most of whom benefitted from the privatized entities through improved pay and better working conditions.

Obstacles in Pursuing Privatization of National Airlines

National carriers are often burdened with obligations in the name of national or public interests, including promotion of employment. These obligations may take several forms. In India, the route dispersal guidelines have been imposed on all carriers, especially on the national carrier (Jain 2006). In Bangladesh, Biman was required to serve domestic routes using wide-bodied aircraft (Hossain et al. 2007). In Pakistan, the *Business Recorder* (2008) urged the Pakistani government to grant full powers to the PIA management team so that they could take personnel and commercial decisions without government interference. Even though Sri Lankan has been partly privatized, interference from the government is reported occasionally. The failure to respond to a request from senior officials to clear 35 seats for a government team on an over-booked flight from London to Colombo in December 2007 might have triggered the government re-taking the management rights of the national carrier (Ionides 2008). We have not found any substantial intervention in other countries.

Foreign Equity Participation of the Domestic Airline

The ownership restrictions for airlines that have been a norm in almost all the countries in the past few decades underpin the system for designation and authorization of airlines in bilateral agreements (Doove et al. 2001). While this norm has been challenged in the last 20 years, it has not been uprooted. For example, in some countries, such as Australia, the domestic market is open to a foreign-owned carrier, but the international route operating rights are still designated to the carriers that are 'substantially owned and effectively controlled' by the country or nationals of that country.

Countries in South Asia that have a 49 per cent cap on foreign ownership include India, Sri Lanka, and Nepal. Bangladesh, Pakistan, and the Maldives have had private carriers wholly owned by foreign companies, so we assume there is no upper limit for ownership. Bhutan is a special case as it has only one carrier and we have no information about the maximum percentage that a foreigner can own.

Investment in Domestic Air Transport Services by Foreign Airlines

Except India, which has clearly stated that foreign airlines are not allowed to invest in domestic air transport services, we have not found similar regulations in any South Asian country.

Existence of Private Airlines/Low-cost Carriers

Private airlines need not necessarily be low-cost airlines. However, many new private entrants take a low pricing strategy to increase their market share. Many private airlines were created simply because they see the prosperity of the operation of low-cost carries. Except for Bhutan, all other countries under study have had private or low-cost carriers, or both. This has contributed to the higher levels of competition now present in these markets compared to ten years ago.

Number of Existing Carriers

This indicator considers only airlines that are already in operation and only scheduled passenger carriers. In general, a large number of competitors in a market indicate a low legal entry barrier and a liberal aviation environment.

Airport Privatization or Handover Management Right to Foreigners

Hooper (2002) summarized some of the motives towards privatization of airports. These include: pursuing efficiency by exposing airports to competition; introducing private sector incentives and forms of organization; easing governments' financial commitments; and decentralizing decision making for airports. Many major airports in South Asia have suffered congestion and shortages of funds to upgrade existing airport facilities. In some countries, such as the Maldives, tourism is poised to expand, but the inadequate infrastructure has become a bottleneck for its growth. However, although many countries have the intention to invite private investment or private management, only India has put this intention into action. The extent of airport privatization is another element of the index.

International Market Index

Bilateral air services agreements continue to be the prevailing approach to expanding international air transport services. According to the ICAO (2006) Information Paper, during the period from 1995 to 2005, about 900 bilateral air services agreements (including amendments or memoranda of understanding) were negotiated, over 70 per cent of which contained some form of open skies arrangements, including unrestricted traffic rights such as third, fourth, and in some cases fifth freedom traffic rights, multiple designation with or without route limitations, free determination of capacity, a double disapproval or country of origin tariff regime, and broadened criteria of air carrier ownership and control. In recent years, provisions dealing with new types of commercial activities, such as computer reservation systems (CRSs), airline code-sharing, leasing of aircraft, and intermodal transport have been included in bilateral agreements.

Led by the US, the concept of 'open skies' was first incorporated in the agreement between the Netherlands and the US. The US has actively sought to establish open skies agreements with other countries. The fact sheet provided by the Under Secretary for Economic, Energy and Agricultural Affairs of the US Department of State (2006)[2] details the following key provisions of open skies:

1. Free market competition: No restrictions on international route rights; number of designated airlines; capacity; frequencies; or types of aircraft.
2. Pricing determined by market forces: A fare can be disallowed only if both governments concur—'double-disapproval pricing'—and only for certain specified reasons intended to ensure competition.

[2]Available at http://www.state.gov/e/eeb/rls/fs/2006/208.htm, accessed on 15 June 2008.

3. Fair and equal opportunity to compete: For example,
   - All carriers—designated and non-designated—of both countries may establish sales offices in the other country, and convert earnings and remit them in hard currency promptly and without restrictions. Designated carriers are free to provide their own ground-handling services—'self-handling'—or choose among competing providers. Airlines and cargo consolidators may arrange ground transport of air cargo and are guaranteed access to customs services.
   - User charges are non-discriminatory and based on costs.
4. Cooperative marketing arrangements: Designated airlines may enter into code-sharing or leasing arrangements with airlines of either country, or with those of third countries, subject to usual regulations. An optional provision authorizes code-sharing between airlines and surface transportation companies.
5. Provisions for dispute settlement and consultation: Model text includes procedures for resolving differences that arise under the agreement.
6. Liberal charter arrangements: Carriers may choose to operate under the charter regulations of either country.
7. Safety and Security: Each government agrees to observe high standards of aviation safety and security, and to render assistance to the other in certain circumstances.
8. Optional seventh freedom all-cargo rights: Provides authority for an airline of one country to operate all-cargo services between the other country and a third country, via flights that are not linked to its homeland.

By 30 May 2008, the US had concluded open skies agreements with 92 countries and territories and by February 2008, worldwide, 142 bilateral 'open skies' agreements had been signed, involving 91 countries and territories (ICAO 2008). Over 60 per cent of the agreements grant seventh freedom traffic rights for all-cargo services, 11 agreements grant seventh freedom traffic rights for passenger services, and 10 agreements grant eighth freedom traffic rights or consecutive cabotage rights for all services (ICAO 2008). Understanding that some countries have difficulty in implementing the liberal agreement immediately, some transitional arrangements were made, allowing for the phasing-in of higher frequencies, fifth freedom traffic rights, seventh freedom traffic rights for all-cargo, third country code-sharing, charter services, and ground handling.

The open skies agreements have been assessed to make a significant difference to transport costs. In a study of freight routes from the US, Micco and Serebrisky (2006) found that signing an open skies agreement reduced rates by 9 per cent and increased by 7 points the share of imports arriving by air (they did not however test the effect of entry by third country carriers onto routes covered by the agreements).

With regard to bilateral agreements for air transport service liberalization, ICAO (2008) reports examples of attempts at regional and plurilateral liberalization. The World Trade Organization (WTO), the intergovernmental organization known as the General Agreement on Tariffs and Trade (GATT) before 1995, is responsible for the rules governing trade in goods and services and trade-related aspects of intellectual property. The Annex on Air Transport Service to the General Agreement on Trade in Services (GATS) under the WTO has applied trade rules and principles such as most-favoured-nation (MFN) treatment, national treatment and transparency to three specific so-called 'soft' rights: aircraft repair and maintenance, selling and marketing of air transport, and CRS services. However, the traffic rights (or hard rights) are excluded from the WTO framework. In 2000, the WTO initiated a review of the annex with the possibility of expanding its coverage, but received no global consensus. The second-round review of the annex on Air Transport Service starting from 2005 has yet to reach any conclusion. A multi-agreement under the WTO framework to liberalize air transport services is not likely in the short term, and certainly not within the current round of negotiations. It may be easier for a small group of countries to achieve this on a regional/plurilateral basis. ASEAN is on the way towards this goal.

According to the ICAO (2006) some countries have sought to liberalize air transport services, in whole or in part, on a unilateral basis at selected airports and/or for limited periods. Such 'open skies' policies for foreign airlines' international air services have been temporarily or permanently adopted in Bahrain, Cambodia, Chile, China, Ecuador, Guatemala, Honduras, India, Lebanon, Pakistan, the Philippines, Sri Lanka, Tunisia, and the United Arab Emirates, among others.

We now consider the following indicators in constructing an index for international market regulation and liberalization constraints. Some indicators used for domestic market index construction also have implications for international air service liberalization and are therefore also included (the existence of a comprehensive air liberalization programme and airport privatization/leasing management right to foreigners). The additional indicators are:

Adopted Unilateral Short-period Open Skies Policy in the Past

We mentioned earlier that for one reason or another many countries have adopted the unilateral open skies policy for a short period, primarily when the national carrier has failed to provide sufficient capacity in the high air travel demand period. A country with such experience usually has a better understanding of the benefit and cost of the open skies policy and is more likely to embrace such a policy in the future.

Signed an Open Skies Agreement with at Least One Country

As countries have realized that its implementation will boost tourism and the movements of goods and people they have gradually embraced the US-led open skies policy. India, Pakistan, Sri Lanka, and the Maldives have signed bilateral open skies policies with a number of countries (Table 8.5). Other countries have not entered into any open skies agreements.

TABLE 8.5   Open Skies Agreements Concluded by
South Asian Countries

Country	Countries with which Open Skies Agreement Signed
India	United States (2005)
Pakistan	United States (1999), Switzerland (1998)
Bangladesh	None
Sri Lanka	United States (2001), Thailand (2004), Singapore (2005), Malaysia (2005), Switzerland (2005)
Maldives	United States (2005)
Nepal	None
Bhutan	None

The Open Skies Agreement(s) Signed Include(s) Seventh Freedom All-cargo Rights

In the open skies agreements signed between the US and India and the Maldives, all-cargo seventh freedom rights are permitted, that is, airlines of these countries can perform international cargo operations without a connection to their homeland. The open skies agreement between Sri Lanka and Singapore concluded in 2005 also contains the seventh freedom right.

Eighth and Ninth Freedom Rights (Consecutive Cabotages) Granted for Foreign Airlines

Findlay (2003) argues that bilateral open skies arrangements do not achieve a full standard openness of markets on the grounds that coverage

has not been extended to domestic routes. So far none of the South
Asian countries under study have opened up their domestic markets to
foreign airlines.

Pursuing More Liberal Bilateral Agreements

While it appears to be difficult for some countries to conclude bilateral
open skies agreements at this stage, almost all the countries under study
are pursuing more liberal bilateral arrangements with other countries on
a reciprocal basis, such as increasing the number of designated airlines,
capacity, frequencies, etc. (MoIC 2007; *Financial Express* 2008).

Private Airlines are Allowed to Fly International Routes

In recent years private carriers have become the designated carriers flying
international routes in many countries but they still face some restrictions.
This policy has implications for market structure and airline competition.
We include an indicator to show how private carriers are treated in the
international markets. Bhutan has no private carrier and even the Maldives'
national carrier only launched its international arm recently.

RESULTS

Figures 8.1 and 8.2 present the total scores, ranging from 0 to 8, for the
domestic market and international market, respectively.[3] The higher the
score, the higher is the level of restrictiveness. There appears a converging
trend in the policies in domestic markets from 2000 to 2006 while policy
in international markets shows more variation. In particular, India,
followed by Pakistan, shows relatively open policies on international
routes. India has taken the lead in policy change.

It is worth noting that for the domestic index, indicators 4 and 5,
namely, foreign equity participation in domestic airlines and foreign
airline investment in domestic airlines, are the sources of discrimination
on foreign firms in the domestic market before a country opens up the
eighth and ninth freedoms. These two indicators distinguish a foreign
firm from a domestic firm. However, if foreign investment is permitted
without such restrictions, then foreign-owned firms are treated largely the
same as domestic firms. In fact, many of the private airlines in South Asia
are partly or wholly owned by foreigners but they are treated the same
as the local businesses. Figure 8.3 presents the difference in index score
faced by foreign firms and domestic firms around 2006. The difference

[3]Detailed scores are available from the authors on request.

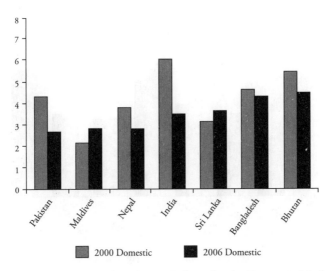

FIGURE 8.1   Restrictiveness Indices for the Domestic Market
in Periods around 2000 and 2006

Source: The authors' calculation.

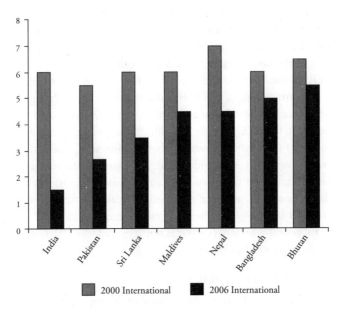

FIGURE 8.2   Restrictiveness Indices for the International Market
in Periods around 2000 and 2006

Source: The authors' calculation.

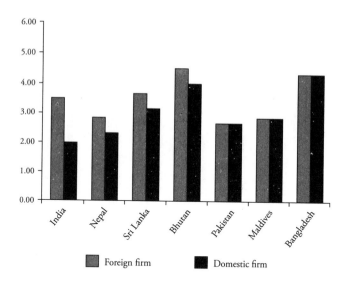

FIGURE 8.3   Index Scores Faced by Foreign and Domestic Firms

Source: The authors' calculation.

in values comes from the restrictions in indicators 4 and 5. The highest score that a domestic firm could gain is therefore 6, not 8. The figure shows a relatively high degree of discrimination in the application of policy in the case of India but less so in other countries.

Of all the indicators discussed earlier, ownership is central. Once the ownership control has been loosened, it is likely that government interference will be reduced and further liberalization measures would be expected to follow. Otherwise, it is difficult for private carriers to compete, since any further move towards liberalization would take the national carriers' interests into consideration. For example, national carriers will strongly influence the open skies negotiation process. Also, direct or indirect financial assistance may be inevitable if a firm is substantially controlled by the government. These all imply that if the substantial control over the national carrier is not removed, the effect of any future liberalization will be limited.

IMPACT OF THE POLICY

In this section we return to the question of the impact of policy measures on the performance of the air transport system. In this section, we refer to the experience of airlines performance, logistics performance, and traffic growth.

As noted, we are limited by the availability of data and the small sample size, so we cannot employ an econometric model to establish a statistical relationship between the aviation regulatory environment and the performance of the carriers. However, the commonly used indicators of airline performance and efficiency and their correlation with the conditions of their operating environment are of interest.

Dee (2003) explained that the welfare effects of services policy reform depend on whether the policy measures are cost or profit increasing. The former might include restrictions on the operating environment (community service obligations, for example) and the latter might include barriers to entry. Some measures have both sorts of effects, but removing cost-increasing measures will have more significant welfare effects. The earlier discussion suggests that what matters in regard to the allocation of the effect of policy measures between cost and profit is the condition of ownership of the carriers: a change of ownership structure would add to national welfare even without a change in other aspects of policy through its contribution to lower costs.

Leinbach and Bowen (2004) examine the determinants of the choice of air freight in the electronics supply chains in Southeast Asia. They identify a number of factors which explain the likelihood of using what they call air cargo services (that is the bundle of air freight and the set of complementary services). They stress factors beyond the value of the cargo relative to its weight, which is a standard explanatory variable. They highlight the rapidity of the product cycles, and also the risk of damage and the cost of that damage in sea freight, as well as the nature of inventory control systems. They stress how conventional airport to airport services have been embedded into logistics services and how the provision of this bundle of services has facilitated the participation of particular regions in global production networks.

We can explore the relationship with logistics services using the World Bank's Logistics Performance Index (LPI) for 150 countries (Arvis et al. 2007). The LPI is based on a survey of multinational freight forwarders and express carriers. The index was constructed from the view of these professionals and reflects the logistics 'friendliness' of the countries where they are based and those with which they trade. The LPI values range from 1 (worst) to 5 (best), aggregated from the indicators covering customs procedures, logistic costs, infrastructure quality, the ability to track and trace shipments, the time taken to reach a destination, and the competence of the domestic logistics industry.

Figures 8.4 and 8.5 show the relationship between LPI and the air transport restrictiveness indices. There is no apparent relationship to domestic policy but we find an inverse relationship between LPI and the aviation environment index for the international market. A less restrictive environment is associated with better LPI scores. When a country such as India or Pakistan has a more liberal operating environment the views of the freight forwarders are relatively positive while countries where the aviation policies are relatively less open fail to achieve a higher performance score.

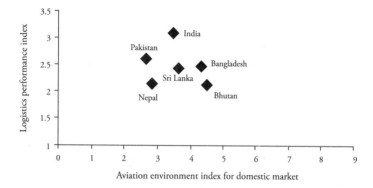

FIGURE 8.4   LPI and Air Transport Restrictiveness Index Values in Domestic Markets

Source: The authors' calculation.

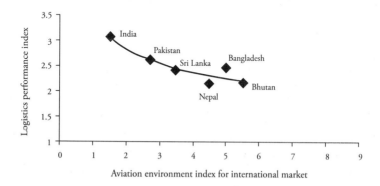

FIGURE 8.5   LPI and Air Transport Restrictiveness Index Values in International Markets

Source: The authors' calculation.

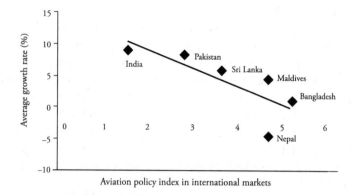

FIGURE 8.6   **Average Growth Rate (geometric) of International Arrivals (2000–6) and International Market Restrictiveness Index Values**

Source: The authors' calculation.

Figure 8.6 presents the relationship between the annual growth rate of international arrivals since 2000 and the restrictiveness index values for the international market in the later period. Aviation policies involving fewer restrictions are associated with higher annual average tourist arrival growth rates. Work reported in Annexure 8A.1 explores the link with traffic flows using econometric methods to control for the influence of other determinants of traffic growth, and the relationship apparent in Figure 8.6 appears to be significant in statistical terms.[4]

REFORM PATHS AND IMPACTS

We observed earlier how differences in ownership structures could affect performance and the distribution of the impacts of restrictive policies between rent and cost. However, the success of private carriers such as Jet Airways does not mean all private carriers have been successful. Some, such as GMG and Airblue, have won popularity in their domestic markets, but their fleets are small with only five to six aircrafts in operation; others are struggling for survival. The restrictions on their operations on international routes are part of the problem. Further liberalization in the aviation sector would provide more opportunities for them to grow and to compete and thereby add to the performance of the markets. The

[4]More recent work by the WTO, released after this essay was first prepared, find a 'positive and significant relationship between the volumes of traffic and the degree of liberalization in the air transport market'. See Piermartini and Rousova (2008).

removal of impediments to entry in domestic markets, including those applying to foreign carriers, would add to competitive pressures.

A method of achieving these results, and at the same time removing impediments to entry by at least some foreign suppliers, is to negotiate more open skies agreements, including giving attention to domestic market entry conditions.[5] What are the priorities for implementation of that approach? What are the impediments to its implementation? Are there policy packages that might be considered valuable complements to liberalization in this sector? What would be some of the consequences of success? These are the questions of interest in this section.

The most important criterion to be applied to the design of open skies initiatives is the significance of distortions in the markets and the contribution to economic welfare of their removal, which we proxy by the expected growth in traffic. This does not preclude policy initiatives in markets where traffic volumes are already relatively high. Even in those markets, there may be scope for further growth in traffic. Markets that are already large have the further advantage of providing scope for immediate entry by new providers, including privately owned firms. There is additional value from this perspective in seeking integration of domestic and international markets.

A second consideration is the ability to achieve a large scale of operations and to realize the benefits of the economies of density through the ability to construct efficient networks. Optimal airline network designs need not correspond to national borders (hub and spoke systems, for example) and the current system of bilateral agreements constrains airline network construction. Again, construction of networks across domestic and international routes should be facilitated.

A third consideration is the scope to reorganize the airline business. The following is a summary by Lafourcade and Thisse (2008: 20) of results of Robert-Nicoud (2008) with respect to fragmentation and outsourcing.

Robert-Nicoud (2008) stresses a different aspect of the fragmentation process, which allows firms to simultaneously reap the benefit of agglomeration economies in the core regions and of low wages in the periphery. Specifically, the reduction of employment in some routine tasks in rich regions helps sustain and reinforce employment in the core competencies of firms in such regions. Consequently, the loss of some (unskilled) jobs (allows the retention of) firms' 'core competencies' in the core regions as well as the corresponding (skilled) jobs.

[5]Generally, airlines of economies not party to the open skies agreement do not have access to its conditions. In that sense these agreements are not accurately described as being 'open': they remain discriminatory.

By contrast, preventing firms to outsource abroad their routine tasks is likely to induce them to relocate their entire activities in the periphery, thus destroying all jobs in what was the core.

Removal of the impediments through the reform process and the relaxation of ownership rules allows airlines to benefit from the process of fragmentation and sourcing inputs and services from locations outside their headquarter location. With emerging wage differences in South Asia, the benefits to the airlines from this reorganization may be significant. The gains to regions that participate in the relocation of activities may also be significant. The design of open arrangements might then deliberately consider the interests of economies with 'lagging regions' that might participate in this process.

It is also noticeable in Table 8.3 that a large percentage of flights operate within the South Asian region. Therefore, with respect to the network design criterion, the first step is to consider a regional and plurilateral open skies arrangement in the whole South Asia region.

The South Asian Association for Regional Cooperation (SAARC), established in 1985 by India, Pakistan, Bangladesh, Sri Lanka, the Maldives, Nepal, and Bhutan, resulted in the South Asian Free Trade Area (SAFTA) pact in Islamabad in 2004. The free trade area came into effect on 1 January 2006. The implementation of FTA calls for cooperation in improving the transport infrastructure in road, rail, air, and port networks in South Asia. The model of reform discussed by Forsyth et al. (2006) in the ASEAN case could be applied.

India is a dominant power in many respects in SAARC, and others in the region are uneasy about the distribution of the benefits of regional cooperation (Thapar 2006). For example, the smaller countries in particular are concerned about India's control over their world trade and transit links (Schaffer and Schaffer 1998). Mechanisms for dealing with these perceptions of risk in regional cooperation will be valuable.

Sub-regional and bilateral talks aimed at liberalizing trade more broadly may provide part of the solution. There have been some initiatives, including the Bangladesh–Bhutan–India–Nepal Growth Quadrangle Initiative (BBIN–GQ), Bangladesh–India–Sri Lanka–Thailand Economic Cooperation (BIST–EC), India–Bhutan Economic Cooperation, India–Nepal Economic Cooperation and Pakistan–Nepal Agreement (Otsuki and Wilson 2007). FTAs signed in this region include the Pakistan–Sri Lanka FTA, India–Bangladesh FTA, and the Sri Lanka–Maldives FTA.

Open skies arrangements could be negotiated in similar ways on a bilateral basis at the initial stage, but subject to principles of openness that we discuss below. Again, the issue is the distribution of benefits. It might be assumed that the benefits would be concentrated in India, which has a more open arrangement, and thus some smaller countries might resist participation. For example, only Sri Lanka has a relatively liberal bilateral agreement with India. Pakistan has said it would discuss such an agreement but there has been no progress on this agreement although a new aviation policy under consideration may change this situation.

India, however, is also the source of gains from reform for other countries in the region. With respect to activities that are complementary to air transport, a regional agreement that leads to policy reform is likely to have a significant effect on the costs of travel, according to the material on the impact of reform discussed in this essay. A South Asian regime would therefore be expected to lower fares relative to routes outside the region. Local tourists would be likely to switch to destinations within the region. The impact could be significant, in the context of the expected growth of outbound tourism from India for example.[6] A South Asia reform programme provides an opportunity for the tourist sectors in other economies to 'bid' for travel out of India.

Options for the integration of air transport markets beyond South Asia are worth attention, for the purposes of achieving gains of the types listed above and the larger likelihood of a greater scale of benefits, as well as providing some countervailing participation by other larger countries at the negotiating table. Table 8.5 shows the significance of flights to the Middle East and Southeast Asia from South Asia. These data prompt the suggestion that South Asia should seek new arrangements with those two regions and indeed could act as an 'air bridge' (that is, leading the establishment of a larger club of countries) between regional arrangements in both those areas. The changing policy environment in all three regions adds to the opportunities for South Asia to play that role.

In 2004, ASEAN members adopted the Roadmap for Integration of the Air Travel Sector (RIATS) with the aims 'to advance the full liberalization of air transport services in ASEAN, to achieve the ASEAN Leaders' vision of Open Sky in the ASEAN region'.[7] In line with the

---

[6]According to E.K. Bharat Bhushan, joint secretary in the tourism ministry, 'outbound tourism [is] growing at an annual rate of around 25 per cent with the country's growing middle class spending more and more on foreign travel'. 'Outbound tourism from India is increasing steadily with 8.34 million Indian tourists travelling overseas in the year 2007. The figure is likely to reach 50 million by 2020.' Available at http://overseasindian. in/2008/may/news/20080805-110255.shtml, accessed on 20 May 2008.

[7]See http://www.aseansec.org/16666.htm, accessed on 20 May 2008.

RIATS, open skies policy will be implemented by 2015 as part of the ASEAN Single Aviation Market. The full liberalization will be achieved through a staged and progressive approach. The RIATS encourages two or more members to negotiate and sign liberal bilateral or multinational agreements on a sub-regional basis in the move to full liberalization among all the members. A full discussion of ASEAN open skies programme can be found in Findlay (2005) and Forsyth et al. (2006).

There have also been calls by the air transport sector for similar arrangements in the Middle East.[8] A dialogue with both the Middle East and East Asia at the same time as South Asia designs its own regional arrangements would be important for the implementation of the open club principles.

The agreement between the US and the EU on air transport[9] is significant in this context. It demonstrates that region-to-region negotiations can be concluded. It will also create spillover effects into other regions through impacts on the efficiency of carriers of both regions, which will be another motivation for liberalization and improved airline performance across Asia. Finally, the terms of that agreement provide a relevant benchmark for an Asian arrangement (subject to its consistency with the principles identified below).

COMPLEMENTARY MEASURES

In this section we discuss complementary policy measures that add to the probability of successful reform in air transport.

As already noted, air cargo services are important in the design and operation of supply chains for manufactured goods. For example, it is competitive for goods where transit time is important, or where security matters (for high unit-value items) and flexibility is important (for example, to meet unexpected shifts in demand). The reform process lowers transport costs across a network. Leinbach and Bowen (2004) stress the importance of the air cargo services package, including logistics, but the literature on the new economic geography (Lafourcade and Thisse 2008) provides further insights. Firms are interested in fragmenting their production to take advantage of differences in labour costs, for example. In the management of fragmentation, transport and communications costs both matter. Fujita and Thisse (2006) find (following the review of Lafourcade and Thisse 2008) that:

[8]Available at www.meed.com/news/2008/06/airlines_call_for_regional_open_skies_agreement.html, accessed on 25 May 2008.

[9]See http://www.state.gov/p/eur/rt/eu/c21824.htm, accessed on 25 May 2008.

when communication costs are high, reducing transport costs actually concentrates activity in the core; that is, the reduction in transport costs works against fragmentation, when communications are sufficiently low, a fall in transport costs leads to a relocation out of the core, and below some threshold this process occurs quickly over a small range of transport costs.

These results suggest that the value of a package of reforms is important. That is, not only transport (in all modes) as well as complementary logistics activities but also communications policy matters when building supply chains in a region. Giving attention only to transport costs without paying any regard to communications and these other services might strengthen the existing core rather than disperse production. This point reflects some of the concerns of the smaller economies in the South Asian grouping.

Pursuing further bilateral or regional open skies arrangements, removing barriers to entry by new providers into international and domestic routes, and including the domestic private carriers as designated carriers on international sectors will create challenges for the existing carriers. Findlay (2005) discusses a set of complementary policy reforms designed to

support the process of adjustment by the national carriers and ameliorate the resistance to reform that has been evident so far in reform programmes in South Asia, and respond to some important public policy concerns about the impact of liberalization and new issues that might arise.

These complementary measures include attention to ownership rules that have already been discussed. New rules help to raise funds and facilitate adjustment, including outsourcing. In addition, valuable complementary measures include: (a) the treatment of state aid, since governments remain concerned about the provision of services on smaller routes, (b) competition policy, which may be challenged by mergers and acquisitions in a more open regime, and (c) consumer protection, since more intense competition adds to the risk of failure.

A final point of attention in the reform package is the rules of the design of the open arrangements. There are some risks, for example, that new arrangements will set up a larger market but that this will be closed to those outside its formation. Regional open skies, in the extreme, may simply protect inefficiency (monopoly power, for instance) in a larger space. It will be important to design any new plurilateral agreement to avoid this risk.

Principles of pursuing an open regime are laid out in Lawrence (2006) and other work on variable geometry in regional trading arrangements, which provides an argument for the club approach to reform discussed here, but with the application of the following principles: (a) all potential members be involved in the design of the constitution of the arrangement but need not join immediately, (b) new members should be allowed to join if they are willing to accede to the rules of the club (not by negotiation with existing members), (c) dispute settlement processes be set up but with the application of sanctions only within the set of measures of the club, and (d) capacity building be provided (for example, on competition policy and the design of policy on state aid and community service obligations).

Air transport is an intermediate input in a large range of other goods and services transactions. Air transport is clearly complementary to other services such as tourism but also many other service providers operate internationally in a way that requires the movement of staff. Production networks in goods such as electronics are large users of air transport services. A more efficient air transport system adds to the productivity and competitiveness of these customer sectors.

The link between policy and performance of customer sectors is illustrated in this chapter. Indices were created to summarize the features of the civil aviation environment of each country in the region. There are inverse relationships between policy restrictiveness and the logistics performance, traffic flows, and international tourist arrivals. In general, liberal aviation policy promotes the growth of the movements of goods and people, including not just tourist arrivals but also outbound internationally mobile workers.

A number of policy measures were discussed. There is value in a focus on ownership reform. There are returns to extending the coverage of bilateral open skies agreements, with provision for designation of private carriers. These agreements are even more valuable if they are embedded in a regional agreement, such as one encompassing South Asia, because of its additional contribution to efficient network design, to achieving economies of scale and density, and also the scope for competition through third country entry to particular routes.

South Asia could set up an 'air bridge' between regional arrangements in the Middle East and ASEAN. Principles for the openness of plurilateral arrangements indicate that South Asia should in any case be designing its own regional initiative in ways consistent with its subsequent extension or amalgamation.

Complementary to a regional initiative would be a concurrent transregional dialogue on the routes for air transport reform. It is valuable

374 The Service Revolution in South Asia

to complement open skies strategies at the bilateral or regional level with a policy on refinancing the national carriers, as well as attention to competition policy, to the provision of state aid and to consumer protection issues.

There are in addition important complementarities between reform in this sector and those in other services sectors, particularly communications but also logistics. The experience elsewhere is that access to a package of services facilitates participation in global production networks.

ANNEXURE 8A.1 ONLINE FARES (LOWEST ECONOMY CLASS) FROM MAJOR SOUTH ASIAN CITIES TO EUROPE, NORTH AMERICA, THE MIDDLE EAST, SOUTHEAST ASIA, AND EAST ASIA ON 29/30 SEPTEMBER 2008

City pair	Airline	Fare	Tax	Total	Note
Male–London	Qatar Airways	Rs 30,180	Rs 6,043	Rs 36,223	Indirect flight
Colombo–London	Qatar Airways	Rs 25,060	Rs 4,346	Rs 29,406	Indirect flight
Dhaka–London	Etihad Airways	Rs 21,950	Rs 5,797	Rs 27,747	Indirect flight
Delhi–London	Gulf Air	Rs 17,089	Rs 5,797	Rs 27,747	Indirect flight
Islamabad–London	Gulf Air	Rs 10,620	Rs 5,748	Rs 16,368	Indirect flight
Male–Singapore	Malaysian Airlines	Rs 9,880	Rs 9,267	Rs 19,147	Indirect flight
Colombo–Singapore	Jet Airways	Rs 10,710	Rs 7,779	Rs 18,489	Indirect flight
Dhaka–Singapore	Biman	Rs 12,345	Rs 3,972	Rs 16,317	Direct flight
Delhi–Singapore	Air India	Rs 8,500	Rs 4,930	Rs 13,430	Direct flight
Islamabad–Singapore	Etihad Airways	Rs 15,575	Rs 5,924	Rs 21,499	Indirect flight
Male–Bahrain	Qatar Airways	Rs 18,290	Rs 5,622	Rs 23,912	Indirect flight

(contd...)

Annexure 8A.1 (contd...)

City pair	Airline	Fare	Tax	Total	Note
Colombo–Bahrain	SriLankan	Rs 10,510	Rs 2,793	Rs 13,303	Direct flight
Dhaka–Bahrain	Etihad Airways	Rs 13,260	Rs 3,983	Rs 17,243	Indirect flight
Delhi–Bahrain	Jet Airways	Rs 8,000	Rs 3,899	Rs 11,899	Indirect flight
Islamabad–Bahrain	Etihad Airways	Rs 7,210	Rs 4,609	Rs 11,819	Indirect flight
Male–New York	Qatar/American Airlines	Rs 83,805	Rs 12,848	Rs 96,653	Indirect flight
Colombo–New York	Etihad Airways	Rs 32,495	Rs 6,627	Rs 39,122	Indirect flight
Dhaka–New York	Gulf Air	Rs 33,470	Rs 9,931	Rs 43,401	Indirect flight
Delhi–New York	Etihad Airways	Rs 18,920	Rs 9,580	Rs 28,500	Indirect flight
Islamabad–New York	Qatar Airways	Rs 16,830	Rs 9,201	Rs 26,031	Indirect flight
Male–Shanghai	China Eastern	Rs 30,180	Rs 4,695	Rs 34,875	Direct fight
Colombo–Shanghai	Malaysia Airlines	Rs 13,785	Rs 10,836	Rs 24,621	Indirect flight
Dhaka–Shanghai	Malaysia Airlines	Rs 19,660	Rs 12,170	Rs 31,830	Indirect flight
Delhi–Shanghai	Air China	Rs 14,990	Rs 5,364	Rs 20,354	Indirect flight
Islamabad–Shanghai	Etihad Airways/ Air China	Rs 34,795	Rs 7,434	Rs 42,229	Indirect flight

Source: http://Cheapfaresindia.Makemytrip.Com, accessed on 25 September 2008.

ANNEXURE 8A.2   ECONOMETRIC RESULTS ON TRAFFIC FLOWS

A multivariate regression was run to test the effect of policy reform on traffic flows. The model used is:

$$\text{Lntraffic} = \beta_0 + \beta_1 \ln(\text{GDPpc1}) + \beta_2 \ln \text{GDPpc2} + \beta_3 \text{distance} + \beta_4 \text{internationalindex} + \beta_5 \text{failingcarrierdummy} + \varepsilon$$

The dependent variable is the outbound passenger and cargo traffic flows, respectively, from the South Asian countries in 2000 and 2006; GDPpc1 is the departure country's GDP per capita while GDPpc2 is the destination country's GDP per capita; distance is the distance between two countries' capital cities. International index is the aviation environment index for international markets in the periods around 2000 and 2006; and failingcarrierdummy is a dummy variable indicating that the networks of two national carriers, Biman of Bangladesh and PIA of Pakistan, shrank significantly around 2006 owing to a financial crisis.

The sample contains the traffic of two periods, 2000 and 2006. The traffic data are from ICAO, consisting of the traffic between major international airports of two countries. If the 2006 traffic data are not available, the nearest year's data are used (for example, the traffic of 2005). The departure countries are the South Asian countries under study, and the destinations include countries in South Asia, Southeast Asia, the Middle East, and Europe. The GDP data are from the International Monetary Fund while the distance can be found at the website: http://www.macalester.edu/research/economics/PAGE/HAVEMAN/Trade.Resources/Data/Gravity/dist.txt.

Table 8A.2.1 reports the OLS results for the freight and passenger equations. The model fit measured by R^2 is not very high in either regression, so we should be cautious in using the results. However, the policy indicator variables are significant with the signs expected. Given the semi-log form, the coefficient of the aviation index may be interpreted as the percentage impact of an incremental index score on traffic flows. For example, an increase in the index by one point (more restrictive in aviation

TABLE 8A.2.1   OLS Estimation Results

	Passenger Traffic		Freight Traffic	
	Coefficient	Std Error	Coefficient	Std Error
lnGDPpc1	−0.4510	0.2518	−0.9817**	0.3359
lnGDPpc2	0.3235**	0.0904	0.6311**	0.1206
Distance	−0.0003**	0.0001	−0.0002*	0.0001
internationalindex	−0.1825*	0.0764	−0.2265*	0.1019
failingcarrierdummy	−0.8876**	0.2692	−0.9784*	0.3592
Constant	13.4040**	1.9760	11.0148**	2.6361
Adjusted R^2	0.22		0.30	
F	6.55		9.14	
N	98		98	

Note: *significant at 5 per cent and **significant at 1 per cent.

policy) results in 18 per cent and 23 per cent decreases in passenger and freight traffics, respectively, holding other conditions fixed.

These results can be used to derive a price effect that is associated with changes in the level of restrictiveness. Demand for air transport is elastic. A recent IATA report referring to studies of demand elasticities reports route-level long-haul values of 1.3 in Asia (IATA 2008). A meta-analysis by Brons et al. (2002) finds a mean elasticity estimate of 1.2 (SD of 0.6). Even at an elasticity value of 1, a rise in one point in the restrictiveness over current ranges has the same effect on passenger traffic as a price rise of 18 per cent.

REFERENCES

Arvis, Jean-Francois, Monica Alina Mustra, John Panzer, Lauri Ojala, and Tapio Naula. 2007. 'Connecting to Compete: Trade Logistics in the Global Economy—The Logistics Performance Index and Its Indicators'. Washington, D.C.: World Bank.

Backx, M., M. Carney, and E. Gedaljovic. 2002. 'Public, Private and Mixed Ownership and the Performance of International Airlines', *Journal of Air Transport and Management*, 8(4): 213–20.

Brons, M., E. Pels, P. Nijkamp, and P. Rietveld. 2002. 'Price Elasticities of Demand for Passenger Air Travel: A Meta-analysis', *Journal of Air Transport Management*, 8: 165–75.

Business Recorder. 2008. 'PIA Woes', Editorial, 14 April 2008.

Dee, P. 2003. 'Modelling the Policy Issues in Services Trade', *Economie Internationale*, 2Q–3Q: 283–300.

Doove, S., O. Gabbitas, D. Nguyen-Hong, and J. Owen. 2001. 'Price Effects of Regulation: Telecommunications, Air Passenger Transport and Electricity Supply', Productivity Commission Staff Research Paper, AusInfo, Canberra.

Financial Express. 2008. 'New Air Deal with India to Boost Bangladesh's Private Airlines', 18 February, Dhaka. Available at 'http://www.financialexpress.com/news/Bangladesh-to-sign-Air-service-deal-with-India/268290/'http://www.financialexpress.com/news/Bangladesh-to-sign-Air-service-deal-with-India/268290/, accessed on 10 May 2008.

Findlay, C. 2003. 'Plurilateral Agreements on Trade in Air Transport Services: The US Model', *Journal of Air Transport Management*, 9(4): 211–20.

———. 2005. 'Strategic Directions for ASEAN Airlines in a Globalizing World Overview', REPSF Project No. 04/008, Final Report, August.

Forsyth, P., J. King, and C.L. Rodolfo. 2006. 'Open Skies in ASEAN', *Journal of Air Transport Management*, 12(3): 143–52.

Fujita, M., and J-F. Thisse. 2006. 'Globalization and the Evolution of the Supply Chain: Who Gains and Who Loses?', *International Economic Review*, 47(3): 811–36.

Gonenc, R. and G. Nicoletti. 2000. 'Regulation, Market Structure and Performance in Air Passenger Transportation', OECD Economics Department Working Paper 254, Paris.

Hoekman, B. 1995. 'Assessing the General Agreement on Trade in Services', in W. Martin, and L.A. Winters (eds), *The Uruguay Round and the Developing Economics*, pp. 3227–64, Discussion Paper 307. Washington, D.C.: World Bank.

Hooper, P. 2002. 'Privatization of Airports in Asia', *Journal of Air Transport Management*, 8(5): 289–300.

Hossain, M.A., A.M. Shamsuddula, and M.N. Alam. 2007. 'Biman Bangladesh Airlines: A Diagnostic Study'. Dhaka, Bangladesh: Transparency International Bangladesh.

IATA (International Air Transport Association). 2008. 'Air Travel Demand', IATA Economics Briefing No. 9, InterVISTAS Consulting Inc. on behalf of IATA.

ICAO (International Civil Aviation Organization). 2006. 'Regulatory and Industry Overview', Presented by ICAO Secretariat, 15 August. Available at 'http://www.icao.int/icao/en/atb/ecp/dubai2006/RegulatoryIndustryOverview.pdf'http://www.icao.int/icao/en/atb/ecp/dubai2006/RegulatoryIndustryOverview.pdf, accessed on 20 July 2008.

————. 2008. 'Overview of Trends and Developments in International Air Transport', Presented by ICAO Secretariat, 7 March. Available at ERLINK 'http://www.icao.int/icao/en/atb/epm/Ecp/OverviewTrends.pdf'http://www.icao.int/icao/en/atb/epm/Ecp/OverviewTrends.pdf, accessed in July 2008.

Ionides, N. 2008. 'Emirates to Pull Out of Sri Lankan', *Airline Business*, 24(2): 25.

Jain, S. 2006. 'Competition Issues in Transportation Sectors', in Pradeep S. Mehta (ed.), *Towards a Functional Competition Policy for India*, chapter 18. Haipur: Academic Foundation in Association with Consumer Unity and Trust Society (CUTS International).

Kelegama, S. 1995. 'The Impact of Privatization on Distributional Equity: The Case of Sri Lanka', in V.V. Ramanadham (ed.), *Privatization and Equity*, pp. 143–80. London: Routledge.

Kemal, A.R. 2000. 'Privatization in Pakistan', in G. Joshi (ed.), *Privatization in South Asia: Minimizing Negative Social Effects through Restructuring*, pp. 143–73. New Delhi: International Labour Organization.

Knight-John, M. and P.P.A.W. Athukorala. 2005. 'Assessing Privatization in Sri Lanka: Distribution and Governance', in John Nellis and Nancy Birdsall (eds), *Reality Check: The Distributional Impact of Privatization in Developing Countries*. Washington, D.C.: Center for Global Development.

Lafourcade, M. and J. Thisse. 2008. 'New Economic Geography: A Guide to Transport Analysis', PSE Working Papers, 2008–02, PSE, Paris.

Lawrence, R. 2006. 'Rulemaking Amidst Growing Diversity: A Club-of-Clubs Approach to WTO Reform and New Issue Selection', *Journal of International Economic Law*, 9(4): 823–35.

Leinbach, T.R. and J.T. Bowen. 2004. 'Air Cargo Services and the Electronics Industry in Southeast Asia', *Journal of Economic Geography*, 4(3): 299–321.

Martin, S. and D. Parker. 1997. *The Impact of Privatization: Ownership and Corporate Performance in the UK*. London: Routledge.

McGuire, G. and M. Schuele. 2001. 'Restrictiveness of International Trade in Banking Services', in Christopher Findlay, and Tony Warren (eds), *Impediments to Trade in Services: Measurement and Policy Implications*, pp. 201–14. New York: Routledge.

McGuire, G., M. Schuele, and T. Smith. 2001. 'Restrictiveness of International Trade in Maritime Services', in Christopher Findlay and Tony Warren (eds), *Impediments to Trade in Services: Measurement and Policy Implications*, pp. 172–88. New York: Routledge.

Micco, A. and T. Serebrisky. 2006. 'Competition Regimes and Air Transport Costs: The Effects of Open Skies Agreements', *Journal of International Economics*, 70: 25–51.

MoIC (Ministry of Information & Communications). 2007. 'Information, Communications and Transport Sectors in Bhutan: A Special Report', Ministry of Information & Communications, Royal Government of Bhutan, July.

Naresh Chandra Committee. 2003. 'Report of the Committee on a Road Map for the Civil Aviation Sector', Ministry of Civil Aviation, Government of India, New Delhi.

Nguyen-Hong, D. 2000. 'Restrictions on Trade in Professional Services', Productivity Commission Staff Research Paper, AusInfo, Canberra.

Otsuki, T. and J. Wilson. 2007. 'In South Asia: What Role for Trade Facilitation?', Policy Research Working Paper Series 4423, World Bank, Washington, D.C.

Pickrell, D. 1991. 'The Regulation and Deregulation of US Airlines', in K. Button (ed.), *Airline Deregulation: International Experiences*, pp. 5–47. New York: New York University Press.

Piermartini, R. and L. Rousova. 2008. 'Liberalization of Air Transport Services and Passenger Traffic', Staff Working Paper ERSD-2008–06, World Trade Organization, December.

Robert-Nicoud, F. 2008. 'Offshoring of Routine Tasks and (De)industrialisation: Threat or Opportunity—and for Whom?', *Journal of Urban Economics*, 63(2): 517–35.

Schaffer, H. and T. Schaffer. 1998. 'Better Neighbours? India and South Asian Regional Politics', *SAIS Review*, Winter–Spring.

Thapar, R. 2006. 'SAARC: Ineffective in Promoting Economic Cooperation in South Asia' *Stanford Journal of International Relations*, 7. Available at http://www.stanford.edu/group/sjir/7.1.03_thapar.html, accessed on 15 July 2008.

US Department of State. 2006. 'Open Skies Agreements Highlights', Economic, Energy and Business Affairs Fact Sheets, Office of Aviation Negotiations, Washington, D.C., 1 June.

Warren, T. 2001. 'The Identification of Impediments to Trade and Investment in Telecommunications Services', in Christopher Findlay and Tony Warren (eds), *Impediments to Trade in Services: Measurement and Policy Implications*, pp. 71–84. New York: Routledge.

World Bank. 2008. *South Asia—Trade and Transport Facilitation*. Report No. 44061-SAS, Sustainable Development Unit, South Asia Region.

Contributors

MAARTEN BOSKER is a postdoctoral researcher, Faculty of Economics and Business, University of Groningen, The Netherlands.

BARRY BOSWORTH is Senior Fellow, Economic Studies, Global Economy and Development, The Brookings Institution, Washington, D.C.

CAROLINE CECOT is a PhD candidate, Law and Economics, Vanderbilt Law School, Vanderbilt University, USA.

CARL J. DAHLMAN is Associate Professor, Georgetown University, Washington, D.C.

RAFIQ DOSSANI is Senior Research Scholar and Director, Center for South Asia, Stanford University, USA.

CHRISTOPHER FINDLAY is Professor and Head, School of Economics, University of Adelaide, Australia.

HARRY GARRETSEN is Professor of International Economics and Business, University of Groningen, The Netherlands.

EJAZ GHANI is Economic Adviser, South Asia Poverty Reduction and Economic Management, The World Bank, Washington, D.C.

Homi Kharas is Senior Fellow, Global Economy and Development, Wolfensohn Center for Development, The Brookings Institution, Washington, D.C.

Annemie Maertens is a PhD candidate in Applied Economics and Management, Cornell University, New York.

Sanket Mohapatra is Economist, Development Prospects Group (DECPG), The World Bank, Washington, D.C.

Çağlar Özden is Senior Economist, Development Research Group (DECRG), The World Bank, Washington, D.C.

Scott Wallsten is Vice President for Research and Senior Fellow, Technology Policy Institute, and Senior Fellow, Georgetown Center for Business and Public Policy, Washington, D.C.

Yahua Zhang is Lecturer, School of Accounting, Economics and Finance, University of Southern Queensland, Australia.